Administration of
Programs for Young Children

Administration of Programs for Young Children

EIGHTH EDITION

Phyllis M. Click

Kimberly A. Karkos

WADSWORTH
CENGAGE Learning

Australia • Brazil • Japan • Korea • Mexico • Singapore • Spain • United Kingdom • United States

Administration of Programs for Young Children, Eighth Edition
Phyllis M. Click and Kimberly A. Karkos

Executive Editor: Mark Kerr

Development Editor: Diane Colwyn

Assistant Editor: Caitlin Cox

Editorial Assistant: Linda Stewart

Media Editor: Ashley Cronin

Marketing Manager: Kara Kindstrom

Marketing Communications Manager: Martha Pfeiffer

Marketing Coordinator: Dimitri Hagnere

Editorial Production: Matt Ballantyne

Art Director: Maria Epes

Print Buyer: Rebecca Cross

Permissions Editor (text): Roberta Broyer

Permissions Editor (image): Leitha Etheridge-Sims

Production Service: PrePressPMG

Text Designer: Marsha Cohen

Photo Researcher: PrePressPMG

Cover Designer: Marsha Cohen

Cover Image: Cengage Learning

Compositor: PrePressPMG

For product information and technology assistance, contact us at
Cengage Learning Customer & Sales Support, 1-800-354-9706

For permission to use material from this text or product, submit all requests online at **cengage.com/permissions**
Further permissions questions can be emailed to
permissionrequest@cengage.com

Library of Congress Control Number: 2010920866

ISBN-13: 978-0-495-80898-5

ISBN-10: 0-495-80898-9

Wadsworth
20 Davis Drive
Belmont, CA 94002
USA

Cengage Learning is a leading provider of customized learning solutions with office locations around the globe, including Singapore, the United Kingdom, Australia, Mexico, Brazil, and Japan. Locate your local office at: **international.cengage.com/region**

Cengage Learning products are represented in Canada by Nelson Education, Ltd.

For your course and learning solutions, visit **academic.cengage.com**

Purchase any of our products at your local college store or at our preferred online store **www.CengageBrain.com**

Printed in the United States of America
1 2 3 4 5 6 7 14 13 12 11 10

Contents

#1 priority is always the children enrolled!

Preface

Rational

Administration of Programs for Young Children was first published in 1976, when interest in the education of very young children was just beginning. Today the importance of those early years is well established, and there is universal recognition that quality programs must have well-trained and knowledgeable teachers as well as leaders or directors who can meet the challenges of operating these programs. Each year new research offers additional insight into the needs of young children. The job of an administrator is so multifaceted that it is imperative that every leader be well versed in the latest information. Therefore the availability of courses and up-to-date training materials is essential. This book can serve that purpose. The text is appropriate for a course at a two-year college, a four-year university, or a graduate level. It can also be a source for working directors, planners of training programs, or people wanting to start a child-care program.

Organization

The organization of this edition reflects a logical progression of information needed by a director. It is divided into five sections with chapters containing relevant information.

Part I—Administration, includes the general responsibilities of a director and discusses the different kinds of settings. Chapter 1 emphasizes the importance of creating a democratic or collegial environment for staff members. Chapter 2 discusses the different kinds of programs and how each affects the job of the administrator.

Part II—Planning: Program and Environment, details the process for designing the program. Chapter 3, Family Child Care, is new to this edition and reflects the growing number of children placed in a family setting. Chapter 4 discusses how to plan a curriculum by setting goals and developing objectives. The reader is taken through the steps that lead to the development of a set of goals, then shown how to use these to develop objectives. Chapters 5 to 7 document planning for three age levels: infants and toddlers, preschool children, and school-age children. Each highlights developmental milestones, then discusses how to plan a developmentally appropriate program and arrange the environment. In each chapter there are specific guidelines and suggestions for activities and areas to include in both the indoor and outdoor environment. This enables the reader to get a complete picture of how to plan for each age level.

Part III—Staff Administration, covers hiring staff and developing personnel policies that encourage staff retention. Chapter 8, Staff Selection/Personnel Policies, takes the director through the process of determining staff qualifications, recruiting, and selecting. There are also sections on developing personnel policies, preventing staff turnover, and writing a personnel manual. Chapter 8 also has a section on managing substitute personnel. Chapter 9, Staff Supervision and Training, suggests effective methods of supervising and evaluating staff as well as planning for staff development and training activities.

Part IV—Management, includes the tasks that are needed to successfully operate a program. Chapter 10 details the process of putting together a budget, including a break-even budget, and operating a program using effective business practices. Chapter 11 discusses maintaining a safe environment, ensuring the health of children. Chapter 12 shows the director how to operate a food program that is economically feasible and is sensitive to cultural differences. Chapter 13, Beginnings: A New Program/A New Year, discusses the processes that are needed to start a new program or begin a school year after a summer break.

Part V—Beyond the School Itself, takes the reader outside the facility to consider external influences. Chapter 14, Including Families and the Community, considers the role of families in early childhood education and how the surrounding community can impact the program. The final chapter, Maintaining the Quality of Child Care, addresses the issues of how to determine quality, how to measure it, and how to maintain it. This chapter also contains a discussion of the laws and issues that pertain to personnel and families as well as a discussion of liability insurance coverage.

Appendix A still contains information about computer software programs that are useful to the administrative process. It has been updated. All vendors were contacted and asked to highlight additions or changes to their product. **Appendix B** lists professional organizations and sources of information for students and directors. **Appendix C** contains a list of publishers and suppliers of early childhood materials, equipment, supplies, and books. **Appendix D** lists the contact information for child-care licensing offices in every state. **Appendix E** is new and contains the complete NAEYC Code of Ethical Conduct.

This edition of the text addresses the requests by reviewers for the latest information and responds to their concerns and requirements. However, the changes may not always meet the needs of each group of students or individual instructors. The order of chapters can be changed as each situation warrants.

Features

The reader will still find the vignettes "A day in the life of . . ." in this edition. These snapshots of a director's activities give the student an opportunity to glimpse what it is like to be a program leader. They also sometimes provide a bit of humor to spark interest in the content and are not meant to be examples of appropriate practices.

Each chapter begins with a list of Key Terms that pinpoint important concepts. Each chapter ends with a Case Study and Helpful websites. The case study poses questions that foster critical thinking, and the websites provide access to additional information if the student chooses to pursue it.

Internet Disclaimer

The authors and Cengage Learning affirm that the website URLs referenced herein were accurate at the time of printing. However, due to the fluid nature of the Internet, we cannot guarantee their accuracy for the life of the edition.

New to This Edition

This edition reflects the changes that are taking place in early childhood education. The following topics have either been expanded or added to this edition.

- Updated References within the text.
- Updated Selected Further Reading.
- Additional information about child care in other countries.
- Entire NAEYC Code of Ethical Conduct in Appendix E.
- Expanded historical, philosophical, and societal foundations of education including Pestalozzi, Rousseau, Montessori, and Dewey.
- Foundation of language development.
- Section of managing aggressive or violent children.
- Updated salary information.
- Changes in organization names or websites.
- Updated information on software programs for computerized data management.
- Information about franchise programs.
- A NEW Video Case related to financial planning for Early Childhood programs is available on the Education CourseMate website.

RESOURCES FOR STUDENTS

Education CourseMate

Cengage Learning's Education CourseMate brings course concepts to life with interactive learning, study, and exam preparation tools that support the printed textbook. This text-specific website offers access to the TeachSource Videos including Video Cases with exercises, transcripts, artifacts, and bonus videos. The website also includes other study tools and resources such as links to related sites for each chapter of the text, tutorial quizzes, glossary flashcards, downloads, and more. Go to www.cengage.com/login to register your access code. If your text does not include an access code card, you can go to Cengage-Brain.com to purchase an access code.

RESOURCES FOR INSTRUCTORS

Instructor's Manual with Test Bank

The Instructor's Manual with Test Bank contains resources designed to streamline and maximize the effectiveness of your course preparations. The contents include Chapter Outlines, Classroom Activities, Audio/Visual Aids, and Guidelines for Answering Review Questions as well as the full test bank.

The instructor website offers access to password-protected resources such as an electronic version of the instructor's manual and PowerPoint® slides. Go to www.cengage.com/login.

PowerLecture with ExamView

This one-stop digital library and presentation tool includes preassembled Microsoft® PowerPoint® lecture slides. In addition to a full Instructor's Manual and Test Bank, Power-Lecture also includes ExamView® testing software with all the test items from the printed Test Bank in electronic format, enabling you to create customized tests in print or online, and all of your media resources in one place including an image library with graphics from the book itself and TeachSource Videos.

WebTutor Toolbox

With WebTutor™ Toolbox for WebCT™ or Blackboard®, jumpstart your course with customizable, rich, text-specific content within your Course Management System. Robust communication tools—such as course calendar, asynchronous discussion, real-time chat, a whiteboard, and an integrated e-mail system—make it easy for your students to stay connected to the course.

How to Use This Text

The sequence of chapters provides the student with a logical progression of topics that have been field-tested by many instructors using the text. The order can be adopted as is or changed to suit the needs of a particular setting. Review questions and activities at the end of each chapter also make it applicable to a self-study plan by individual readers.

A significant resource for students is the list of websites at the end of each chapter. Many students have computers and are comfortable searching for information on the Internet. The instructor can assign topics or pose questions to be answered by logging on to one of the sites. Additionally, the premium website provides the instructor with ways to enhance students' learning. Downloadable forms can be used as worksheets for in-class discussions or reproduced as transparencies to accompany lectures. The case studies are a rich source for augmenting learning. Students can read and discuss the studies online or in groups during class time. The author has posed questions at the end of each, but the instructor may want to pose other questions.

About the Authors

Phyllis Click obtained her bachelor and master's degrees from the University of California at Berkeley in psychology and child development. Throughout a long career, she worked in various settings with both children and adults. She taught in preschools, worked in summer camps, and developed and taught in a program for autistic children. She began working with adults, teaching college students, administering grant programs, and designing a curriculum for a private college for prospective teachers.

Now retired, she has been a consultant, helping others start or administer programs, and has published widely. Her publications include another textbook, articles in professional journals, and ancillary materials for other authors' texts. She belongs to the National Association for the Education of Young Children, the California School-Age Consortium, and the Association for Childhood Education International.

Kimberly Karkos was awarded a bachelor's degree in early childhood education and family relations from the University of Connecticut and a master's degree in early childhood development from St. Joseph College in Connecticut. She received a director's Administrative Credential from the National Institute of Childcare Management in 2004. She has been an administrator for various early childhood programs for over 35 years.

Ms. Karkos currently is a Child Development faculty member at Oxnard college and serves as the Director of the laboratory school. Previously, she has worked as a consultant, grant writer and also has conducted research. She has had extensive experience designing and conducting various training programs; workshops; and courses for child-care staff, family day-care providers, and parents. She belongs to the National Association for the Education of Young Children and is an active of the Ventura County Child Care Planning Council and several other community boards.

Acknowledgments

Our thanks to those who generously gave of their time to make this edition of *Administration of Programs for Young Children* an effective tool for both new and experienced administrators. Our special thanks to Christopher Shortt, Acquisitions Editor, and Diane Colwyn, Developmental Editor. We want to express our appreciation for the other Wadsworth Cengage Learning staff members who carried the project from one step to another until the final pages were put together.

A special thanks to the reviewers who took the time to read the previous edition as well as the eighth edition draft manuscript and offered excellent suggestions for changes and additions to this edition:

Toni A. Campbell	San Jose State University
Sandra Duncan	Nova Southeastern University
Colleen Fawcett	Palm Beach Community College
Kay Gillock	Gillock Gang's Home Child Care
John R. Hranitz	Bloomsburg University of Pennsylvania
Jerri J. Kropp	Georgia Southern University
Herman E. Walston	Kentucky State University

PART I

Administration

The Director: A Broad View

Objectives

After reading this chapter, you should be able to:

- State the responsibilities of a director.
- Describe management styles and methods.
- Identify ways a director allocates school resources.
- Discuss the role of a director as a communicator.
- Devise and use a self-evaluation tool.
- Discuss the relationship of a director to a board of trustees.

KEY TERMS

ethics

leadership

management

morality

nonverbal messages

values

A day in the life of . . .

A Director of a For-Profit Center

6:30 A.M. Arrive to open center. One parent waiting, the first teacher is late. The phone is ringing, it's a sick teacher. Child and I go to classroom to set out a few materials. Finally a teacher arrives.

6:45 A.M. I go to my office; there are notes from my assistant on my desk. They concern a request from Michelle (an assistant teacher) to leave early; an upset mother; two requested tours with prospective families; and that it is time to order rubber gloves, paper towels, and tissues. The parents are arriving and the phone continues to ring, heralding further changes in attendance. I take out my daily schedule to make the changes, then call a substitute teacher from our list. She will come, but cannot get there for an hour and a half. No substitute assistant teacher, so Michelle cannot leave early. Maybe I'll be able to figure it out later.

7:00 A.M. Jordan's mom comes into the office and without closing the door demands to talk to me. "I thought you had a policy that you won't release a child to anyone other than who is listed on the enrollment form by the parents!" Yesterday her daughter was released to her uncle. Even though he was known to the staff, he should not have been allowed to pick her up. "I expect that you are going to look into this and give me a full report. And I just want you to know how upset I am!"

I apologized and assured her that I would investigate it and that this was not reflective of our policy. I told her I would give her a report by the end of the day.

7:30 A.M. I am in the toddler room welcoming parents, explaining why I am there and that the regular teacher was sick, reassuring them, however, that a substitute teacher was on her way. I spend 45 minutes in the room helping the children separate from their parents. The phone continues to ring. I answer from the classroom. Three more children have called in sick.

The cook enters the room to tell me that the milk expired yesterday and that there is no pancake mix for the morning snack. She stays in the room while I get petty cash so she can go to the store for more. I have to remember to tell the teachers that the snack will be about 20 minutes late.

8:20 A.M. The substitute has arrived. I walk through the classrooms to see if everything is fine. I count to check that the teacher/child ratio is correct. A parent comes in and hands me her tuition check. She waits for a receipt and requests a conference with her child's teacher. She wants me to be there because the teacher intimidates her.

8:40 A.M. I finally get to my desk. A staff member comes to request a day off the following week. I talk to a prospective parent for 10 minutes and schedule a tour for this afternoon at 2:00.

9:00 A.M. My administrative assistant arrives. We talk briefly about what needs to get done today and what transpired yesterday afternoon. She takes messages off the answering machine. By now there is an extra teacher in one room.

I begin to work on the payroll report, the cash flow report, and the payment status log. This usually takes one hour if there are no interruptions. I almost finish, but my tour arrives 10 minutes early. We tour the building, then sit in the office.

10:30 A.M. The tour leaves, and I return to my paperwork. I meet with the staff who let the child go yesterday with her uncle. I reiterate our policy and ensure they understand their responsibility.

11:00 A.M. The phone rings with another inquiry from a prospective parent. I take her phone number and promise to call back.

12:00 P.M. I leave the building to make a bank deposit and to purchase tomorrow's supplies. I return to the center in time for some leftovers from lunch and again review the daily schedule to decide if I can let Michelle leave early. I decide to shift an extra teacher to Michelle's room. She's very happy.

I begin tomorrow's schedule and look at my to-do list for today. I call the upset parent and give her a full report. I write a thank you note to the parents who partici-pated in last week's fundraiser, ask my assistant to send reminders to 10 parents to pay tuition, and call back the prospective parent who wants to tour the school. I begin work on a grant application that is due next week.

2:00 P.M. My tour arrives, and we spend about 20 minutes together. I give my assistant a list of three things to do that I did not get done today. I make a new list for tomorrow.

3:00 P.M. I begin the agenda for Friday's staff in-service. My doctor's office calls to inform me that I missed my appointment this morning and will be charged for that.

I look at the clock and realize I am going to be late for a Child Care Planning Council meeting. I run out of the building and tell my assistant to call my cell phone if there are any emergencies.

Karen, Director of Kiddie Academy

Child Care in the United States: A Brief History

Throughout history, families have relied on others to care for their children (Gotts, 1988). The beginning of the day-care movement originated with the welfare and reform move-ments of the 19th century. "Day care grew out of a welfare movement to care for immi-grant and working class children while their impoverished mothers worked" (Boschee & Jacobs, 2006). Today's day-care centers evolved from these day nurseries, which began in Boston in the 1840s.

The nurseries cared for children of economically deprived working wives and wid-ows. Settlement houses promoted day care for immigrant children. Day care was founded to alleviate the child-care problems of working parents and to prevent children from wan-dering the streets.

Child care in the United States, like many other enterprises, has been a melting pot of ideas and interests (Boschee & Jacobs, 2006). During the Great Depression, the Federal Government sponsored day care. The desire to employ out-of-work adults—not a belief in the value of early education—motivated this sponsorship.

During World War II, the Federal Government sponsored day care for 400,000 preschool children so that their mothers could work in industries producing war materials. After the war, the government removed all support for day care, and it encouraged women to stay home and care for their children. Many women, however, rejected that advice. Consequently, the ranks of working women have been steadily increasing since World War II (Boschee & Jacobs, 2006).

In 1943 a unique program began in Portland, Oregon. The Kaiser shipyards opened two child-care centers. They built these centers as an effort to reduce the rate of absenteeism among their working mothers. These were the world's largest child-care centers, open 24 hours a day, and models of child-centered construction. Each center had a nurse for sick children, and each provided hot meals for mothers to take home. Cost of the care was shared by parents and Kaiser. In the two years that they were open, the centers served 3,811 different children (Gordon & Browne, 2007).

CHILD-CARE TRENDS

Today more businesses are providing on-site child-care centers for their employees. New innovations in corporate, intergenerational, day-care centers provide services to toddlers, preschoolers, and the elderly. Two hotel chains in Atlanta have combined to build a 24-hour-a-day, subsidized child-care center, offering family-support services, immunizations, and parenting classes. Eighty percent of their 250 openings are reserved for children from low-income families (Shellenberger, 1994).

The dramatic increase in the labor force participation of mothers has been the most important factor affecting the demand for child care in the last quarter century. Currently, in a majority of American families with children, including those with toddlers, the mother works. According to the 2008 Yearbook on The State of America's Children, 65 percent of married women with children and 70 percent of single women with children are in the workforce. According to their figures, however, only one in seven child-care centers and one in 10 family child-care homes are high enough quality to enhance children's development (Children's Defense Fund, 2008).

Similarly, an increasingly significant trend affecting the demand for child care is the proportion of mothers who are the sole or primary financial supporters of their children. Additionally, child care has been a significant issue in debates over moving welfare recipients toward employment and self-sufficiency; mothers on welfare may have difficulty entering the labor force because of child-care problems. Finally, the impact of child care on children is the subject of ongoing discussions about whether low-income children benefit from participation in programs with an early childhood development focus. *NC Pre-K*

According to the U.S. Department of Labor, "The need for programs that serve young children and their families will continue to grow. The need for day care providers and child-care workers is projected to increase faster than the average of all occupations through the year 2008" (2006).

As women's labor force participation has grown over the past several decades, concerns about the quality of child care have increased. Highly publicized research on brain development in infants and children younger than age three has drawn attention to the role that child care may play in children's cognitive and social development. The relationship between quality of child care and children's development is of increasing interest to parents,

[handwritten margin note: A daunting challenge / An exhausting Job / 40+ hrs/wk]

researchers, and policymakers. A growing body of research is examining the elements that correspond to quality child care, measurements of those elements, and their effects on children both in the short and long term.

Knowing that the quality of early care and education that young children receive lays the building blocks for future success in school urges child-care programs and day-care providers to meet higher standards. Thus, organizations such as the National Association for the Education of Young Children (NAEYC), the National Child Care Association (NCCA), the National School Age Childcare Association (NSACA), and the National Association for Family Child Care (NAFCC) promote professional development, accreditation, and other quality care initiatives.

MODERN DAY REALITY

Running a successful business while providing quality services to children and families is a complex task, which makes child-care administration a daunting challenge. How do you retain competent staff, offer a program that prepares children for later school success, and manage a business at the same time? It becomes harder every day. During slow economic times, businesses of all sizes face layoffs, closures, or restructuring. Employees may have shortened hours, a lack of raises, reduced pay, split shifts, and/or multiple jobs to make ends meet.

Directors know the impact of these modern day realities: shifting enrollments, more part-time enrollments, and difficulty collecting fees. There is also increased competition, increased costs, and a growing number of "customers" with few resources. What can the child-care provider and the business owner do? First, they can revisit the basics of sound business practices for small businesses. Small businesses all face stiff competition, rising costs, and shifting consumer demand. Many do not survive. However, many last because they monitor consumer needs, customer satisfaction, and cost controls.

A successful program director needs more than a strong commitment to children and families. Minimally, such a director must be a knowledgeable manager and a wise leader. The following is a description of some salient elements of both of these necessary and valuable roles.

Management

[handwritten note: Goal: Be a Knowledgeable manager and a wise leader]

Managing a child-care facility can be an exhausting job that requires much more than a typical 40-hour workweek. Stress and burnout often occur, resulting in substandard child care. The child-care program manager in the 21st century must learn to work smarter, not harder. What does intelligent management include? Knowing that the quality of **leadership** can determine program success, how can someone be an effective leader?

Successful program **management** today includes such valuable practices as:

- learning how to run a successful business.
- automating the facility for maximum efficiency: management software keeps track of children and families; keeps records updated; monitors fees to collect, bills to pay, and reports to write; and much more. Using such software you can accomplish tasks significantly faster.
- sound financial planning: maintaining a balanced budget; developing profit and loss forecasts, break-even points, and strategies to identify cash flow or funding gaps; and creating strategies such as fundraising, grants, and gifts to meet funding gaps.

- establishing effective marketing and public relations strategies to promote the services: staying abreast of market trends in the area; and maintaining a competitive edge.
- knowing, implementing, and, often, exceeding licensing standards.
- being aware of legal issues including legislation affecting child care: national standards, health and safety, fire safety and first aid, child protection, equality of opportunity, employment law, insurance, and environmental health.
- developing a work plan, including assigning roles and responsibilities and developing timetables of work and a SWOT analysis. (SWOT analysis is a tool for auditing an organization and its environment. SWOT stands for strengths, weaknesses, opportunities, and threats. Strengths and weaknesses are internal factors. Opportunities and threats are external factors.)
- regularly evaluating the strengths and weaknesses of your operation, and developing action plans to improve program performance.

Leadership

I don't want to be just a manager. I want to be a leader

Understanding the difference between leadership and management is as important as understanding what each is. Leadership is setting a direction or vision for a group to follow. A leader provides guidance for that direction. Management controls or directs resources according to established principles. Management without leadership works to maintain the status quo and ensures that things happen according to established plans. Leadership combined with management designates a new direction and manages the resources to achieve it.

A transformational leadership approach, which emphasizes behaviors that inspire and nurture others, is especially beneficial in child-care settings. This method of leadership meets both the challenges of a rapidly changing environment and the need to engage everyone emotionally within the program.

Transformational leadership behaviors include:

- developing and sharing an inspiring vision of the program's future.
- behaving in ways that bring out the best in individuals and teams.
- showing genuine concern and respect for others.
- investing continuously in the development of oneself and others.
- developing a culture of collaboration, where change is welcomed as an opportunity rather than one of command and control, where change is viewed as a threat.
- recognizing that leadership needs to be demonstrated at times by everyone in the organization.

THE FIVE C'S OF LEADERSHIP

1. **Character:** People will not follow someone whom they cannot trust. Leaders have to be trustworthy to produce sustainable results.

2. **Caring:** The old cliché is true: "People don't care how much you know until they know how much you care." Leaders demonstrate care for their team personally and professionally. A leader is interested in staff concerns, while sensitive to individual needs; is patient, creative, and flexible; is respected as knowledgeable and fair; is able to share responsibility and credit with others; promotes consensus, compromise, and trade-offs; and integrates different perspectives.

Touchone

3. **Commitment:** There is a poster on the gym wall in Clint Eastwood's movie *Pretty Baby* that says "Winners do what losers won't do." Leaders have that quality too. Leaders are doers. Their high level of commitment is the inspiration that motivates their staff to achieve program goals.

4. **Confidence:** Leaders are confident about what must be done and in their own capabilities to accomplish those tasks. Furthermore, they want others to be successful with them. They instill confidence in others and make everyone on the team feel like a winner.

5. **Communication:** Leaders have compelling visions and clearly communicate those visions to their staff. Leaders utilize good communication and group interaction skills. In his book, *Leadership*, Rudolph Giuliani (2002) explains his insistence on his routine morning meeting. "I consider it the cornerstone to efficient functioning within any system. . . . We accomplish a great deal during that first hour, in large part because the lines of communication were so clear." In addition to being clear and understandable, leaders are exceptional listeners. Managers who develop these qualities will create an environment where their teams will willingly do more tasks.

Gotta work on that!

TO LEAD OR TO MANAGE

The answer is to employ a combination of skills, and as the old proverb says, "leadership is doing the right thing; management is doing things right." Both are required for effective program coordination:

> There is a direct correlation between the way people view their managers and the way they perform themselves. Strong leadership is imperative for shaping a group of people into a force that serves as a competitive business advantage (Stevens, 2001).

Cengage Learning

The director acts as organizer, manager, and communicator of the institution.

DIFFERENCES BETWEEN WHAT LEADERS AND MANAGERS DO

The role of the classic manager is to work within the existing system to maintain status quo, minimize risks, enforce organizational rules, steer people in the right direction, react, and provide instruction and direction.

Leaders work "on" the system to create new opportunities, transform organizational rules when necessary, provide a vision and strategic alignment, coordinate efforts, and support and empower people. Leadership requires motivating people to abandon out-moded habits and achieve new results. Therefore, it is about change and, subsequently, about inspiring, helping, and sometimes enforcing change in people. "While there can be effective management absent ideas, there can be no true leadership" (O'Toole, 1996).

The Director Has General Responsibilities

Determines requirements that must be met regarding licensing, health, and safety regulations from the state and local regulatory agencies. Works with agencies to meet requirements.

Serves as an ex officio member of the board of directors and attends committee meetings as necessary.

Provides leadership for setting overall goals for the school—to be used as a basis for curriculum objectives.

Creates reports on the school as required by the board or corporation.

Evaluates own work as a director and plans for continuing professional growth.

The Director Has Enrollment Duties

Enrolls children and keeps an accurate waiting list.

Interviews prospective parents, providing information about the school.

Plans orientation for new parents.

Knows the changing needs of the community in order to maintain full enrollment.

Prepares a parent handbook and keeps it current.

The Director Supervises Curriculum

Provides direction to staff in setting curriculum objectives appropriate to the school goals.

Works with staff to implement and maintain goals and objectives.

Provides leadership in evaluating curriculum.

Provides up-to-date information on curriculum issues.

The Director Is Responsible for the Physical Plant and Equipment

Plans, allocates, and uses space effectively.

Maintains the physical plant by providing custodial care and repair services.

Plans for the future space and equipment needs of the school.

Keeps records such as inventories, repair schedules, and purchase information.

Manages supplies, reordering as needed.

Monitors the health and safety aspects of the environment.

Playground Safety

The Director Is in Charge of Finances

Plans a budget.

Controls budget expenditures.

Collects fees and tuition.

Manages disbursements for payroll, equipment, and supplies.

Keeps adequate records of income and expenditures.

Handles petty cash disbursements.

Prepares monthly reports on expenditures to date.

Prepares a year-end analysis of budget and expenditures.

Reports to board or corporation.

The Director Is Concerned with Staff Relationships

Recruits and hires staff.

Plans and conducts staff orientation.

Prepares job descriptions for each position.

Formulates and implements personnel policies.

Assists staff in implementing school goals.

Provides a continuing assessment of staff development needs.

Plans with staff for in-service training.

Encourages staff involvement in community activities.

Meets with staff members to resolve problems.

Prepares a staff handbook and keeps it current.

Keeps personnel records.

The Director Provides Leadership in Parent Involvement and Education

Communicates goals of the school to parents.

Plans and implements parent education activities.

Confers with parents regarding their child's progress.

Encourages various ways for parents to be involved in school activities.

Keeps adequate records of parent involvement and education activities.

The Director Must Plan for Health and Safety

Maintains an adequate health program for the school.

Keeps health records on all enrolled children.

Keeps staff informed concerning the health status of each child.

Confers with parents as needed about child's health and nutritional status.

Refers families to community agencies for special help when necessary.

Continues to be informed regarding legal responsibilities of the school in relation to safety.

Plans activities for staff and children to teach safety.

Effective managers involve staff in planning.

Cengage Learning

The Director Builds and Maintains Good Community Relations

Interprets the school's goals to visitors.

Maintains an effective public relations and advertising process.

Represents the school at community functions.

Establishes contacts with community agencies.

Involves self and staff in professional and legislative activities.

Organization

DELEGATING RESPONSIBILITY

In order to accomplish the many tasks required, directors must be good organizers. This means they must make the best possible use of the resources available to them. The first step is to learn to delegate responsibilities to others. By doing so, they will accomplish more themselves and achieve greater participation from staff members. Many directors find it difficult to delegate responsibility to others, feeling that it puts an unnecessary burden on their staff or that they cannot be certain the job will be done properly. In *The Early Childhood Super Director*, Sue Baldwin (1991) cited the following reasons directors gave for not being able to delegate.

Book to buy →

- Unable to let go of control *(Me)*
- Staff does not measure up to expectations
- Fear of repercussions if delegating occurs

- Perfectionism **Me**
- Concerned about the quality of the job to be delegated **Me**
- Staff perception that the director may be pushing work onto the staff
- Caretaking personality
- Fear of imposing on people
- Staff that will not say "no" to any requests because of the director's position
- Not being able to explain why others should do the tasks
- Lack of organization to get help in time

Directors in all-day centers may have an assistant director who handles some administrative tasks. When a program is open many hours, one person may open the school in the morning, set the daily schedules, and talk to parents as they drop off their children. The other may close the school and help parents and children reunite. In between, they may divide other administrative tasks.

The division of labor between the director and assistant should be based on an assessment of their skills and interests. Some people like to do the necessary myriad daily paperwork; others like to interact with the people involved in the program. Both should decide which jobs each is more comfortable with and does best. Each should have primary responsibility for those tasks. Once their primary responsibilities are assigned, assistants should be allowed to perform those tasks without interference. The director still bears ultimate responsibility for the performance of the assistant; therefore, communication between them is important.

Responsibilities also can be delegated to other staff members. The cook can order supplies, compile information on new equipment to be purchased, or plan schedules for serving snacks and meals. The maintenance person can create the cleaning schedule or suggest ways to recycle and reuse disposable materials. A secretary may assume responsibility for scheduling classroom field trips that have been suggested by teachers or for calling a qualified substitute from a list. The director should decide who can best accomplish a task. This requires the director to assess the necessary skills and then to find the best person for the job. The person who does the task needs to benefit. No one should be asked to perform extra duties merely to help the director with administrative functions. Delegating a task does not mean forgetting about it and expecting it to be done. It is important to establish a schedule and procedure for supervising delegated responsibilities. The director may meet with the staff person once a week or once a month, or they may just have that person provide written updates periodically.

When first delegating responsibilities, some directors may find that the task takes more time than if they had done the work themselves. However, as employees learn and gain confidence, directors find that their time is freed for those tasks that only they can do. They also discover that both they and their staff benefit immeasurably from the team effort.

ORGANIZING TIME

Time is a precious commodity to busy directors. They can accomplish much more each day if they make a list starting with either urgent jobs or daily jobs; these should take top priority. Next come jobs that should be done as soon as possible or need to be done once a week. Last are the jobs that they would like to do or only have to do infrequently.

The director should set aside a specific time to do jobs that must be done every day. Sometimes it helps, for instance, to get to work a half-hour before opening time so that certain jobs can be done before the center becomes busy. Some of the daily jobs can be done later in the day. It may be difficult to follow precisely a schedule for accomplishing these tasks, but if done with persistence, other staff members will begin to honor the time commitments of the director.

It is helpful to schedule one day a week or specific days during the month to do tasks that need to be completed less frequently. Ordering materials, compiling financial reports, and writing a newsletter are examples. The director should mark the day on the calendar, block out some time, go into the office, close the door, and get to work. It is surprising how quickly it will be finished when there are no interruptions.

Directors should plan for those tasks they would like to do when they have time. Reading professional materials, writing an article, or making long-range plans may all fall into this category. These are all important, and directors should not feel guilty about setting aside an afternoon each month to accomplish any of these tasks.

Emergencies will arise—by definition, at the most inopportune times—but if one is prepared, they are manageable. What kinds of emergencies come up in a school for young children? The same kinds that happen in a busy household: the plumbing stops working or leaks occur; the licensing worker is coming to visit and two teachers call in sick; a child falls and is bleeding from a cut on his forehead. No one will panic in any of these situations if procedures have been established ahead of time.

For possible building and equipment emergencies, it is useful to keep an up-to-date list of repairmen. When new equipment is purchased, repair information should be added to the list immediately. For staff emergencies, a list of reliable substitutes is essential. Qualified people can often be found by advertising in a local newspaper.

Students may be found through the local community college or university. If a desirable teacher applies for a position at the school and there is no opening, they should be encouraged to accept placement on the substitute list. A written procedure to care for children's injuries should be posted in a prominent place so that any staff member can follow the correct procedure. Training of the procedure should be part of orientation.

Additionally, several staff members should know first aid and be Red Cross certified, if possible. Other kinds of emergencies arise, depending upon the area of the country. In southern California, schools are required to have an earthquake disaster plan. In some hillside areas, schools have developed a plan for evacuating children in case of a brush fire. A tornado drill for schools in the Midwest, Texas, and New England is appropriate. States along the southeastern seaboard may need plans for managing children in case of a severe

[Handwritten margin note: Tasks 1. urgent/daily 2. Do soon/weekly 3. Infrequently/would like to do]

storm. There may be other disasters requiring an evacuation or lockdown of the building, such as community violence or a bomb scare. Drills should be planned and executed so that all staff members and children react quickly and without panic.

A computer will save the director an incredible amount of time. Although it takes time to learn to use one and to input data, it will be an enormously useful tool for keeping financial records and budgets up-to-date along with records from previous years. A quick comparison of this year's income and expenses is immediately accessible. Many personnel records can be kept on a computer file: dates of employment, attendance, and additional academic work are a few examples. A computer word processing program will make any secretarial task faster and easier. All correspondence, newsletters, memos, and notices can be done faster and with greater possibility for interesting variations such as graphics. Programs for developing address lists are available. Ample databases are useful for lists of addresses of parents, staff, community organizations, food and equipment vendors, or people who have visited the school. Within the last few years, some software manufacturers have developed programs specifically for preschool management. These programs and systems vary considerably in quality and price. Although specific references to computers appear in later chapters, Appendix A contains a lengthy discussion.

PLANNING

Faced with the pressures of everyday activities, it is easy to overlook any kind of planning, yet it is an essential part of managing a child-care center. Each day is filled with so many occurrences that must be dealt with immediately that it is difficult to find time to focus on what should happen the next day, let alone the next month.

However, both short- and long-term planning are necessary for the smooth operation of the facility. Short-term planning ensures the smooth running of each day and provides contingency plans when the unexpected occurs. At the beginning of each day and each week, the director must know what has to be done, and then he or she must ensure that those tasks are finished throughout the day or week. However, there will be inevitable emergencies. It is important to think ahead about the kinds of emergencies that have occurred in the past and are likely to happen again, and then develop backup plans. This will not eliminate temporary disruptions caused by emergencies, but they will be easier to manage.

Long-term planning will help the director to provide the kind of environment and services that are set forth in the goals for the center. The director decides which goals should be addressed at a particular time and then sets a schedule for implementation. For example, one of the program goals might be that The Child Learning Center will offer various experiences designed to help children acquire the skills needed for kindergarten entrance. To implement that goal, staff members need to know which skills are included, when it is developmentally appropriate to introduce experiences designed to teach those skills, and how to evaluate children's progress. The director should carefully plan a series of learning experiences to inform the teachers. This project may take place over several months or even a year.

The most effective planning will involve the staff as much as possible. Everyone should have a copy of daily and weekly schedules as well as changes for rainy days. Additionally, they should identify long-term goals to work toward during a particular period of time. The director should solicit suggestions for implementing the goals and provide a method for obtaining feedback to evaluate progress.

Communication (verbal, non-verbal, written)

Directors spend a great deal of time talking to people. It is important to develop communication skills to prevent problems as well as to provide a model for other staff members. Everyone experiences some difficulty in communicating with others. We know what we mean, and we are sure the other person understands. Often, though, we are surprised at how others interpret what we have said. We think, "How could they have gotten that meaning out of what I said?"

VERBAL MESSAGES

Words are a coding system and the means by which our thoughts are conveyed to others. Although each word in a language has a meaning, coloration of that meaning comes from our own experiences. Problems occur because we do not all share the same experiences. Words may have different meanings to each of us based on our past. When we use words, what we mean comes from our own experiences. People hearing our words bring their own interpretations. As a result, the message being conveyed may be misunderstood.

Reason for misunderstandings

Sometimes a particular word triggers an emotional response based on a past experience or an association. This causes us to stop listening to the rest of the communication and focus on that one word. The speaker's tone of voice or the emphasis on one word may result in a similar response. "How are you today?" can convey many messages depending on the way it is uttered. It can be merely a polite contact, a real concern, or an irritated inquiry meaning "Are you really all right today since usually you are not?"

NONVERBAL MESSAGES (roadblocks to hearing)

Another reason for problems in communication is that we communicate nonverbally as well as verbally. **Nonverbal messages** are facial expressions, movements, and postures we use while speaking. Additionally, we maintain eye contact or we look away. We sit or stand close to the listener, or we maintain a distance between ourselves and the listener.

Each of these behaviors communicates a meaning, and we are not always aware that our words are saying one thing and our behavior is saying something quite different. (It is interesting to note that different cultures also interpret these behaviors differently.) Not everyone notices these subtle expressions, but others see them clearly and react accordingly. The nonverbal message gets in the way of their hearing our verbal message clearly.

PREVENTING PROBLEMS IN COMMUNICATION

Because so much of a director's work is done through communicating with others, it is important to develop methods that avoid as many problems as possible. The first step is to decide what you want to relay. Are you merely giving information without expecting a response? "There will be two prospective parents visiting your classroom today." Are you stating a problem and do you expect a response from the listener? "I'm wondering if you have any suggestions about how we can make cleaning up the playground at the end of the day any easier?"

Goal:

The second step is to consider when to convey the message. If the content is important, do not do it when the listener is busy and cannot give full attention. For example,

Timing

a director should not tell a teacher something important when they are busy in the classroom. It is better to wait until the children are gone or until the teacher can take a few minutes away from the children.

The third step is to allow enough time to receive feedback. Words spoken on the run are likely to be misunderstood. If the listener does not grasp your message, he or she can ask for clarification, and you can question whether your message was clear.

The fourth step is to decide where a message should be conveyed. When talking to a teacher in an office with the door closed, an atmosphere of confidentiality, or perhaps seriousness, is conveyed. When the conversation takes place on the playground or in the staff lounge, the message will seem more casual. Each place may be appropriate for different kinds of communications.

The fifth step is to decide how to present the message. Is it something that can or should be written? Sometimes it is important for others to see something stated clearly in written form. When information needs to be distributed to all staff members, this may be the most efficient way. Remember, though, the written message is less personal than face-to-face communication and does not allow for immediate feedback, so statements have to be clear.

It is often necessary to follow up on a message. For example, it is apparent that a teacher has misunderstood what was said or is still confused when the expected response is not forthcoming. It will help to consider the way in which the message was conveyed. Sometimes body language conveys one meaning and words another. Is there another way the message can be stated? Did some of the words cause an emotional reaction? It is also helpful to ask for feedback. "You still seem confused. What is it you do not understand about what I have said?" or "Let me say it in a different way. What I meant was. . . ." If the atmosphere encourages open discussion, staff members will likely ask for further clarification when they do not understand. A healthy give-and-take discussion helps resolve a situation. This can help prevent misunderstanding. ✱

LISTENING

I need to work on this.

Part of being an effective communicator is the ability to listen while others speak. Sometimes we only partly listen, letting our minds wander to other topics that seem more urgent. At times, we listen only until there is a point at which we can respond with information, sympathy, a solution, or a denial. One of the most important communication skills a director can develop is to really listen to what others say and to allow them to express their thoughts fully before responding. The following list describes the process of active listening.

Practice listening! ✱

1. Stop talking. That sounds obvious, but it is often forgotten. Do not interrupt.
2. Be mentally ready to listen. Put other thoughts out of your mind and give your full attention to the speaker.
3. Listen to the content of the message. Do not get distracted by the speaker's method of delivery or his or her appearance.
4. Use body language that conveys your interest. Maintain eye contact and assume an attentive posture. Sit or stand in an alert position. Do not slouch or turn away.
5. Try to determine the speaker's intent. Why is the speaker telling you this? If you can answer that question, it will help you to focus on what you hear.
6. Listen for the main ideas. What are the most important concepts or pieces of information, and which are irrelevant? *decipher. . .*

7. Listen for what is not said. You can sometimes learn a great deal from what the speaker leaves out or avoids.

8. Give feedback. Nonverbal feedback, such as a nod or a smile, encourages the speaker to continue. You can also use encouraging phrases such as "go on, tell me more," or "I understand."

9. Check your own understanding of the message. "I hear you saying. . . . Am I hearing you correctly?"

10. Summarize the message. "So the main points of what you have been telling me are. . . ."

Goal → When directors have developed both their speaking and listening skills, they will find that interactions with people will change. They gain in understanding others and demonstrate that they are truly interested in others' concerns and problems. Their relationships with staff members, parents, and even children will be enhanced. Problems will not disappear, but they will be more easily resolved because each party has a greater appreciation of what is involved.

WRITTEN COMMUNICATION

It is sometimes difficult to decide when to convey a message orally and when to write a report, memo, or note. If the message is important and affects more than one person, it should be written. A written record is permanent and far less likely to be misunderstood.

One type of written communication a director must prepare is a report concerning finances. A board of trustees should have a monthly report of cash flow including income and expenses as well as to-date expenditures compared to the budgeted amount. There should be a schedule for submitting preliminary budgets and a final budget for the next year. Although this kind of information can be compiled manually, a computer will allow financial reports to be prepared more efficiently.

A monthly newsletter to parents is another written communication that many directors find effective for disseminating information. Parents want to know what their children are learning, what they have for lunch and snacks, and what plans there are for field trips. A newsletter will give them a sense of involvement and will help to establish a bridge between home and school. As with financial reports, a computer makes it fairly easy to generate a good newsletter.

It often helps to distribute written memos or notices to teachers and parents when changes are going to take place. Shifts in staff assignments, alterations of schedules, substitutions of menu items, or change of plans for celebrating holidays are examples of information that should be conveyed in writing. Everyone receives the same information, so no one will be surprised or feel excluded. Additionally, a written message is less likely to be forgotten because it can be reread.

Written messages can be used to give positive reinforcement. Everyone likes to be told their efforts have been appreciated, and a written message is a tangible reminder that they are valued. A teacher will appreciate a note recognizing an especially effective project. "I heard many comments from parents about how the children really enjoyed the lessons on different artists. The parents said they, too, learned some things they hadn't known before. Thanks for making school an exciting place for our children."

Ethical Practices

The stresses and strains directors experience on any given day are exacerbated by a lack of guidelines to help them confront difficult situations. What should they do when a demanding parent wants her child spanked for hitting other children? Or what should they do when they are asked by a board member to enroll his child ahead of others on the waiting list? The decisions they make are frequently based upon their sense of **morality,** their view of what is good or right. Morality also includes beliefs about how people should behave and the kinds of obligations we have to each other. **Values** are another part of the decision-making process, particularly when faced with a dilemma. Values are the qualities that we believe are intrinsically desirable and that we strive to achieve. The difficulty, however, is that not everyone agrees on issues of morality and not everyone has the same values. There needs to be a link between personal morality, values, and a professional code of behavior. NAEYC (2009) has compiled a statement of core values central to a code of ethical conduct. The organization defines core values as commitments held by a profession. The statement of core values set forth by the organization is based on a long history in the field of early childhood education and care. The statements in the code indicate a commitment to the following core values:

- Appreciate childhood as a unique and valuable stage of the human life cycle
- Base our work on knowledge of how children develop and learn
- Appreciate and support the bond between the child and family
- Recognize that children are best understood and supported in the context of family, culture, and society
- Respect the dignity, worth, and uniqueness of each individual (child, family member, and colleague)
- Respect diversity in children, families, and colleagues
- Recognize that children and adults achieve their full potential in the context of relationships based on trust and respect

Ethics, the study of right, wrong, duty, and obligation, also attempts to provide a link to help in decision making. Ethics and morality are closely related and are often used interchangeably. The NAEYC tried to help educators find the answer to the dilemma of determining ethical behavior. Insights were gathered through surveys, focus groups, and professional input and were compiled as the NAEYC Code of Ethical Conduct, first published in 1989 and revised in 2009 by Carol Copple and Sue Bredenkamp (Copple & Bredenkamp, 2009). The code focuses on the daily interactions with children from birth through age eight and on their families, and the code sets standards for ethical behavior.

The code of ethical conduct is divided into four sections: (1) children, (2) families, (3) colleagues, and (4) community and society. Each section addresses responsibilities, ideals, and principles. The intent of the code is to show exemplary professional behavior and define practices that are required, prohibited, and permitted.

Each section has statements of ideals that reflect the aspirations of practitioners and principles that are intended to guide their conduct and assist them in resolving ethical dilemmas. The entire code can be found in Appendix E.

Every director should be familiar with the code and use it as a guide when making decisions or interacting with others. Additionally, all staff members should have copies, and there should be training workshops to discuss the content and its application to daily experiences. Discussions at staff meetings often center around the challenges teachers meet, and these are additional opportunities to consider solutions based upon the code. Further discussion of training staff members is found in Chapter 8.

Professional Development

First-time directors often express their frustration about their jobs and their abilities to perform them adequately. Bloom (1997) found that only 32 percent felt confident and self-assured when they first became directors. Many had been coaxed and coerced into becoming leaders after success in the classroom, and most felt they were not prepared for the kinds of situations and problems they encountered. Eventually they learn by doing but the journey is a difficult one.

I want to be prepared...

Bloom quotes some comments about their experiences. They said being a director was like ". . . going on a trip—lots of surprises, a few roadblocks and detours, but never a dull moment"; ". . . going through a large maze without a map to guide me—I encounter many twists and turns, often unsure where I am going exactly"; "riding a roller coaster—the ups and downs are exhilarating and usually unpredictable." Bloom found that directors go through several career stages that correspond to career stages of teachers as delineated by other researchers (Fessler & Christensen, 1992). The stages are survival, competence building, enthusiastic and growing, career frustrations, reflective and inspiring, and career wind-down. The survival stage is the period when directors are merely getting through each day, and when they often feel extremely inadequate. By approximately the second year, directors begin to feel competent, having learned how to perform the basic tasks required of them. Bloom uses a wonderful phrase to describes this shift as, "from struggling to juggling." An important realization occurring at this stage is that the qualities that made them good teachers are not always the same qualities that lead to success in their leadership roles. The third stage, enthusiastic and growing, is typical of a master director. These people feel confident, while still juggling the many demands made on them. At the reflective and inspiring stage, directors have reached a high level of competence. They are often seen as leaders and mentors by colleagues. The last stage, career wind-down, is reached as directors prepare for retirement or a career change.

Bloom's research indicates the need for a plan to prepare people to move into administrative positions. Some states have requirements that include specific courses for directors and site supervisors in publicly funded programs. However, professionals feel there is a need for a credential specifically designed for directors or supervisors. This would help to prepare new administrators.

ADMINISTRATIVE CREDENTIAL

The state of Illinois has developed a credential to address the concerns of professionals for director competency. After considering the requirements, the developers outlined a Director Credential that is earned through demonstrating accomplishments in five competency components.

I want to be competent

- General education
- Knowledge and skills regarding early childhood/school-age children: fundamentals of development, care, and education
- Management knowledge and skills: delineates 10 management knowledge and skill competencies

- Experience: on-the-job experience
- Professional contributions: contributions to the profession in six leadership and advocacy situations

The credential is awarded at three levels. The individual must have attained an associate degree for level I, a baccalaureate degree for level II, and a master's degree or other advanced degree for level III. At each level, the candidate must demonstrate the five competency components.

Individuals can achieve the credential in two ways. The first is the entitled program route, accomplished by completing an approved program at an Illinois Director Credential Commission–entitled institution of higher education. The second is the direct application route, accomplished by completing the Illinois Director Credential requirements and submitting documentation to the Illinois Director Credential Commission. For option one, the individual enrolls in an approved program or an entitled institution of higher learning and completes the coursework requirements for the credential. The institution verifies the attainment of each of the requirements. For option two, the individual makes direct application to the commission by submitting a portfolio that includes transcripts, verification of experience, and documentation of professional contributions. The credential is conferred by the Illinois Network of Child Care Resource and Referral Agencies on the recommendation of the Illinois Director Credential Commission.

Although there has been no universal acceptance or adoption of a special credential for administrators of programs, there may be movement toward it in the future. For more information about the Illinois model, contact:

INCCRRA
1226 Towanda Place
Bloomington, IL 61701
309-829-5327 or 800-649-1884
309-828-1808 (fax)

E-mail: inccrra@ilchildcare.org
Website: http://www.inccrra.org

The Director's Evaluation

COMPETENCIES

Assessing director competencies is a difficult and multifaceted task. Bloom (2000) believes that difficulty also occurs because there is not a clear definition of competence. Many educators use a statement put forth by Fenichel and Eggbeer (1990) that competence "is the ability to do the right thing, at the right time, for the right reason." According to Fenichel and Eggbeer, competence requires the ability to analyze a situation, consider alternatives, evaluate the outcomes, and state a rationale for the chosen process. How one measures any of these criteria is purely subjective and therefore difficult to quantify.

Additional problems assessing competency stem from the diverse abilities that different programs require of their leaders. The director of a small center may have limited administrative tasks to perform and may even teach in a classroom part-time. This person must have an extensive knowledge of child development and curriculum planning. The director of a large program with several sites requires quite different skills. The ability to interact with people effectively and to organize a diversified workload would be essential in such a case. The director of an on-site center at a business must work within the corporate structure with people who have business rather than education backgrounds. In addition to a background in early childhood education, this director must have a strong grounding in business methods.

Bloom (2000) believes that competence is comprised of three components: (1) knowledge competency in areas such as group dynamics, organizational theory, child development, teaching strategies, and family systems; (2) skill competency encompassing technical, human, and conceptual skills that are needed to do various tasks from formulating a budget to solving problems; and (3) attitude competency that includes personality and emotional components such as beliefs, values, dispositions, and emotional responses that support the best performance from others.

Directors can evaluate themselves, but it is difficult to be objective. A director can start by listing everything that is done well. This should be followed with a list of things needing improvement. As an example, some directors feel they have not done enough to encourage staff to increase their skills. It is important that they answer the questions of why not. Was it lack of time? Was it lack of knowledge about what is needed? After these questions are answered, determining necessary changes becomes easier.

Another method is listing goals at the beginning of each year and periodically checking whether the goals are being met. If not, how can they be implemented? At the end of the year it is important to check the list and mark items that were not done. Why were they not completed? Was it a lack of skills, of knowledge? Were there other reasons that prevented the attainment of goals? The answers will give directors valuable information about what to change.

SELF-EVALUATION TOOLS

Written evaluation tools can be used to analyze the director's performance. These will be similar to those used to evaluate other staff members. There are two basic types: an evaluation sheet containing a list of questions and a rating scale.

The evaluation sheet asks questions about specific areas of the job. It should be based on either the job description or the goals that have been set for the year. It will ask, "Have I . . . ?"

Some sample questions are:

- Have I created an open climate for discussion among staff members?
- Have I used my time efficiently?
- Have I sufficiently conveyed my understanding of parents' problems and pressures through my contacts with them?

A rating scale can also be used. It addresses specific skills such as organization, planning, or initiative. It also includes a way of rating the skills comparatively, such as good versus unsatisfactory, or on the frequency of occurrence. It might look like the following example:

I show consideration for the feelings of my employees.	☑ Often	❏ Sometimes	❏ Never
I try to praise rather than criticize.	☑ Often	❏ Sometimes	❏ Never
I welcome suggestions from others.	❏ Often	☑ Sometimes	❏ Never

A numerical scale asks individuals to rate their own abilities on a scale of 1 to 5, with 1 being the most adept. It might look like this:

Schedule and organize work	☑1	❑ 2	❑ 3	❑ 4	❑ 5
Plan for future needs of the school	❑ 1	☑2	❑ 3	❑ 4	❑ 5
Communicate clearly with staff	☑1	❑ 2	❑ 3	❑ 4	❑ 5
Resourceful in resolving problems	❑ 1	☑2	❑ 3	❑ 4	❑ 5

● ● ● ● ● ● EVALUATION BY STAFF MEMBERS

A more recent trend is peer rating, whereby directors are evaluated by staff members. This is best accomplished through periodic attitude surveys of how employees view the organizational climate of the child-care center. A general survey of various aspects can be included in one survey, or individual surveys can focus on specific parts of the work environment. In the example (Table 1-1), teachers are asked to determine whether specific conditions exist most of the time.

Many other items could be added to fit the needs of a particular setting. There should also be a place at the end of the document for comments or suggestions to improve the organizational environment.

TABLE 1-1

Example of a Teacher Evaluation of the Director

CHECK ALL THE RESPONSES THAT APPLY

OPEN COMMUNICATION
Does your director . . .
_encourage questions and discussions of problems?
✓allow staff members to express feelings?
_create a team feeling among all staff members?
_solicit ideas for improving working conditions?

PROFESSIONAL DEVELOPMENT
Are you encouraged by the director to . . .
✓attend workshops to learn new skills?
_share resources with other staff members?
_visit other classrooms?
_attend college classes and obtain reimbursement for tuition?
_read professional journals and books?

LEADERSHIP CHARACTERISTICS
Which characteristics apply to your director?
_is supportive
_gives frequent feedback
✓is often critical
_is willing to share information with others
✓very seldom visits classrooms
_is fair when evaluating staff
_is usually available when needed

EVALUATION BY A BOARD OF DIRECTORS

In a child-care center governed by a board of directors, periodic evaluation of the administrator is essential. However, this kind of evaluation has some drawbacks that need to be addressed before proceeding. Board members may not have frequent contact with the daily functioning of the center. They may also be laypersons with limited knowledge of either early childhood education or of organizational management. Additionally, directors do not always know in advance the criteria to which they are being held accountable.

These problems are avoidable, and the process can even enhance the director's effectiveness. One of the first issues to be addressed is the frequency of evaluation. A usual period is once every 12 months, although a board may choose a six-month period for a new employee. Next, the board and director should agree upon the criteria to be used in the assessment. Two broad categories are standard. First, how is the director furthering the overall goals of the program (Table 1-2)? Second, how effective are the director's leadership and managerial qualities (Table 1-3)?

The director's job description is a good place to start because it is important to know whether specific tasks were done and how well they were done. Some criteria are easy to assess, whereas others are more difficult. For instance, it is easy to determine whether enrollment information is being kept up-to-date and whether reports are presented on time. It is more difficult to decide whether the director communicates effectively. In this case, a rating scale is useful.

Usually a committee comprising several board members works out the wording of the rating instrument, which the entire board then approves. Whenever possible, the same people who developed the scale should be involved in conducting the evaluation. Before beginning, they should review the criteria and agree upon how to assess them. Directors should submit a written report on their compliance, accompanied by any specific materials that support the report. The committee can then seek further information from others: parents, fund-granting agencies, or other directors.

The merits of gathering information from staff members are debatable. Some professionals feel this undermines the relationship between the director and employees.

After collecting all the information, the committee meets with the director to discuss each item. This meeting can also include a discussion about improving performance or

TABLE 1-2 **Achievement of Center Goals**

CIRCLE THE APPROPRIATE MEASURE OF ACHIEVEMENT

The director:

1. maintained at least an 80% full-time equivalent enrollment.
   Seldom   Often   Always

2. ensured the safety of children by scheduling periodic safety checks.
   Seldom   Often   Always

3. worked with the licensing agency to comply with regulations.
   Seldom   Often   Always

4. planned and implemented a staff training program to upgrade the quality of the overall program.
   Seldom   Often   Always

5. publicized the center by speaking to community groups about the center's philosophy.
   Seldom   Often   Always

TABLE 1-3   **Achievement of Leadership Goals**

CIRCLE THE APPROPRIATE MEASURE OF ACHIEVEMENT

The director:

1. communicates effectively with board members, staff, and parents.

1................................2................................3................................4................................5

Incompetent   Excellent

2. is available to provide information to board members.

1................................2................................3................................4................................5

Incompetent   Excellent

3. is viewed by other directors as a leader and a mentor.

1................................2................................3................................4................................5

Incompetent   Excellent

4. is viewed by parents as knowledgeable and supportive.

1................................2................................3................................4................................5.

Incompetent   Excellent

5. follows through with board directives.

1................................2................................3................................4................................5

Incompetent   Excellent

a response from the director with further information. The committee members and the director sign the report and present it to the board. The final step in the evaluation process is to plan for the next evaluation.

The Director's Relation to Boards of Directors

BOARDS OF DIRECTORS

Historically, the majority of board-governed schools were nonprofit ones sponsored by churches, community organizations, or social agencies. This category now includes programs funded by some level of government: Head Start, migrant worker centers, child-care centers, and facilities for children with special needs. More recently, there has been a significant rise in the number of multisite, profit-making corporation-schools governed by a board. Additionally, many businesses now operate on-site child-care centers or participate in a consortium that is established as a corporation.

In order to work effectively, a director must understand the composition and function of the boards. Two basic types of boards exist: governing and advisory. A governing board creates and enforces policy that is then implemented by the program administrator. An advisory board has no power to enforce; instead it suggests policies and procedures or provides information to those who administer a program. The bylaws of an organization should clearly state the purpose and functions of a board of directors.

The composition of a board will vary according to the type of center it administers. A nonprofit board will include members chosen from the population it represents. Frequently, these members will be parents of children attending the school or members of the sponsoring church. Additionally, the board may include early childhood education professionals and community leaders. Substantial consideration is usually given to making the board diverse—based on the members' backgrounds, occupations, ethnic groups, ages, genders, and points of view. Board members may be appointed or elected, and membership is contingent upon the individual's willingness to serve.

The board of directors of a for-profit corporation is selected by the shareholders or investors. This type of board usually consists particularly of people with business expertise. Sometimes, parents may also be shareholders and therefore eligible for board membership. The board may decide to include nonshareholder parents, early childhood professionals, or community representatives.

No ideal number for a board of directors exists, although some state laws specify a required number. Some boards have three members whereas others have 25 members. A small board is more manageable. It is easier for members to become acquainted and to work together effectively, but there are fewer people to perform the necessary tasks. Conversely, a larger board may be unwieldy. However, it provides greater diversity of ideas and expertise, and there are more people to assign to committees.

Board members may serve terms of one to three years. One year may not allow an individual enough time to become a fully functioning participant. However, some people may be unable or unwilling to serve for a longer period. Many boards institute three-year terms in order to maintain continuity. This is particularly effective with large boards, where terms can be staggered. The board always has seasoned members and some newcomers.

Board member term limits should be stated in the bylaws. The bylaws should also contain a clear method for filling vacancies. The bylaws should include a provision for removing board members—either at their own request or at the request of center personnel, parents, or fellow board members.

BOARD DUTIES

One of the first duties of a new board of trustees is to research, draft, and publish an appropriate set of bylaws. In an existing school, bylaws should be periodically reviewed to determine whether changes or updates are needed. The bylaws constitute the basic charter of the school and should include the following:

- official name of the school.
- purpose.
- composition of the board.
- terms of office and procedure for selection or replacement.
- officers and procedure for selection.
- participation by staff members.
- board duties.
- standing committees and their duties.
- guidelines for regular or special meetings.
- procedures for amending bylaws.

A typical set of bylaws is shown in Figure 1-1. Some programs may require additional items. When the bylaws are completed, the rest of the board's work can begin. The board should determine the philosophy of the program. Philosophy is discussed in Chapter 3; basically it is a condensed version of the ideas, beliefs, and values held by those

(Official Name and Address of School)

Article I. Board of Trustees

Section 1.   The board of trustees shall consist of not less than _____ nor more than _____ people.

Section 2.   Members of the board of trustees shall be elected at the membership meeting in _____ (month) and such trustees shall be elected for terms as hereafter provided.

Section 3.   The terms of office shall be for _____ years, beginning _____ .

Section 4.   The board of trustees shall meet at least _____ times a year. A special meeting may be called at any time by _____ .

Section 5.   A quorum shall be constituted by _____ of the membership.

Section 6.   A vacancy on the board may be filled by the board, pending the next meeting of the membership.

Article II. Officers

Section 1.   The officers shall consist of _____ .

Section 2.   All officers shall be elected for a term of _____ .

Section 3.   Officers shall be elected at the membership meeting in _____ (month).

Section 4.   The chairperson shall have the following duties: _____ .

Section 5.   The vice chairperson shall have the following duties: _____ .

Section 6.   The treasurer shall have the following duties: _____ .

Section 7.   The following officers may be elected if desired: _____ .

Section 8.   The director of the school will serve as an ex officio member of the board.

Article III. Standing Committees

Section 1.   The following standing committees shall be appointed by the _____ .

Section 2.   The function of the (curriculum, finance, personnel, building, etc.) committees shall be _____ .

Article IV. Membership Meetings

Section 1.   The regular annual meeting of the membership may be held during the month of _____ .

Section 2.   Special meetings of the membership may be called by _____ .

Article V. Amendments

These bylaws shall be subject to amendment by _____ vote of the membership.

FIGURE 1-1   Sample board bylaws.

formulating the statement. The philosophy statement is the foundation for all policies. Policies are general instructions for future actions and should allow personnel to make daily decisions. Broad statements will allow the center director to develop procedures that fit new or unpredicted situations. When policies are too limited, the director may have to request policy changes frequently. Most directors would balk at that kind of restriction.

Standing committees have the responsibility for developing policies that the entire board approves. Committee members are appointed by the board chairperson because of their interests or expertise. They should also provide a balanced representation of the board membership in terms of gender, race, and points of view. Although standing committees may vary from one program to another, there are some basic types that appear frequently.

Executive committee: comprises officers, with the program administrator as an ex officio member. Meets more often than the full board, particularly as emergencies arise or as changes are needed.

Finance committee: is responsible for the budget and soliciting funding sources. The committee may meet with the center director to gather information for budget preparation or may merely approve a budget prepared by the director.

Personnel committee: hires the director, and may also help in the creation of job descriptions for all staff members. It participates in interviewing job candidates and makes final recommendations to the board.

Program committee: is responsible for the children's program, staff in-service, and parent education activities. Frequently, the center director and staff determine the specifics, but the committee formulates overall policies regarding these areas. It may also make recommendations to the director.

Building committee: finds a building appropriate for the type of program and plans for future additions or remodeling as needed. It also oversees maintenance, plans preventive measures, and approves emergency repairs.

Nominating committee: screens potential new board members and prepares a slate for election by the board. This committee may also plan and conduct orientation activities for new members.

Grievance committee: serves as a mediator after allowing reasonable time for the director to resolve problems. Parent complaints and staff differences with the director are examples of situations this committee might handle. Care should be taken, however, not to undermine the authority of the director, thus creating even greater problems.

COMMUNICATION WITH THE BOARD OF DIRECTORS

Responsibility for the operation of an early childhood center is shared by the board and the director. Effective communication between the two levels is essential. Ineffective communication can lead to distrust, disagreements, and unresolved problems. It may be necessary to provide training so that everyone involved can learn to express their ideas clearly and to discuss problems in a nonthreatening manner, which leads to solutions.

Communication must be bidirectional, from the board to the director and from the director to the board. The board must inform the director of policy changes and provide reasons for making those changes. A well-functioning board will seek information from the director before suggesting policy changes. The director must keep the board informed as well. There should be sharing of problems arising at the center that might require personnel changes or revisions of job descriptions. The board needs to be informed when parents or staff request changes or additions to the center's program. The board must also be aware of changing community needs that additional services could address. Communication can take place either through direct contact or by written reports. Both have a purpose. Often, directors keep closest direct contact with the chairperson of the board, either through frequent telephone conversations, emails or by scheduled meetings. Sometimes a lunch away from the distractions of administrative responsibilities accomplishes plenty. As an ex officio member of the board, the director also attends board meetings and can present information, discuss problems, or make suggestions. Periodic written reports to the board are also required: enrollment reports, personnel changes, and budget information are examples.

THE CORPORATION

In some corporate settings the director does not have direct contact with a board. In national corporate chains such as Children's World Learning Centers or KinderCare, a director communicates with an area supervisor. That person sends the information to the next administrative level. It gets passed up the management chain until it reaches the board. Correspondingly, in business settings, the director usually works with an executive, such as the director of personnel or a vice president, who then passes along the information. Some directors find this kind of structure frustrating and impersonal. Others find it easier to be responsible to one person rather than several. Working with a supervisor or business executive takes practice. It is important that both director and supervisor have similar goals and philosophy, and that each respect the other's competency. Here again, communication skills are essential. Directors must be able to state their ideas clearly, discuss problems openly, and give information concisely. They must be able to write complete and comprehensible reports. Written information assumes added importance because it may be the primary means to gain access to the board. Being part of a corporation has many benefits. Directors can summon resources that are not usually available in single schools. They can profit from the experience and knowledge of specialists who plan curricula. There are others to help resolve problems with staff or parents. Even more important, there are often opportunities to advance to higher levels of management within the organization.

In national child-care chains, directors can become area supervisors, specialists, or consultants. In these corporations, or in businesses, a director may eventually become an executive.

Throughout this chapter, we have investigated the characteristics of an effective director and discussed various skills and knowledge the position requires. The director's job is challenging, but it has many rewards. The rewards are different from those of teaching, but they retain some similarities. The following chapters explore the similarities and differences.

A director needs some specific skills to be successful. Management skills enable the director to coordinate all parts of an organization to meet individual and group goals. Directors must know good educational practices and understand how children develop. Certain personality characteristics are necessary for the effective director: ability to lead others, enjoyment of interacting with people, and self-confidence. A manager is the person who maintains the direction of an institution and who manages the resources of that institution. In a child-care setting, the resources are the people involved, the financial base, and the physical facility.

The director is also a leader who affects everyone who is involved in a child-care facility and who forms the character of the program. This character is the organizational climate.

CASE STUDY

Jill and Lisa are coteachers in a classroom for 20 three-year-olds. Both are experienced teachers, with their own classroom management styles and beliefs about how a program should be run. Jill recently talked to the director about her frustrations with Lisa. According to Jill, there are far too many transitions from one activity to the next and not enough time is allowed for cleanup. Consequently, the room is usually disorganized and messy. Moreover, Jill was embarrassed recently when a prospective family visited. The room was scattered with materials, the children were undirected, and several arguments broke out between children.

When the director asked Jill how Lisa responded to her concerns, Jill replied, "Well, I haven't mentioned it. It's hard for me to confront someone and I don't want to hurt her feelings." The director responded, "Please talk with her about it. You can be gentle and respectful, but you are really the one who should discuss your feelings with her." Jill was upset with this reaction and felt that it was the director's job to talk to Lisa.

1. What do you think is the problem between these two teachers?
2. What would you suggest that Jill do to resolve the problem?
3. What can the director do to prevent future difficulties between these teachers?
4. If you were the director, how would you follow up on this situation?

SUMMARY

The day-care movement originated with the welfare and reform movements of the 19th century. Today child-care programs are essential for meeting the needs of the large number of women in the workforce.

Leadership is setting a direction or vision for a group to follow.

Management controls or directs people/resources in a group according to established principles or values.

The five C's of leadership are character, caring, commitment, confidence, and communication.

Much of a director's day is spent talking to people. Therefore, communication is an important part of a director's job.

Both verbal and nonverbal messages must be clear and unambiguous. There are ways to prevent problems in communication. Consider what is to be conveyed and when is the best time. Allow enough time for feedback. Decide whether the message will be verbal or written, and then follow up to be sure the message has been understood. Written communications are appropriate for periodic reports to a board or to report financial information. A monthly newsletter to parents keeps them informed. Memos to staff members provides the same information to everyone at the same time. An effective use of written messages is to reinforce a teacher's accomplishments.

Directors go through several stages in their professional development: survival, competence building, enthusiastic and growing, career frustrations, reflective and inspiring, and career wind-down. There is a need for programs to prepare people to move into administrative positions as well as programs to help directors as they move through the stages.

Directors face many situations during any given day that call for difficult decisions. They use their own sense of what is right or wrong, but they need firmer guidelines to help make decisions based on ethics and professionalism. NAEYC has developed a Code of Ethical Conduct designed to help. Assessing director competencies is a difficult task because the job is multifaceted. Bloom believes that competence has three components: knowledge, skills, and attitudes.

The state of Illinois has developed a credential specifically designed for people in administrative positions that addresses competencies needed for that position.

STUDENT ACTIVITIES

1. Visit a school for young children. With permission, follow the director for an hour or so. Count the number of people spoken to and note any follow-up actions.

2. Think of your most flagrant failure in communicating with someone. What caused it? Is such failure common? How can it be remedied?

3. Who has the ultimate authority at your school? How does this power most often make itself felt? Suggest improvements.

4. Attend a board of trustees or advisory committee meeting. What topics were discussed? If decisions were made, how was this accomplished? Share with classmates your perception of the function of these bodies.

5. Discuss how directors might resolve the following problems. Cite the statement in the NAEYC Code of Ethical Conduct that could be used as a basis for the resolution.

    a. A parent comes into the director's office to say she is upset because her child doesn't want to come to school. The child says his teacher doesn't like him.

    b. A teacher comes in late for her morning shift, leaving 18 children with only one teacher for 15 minutes.

    c. During the coldest winter months, some parents wanted their children to play indoors and not go outside. The teachers felt they should have time outdoors.

    d. One parent is chronically late in picking up her child. She always seems to have a good reason, but a staff member must stay overtime to be with the youngster.

    e. The budget for art materials is being used up much too quickly. At this rate there will no paper, paint, or glue by the end of the year.

    f. The teachers are complaining that the bathrooms are not cleaned thoroughly enough by the evening cleaning crew. There is always an unpleasant smell, and they are afraid the area is unhealthy for the children.

REVIEW

1. What is the difference between leadership and management?
2. List the five C's of leadership.
3. List five reasons directors cite for not delegating responsibility to others.
4. In what ways can a busy director organize time so that necessary tasks are completed?
5. Why are verbal messages often misinterpreted by the listener?
6. List things you can do to prevent problems in communicating.
7. Part of being a good communicator is the ability to listen. State five suggestions for being a better listener.
8. Describe two methods directors can use to evaluate themselves.

9. Compare membership on a board of a nonprofit early childhood center with one that is part of a profit-making enterprise.

10. Standing committees develop policies that are then approved by the full board of directors. List the committees and briefly describe their functions.

REFERENCES

Baldwin, S. (1991). *The early childhood super director.* Mt. Rainier, MD: Redleaf Press.

Bloom, P. J. (1997). Navigating the rapids: Directors reflect on their careers and professional development. *Young Children, 52*(7), 32–38.

Bloom, P. J. (2000). How do we define director competence? *Child Care Information Exchange, 132,* 13–18.

Boschee, M. A., & Jacobs, G. M. (2006). Child care in the United States: Yesterday and today. *National Network for Childcare.* Retrieved March 10, 2006, from http://www.nncc.org.

Children's Defense Fund. (2008). *Yearbook on the state of America's children.* Washington, DC: Author.

Feeney, S., & Freeman, N. (2003). *Ethics and the early childhood educator: Using the NAEYC Code.* Washington, DC: NAEYC.

Fenichel, E. S., & Eggbeer, L. (1990). *Preparing practitioners to work with infants, toddlers, and their families: Issues and recommendations for educators and trainers.* Arlington, VA: National Center for Clinical Infant Programs.

Fessler, R., & Christensen, J. (1992). *The teacher career cycle.* Boston: Allyn & Bacon.

Giuliani, R., & Kurson, K. (2002). *Leadership.* New York: Hyperion.

Gordon, A., & Browne, K. W. (2007). *Beginnings and beyond.* Clifton Park, NY: Thomson/Delmar Learning.

Gotts, E. E. (1988). The day-care debate. *Parents, 63,* 114–116.

NAEYC. (2009). Code of Ethical Conduct., Carol Copple & Sue Bredenkamp, eds. NAEYC, Washington D.C.

O'Toole, J. (1996). *Leading change.* London, England: Random House.

Shellenberger, S. (1994, July 20). Companies help solve day-care problems. *The Wall Street Journal,* 5.

Stevens, M. (2001). *Extreme management.* Clayton, Victoria: Warner Books.

The Center for Career Development in Early Care and Education. (1996). *Child care licensing: Training requirements for roles in child care centers and family child care homes.* Boston: Wheelock College.

U.S. Department of Statistics. Retrieved March 12, 2006, from http://www.bls.gov.

SELECTED FURTHER READING

250 management success stories by child care center directors. (1995). Reprinted from Child Care Information Exchange. Redmond, WA: Exchange Press.

Bloom, P. J. (2005). Dedication doesn't have to mean deadication. *Child Care Information Exchange, 164,* 74–76.

Hnatiuk, P., & Gerbretensae, H. (2005). Culture and leadership. *Child Care Information Exchange, 163,* 8–13.

Kagan, S. L., & Bowman, B. T. (Eds.). (1997). *Leadership in early care and education.* Washington, DC: National Association for the Education of Young Children.

Reno, H., Stutzman, J., & Zimmerman, J. (2007). Handbook for early childhood administrators: Directing with a mission. Allyn & Bacon: Los Angeles, CA.

Staff challenges: Practical ideas for recruiting, training, and supervising early childhood employees. (2008). Compiled by Child Care Information Exchange, Redmond, WA, Exchange Press.

HELPFUL WEBSITES

Disclaimer: Links to Internet sites throughout this book are provided for your convenience and do not constitute an endorsement.

NAEYC Code of Ethical Conduct:	**http://www.naeyc.org**
Illinois Director Credential Information:	**http://www.inccrra.org/**
National Child Care Information Center:	**http://nccic.org**

For additional resources related to administration including videos, links to related sites for each chapter of the text, tutorial quizzes, glossary flashcards, and more, visit the Education CourseMate website for this book at www.cengage.com/login.

CHAPTER 2

Choices: Schools and Programs

Objectives

After reading this chapter, you should be able to:

- State the differences between a half-day school and a full-day school.
- Describe the characteristics for each type of privately and publicly funded program.
- Discuss the advantages and disadvantages of each type of program.

KEY TERMS

child–care resource and
referral networks

church–sponsored
program

cooperative school

corporate child–care
center

employer–sponsored
programs

family child–care home

for–profit proprietary
school

laboratory schools

A day in the life of . . .

A Director of a Church-Affiliated School

Each class in our school goes to chapel weekly. Our pastor knows sign language and teaches the students to sign some of the songs. Christina's mother was picking her up after chapel time and I heard Christina say, "Mommy, Pastor John knows how to do the Macarena, and he's teaching it to us."

According to the Children's Defense Fund report, *The State of America's Children 2005,* 12 million children, including six million infants and toddlers, were in child care that year. Of these, 22 percent were in child-care centers and 17 percent were in family child-care settings. The others had in-home care or were with relatives.

The number of working mothers in two-parent and single-parent families continues to increase. The U.S. Census Bureau (2005) reported that in 2000, 58.6 percent of married couples had children and both spouses worked. Additionally, in 1999, 71.5 percent of single mothers had jobs. Passage of the 1996 Personal Responsibility and Work Opportunity Reconciliation Act increased the number of welfare recipients in the workforce. In 1999, 58 percent of recipients worked at some time during the year, compared to 40 percent in 1995. Finding affordable child care is difficult for families, and it will likely become worse. Full-day child care may cost between $4,000 and $10,000 per year. This cost is prohibitive to the one-quarter of American families with young children who earn less than $25,000 a year.

Older children often care for themselves, but an increasing number are enrolled in group programs. Boys and girls clubs, recreation programs, and community organizations offer some excellent before- and after-school activities for these children. Many early childhood centers are extending their offerings to include programs for children's out-of-school hours, including special summer sessions.

The quality of care given to children influences more than just the children's safety each day; it also has long-term effects. Children who have been in quality programs tend to have fewer behavior problems, get along better with their peers, and have better academic skills (Weaver, 2002).

Individuals who care for a single child, or family child-care providers watching a small group of children, can provide quality care. However, because of the knowledge and expense required to design and operate a quality program, group-based settings are more common. Later chapters include extensive information concerning the components of quality child care. A summary is outlined here.

- Well-trained staff capable of providing interactions with children that meet their developmental needs
- Maintenance of consistent child–caregiver relationships via low staff turnover *low movement from room to room*
- Promotion of good health through health and nutrition practices
- Safe, well-maintained, adequately supervised physical environment
- Developmentally appropriate activities for the age level of the children
- Collaboration with parents concerning the introduction of cultural activities and information
- Involvement of parents through open access and sharing of decisions that affect their children
- Sensitivity to cultural differences and a commitment to preserve each child's cultural uniqueness

As a director, it is important to know the possibilities and limitations of the various types of child-care arrangements. Although all share many common attributes, each type has unique features. The characteristics are determined by the hours of operation, the philosophy underlying the goals, and the sponsorship.

Types of Programs

HALF-DAY SCHOOLS

Half-day schools have sessions of four hours or less. Their primary purpose is to provide an enriched educational experience for children before they are old enough to attend elementary school. They are called preschools, learning centers, and early childhood education centers. They usually serve children between the ages of two and six years. Some schools have extended their offerings to include infant and toddler programs.

There has been a rise in the number of state-supported programs for three- and four-year-olds, usually called Pre-K programs. Forty states have at least one state-funded program, and other states are planning programs. The primary focuses of these settings are to facilitate children's development, provide early educational experiences, and promote school readiness.

Fewer traditional half-day schools are currently available. The two main reasons for their decline are that parents need all-day care for their children, and that the expense of operating a school cannot be met with a half-day session.

Among those remaining are church preschools, which function as an adjunct to the church's educational program. The church may cover the cost of space and certain services. Cooperative schools, with their decreased costs due to high parent participation, are usually half-day programs. Colleges or universities may operate a half-day school as part of their early childhood education curriculum. Private proprietary schools may meet expenses if they schedule morning and afternoon classes.

An effective preschool will provide for all parts of the child's development: social, emotional, cognitive, and physical. There will be many opportunities for interaction with both adults and children so that the child can develop social skills and language. Responsive adults encourage independence, self-confidence, and impulse control.

Learning centers or individualized activities allow the child to explore and develop cognitive skills. Outdoor play with wheel toys, climbing equipment, sandboxes, and large blocks helps develop large muscles. Cutting, painting, and manipulating materials indoors help the child develop fine muscle coordination. Because the primary focus of this type of school is the education of the child, the staff should have an especially strong background in an early childhood curriculum.

Teachers should be able to plan stimulating activities for children and to take advantage of the many spontaneous learning experiences available in the environment. Both director and staff should be motivated to continue learning by attending workshops and special classes.

ALL-DAY SCHOOLS

All-day schools are in session for more than four hours each day, many as long as 10 or 12 hours. Their primary purpose is to provide safe care and a stimulating, age-appropriate environment for children while their parents work. They operate 12 months of the year, closing only for a few holidays. A large proportion of child-care centers are operated by profit-making corporations, some of which have schools throughout the United States. The largest, KinderCare Learning Centers, has over 1,000 locations, while La Petite Academy and Children's World Learning Centers have over 500 each. Corporations exist with only 10 sites, and others have more than 50. Individually owned for-profit schools also offer child care, often providing space for infants as well as preschool and school-age children. Churches and community organizations may also provide all-day

FYI

Head Start has immediate positive effects on children's development. After only a half year in a program, children show higher cognitive and language skills, and they increase their self–esteem, achievement motivation, and social behavior. By the end of one year, Head Start children score higher in all categories than their non–Head Start peers.

SOURCE: National Head Start Association. http://www.nhsa.org

A daily schedule for any group of children will vary according to their age level. The following is one way of scheduling a morning for a group of three-year-olds:

8:00–8:15 A.M.	arrival, greeting, free choice of activities
8:15–8:30 A.M.	group greeting, group activity, explanation of learning activities available
8:30–10:15 A.M.	free choice of learning activities
10:15–10:30 A.M.	cleanup, toileting, wash hands
10:30–10:45 A.M.	snack
10:45–11:15 A.M.	outdoor play
11:15–11:30 A.M.	indoor story
11:30 A.M.	greet parents, dismissal

FIGURE 2-1 Sample schedule for a half-day program.

care. Many businesses, hospitals, and governmental agencies have begun to offer child care for their employees.

The daily schedule of the child-care center must meet the total developmental needs of children because much of their day will be spent there. There should also be time for the enriched learning activities that take place in a half-day school. Furthermore, enough time must be allowed for children to take care of their own health needs, such as brushing their teeth, getting enough rest, and eating a nutritious diet. Children must be encouraged to develop independence and language skills.

A developmentally appropriate program will allow time for children to be by themselves and to be involved in activities that can be done alone. The pace of the day in an all-day setting should be slower than in a half-day center, alternating quiet times with active times to avoid overstimulation and fatigue (see Figures 2-1 and 2-2 for a comparison of typical schedules).

The director of a full-day child-care center will have different management problems from those of a half-day school. One administrator cannot be present during all hours the program is open. An assistant director is needed to share administrative tasks. This can be either a separate position or the work of a head teacher who performs administrative tasks when not teaching. One person may work from the opening of the school until early afternoon. The other will be there during the middle of the day and assume responsibility for the late afternoon to closing time.

An all-day school needs additional staff. Each group of children will have two shifts of teachers, some who arrive early in the morning and others who stay until closing. Most all-day schools have at least a part-time person who works in the kitchen. Many hire drivers to pick up children at home or at their elementary schools. A secretary and a bookkeeper might also be members of the staff.

Staff members in an all-day school should have qualities that help make school a secure and happy place for children. Each person should enjoy being with children. The cook who welcomes children into the kitchen or ensures that good cooking smells permeate the school helps to create a pleasant atmosphere. Drivers often must help children separate from home, and therefore they should be warm and reassuring people. Even a

Schedules will vary for different age levels and according to the weather. This is one possibility for a group of four-year-olds:

6:30–7:45 A.M.	arrival, greeting, time with parents or friends, free play indoors or outdoors (weather permitting)
7:45–8:00 A.M.	group greeting, story
8:00–8:30 A.M.	wash hands, breakfast
8:30–8:45 A.M.	clear breakfast dishes, toileting, wash hands, brush teeth
8:45–9:30 A.M.	outdoor play
9:30–9:45 A.M.	group music, language, or learning activity
9:45–11:30 A.M.	free choice of learning activities
11:30–11:45 A.M.	cleanup, toileting, wash hands
11:45–12:15 P.M.	lunch in small groups
12:15–12:30 P.M.	brush teeth, toileting, wash hands
12:30–2:00 P.M.	rest or naps, soft music
2:00–2:30 P.M.	toileting, wash hands, snack
2:30–3:30 P.M.	outdoor play (weather permitting)
3:30–5:00 P.M.	indoor play: art, music, dramatic play, block building
5:00–5:30 P.M.	preparation for departure, group story

FIGURE 2-2   Typical Daily Schedule, full day.

secretary will have contact with children and should be able to respond appropriately. Teachers should be able to allow children to develop at their own pace, not rushing them to perform at unrealistic levels. They also should be nurturing and responsive to children's needs. Everyone working for an all-day school should be healthy and energetic.

Communication becomes extremely important in an all-day school because many people are involved. The director and assistant must talk to each other every day. The morning teacher must tell the afternoon teacher about any unusual occurrences. The cook, driver, and secretary all need to be a part of the "communication loop," which focuses on what is happening with the children. Parents, too, want to know what their children did at school during the day and should be encouraged to let the school know about home occurrences.

One of the biggest problems for the staff in a child-care center is fatigue. The long hours with children and the minimal vacation days can put a tremendous burden on the staff. This results in low morale or, in the extreme, burnout. If directors are sensitive to the needs of adults, they will provide time for teachers to be away from children each day. Varying responsibilities for outdoor supervision and for naptime duty can help overcome fatigue. Staff meetings at which teachers can discuss problems and find solutions will also help. Social activities may promote staff cohesiveness.

Types of Programs—Characteristics

• • • • • ● PRIVATE FOR-PROFIT SCHOOLS

Proprietary School

The private **for-profit proprietary school** is owned by one or more individuals who profit while providing this service. Tuition is the primary source of income; it must cover expenses and allow for a profit margin. Often the owner(s) is an active participant(s), alternating administrative tasks with teaching a group of children. These schools can be half-day programs, but increasing numbers are offering a full-day session.

Two factors are important to the director/owner of this kind of school. First, there is the freedom to initiate a program based on the owner's ideas. The program can emphasize cognitive development of children or can focus on the children's creative expression. For example, some owners may want to develop a program using the Montessori method and materials. The opportunity to have "the kind of school you've always wanted" appeals to many people.

The second factor is a disadvantage. It is the likelihood of constant financial worry. Each school is licensed for a specific number of children, so the potential income is limited. Child care is expensive, and it is difficult to keep tuitions high enough to pay expenses but low enough so that parents can pay.

Many schools meet this challenge by adding programs. Before- and after- school care programs for older children can fill the time slots when enrollment of other children may be less. If most of the preschoolers do not arrive until 8:30 or 9:00, there is space and time for children before they go to elementary school. The same is true at the end of the day after some of the younger children have gone home. The additional outlay for materials and staff can be outweighed by the additional income generated. Having children who come two or three days a week can also add income. The total income from two part-time tuitions can be greater than that gained from one child attending full time.

Directing a for-profit school must be approached like any small business. Costs must be controlled without jeopardizing quality. Income must cover all expenses and allow for a profit. However, many director/owners do not expect to make a profit beyond their own salary. If they own the building that houses their school, additional compensation may come from equity in the real estate.

Child-Care Corporations

As a business, child-care corporations operate multiple facilities at many different sites, often in different states. Income still comes primarily from tuition. The **corporate child-care center** functions like any big business with a board and a chief executive officer. Ideas may be developed at corporate headquarters, sometimes resulting in considerable similarity between child-care centers. The building, curriculum, and teacher training may be the same in a center in Oregon as in a center in Georgia. Other corporations allow more local autonomy. General guidelines may be proposed by corporate headquarters, but implementation may be done at the discretion of the director and staff at each center.

These corporations aim to sell a trusted product to the public. They spend effort and money to create a recognizable image—either a name or a symbol. The originator of KinderCare's red tower has said he wanted that symbol to be as familiar as the McDonald's arches.

Advantages of a Corporation (handwritten margin note)

There are advantages to being the director of a corporate child-care center. Financial problems for an individual center are lessened by the greater resources of the corporation. When one center is temporarily under-enrolled, there is financial support until enrollment increases. More money for materials and equipment is available because the company purchases in large quantities. Maintenance and repair people are often available. Area supervisors provide extra support. They help the director plan in-service training, resolve problems, and develop recruitment strategies. Other corporate directors in the area are available by telephone to share ideas, problems, substitute teachers, and even materials. Directors are sometimes able to transfer to another child-care center within the corporation if they change their residence. For many, the greatest advantage is the ability to move up the "corporate ladder." Advancing to area supervisor, and then into other positions within the corporation, is a possibility.

There are also some disadvantages. Directors of corporate child-care centers report a tremendous amount of paperwork; everything has to be accounted for, sometimes minutely. They may find constraint on planning the curriculum if this is preplanned at the corporate office. A business orientation and the corporation's profit are stressed. Costs must be kept within specified budget limits. This can affect salaries.

Franchises

Kiddie Academy, based in Abingdon, Maryland, is a franchise business that offers support, training, and third-party financing to persons wishing to open a for-profit child care facility. They provide a design for a curriculum that is accredited by the Commission on International and Trans-Regional Accreditation (CITA). They have building plans that can be adapted to meet local codes and marketplace needs. Construction teams help the operator during the start-up period whether the choice is to build, lease, renovate, or purchase an existing facility.

The franchise includes initial training of staff as well as ongoing training and support. They also offer refresher training programs and site visits. The main advantage of a franchise program is that everything is planned. Perhaps a disadvantage is that the operator of this kind of program has little opportunity for innovation (Retrieved from Internet, January 2009).

Employer-Sponsored Programs

Employer-sponsored programs have proliferated in recent years in response to the needs of working families. Only a few companies offer direct assistance, and those that do often focus on care for very young children. However, a wider focus is emerging. Some companies now extend their work/family coverage to include elder care, special activities for school-age children and adolescents, and care for children who are mildly ill. Diane Harris, in a 1993 article in *Working Woman* magazine, stated that only one-tenth of one percent of companies offer these kinds of direct care, but the ranks swell to 60 percent when counting corporations that offer indirect services. These include free access to child care–information services, tax breaks, and time off to take care of family needs. Today, work/family issues are clearly part of the workplace. Unfortunately, as economic changes occur employers may be unable or unwilling to incur this expense.

In 1993, about 600 companies in the United States supported on-site or near-site centers. If you add hospitals, the number increases to 1,400. These centers are open during hours that meet the needs of the employees. The primary advantage is location at the work site, or near enough to eliminate transportation time.

Another advantage is that parents can visit their child at lunchtime or during breaks. Parents are also accessible if a child needs additional comfort. A director of this kind of center may find this advantage can also lead to problems. One director said, "The eyes of the whole company are looking at us all the time." She explained that a parent may visit and observe a teacher trying to manage a problem with someone else's child. When that parent goes back to a workstation, he or she might report the incident, creating a possibility for misunderstanding. For some directors without business experience, another disadvantage is working within a hierarchy.

A company may use **family child-care homes** as satellites to a center program. The homes are usually located near the business or near elementary schools. The operators of the homes may receive some salary support and benefits from the company. A few companies have a staff person who works with the home operators to provide training or a toy-loan service.

Some companies indirectly support child care. In 1980, Merck & Co. in New Jersey provided a grant to start a center in a nearby community. The center was run by a local group as a nonprofit enterprise.

Space was made available for infants and preschoolers of Merck employees. Continued income for the center comes from tuition, fund-raising activities, and in-kind services. A similar kind of arrangement is the voucher, whereby some companies allow their employees to use the child-care setting of their choice. The company then pays part of the tuition. A variation of the grant method is being tried by some companies. Several form a consortium to provide funds to build a child-care center.

Some companies have instituted a resource and referral service rather than operating an on-site child-care center. Either a person within the company or someone outside the company establishes an information service for parents seeking child care. Xerox Corporation has contracted with Work/Family Directions, a community-based agency, to provide this service to its employees throughout the United States.

The service supplies parents with various child-care options. An agency employee visits each of the approved locations before it is placed in the directory. Parents are given guidelines to help them choose the appropriate care setting for their child. A list of child-care providers, especially those available to care for a sick child, is often included in the directory. In addition to information about child care, some companies offer flexible benefit plans in which a parent can choose support for child care over dental coverage, for instance.

Cengage Learning

At an on-site center, a mother can still breastfeed her baby.

Child Care for Mildly Ill Children

As more children enter out-of-home child-care situations, the risk that they are sick more often also grows. A working parent with a child under the age of five years can expect the child to have six to nine illnesses per year, which last three to seven days in length. Working mothers and fathers miss from five to 29 days of work per year on average due to a child's illness. Employee absenteeism resulting from child care–associated illnesses is estimated to cost businesses in the United States between $160 million and $400 million each year. Awareness of these statistics has increased the demand for child-care centers for mildly ill children. According to the National Association for Sick Child Daycare (NASCD), only 36 sick-child-care facilities existed in 1986. Today there are at least 324 nationwide.

Of these existing programs, 50 percent are hospital-based programs (created for hospital employees and community members), 25 percent are child-care center infirmaries (attached to a licensed child-care facility), 17 percent are freestanding facilities, 12 percent are in-home care programs, and 2 percent are affiliated with family child-care homes. Licensing regulations have already been developed in many states for mildly ill child-care programs, and many other states are in the process of developing standards.

The daily schedule for children in a quality, child-care program for the mildly ill is similar to that of a regular care center. Teachers and staff will need to carefully monitor and document the children's symptoms and follow stringent hand washing and cleaning policies. Children are often involved in relaxing and low-key play such as art activities, stories, board games, and dramatic play.

Children's videos and computer games—which may not be appropriate for other early childhood programs—can be appropriate for the more restful play a sick child needs.

Most programs developed for mildly ill children cannot operate solely on parent fees. This is because of the highly variable daily attendance and because staffing requirements are generally more restrictive.

Successful programs rely heavily on corporate partnerships, grants, and/or adjoining child-care facilities where costs can be shared. Research suggests that for every dollar an employer invests in sick-child day care, it saves at least three dollars through increased productivity and not needing to replace an absent employee. Companies are becoming more aware of these benefits and are helping to resolve the problem for worried parents. Some provide the resources for care, whereas others cover the full cost of care for their employees. According to the Families and Work Institute (FWI), only about 5 percent of all employers (9 percent of those with 1,000 or more employees) offer some type of care for children with mild illnesses. This number is expected to steadily increase as many companies become more sensitive to the balance between family and work.

• • • • • NONPROFIT SCHOOLS

Cooperative School

The **cooperative school** is privately owned but is operated as a nonprofit enterprise. This type of school usually has a half-day session. A co-op, as it is often called, is owned by all the parents who currently have children enrolled in the school. Ownership ends when enrollment ends. This type of school may be incorporated and have a board of trustees elected by the members. Tuition is the primary source of income; additional income may come from fund-raising activities. Tuition is usually less than that of profit-making schools.

The co-op employs a teacher/director with dual responsibilities for teaching and directing. Parents perform many of the administrative tasks such as purchasing supplies and overseeing finances. Parents also assist in the classroom regularly. The number of

Cengage Learning

Mother holding her child in a co-op school.

co-op schools has decreased in the last decade because few working parents can spare the time necessary for participation.

The cooperative school is a good place for a director who likes working with adults as well as children. There is significant daily interaction with parents as they participate in the classroom. This provides many opportunities for parent-education activities.

In addition to work in the classroom, parents often build and maintain equipment, or make materials for the school. The director spends significant time in meetings, discussing administrative matters and conducting parent-education activities.

One director of a co-op reported that the children in her school often "played meetings" because that was what their mothers did. The children got dressed up in high heels and long dresses, took their purses, paper, and pencils, and sat at a table "having a meeting."

Some early childhood educators find that having to share administrative and teaching responsibilities with parents is a disadvantage. It may be difficult to mediate the differences of opinions and ideas. Furthermore, there is limited income to purchase equipment or materials. Few co-ops can afford their own building, so they may be housed in a community center, a church building, or a park. Storage facilities may be minimal.

Church-Sponsored Programs

A **church-sponsored program** may be a half-day preschool, a kindergarten, or an all-day center. These are set up as an extension of the church educational program or as a service to its members. Enrollment might be limited to church member families or be open to the community. These schools are expected to pay for their own expenses with income from tuitions, although some costs may be shared by the church. Space is usually given to the school for free or at minimal cost, maintenance service may be provided, and insurance may be covered through the church policy.

The church board or a committee appointed by the board determines the general policies for the program. They may specify the inclusion of religious teaching along with traditional early education activities. They may also set guidelines for hiring staff or creating a budget. Directors can decide how those policies will be implemented in the program. Learning to work cooperatively with the board or committee members is essential in this setting.

Directors may confront other special challenges in a church-sponsored program. The center often has to share space with church activities. The classroom may be used for Sunday school or social functions. Directors have to develop creative ways to use space or to store equipment.

Laboratory Schools

Colleges and universities often operate **laboratory schools** as part of their instructional program in early childhood education, teacher training, or psychology. Some of these schools are half-day programs, but according to the National Coalition for Campus Children's Centers, the majority (81 percent) are full-day programs. Enrollment includes children from student or faculty families, but may also include children from the wider community. Although tuition is charged, one or several departments of the college or university supplement operational expenses.

The laboratory school has several purposes. It is designed to teach students about the materials and techniques appropriate for working with young children. It provides a supervised setting for students to practice teaching. The school often is a site for research studies conducted by campus personnel in various disciplines. Lastly, the school may serve as a model for other programs in the community.

Laboratory schools usually have high standards, well-planned facilities, and a wide variety of materials and equipment because they serve as models. The curriculum varies among schools and is often based on a particular philosophy or approach. Some schools design a curriculum using developmental psychologist Jean Piaget's ideas, in which children are allowed freedom to explore and construct their own knowledge. Other schools base their methods on behaviorist theory, with emphasis on structured learning experiences and a system of rewards for positive reinforcement. Still other schools adopt the ideas of Maria Montessori and use the materials developed by her. Montessori materials are graded in difficulty, and the procedures for using the materials have self-correcting features.

Some model laboratory schools are now using an approach disseminated by the HighScope Educational Research Foundation. The content of the HighScope curriculum supports children's development and learning through key experiences in an active learning environment (Hohman & Weikart, 1995). The curriculum stresses active child participation in learning centers with various developmentally appropriate materials. The children are encouraged to solve problems as they plan their day, complete their plan, and, finally, review their accomplishments. Key experiences include creative representation, language and literacy, initiative and social relations, movement, music, classification, seriation, number, space, and time.

The HighScope curriculum is similar to Piagetian theory, and it strongly supports Lev Vygotsky's theory of social interaction. According to Vygotsky, children learn when they interact with people and materials in their environment. Both Piaget and Vygotsky stressed the importance of encouraging children to construct their own knowledge from many different activities, along with the importance of adult support to help children move to higher levels of cognition.

The director of a laboratory school has two distinct responsibilities. One is to the instructional program of the college or university. This means that the adult students are the primary focus. Their need for learning experiences must be met. The program should allow students to plan activities, implement them in a day's schedule, and evaluate their lessons.

The second focus is the fostering and maintenance of a superior educational program for the children. This means a delicate balance between the adult students' needs for experimentation with activities, and what is acceptable and appropriate for the children.

It is also important to become part of the campus community. Directors must work within the campus administrative structure. Sometimes this means convincing administrators or faculty to maintain or increase the program's budget. Directors should be active in the wider community, participating in conferences, speaking to groups, and generally informing others about the program. These activities are essential to recruiting new students.

PUBLICLY FUNDED SCHOOLS

Children's Centers

Children's centers, also called state preschools, are sponsored by public agencies and are maintained primarily to meet the needs of working mothers or one-parent families with limited incomes. Today's centers are an outgrowth of the child-care centers started during World War II to care for the children of women working in war industries. They are all-day programs, open 10 or 12 hours a day, five or six days a week. Funding comes from

A father brings his child to child care.

a combination of federal, state, county, and city sources. Tuition may be charged on a sliding scale according to family income. The local school district usually operates the school. The centers are often housed on the school grounds and are sometimes referred to as child development centers.

Hired by the local school board, the director of a children's center carries out the policies of the board. Guidelines and regulations for parent fees, curriculum, staff qualifications, salary scales, purchasing, facility plans, and maintenance procedures may all be covered by board policy. Federal and state guidelines may include additional restrictions on administrative procedures and additional program requirements.

The director of such a center is part of the school district and therefore must work within the system. A distinct advantage of this type of school is that income does not depend upon tuition; therefore, there is usually more money for materials and equipment. Standards for teachers may be higher than in other schools, and salaries may be proportional. Resources throughout the school district such as psychologists, nutritionists, and curriculum specialists may be available as needed.

A disadvantage of such a center is that directors may not be free to design their own curriculum—instead, they must implement the guidelines given by the funding source. For some people, the restrictions of working within a public school system may be difficult.

Head Start

Head Start is a compensatory educational program begun in 1965 by the Office of Economic Opportunity. It evolved from political and social attempts to break the cycle of poverty by providing a comprehensive preschool program for young children. It is now administered by the Administration for Children, Youth and Families, Office of Human Development in the U.S. Department of Health and Human Services. Funds go either to an agency that operates the various centers or to a delegate agency that disburses funds to nonprofit organizations, which operate centers.

When Head Start began, it was a half-day program that included breakfast and a hot lunch. The program has since added more features that meet the needs of families. Among them are Early Head Start and Wrap-Around programs, which, respectively, serve children from birth to three years of age and provide all-day care for children of working parents.

Early Head Start began in response to growing bodies of research that showed care for infants and very young children in centers is inadequate. In one study (Helburn, 1995), the researchers found that only 8 percent of the centers surveyed met children's needs for "health, safety, relationships, and learning."

Even within this 8 percent, two out of every five centers (3.2 percent of all centers) only minimally met the standards. In poor-quality settings, basic sanitary conditions were not met, children did not have supportive relationships with adults, and there was a lack of appropriate learning materials. New guidelines were developed to meet the needs of these children in group settings. Some Early Head Start programs also help parents develop better parenting skills. Head Start has several clearly defined program goals as stated in their Performance Standard guidelines (DHHS Publication No. 84-31131).

The overall goal of the Head Start program is to bring about a greater degree of social competence in children of low-income families.

To accomplish this goal, Head Start objectives and performance standards provide for:

1. the improvement of the child's health and physical abilities, including the family's attitude toward future health care.

2. the encouragement of self-confidence, spontaneity, curiosity, and self-discipline, all of which will assist in the development of the child's social and emotional health.

3. the enhancement of the child's mental processes and skills with particular attention paid to conceptual and communication skills.

4. the establishment of patterns and expectations of success for the child, which will create a climate of confidence for present and future learning efforts and overall development.

5. an increase in the ability of the child and the family to relate to each other and to others.

6. the enhancement of the sense of dignity and self-worth within the child and his or her family.

Head Start achieves its goals by providing medical and social services to families and by requiring active involvement of parents. Parents serve on policy boards, assist in the classroom, and are active in various support committees. In addition to fostering parent participation, Head Start encourages staff to upgrade their skills. Teachers receive financial support to attend classes at local colleges or universities. Some enter a structured training program leading to a Child Development Associate credential administered by the National Association for the Education of Young Children.

Many Head Start centers are single-classroom schools; therefore, a head teacher is also the director. This person supervises all other staff in addition to their teaching duties. Responsibilities include coordinating the center's activities, receiving and distributing information from the Head Start office, ordering supplies, and organizing staff meetings.

This position is not the same as that of a director in other kinds of schools, but it provides an opportunity for someone with a background in early childhood education. The head teachers in these centers need to be sensitive to the needs and interests of the communities they serve. They should be able to work with families of diverse ethnic and cultural backgrounds. Ability to speak the parents' language(s) is helpful, but not a requirement of employment. An advantage of working in this kind of program is higher wages than those of private schools. Staff also enjoy benefits such as health coverage and retirement benefits. One of the most noteworthy disadvantages is the tremendous amount of paperwork required; records must be kept and reports submitted on all aspects of the center's functioning. Guidelines for curriculum are specific and mandatory, although the staff has freedom to implement them.

Each preschool or child-care setting has its own characteristics, advantages, and disadvantages. As shown in Figure 2-3, there is variation among types of schools. Directors must understand the differences. They must know the characteristics of the specific school in which they serve in order to be effective leaders. Knowledge of the differences also helps a prospective director to choose a program that matches his or her personality, interests, and experience.

Military-Based Child Care

The military contains many young families, who combined have approximately 500,000 children under five years of age and 440,000 children from six to 11 years of age. About half the military families have at least one child younger than school age, and both parents work in 60 percent of these families. The Department of Defense reported that in 2005 there were 215,000 children of active-duty military families who needed child care. Eighty-five percent of those were already enrolled in programs, meaning there were still 32,000 who needed to be in child care but were not.

The military child-care system has undergone many changes in the last decade and is becoming a national model for child-care reform. The military's programs are known

Low pay

TYPE	SPONSORSHIP	INCOME	CHARACTERISTICS
Private Schools			
For-profit	One or more individuals	Tuition	Profit making. Freedom to initiate programs. Limited resources for income. Must use good business practices.
Corporate	Group of people	Tuition	Goals set by corporation. Director must be business oriented. **Advantages:** Shared resources for purchasing, maintenance. Financial problems shared. Support from area supervisors. Director can be promoted to other jobs. **Disadvantages:** Many aspects preplanned at corporate headquarters. Need to show a profit. May pay lower salaries.
Employer-supported	Business, hospital, government agency, building developer	Tuition, fund-raising	Set up as fringe benefit for employees. Close to parents' work. **Advantages:** Parents can visit during day. Parents nearby if needed by child. **Disadvantages:** Must work within business hierarchy. "Eyes" of company may be on school.
Nonprofit Schools			
Cooperative	Member families	Tuition, fund-raising	Intense parent involvement. Less costly to operate. **Advantages:** Opportunity for parent education. Opportunity to work with adults as well as children. **Disadvantages:** Work with untrained staff. Lots of meetings. Have to share administrative tasks with parents. Limited income. May not have own building.
Church	Church	Tuition, fund-raising, supplements	Policies determined by church board. Share church facilities. Is part of church educational program. **Advantages:** Support from the church. **Disadvantages:** Must work with church board. Share space with other church programs.

FIGURE 2-3 Types of Schools.

TYPE	SPONSORSHIP	INCOME	CHARACTERISTICS
Laboratory	College or university	Tuition, supplements	Model program design. Used for practice teaching placements. **Advantages:** Well-planned facility. Good equipment. **Disadvantages:** Must balance needs of children and adult students. Must work within administrative structure of college or university.
Publicly Funded Schools			
Child-care centers	Local school district	Government funds,	Director hired by school district. School board sets policy guidelines. **Advantages:** Not dependent on tuition. More money for equipment and materials. Standards for teachers high; salaries better. Resources of school district available. **Disadvantages:** Not totally free to design own curriculum. For some, working within school district is restrictive.
Head Start	Public or private nonprofit agencies	Government funds	Designed to prepare child for school. Parent involvement. Community participation. Director must be sensitive to diverse ethnic and cultural backgrounds. **Advantages:** Higher pay levels. Opportunity to work with parents. **Disadvantages:** Lots of recordkeeping necessary. Segregated according to income.

High pay

F I G U R E 2 - 3 Types of Schools *(continued)*.

for their quality of care, availability, and affordability. The Military Child Care Act of 1989 allocated funding for child development centers, set fees based on family income, and created subsidies for family child care. It also linked caregiver salaries to training requirements, and it made accreditation a goal of every center. With research continuously demonstrating that quality child care positively affects recruiting, retention, and military readiness, Pentagon policy makers and military commanders have made child care a top priority for their military communities.

The current program comprises a supportive web of more than 800 child development centers (including school-age programs), over 9,000 family child-care homes, and many available resource and referral services. The next step is to work with the civilian sector to improve and expand child care to ensure its availability for military families. A report developed by the National Women's Law Center, entitled Be All That We Can Be: Lessons from the Military for Improving Our Nation's Child Care System, (Campbell,

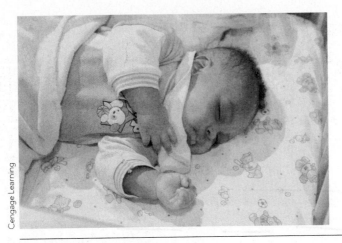

Cengage Learning

In child care, nap time is needed.

Appelbaum, Martinson, & Martin, 2000), provides six key lessons from the military for state and federal policy makers.

advocacy

1. Do not be deterred. It is possible to create dramatic changes in the child-care system.
2. Recognize the seriousness of the child-care problem and the results of inaction.
3. Improve quality by setting standards and rigorously enforcing those standards.
4. Keep parent fees affordable through subsidies.
5. Expand the availability of all kinds of care.
6. Commit the resources needed to get the job done.

The report from the National Women's Law Center can be downloaded at http://www.nwlc.org, under Child Care.

Child Care in Rural Areas

In most rural areas there is a shortage of high-quality child care. Most child care is informal and thus unregulated. Several conditions make delivery of adequate child-care services in rural areas difficult.

Funding is the biggest challenge. Less-populated areas often receive less federal money than urban communities receive, and there are few large employers who can contribute to child-care services. Families must travel long distances to child-care programs, and providers must also travel long distances to training activities.

Demand for child care often fluctuates in rural areas along with seasonal jobs. This makes it almost impossible for providers to stay in business.

One solution to the problem has been to use **child-care resource and referral networks (CCR&Rs)**. These networks help parents find child care and help providers find support and training programs. CCR&Rs operate at the state level and coordinate with local organizations and programs. The passage of the Child Care and Development Block Grant funds in 1991 brought about an increase in the number of these networks. In 2005, there were 850 Resource and Referral agencies across the United States, including satellite and affiliate offices (National Association of Child Care Resource and Referral Agencies, 2005).

A larger state network enables smaller CCR&Rs to offer services to rural residents. Employers may contribute to a lending library, subsidize a newsletter, or support a small, family-child care network. The problem of distance can be overcome through the use of new technologies: telecommuting, telephone conferences, and public television broadcasts. States utilizing these innovations discover that they can improve the quantity and quality of services to rural communities and use their available child-care dollars more efficiently.

Child Care in Other Countries

As more women enter the workforce, countries throughout the world are recognizing the need for child-care facilities. In some countries, child care has been available for a long time, but in others the need has only recently been recognized.

Child care has been available in **China** since the communist revolution. After the revolution, women were expected to work, while recently many more women are working to augment family income. Although grandparents care for many children, many other children attend child-care centers.

China passed a one-child policy in 1979, mandating severe penalties for families who had a second child: denial of medical and educational services for that child plus a fine or possible loss of their jobs. This often leads to overindulgence of the single child by parents and grandparents. Growing concerns about children's social competence even prompted the producers of *Sesame Street* for Chinese audiences to adapt their format to coach children in how to get along with playmates (Tung, 1997). Teachers must help children overcome the effects of "spoiling" and learn the skills they might otherwise develop in a large family of siblings. Teachers plan activities during the daily routines that teach social skills such as sharing, cooperation, and caring for themselves as well as others.

Children are divided by age group, with 20 to 40 children per class. Each day begins with organized exercises, and group activities continue throughout the day. All children participate in the same activity at the same time. The classrooms are sparsely equipped with toys, in stark comparison with a Western classroom where there is an abundance, including duplicates of some toys. Chinese children have to learn to share, wait for their turn, or negotiate with their peers for an opportunity to play.

Teachers even remove some materials as the school year progresses, forcing even more cooperative behavior from the children. When children want to speak in class, they must raise their hand and wait to be recognized. They stand when speaking because it is believed that this helps to overcome self-consciousness. The Chinese child-care settings are a good example of how cultural values and practices are reflected in the education of young children.

The Scandinavian countries have also supported child care for many years. Under the Ministry of Education, **Finland** administers the 1973 Act on Children's Day Care. The act funds preschools and kindergartens to offer education and care for children up to the age of six. These now serve almost all Finnish children under the age of seven. Primary school children have after-school and holiday programs. The curriculum of Finnish centers focuses on fostering all aspects of children's development: cognitive, psychomotor, and affective. Teachers use the basic principles outlined by Piaget. Cognitive concepts are taught through visual and performing arts such as painting, music, drama, and puppetry and through literature. The physical settings are built specifically for children and often are located in neighborhoods or nearby community centers, libraries, or youth centers. Space is carefully planned and used attractively. Child-sized work areas invite children to participate in activities. Overall, Finland's child-care centers are exemplary models of public-supported care.

Denmark's preschool programs are similar to those in Finland; however, there is an interesting difference. By law, preschool children are not allowed to be taught formally. There is a pervasive belief that very young children should be allowed to be children. Learning occurs in informal groups or through cooperative play. Adults read to children, and the children learn by looking at books. They take field trips to their parents' workplaces or to one another's homes. Time is set aside to prepare children for school. They learn to sit and listen to the teacher. Most facilities are separate from the primary school or at least are housed in a special place within the building.

Another innovation in the Danish system is the establishment of discovery playgrounds. These are places where children can raise vegetables, keep chickens, and house ponies. Within the child-care/kindergarten network there are also clubs for young people up to age 18 or 20. Many school-age youngsters and teenagers attend after-school or evening clubs and participate in sports, arts, and swimming.

France, too, has an extensive child-care program serving most three- to five-year-olds. The French system dates back to the beginning of the 20th century, but there has been tremendous growth since the 1950s. The programs are under the auspices of the public school system. Some of the centers are freestanding, but others are housed on primary school campuses. Every child over the age of two years and three months is eligible, although space is still limited for this age level. More than 90 percent of three-year-olds are in school. The hours correspond to the school day, 8:30 A.M. to 4:30 P.M. The curriculum stresses cognitive development, and it is implemented with developmentally appropriate practices. Group size is large, usually 25 to 30 children.

Japanese programs for young children focus on "creating a community spirit to foster the development of children's interpersonal skills in group-oriented environments" (Izumi-Taylor, 2008).

Children are expected to learn to live in a cooperative setting by developing a characteristic called *sunao*. Sunao is related to children's autonomy so teachers stress listening to others, and being honest and cooperative. In order to further develop autonomy Japanese teachers reduce their own authority by encouraging children to have group meetings at which issues that are important to them can be discussed.

In **Kenya** teachers use music to promote a variety of skills in children. When children enter preschool at the age of three they are taught English, which is the official language of the country. Songs and games in English are played both indoors and outdoors. Musical games teach the children important social skills such as taking turns or being obedient, minding parents, and doing chores and schoolwork. There are songs that help children learn to count and remember numbers, develop their physical abilities, and teach personal safety and mastery (Freshwater, Sherwood, & Mbugua, 2008).

Italy has provided education and care programs for children between the ages of three and six for many years. In 1971, infants and toddlers were included. These programs combine both education and social service concepts. One program begun in Reggio Emilia has become a model for others in Italy, in the United States, and in other countries. The principles embodied in the Reggio Emilia centers rely upon the ideas of John Dewey, Jean Piaget, and Lev Vygotsky. One of the system's basic principles is that children should be viewed in relation to other children, to their family, to their teachers, and to their environment. Parents are seen as an essential and active part of their children's learning.

The design of each school encourages choices, problem solving, and discoveries as components of child learning. Thoughtful placement of furniture and materials increases the possibilities of encounters with their teachers and with other children. One of the most important aspects of Reggio Emilia is that the curriculum is not planned. There are general goals, but the curriculum emerges from the children's activities and projects.

Children's progress is carefully documented through photographs, videos, and written transcripts. This recordkeeping serves several functions. It allows parents to maintain their involvement by sharing their children's experiences. It also helps teachers to understand children better, thus enhancing their professional development. The records also allow educators to share information. Possibly the most important function is that children become aware that their efforts are valued.

CASE STUDY

Andrea is the director of a large church–sponsored preschool and is preparing for the new school year. She has met with the returning teachers to assess their abilities and preferences for group assignments. She needs four new teachers to accommodate the increased enrollment for this year. Because the center is church affiliated, she is committed to recruiting candidates for the positions who have a religious belief close to that of the church. She has run advertisements in the local newspapers and has 11 possible candidates to interview.

1. What questions would you ask the candidates if you were Andrea?
2. Think for a moment about the question "What is your personal educational philosophy?" How would you state it to another person?
3. What information could an interviewer gather from your response to the previous question?

SUMMARY

According to the Children's Defense Fund report The State of America's Children 2005, someone other than the parent cares for more than half of children in the United States under the age of six. The others have in-home care or are with relatives. Additionally, an increasing number of school-age children are enrolled in before- and after-school programs.

The quality of care given to the children can improve their safety and can affect development. Children who have been in quality programs have fewer behavioral problems, interact better with their peers, and have better academic skills.

Half-day schools are in session for four hours or less. Their primary purpose is the education of the child.

All-day schools function more than four hours per day. They must provide for the full care of the child. Different management problems are encountered than in the half-day school. Additional staffing is necessary. Communication must be complete for the school to function successfully.

A private, for-profit school is owned by one or more individuals and is expected to make a profit. This type of school has the freedom to experiment and the constraint to operate efficiently.

Family child-care homes are especially suitable for infants and toddlers and such homes can have a flexible schedule.

Corporate child-care centers are relatively new. They are expected to make a profit and have many different locations. They are similar, have a recognizable "style," and often have an interchangeable curriculum. Advantages of these centers include financial strength, increased resources, and the opportunity for professional advancement.

Employer-sponsored programs are growing. The parent company may furnish a building and/or capital for an on-site child-care center. Some employers support satellite programs near the workplace or near employees' homes.

Other companies offer a voucher program whereby employees are given a fixed amount for child care. Another form of support is a resource and referral service where parents seeking child care may obtain reliable information.

Employers are also beginning to respond to another need of working parents—care for their mildly ill children. In 1986 only 36 sick-child programs existed. Today there are 324 programs nationwide, 50 percent of which are in hospitals. The others are in child-care centers, freestanding facilities, or in-home care facilities. Employers are finding that these programs are decreasing employee absenteeism.

The cooperative school, a declining enterprise, is operated as a nonprofit center. The director is also the teacher. Parents fill in as staff, and thus coordination is essential.

Churches characteristically offer a half-day program, which may be religiously oriented. Such a program usually must be self-supporting. Space may be a problem because the school often shares facilities with other church-related functions.

Many colleges and universities operate laboratory schools. These serve at least two functions: teaching and child care. Various orientations exist, and standards are generally high.

Child-care centers are often publicly funded and are usually adjuncts to the local school system. As with public education systems, generally, they have bureaucratic rules, but offer relatively higher salaries and adequate funding.

Head Start is a federal program begun in 1965 primarily for disadvantaged children. It is typically a single-classroom school aimed at raising children to grade level before they enter elementary school. It has been generally successful.

The U.S. military has developed a model program for caring for the children of their personnel. The system comprises a supportive web of more than 800 child development centers, 9,000 family child-care homes, and many resources and referral services.

There is often a shortage of child care in rural areas. One solution is to use resource and referral networks, some of which receive grants through the Child Care and Development Block Grant of 1991.

Countries throughout the world are responding to the need to provide child care for working mothers. China has many centers attached to workplaces. The Scandinavian countries have also supported child care for many years. Centers in Finland serve almost all children up to the age of six. Denmark cares for young children, as well as providing after-school programs for older children and clubs for teenagers.

France has an extensive system that began in the early 20th century. Every child over the age of two years and three months is eligible, although space is still limited. More than 90 percent of three-year-olds are in school, however. Japan stresses the development of autonomy and cooperation in children. Kenya teachers use music and musical games to promote all areas of children's development. Italy provides education for children starting from infancy. A program was begun in Reggio Emilia that has become a model. The design of each school furthers the principles upon which the system is based: learning through encounters, making choices, problem solving, and discovery.

STUDENT ACTIVITIES

1. Visit a half-day school and a full-day school. Return to the full-day school at the end of a day. Observe the similarities and differences during the morning hours of each of the schools. What happens at the end of a day at the all-day school? Report your findings to the class.

2. Make an appointment to visit a family child-care home. Choose a time when the operator will be able to talk to you. Observe the number of children, the kinds of activities that are provided, and the routine of the day. Talk to the operator about the satisfactions and difficulties of conducting this kind of program.

3. Meet with the director of a corporate child-care center. Before the meeting, prepare a list of questions to ask. After the visit, summarize your findings and report to the class. Some suggested questions are the following:

   a. How is your budget prepared?

   b. Is there someone within the corporation you can call when you have problems?

   c. How is the curriculum of your center planned?

   d. What is the process for hiring new staff members? Are you free to determine the salary for that person?

   e. What are the advantages for you in working in this kind of center?

   f. What have you found difficult about working for a corporate child-care center?

4. Visit two other types of schools. Do you observe differences in the character of the job of director in each? Ask the directors to describe the most important aspects of their jobs. Are they different or the same in each school? Is the role of a director the same or different from what you expected before your visit?

REVIEW

1. According to the Children's Defense Fund report *The State of America's Children 2009*, who are the caregivers of the greatest number of children under the age of six?

2. List the components of quality child care.

3. Although an all-day program offers many of the same activities you would find in a half-day program, there are differences. What are they?

4. What is the primary source of income for a for-profit school? In what ways can income be increased?

5. What are the advantages and disadvantages of operating home-based child care?

6. Discuss the advantages and disadvantages of directing a school that is part of a national corporation.

7. List the types of work/family services that businesses are offering to their employees.

8. The laboratory school has several purposes that are usually not found in other programs. What are they?

9. What are the advantages and disadvantages of being the director of a child-care center that is part of a public school district?

10. The overall goal of Head Start programs was cited in this chapter. What is it?

REFERENCES

Bailey, S., & Warford, B. (1995). Delivering services in rural areas: Using child care referral and resource networks. *Young Children, 50*(5), 86–90.

Campbell, N. D., Appelbaum, J. C., Martinson, K., & Martin, E. (2000). Be all that we can be: Lessons from the military for improving our nation's child care system. Washington, DC: National Women's Law Center. www.nwwlc.org. Retrieved 02-19-06.

Children's Defense Fund. (2005). *The state of America's children 2005.* Washington, DC: Author.

Families and Work Institute. www.familiesandwork.org. Retrieved 03-15-06.

Freshwater, A., Sherwood, E., & Mbugua, E. (2008). Music and physical play. *Childhood Education,85*(1), 2–5.

Helburn, S., ed. (1995). *Cost, quality, and child outcomes in child care centers.* Public report. Denver: Department of Economics and Public Policy, University of Colorado at Denver.

Herman, R. E., Koppan, D., & Sullivan, P. (1999). Sick child daycare promotes healing and staffing. *Nursing Management, 30*(4), 45–47.

Hohman, M., & Weikart, D. P. (1995). *Educating young children: Active learning practices for preschool and child care programs.* Ypsilanti, MI: HighScope Press.

Izumi-Taylor, S. (2008). Sunao (Cooperative Children): How Japanese Teachers Nurture Autonomy. *Young Children, 63*(3), 76–79.

National Association for Sick Child Daycare. Retrieved from http://www.nascd.com.

National Association of Child Care Resource and Referral Agencies. (2005). *Child care resources and referral: The shape of things to come.* Washington, DC: Author.

National Coalition for Campus Children's Centers. www.campuschildren.org. Retrieved 03-21-06.

Tung, L. (1997, August 20). How to get to (China's) Sesame Street. *The Wall Street Journal,* p. A12.

U.S. Department of Commerce, Bureau of the Census. (2005). *Current population survey.* Washington, DC: U.S. Government Printing Office.

Weaver, R. (2002). The roots of quality care: Strengths of master providers. *Young Children, 57*(1), 16–22.

SELECTED FURTHER READING

Abbott-Shim, M., Lambert, R., & McCarty, F. (2003). A comparison of school readiness outcomes of children randomly assigned to a Head Start program and the program's wait list. *Journal of Education for Students Placed at Risk, 8*(2), 210–211.

Cartwright, S. (1999). Early childhood care and education in China. *Child Care Information Exchange, 126,* 22–25.

Click, P. M., (2009). *Caring for school-age children* (5th ed.). Clifton Park, NY: Cengage

Cordell, R. L., Waterman, S.H., Chang, A., et al. (1999). Provider reported illness and absence due to illness among children attending child-care homes and centers in San Diego, California. *Archives of Pediatrics & Adolescent Medicine, 153*(3), 275–280.

Gandini, L. (1993). Fundamentals of the Reggio Emilia approach to early childhood education. *Young Children, 49*(1), 4–8.

Gordon, A. M., & Browne, K. W. (2007). *Beginnings and beyond* (6th ed.). Clifton Park, NY: Cengage.

Kennedy, D. K. (1996). After Reggio Emilia: May the conversation begin! *Young Children, 51*(5), 24–27.

MacDonald, B. (2005). Purposeful work: A Montessori approach to everyday challenging behaviors. *Child Care Information Exchange, 164,* 51–54.

Marmer Solomon, C. (2000, December/January). Sic daze. *Working Mother, 40,* 26–30.

Montessori, M. (1967). The *Montessori method* (A. E. George, Trans.). Cambridge, MA: Robert Bentley. (Original work published 1912.)

Neugebauer, Roger. (2008). Employer Child Care Organizations Eye Changing Economics. *Exchange, 30*(4), Issue, 182, 778–780.

Nielson, D. M. (2002). The journey from baby-sitter to child care professional: Military family child care providers. *Young Children, 57*(1), 9–14.

Sciarra, D. J., & Dorsey, A. G. (2003). *Developing and administering a child care center* (5th. ed.). Clifton Park, NY: Cengage.

Sussman, C. (1998). Out of the basement: Discovering the value of child care facilities. *Young Children, 53*(1), 10–17.

HELPFUL WEBSITES

Disclaimer: Links to Internet sites throughout this book are provided for your convenience and do not constitute an endorsement.

Day Care Provider's Beginner Page:	**http://www.oursite.net**
Military Child Development Program:	**http://dticaw.dtic.mil.milchild**
Military Children and Youth Programs:	**http://military-childrenandyouth.calib.com**
National Association for Sick Child Daycare:	**http://www.nascd.com**
National Head Start Association:	**http://www.nhsa.org**

For additional resources related to administration including videos, links to related sites for each chapter of the text, tutorial quizzes, glossary flashcards, and more, visit the Education CourseMate website for this book at www.cengage.com/login.

PART II

Planning: Program and Environment

Cengage Learning

Family Child Care

Objectives

After reading this chapter, you should be able to:

- List the common characteristics of family child-care providers.
- List steps in starting a family child-care business.
- Discuss the reasons that parents choose the family child care.
- State the challenges of running a home-based business.

KEY TERMS

Child Care HOME
Inventory

Family Child Care
Environmental Rating
Scale, Revised Edition
(FCCERS-R)

family, friends, and
neighbors (FFN) care

license-exempt family
child-care providers

provider networks

A day in the life of . . .

A Family Child-Care Provider
Thursday:

5:30 A.M. My youngest son comes to me saying he doesn't feel well. Within a few minutes he has thrown up and is running a fever. I get out my address book to call the other providers that may be able to take care of the four children I have coming in today. I find room for three but no one has an opening for an infant. I then call the four families and break the news. Two families are fine, one family tells me they are uncomfortable taking their child to someone new and will make other arrangements, and the family with the infant is upset and tells me that it is my responsibility to find them care and if I cannot then I need to take their child anyway. I explain that our contract states that due to immediate closure on my part then I will try my best to find them backup care but that they need to have other arrangements in case a situation like this will arise. They are still upset but will find other care. In the end of it all I have to close Friday also and have lost around $200.00 in wages.

Monday:

6:00 A.M. Alarm clock rings. Make myself presentable for children arriving, do sweep of house, make bleach solution, and make sure everything is still clean and orderly from the night before.

6:30 A.M. Wake up C (my 3-year-old son) and H (my 6-year-old son), get them ready for school. First child arrives, M a 2-½-year-old girl, my boys begin a sibling disagreement in the bathroom. I excuse myself to referee. Upon my return M's mom comments that she understands now where M has learned to fight with her brother. I politely smile and ask her how her weekend was. She begins to leave, I remind her to sign M in and for payment of M's tuition. She asks if she can pay me later because she always asks on payment day. I tell her no.

7:20 A.M. J, a 3-½-year-old boy, arrives. His mom says that he is on medication for an ear infection and hasn't eaten breakfast yet. I hurry him to the breakfast table so I can keep on schedule and then run to get the proper paperwork for the medication.

7:35 A.M. We go to the bathroom to wash up and go potty. M is potty training so I make sure she goes. I grab my "trip kit" which has first aid kit, emergency numbers, and medical POAs on all children and leave to take H to school.

9:10 A.M. 10-month-old boy, G, gets dropped off. We sit down for circle time. G crawls behind the couch.

10:00 A.M. Clean up for snack. Warm bottle for G. G begins to fuss. G cries while I get J, C, and M set at table. Daycare regulation states that infants under 1 year old must be held while given bottle. G won't take bottle so I sit on floor with G in my lap. M spills water, hold G with bottle while cleaning up spill. Reposition myself in rocking chair with G. J, C, and M finish snack.

10:30 A.M. Backyard play. Keep everyone on porch until I can remove droppings left by the neighbors' cat. J & C try to keep G from crying.

11:15 A.M. Clean up. Go inside, take everyone to the bathroom, change G's diaper. Get ready to pick up S, (4-½-year-old boy) from preschool.

12:00 P.M. Everyone back inside and sent to wash hands for lunch. G starts to cry again. The older children set the table. Warm bottles for G. Make sure Q has no allergies. Give J medicine and log it on sheet. While getting out the rest of the food I realize my husband has eaten the lunchmeat set aside for the children. Scurry to find another USDA-approved item for lunch.

12:45 P.M. Get the rest of the children into bathroom to brush teeth and go to the bathroom. Get Pull-Up on M. Check G's diaper. Get cots set out and everyone in proper spots.

1:15 P.M. G is back on the cot but cannot get settled. I remember he didn't eat and fix him another bottle. Within a few minutes after eating he is sound asleep.

1:30 P.M. I write out daily reports and observations, log on and enter information into computer about next week's menus and schedules.

3:00 P.M. Pick up H and drive to park where the children play.

4:00 P.M. Back at the house we all sit down at table and do "Homework."

4:30 P.M. J and S get picked up .Get daily paper work filed in proper areas, disinfect and sanitize. Get food and supplies ready for next day, do walk-through of house to make sure all toys, safety items, are still in proper places.

5:00 P.M. End of workday ~ Time to switch from day-care provider to mom and wife!

What Is Family Child Care?

Family child care is an important component of the child-care landscape, serving a large number of children, and providing a critical service to working families. Recent estimates suggest that today in the United States family child-care providers care for between 2 and 3 million children under age six. According to the Bureau of Labor Statistics in 2008 there were 232,923 regulated family child-care homes in the United States. Considering the significant numbers of children enrolled nationally, family child care has, and will continue to play, a major role in determining this country's future.

With the enactment of the Personal Responsibility and Work Opportunity Reconciliation Act in 1996, many states sought to increase the availability of child care for low-income families. In the aftermath of welfare reform, local and state governments are compensating family child-care providers to care for the children of welfare-to-work recipients. Child-care workers held about 1.4 million jobs in 2006. About 35 percent of those child-care workers were self-employed family child-care providers.

What began years ago as an informal approach to providing child care as a way to support working parents has now become big business. Family child-care providers today are making an intentional career choice to offer quality early care and education in their homes.

So what do we know about family child care? Who are these providers? How are these programs regulated? And what does the future hold for this little known and underrepresented segment of providers and the children they care for?

It is with the intention to present a more representative picture of this large and important segment of the U.S. child-care workforce that this chapter has been added.

The following information will focus on the "regulated sector," which includes both licensed and registered family child-care providers. Regulated family child-care homes are owner-operated small businesses and typically contain mixed-age groups and siblings, versus **License-exempt family child-care providers** (also referred to as **FFN—Family, Friends, and Neighbors**) typically care for fewer children, in their own home or in the home of one of the children in their care.

Family child-care homes are facilities where care for a small number of children of mixed ages typically is provided in the caregiver's residence. Many providers are mothers of young children themselves. Most states classify their homes by size as being either family child-care homes (FCCH) or group or large child-care homes (G/LCCH). Generally, FCCH allow up to six children, and G/LCCH allow between seven and 12 children. The age group of the children is sometimes considered in determining the maximum numbers allowed in each type of home.

Family child-care providers nurture and care for children who have not yet entered formal schooling and also supervise older children before and after school. These providers play an important role in children's development by caring for them when parents are at work or away for other reasons. In addition to attending to children's basic needs, providers organize activities that stimulate children's physical, emotional, intellectual, and social growth. They help children explore individual interests, develop talents and independence, build self-esteem, and learn how to get along with others. Helping to keep children healthy is another important part of the job. Child-care workers serve nutritious meals and snacks and teach good eating habits and personal hygiene. They ensure that children have proper rest periods, identify children who may not feel well and, in some cases, may help parents locate programs that will provide basic health and other social services.

Significant research has provided evidence that warm, loving, and home-like settings are natural environments for children during early childhood. While offering the safety and comfort of home, and providing a consistent caregiver throughout the years, family child care is the care of choice for many parents.

· · · · · · REGULATION

Regulatory status distinguishes family child care from informal home-based arrangements. States vary widely in the way they define and regulate family child care. In some states, regulated family child-care providers are licensed, whereas in others they are registered, which is usually a form of licensure. The line between regulated and unregulated care is often blurry.

Most states require the licensure or registration of home-based child-care providers who cared for more than two unrelated children. Additionally, states differentiate small and large family child-care homes, with separate regulations. Small family child-care homes care for up to six children, whereas large or "group" family child-care homes employ an assistant in order to serve between seven and 12 children.

Though research has tried to determine which regulations are effective in promoting quality in family child care there are few conclusive results. What is clear is that the unintended consequence of increased regulation and oversight is moving some providers to leave the market or regulated system. This is a cause for concern among policy makers and researchers.

Regulations concerning family child care are administered at the state level and typically include standards governing the maximum number of children in care or families served, hours permitted, health and safety measures, minimum indoor and outdoor usable space, provider training, and sometimes provider criminal background checks.

It is worth noting that as of 2004, NCCIC reported that 20 percent of states required a Child Development Associate (CDA) or Associate's degree to obtain a small family child-care

Cengage Learning

Home-based child-care programs strive to meet the individual needs of young children in a nurturing setting.

license, whereas 60 percent of states required no preservice training. Most states (34) require ongoing training, ranging from one hour to 20 or more hours per year. Licenses often require scheduled or unscheduled site visits and must be renewed every one to three years.

THE CHOICE OF FAMILY CHILD CARE

Parents perceive family child-care homes (FCCH) as offering several advantages including close supervision, warmth, and responsiveness to children's needs and environments that are often considered more intimate and familiar. Frequently family child-care sites are located in neighborhoods and communities where families live and are generally cheaper than either a nanny or center-based care. The family child-care option is also attractive to parents as they are seen as comfortable settings for infants and toddlers in that they offer a consistent caregiver in a stable setting. Additionally, family child-care homes provide opportunities for sisters and brothers of different ages to be together which reflects a more homelike atmosphere. Individual providers are often willing to offer a more flexible schedule including evening and weekend care.

Some disadvantages of family child care are that not all FCC providers are licensed/regulated. Most providers are not required to have background experience in child development or early education and not all settings offer an academic program. Exposure to extracurricular activities, such as dance and art, may be limited. And providers may not have the funds to provide the same type of equipment, activities, and learning experiences as a center-based program. If the provider is ill, parents may need to find backup placement or take a day or more off of work. Equally of concern is that without a contract, providers can terminate services at any time.

The results of one large nationwide study conclude that the majority of parents using both regulated and unregulated home-based care are satisfied with their care arrangement and believe that their children receive more individual attention in home-based settings.

PROVIDER CHARACTERISTICS

Family child-care providers vary widely in race, age, educational attainment, and socio-economic status, however more than 90 percent of providers are female and are parents themselves. Approximately 33 percent care for their own children in addition to others. In California the typical licensed family child-care provider is in her mid-forties and has been taking care of children in her home for 10 years; 7 percent are age 29 or younger, and 21 percent are age 55 or older. Average tenure is 12 years for providers licensed to care for 14 children, and 8 years for those licensed for eight children.

Statistics show that education levels in home-based early childhood education (ECE) are much lower than center-based ECE. Only about one in nine home-based early child-hood educators has a college degree compared to nearly one in six in center-based ECE. Twenty-one percent of home-based early childhood educators have less than a high school degree compared to 12 percent of center-based staff.

Family child-care providers work out of their own homes. Although this arrangement provides convenience, it also requires that their homes be accommodating to young children. Providers' private homes become places of business, and both they and their families must confront issues of privacy and work/life balance, potentially producing conflict within the caregiver's family.

Helping children grow, learn, and gain new skills can be very rewarding, though physically and emotionally taxing, as providers constantly stand, walk, bend, stoop, and lift to attend to each child's interests and problems. Additionally the work hours of providers vary widely. Family child-care providers have flexible hours but they may work long or unusual hours to fit parents' work schedules.

Work and personal life can often become enmeshed, especially when the provider is caring for her own children. Additionally, personal relationships with clients (ie, the families of children in her care) can interfere with the business aspects of child care. In one statewide survey (New Jersey), family child-care providers reported that an overall lack of respect for their work and for their policies, mainly from parents, was a major issue, often resulting in difficult attitudes, late pick ups, and late or inadequate payments.

Providers also report more stress, longer hours, and less income than other working mothers. One result of the stressful working conditions in family child care is high turn-over. Most recent estimates range from 15 to 25 percent.

Surveys and qualitative studies have revealed that both personal reasons (eg, own children aging out of child care, unfulfilled need for adult contact, problems with parents) and economic factors (eg, income instability, lack of affordable liability and health insur-ance and retirement benefits) influence the decision to leave or remain in the child-care field. Despite challenging work conditions and low wages, most providers report being satisfied with their work.

Because many providers have infrequent opportunities to interact with other adults, social isolation is assumed to be a problem in family child care. Research is mixed on this issue. Belonging to a support group or provider association has been associated with higher-quality care and fewer child injuries and fatalities. **Provider networks** are often used as a strategy for combating isolation and turnover.

Although child-care workers as a whole earn low wages, family child-care providers are among the lowest paid within the profession. Recent data is lacking, one analysis used Bureau of Labor Statistics data to report that the median weekly earnings for family child-care providers in 1998 was $211. Earnings of self-employed child-care workers vary depending on the number of hours worked, the number and ages of the children, and the location.

In addition to low earnings, few family child-care providers have health insurance unless they are covered by the policy of a spouse or family member. Some family child-care providers, however, are eligible for Medicaid and publicly subsidized child health insurance plans for dependents.

Low earnings and few benefits leave family child-care providers in a precarious economic situation. There are few financial incentives for providers to stay in the child-care field, particularly when better paying jobs are available in the school system for providers with adequate training and education. Within the family child-care field, providers are also vulnerable to fluctuations in the economy or family emergencies such as a serious illness. Therefore, turnover in the field is high.

One study found that approximately 40 percent of providers leave family child care each year. Among those who left the field, half went to school or found another job. Experts also suggested that another problem is that the family child care field lacks a "career ladder" to provide an incentive for remaining in the child-care field and enhancing training credentials.

The Business of Family Child Care

Family child care constitutes a large number of U.S. small businesses. In 2005, there were 166,514 licensed small and 47,452 licensed large family child-care homes in the United States. Although most family child-care providers operate independently as small businesses with a sole proprietor, some do operate under the sponsorship of an outside organization such as a neighborhood child-care center or family service agency. In such arrangements, programs are members of a family child-care home network where the sponsoring agency takes responsibility for training (and sometimes paying) the family child-care provider and for referring potential clients to the family child-care home.

The work of family child-care providers is unlike many other self-employed careers. Rather than being motivated solely by profit, as are most entrepreneurs, family child-care providers are often also motivated by their enjoyment of working with children and their desire to stay at home with their own children. Most family child-care providers see themselves as caregivers first and business people second. Although many are very entrepreneurial, few have sophisticated businesses or administrative and financial systems.

Revenue from family child care typically contributes about a quarter to a half of total household income although it may constitute the provider's entire household income, particularly if providers are unmarried. Providers caring for their own young children may also benefit from the savings of not paying for their children's out-of-home child care, if the cost of care for their children elsewhere is greater than the provider's additional earning potential of those care slots. In general, family child-care providers average lower earnings and benefits than they could receive in similar skill level jobs.

Regulated family child-care homes have much in common with other forms of self-employment and other home-based businesses in that providers are generally responsible for all aspects of the business, including finances, planning, and service delivery. Providers also often operate with little, if any, external support. In addition, providers have both a business relationship and a caring relationship with the families whose children are in their care, making it more difficult to set and collect fees.

The vast majority of licensed providers report that the most rewarding aspects of their jobs are doing work they consider important and that has an impact on people's lives. Providers spend an average of 52 hours a week directly caring for children, plus an additional 10 hours a week, on average, on tasks related to their family child-care business (such as doing laundry, food shopping, and record-keeping). The most stressful aspects of licensed providers' work are the fact that their earnings are unpredictable and that they often have to juggle conflicting tasks or duties.

In a 2007 California Workforce study of licensed home-based providers, one quarter expect to stop caring for children within the next three years and most of the providers expect that their next job will not be in early child care and education. Providers said they would be more likely to continue as licensed providers if they received retirement savings, better pay, health benefits, and greater respect for the work they do. Support services, such as respite care or local resources, were important to about a third of the providers, but not as important as increased financial rewards.

Earnings of self-employed child-care providers vary depending on the number of hours worked, the number and ages of the children, and the location. On average, family child care is not a lucrative business; most providers have low earnings, have little or no access to employment benefits such as health care and retirement, and work long hours.

The majority of family child-care providers charge fees that are typically lower than centers' but higher than most unregulated home-based arrangements. Many family child-care homes also receive federal or state subsidies for low-income children in their care.

Personal relationships with children's parents may interfere with business aspects of child care, resulting in negative attitudes, late pick ups, and/or late or inadequate payments; providers may feel socially isolated given that they have infrequent opportunities to interact with other adults; however, research is mixed regarding how problematic this is for providers.

QUALITY

The quality of care a young child receives has been shown to dramatically impact their social, emotional, physical, and intellectual development, and ultimately success in school and life. Although research studies show that top predictors of quality child care are educated providers, low staff turnover, low child/staff ratios and above minimum licensure or accreditation of the child-care program, many home-based programs do not meet these criteria.

Experts have identified low earnings among family child-care providers as a primary obstacle to improving quality. Research suggests that in the family child-care field, the provider's education level, a strong indicator of quality service, has little relationship to the level of income that the providers receive. Many experts suggested that the link between quality and earnings could be attributed to high turnover and low commitment to the child-care field. Low earnings may impact a provider's willingness to partake in training and professional development activities. In addition, because family child-care providers generally own their child-care businesses, low profits make it difficult to invest in quality improvement.

Though we are fortunate to have some national averages it is important to note that there is great variation in quality and characteristics within the family child-care sector.

Most observational studies to date suggest that much of family child care is of "adequate" quality. Research suggests that the quality of care is not associated with the provider's age or years of experience, but is positively correlated with the training and education the provider has received.

Research results suggest that policies and programs that encourage continuing education or training for providers – at the level of a CDA credential, college courses in early childhood education, or an Associate's degree or higher in a related or unrelated field— combined with policies that support the entry of better-educated providers into the market, would be likely to raise the quality of licensed family child-care homes. However, the finding that higher-quality family child-care homes cost more to operate than lower-quality homes, require that any policy designed to address quality issues must also address affordability issues and the working conditions of licensed family child-care providers.

Most measures used to study family child care assess characteristics of the care environment, the provider, and children and families. Studies often adapt measures used in child-care centers or private homes. Studies use two approaches to evaluate quality in child-care settings: structure and process.

The **Family Day Care Rating Scale, Revised Edition (FCCERS-R)** and the **Child Care HOME Inventory (CC-HOME)**, and the Arnett Caregiver Involvement Scale (CIS) are research tools for measuring quality specific to family child care.

It is important to note that across all settings, current definitions of quality do not include assessments of the cultural and linguistic diversity and skills of the workforce. This is particularly significant in family child care where caregivers are often from the same cultural and linguistic background as the child. They have the ability to provide culturally appropriate services, and are able to build and reinforce families' cultural values, heritage, and assets.

Additionally, quality measures and definitions also do not currently take parents' definitions of quality into consideration. It is important to consider that parents might choose their care for reasons that do not reflect professional or regulated standards of quality. Instead, this choice may reflect other equally important or more important preferences, such as flexibility, the importance of family bonds, shared values around child rearing, or the desire for cultural and language congruity. Because so many families need child care that is affordable and accessible, protecting the quality of family child care is crucial.

Support for family child care comes from federal, state, and local levels of the government and social service organizations. Several federal programs and block grants to the states are designed to improve access to and the quality of child care. Additionally the U.S. Department of Agriculture's (USDA) Child and Adult Food Program reimburses participating family child-care providers for serving nutritious food to children. At the local level, CCR&R agencies located in all 50 states also provide support to existing child-care providers. They maintain a local calendar of upcoming training and professional development activities and provide training directly.

Implementing promising practices to improve training opportunities, decrease job isolation, and improve earnings and benefits among family child-care providers may significantly elevate the quality of service children receive.

RECOMMENDATIONS FOR SUCCESS

There are many things that a family child-care provider needs to be good at besides caring for children to be a success in business. Things like getting paid on time from parents, writing solid policies and contracts, marketing your business to new potential clients, obtaining the right insurance policy, understanding record keeping and how it affects your taxes, and overall, just getting started in a manner that will optimize success.

The following is a list of recommendations:

1. *Do the proper research on the child-care market in your town or city.* This is a crucial step. It involves spending a few hours, calling around (or maybe visiting some other child-care businesses) and asking key questions. By asking key questions you can potentially uncover an unfulfilled need in your town or city. By taking the time to do this research, you will gain a huge advantage by understanding your market and how you can be successful within that market.

2. *As a small business owner, each provider needs adequate life, health, and disability insurance to protect their family from the loss of their income.* Child-care providers face unique risks such as the financial loss that would result if the provider were found liable or responsible for the injury or death of a child or a child's parent. A homeowner's policy does not provide enough protection, nor the right kind of protection you need for special situations that a day-care owner can face.

3. *Charge the right fees.* Deciding what to charge is simply a matter of making some phone calls or visits to other child-care businesses and setting your prices appropriately.

4. *Manage your child-care business finances.* The potential provider must then decide what his or her revenue model is by sitting down and listing estimated expenses. Then, based on intended charges, calculate how many children you will need to provide care for to breakeven. Anything more than that is profit. Remember, your day care is a business and needs to remain separate from your personal affairs.

5. *Develop a comprehensive policy handbook and well-written contract.* If you use your contract and policy handbook properly, you may save yourself thousands of dollars of lost income.

6. *Market your business to attract future customers.* The best advertising is word of mouth. Some marketing ideas to get you started include: Register with the Child CCR&R office in your area. Once you register with your CCR&R, they will provide your contact information, along with any special information pertaining to your day care, to parents seeking child care. Contact all the elementary schools in your community or on your bus line. Ask to have your name and phone number added to their list of child-care providers, which they provide to parents upon request. Ask for referrals. Tell everyone you know that you are providing child care and ask them if they know anyone who is seeking child care in your area. Place announcements or small ads in community newsletters such as a church, play group, or community group. In your ad, focus on the unique features of your business and the benefits of your program.

7. *Keep good records.* Visit other successful providers and learn what records must be kept for your business and how to set up an organized, efficient record-keeping system. Start a new set of business files and receipts for each year. Keep all business files for at least three to five years for income tax purposes.

8. *Utilize free resources available in your local area.* The best place to start is with your state. Every state in the United States has an agency within their state government that sets the rules for family child-care providers. Simply go to your state's website (such as http://www.California.gov) and look for the appropriate department, or type "child care" in the search box.

9. *Obtain a license or certification from your state.* As for the licenses and requirements in your state, the Administration for Children and Families provide a state-by-state listing of contacts for licensing and regulations governing child-care businesses. Licensing can be beneficial because quality is a selling point.

10. *Work to develop yourself as a professional.* Most States require family child-care providers to complete a specific number of hours of training each year. Local CCR&R agencies can provide information about training opportunities, professional development initiatives, and other resources in your area. Child Care Aware is a national nonprofit initiative that can help you find the CCR&R agency in your area.

UNIONIZATION

Family child-care providers are providing crucial services to children and families but because most are self-employed, they are not entitled to benefits—that is, workers' comp, health insurance, unemployment, disability, or retirement. In most states providers are "really out there by themselves." But times are changing. And in increasing numbers, home-based providers have begun to join together in advocacy, realizing that in order to get these benefits, they need the combined strength of an organization of family child-care providers and in several states have become unionized.

Family child-care providers, across the country today, are increasing their efforts to organize, to boost the quality of their programs, their incomes, and their voice in child-care decision making. California's Child Care Providers United is part of a growing movement to unionize family child-care providers. 11 states, in 2009, now have regulations allowing family child-care providers to bargain collectively with the state, and providers have negotiated contracts providing rate increases and other benefits in many of these states.

This particular unionization movement is unusual because home-based child-care providers are not in traditional employer-employee relationships. Most are self-employed and care for a small number of children in the providers' own homes. This means that home-based providers are not covered by existing labor laws, and unions such as the American Federation of State, County, and Municipal Employees (AFSCME) and the Service Employees International Union (SEIU), which have been the most active in these unionization efforts, have had to advocate for new laws to organize these providers.

Cengage Learning

Despite the challenges of low wages, long hours, and lack of benefits, family child-care providers remain committed to their work with children.

This strategy, which is modeled after unions' successful campaigns to organize home health care workers, relies on the fact that home-based providers that have unionized or currently are pursuing unionization receive a state subsidy to care for low-income children and/or are regulated by the state. It is this connection that allows the state to serve as an "employer"

There are three unions currently organizing family child-care providers: The AFSCME; the American Federation of Teachers (AFT); and the SEIU.

Unions are approaching state governments that regulate providers and that pay providers as part of a state child-care assistance program. Unions are fighting to increase the resources available to family child-care providers. They are turning to states because most providers will never be able to significantly improve their financial well being by raising rates they charge to parents. Unions are lobbying states to allow providers to vote for a union that will represent them in collective bargaining with the state. Unions hope that by negotiating with the state on behalf of a large number of providers they can access public funding that will benefit providers as well as increase the quality of child care for the children they serve.

Unions have begun negotiations in some states to increase subsidy reimbursement rates, improve state child-care regulations to keep children safe, and provide health insurance and other benefits. Some unions are working on local projects to support providers and with other advocacy organizations to improve the quality of child care, such as supporting statewide quality assurance programs. This is a new approach to union organizing, so union activities vary across the country and from one union to another.

The National Women's Law Center's (NWLC) 2007 report, *Getting Organized: Unionizing Home Based Child Care Providers*, analyzes the recent and growing trend to unionize home-based child-care providers. The report suggests that the drive toward unionization is proving to be a promising strategy, not only for improving working conditions for these providers, who are overwhelmingly women and have low earnings and few benefits, but also for securing increased resources for child-care centers and for families needing child-care assistance. *Getting Organized* provides detailed information about the progress of these campaigns in the states in which there has been the most activity.

CASE STUDY

It's 6:30 A.M. and Amy receives a phone call from another provider looking for care for Q, a 6-month-old girl. Amy agrees to care for Q although she has three other children to care for. Q's mom drops her off in a short time without any paperwork, payment, or supplies. She states that she has already paid the provider for the week. Amy tells the parent she will follow up with the provider on payment but paperwork needs to be done. Also the parent doesn't have formula or supplies for Q and Q cannot drink the formula that Amy has available. Q's mom has to leave to get the proper supplies and is upset because she will be late for work. Q cries when mom leaves and will only stop crying if held. She stops crying and goes to sleep as long as Amy holds her. When Q's mom comes to pick her up, Amy tells her about Q's day. As the mother is signing her out she asks where the daily report paper is? Amy tells her she didn't have time to get to it and she just told her everything. Q's mom states that the other provider always has it done, picks up Q, and leaves.

1. How would you have handled this situation differently if you had been the provider?
2. What are the steps that the provider might take to make certain that this did not happen again?

SUMMARY

Reflecting the growing number of working families with young children and the importance of early learning, the United States has witnessed an explosion of early care and education services both in centers and homes over the last 30 years. What was once a relatively small, unnoticed sector of the economy is now viewed as a growing industry with substantial economic impact. At the same time, researchers in cognitive science, psychology, and education, among others, have expanded our understanding of the developmental significance of the early years, underscoring the importance of high-quality early learning settings to ensure that children realize their potential.

Evidence that the quality of early care and education settings can and does influence children's development during and beyond the preschool years has increasingly shifted attention to the early care and education workforce, and the extent to which those who care for young children are adequately prepared to facilitate their learning and well-being. This chapter was intended to identify the characteristics of the current status of family child care.

In California, today more than 50,000 licensed family child-care providers and paid assistants care for approximately 250,000 children, mostly in mixed-age groups. Approximately 80 percent of the children cared for by licensed providers are not yet in kindergarten, and nearly one-half of them are age two or under. A little more than one-half of licensed providers report caring for at least one child who receives public child-care assistance. Twenty percent of licensed providers report caring for at least one child with special needs. More than one-half of all licensed providers in California currently care for at least one child who receives a voucher to cover the cost of child-care services. This is remarkable, considering that a little more than two decades ago, public dollars were not permitted to be spent in licensed family child-care homes.

Today with the support of networks, associations, and unions, family child-care providers are building strength, fast becoming a force to be reckoned with. While addressing challenges of low wages, long hours, and lack of benefits, these providers remain committed to their work with children. Their devotion and strengths are a critical part of the system of care for our nation's families.

STUDENT ACTIVITIES

1. Make an appointment to interview the Family Child Care Coordinator at your local Child Care Resource and Referral agency. Summarize your findings and report back to the class. Some suggested questions include:

    a. What kind of training and technical assistance do they offer to local providers?

    b. What are the common challenges that prospective providers face in the process of opening a family child-care home?

    c. Describe the current family child-care quality improvement initiatives?

2. Make an appointment to visit a family child-care home. Choose a time when the operator will be able to talk to you. Observe the number of children, the kinds of activities that are provided, and the routine of the day. Talk to the operator about the satisfactions and difficulties of conducting this kind of program.

3. Meet with the director of a large family child-care home. Before the meeting, prepare a list of questions to ask. After the visit, summarize your findings and report to the class. Some suggested questions are the following:

   a. How is running a large home-based program different from a small operation?

   b. Who do you contact when you have business problems or need professional support?

   c. How is the curriculum of your program planned?

   d. What is the process for hiring new staff members? Are you free to determine the salary for that person?

4. Attend a local Family Child Care Association meeting and report your experience to the class. Explain why you thought this meeting was valuable for providers or not.

REVIEW

1. List some of the common characteristics of family child-care providers.

2. List the reasons that parents choose family child care over center-based or other options.

3. What are the disadvantages of home-based versus center-based programs?

4. List some of the recommendations for success in operating a family child-care business as mentioned in the chapter.

5. State the challenges of running a home-based business.

6. Why would unionization be attractive to home-based providers?

7. What are some of the tools used to measure quality specific to family child-care homes?

REFERENCES

Barnett, W. S. (2003). *Better teachers, better preschools: Student achievement linked to teacher qualifications. Preschool Policy Matters* (2nd ed.), New Brunswick, NJ: National Institute for Early Education Research.

Bureau of Labor Statistics. http://www.bls.gov/oco/ocos170.htm Accessed May 2009.

Burton, A., Whitebook, M., Young, M., et al. (2002). *Estimating the size and components of the U.S. child care workforce and caregiving population.* Washington, DC, Center for the Child Care Workforce, http://www.hspc.org/publications/pdf/ccw_May2002.pdf.

California Child Care Resource & Referral Network. (2005). *2005 California child care portfolio,* http://www.rrnetwork.org/rrnet/our_research/2005Portfolio.php.

Chalfie, D., Blank, H., & Entmacher, J. (2007). *Getting organized: Unionizing home based providers,* Washington, DC, National Women's Law Center, http://www.nwlc.org/pdf/Getting Organized2007.pdf.

Galinsky, E., Howes, C., Kontos, S., & Shinn, M. (1994). *The study of children in family child care and relative care: Highlights of findings.* New York: Families and Work Institute.

Garcia, E. E. (2005). *Teaching and learning in two languages: Bilingualism and schooling in the United States.* New York: Teachers College Press.

Gormley, W., Gayer, T., Phillips, D., & Dawson, B. (2004). *The effects of Oklahoma's Pre-K Program on school readiness.* Washington, DC: Georgetown University Public Policy Institute.

Helburn, S. W., Morris, J. R., & Modigliani, K. (2002). Family child care finances and their effect on quality and incentives. *Early Childhood Research Quarterly, 17*(4), 512–538.

Herzenberg, S., Price, M., & Bradley, D. (2005). *Losing ground in early childhood education: Declining workforce qualifications in an expanding industry, 1979–2004.* Washington, DC: Economic Policy Institute.

Marshall, N. L., Creps, C.L., Burstein, N.R., et al. (2003). *Family child care today: A report of the findings of the Massachusetts Cost/Quality Study Family Child Care Homes.* Washington, DC: U.S. Department of Health and Human Services, Child Care Bureau, Administration for Children, Youth, and Families.

Morrissey, T. (2007). *Family child care in the United States.* Reviews of Research, Cornell University, Department of Human Development, www.researchconnections.org.

National Economic Development and Law Center. (2001). *The economic impact of the child care industry in California.* Oakland, CA: NEDLC. Note: Similar economic impact reports are available from NEDLC for Hawaii, Illinois, Massachusetts, Minnesota, North Carolina, and Ohio. www.nedlc.org.

Public Policy Institute of California (2005). *Just the facts: California's future population: June 2005.* San Francisco: Public Policy Institute of California. http://www.ppic.org/content/pubs/JTF_FuturePopulationJTF.pdf.

Shonkoff, J.P., & Phillips, D.A., Eds. (2000). *From neurons to neighborhoods: The science of early childhood development.* Washington, DC: National Academy Press.

U.S. Census Bureau (2000). *Census 2000 Summary File 4.* Data retrieved March 3, 2005, from http://factfinder.census.gov.

Whitebook, M., Bellm, D., Lee, Y., & Sakai, L. (2005). *Time to revamp and expand: Early childhood teacher preparation programs in California's institutions of higher education.* Berkeley, CA: Center for the Study of Child Care Employment, University of California at Berkeley.

Whitebook, M., Kipnis, F., Sakai, L., Voisin, I., & Young, M. (2002). *California child care workforce study: Family child care providers and assistants in Alameda, Kern, Monterey, San Benito, San Francisco, San Mateo, Santa Clara and Santa Cruz Counties.* Washington, DC: Center for the Child Care Workforce.

Whitebook, M., Phillips, D., Bellm, D., et al. (2006). *Two years in early care and education: A community portrait of quality and workforce stability.* Berkeley, CA, Center for the Study of Child Care Employment, University of California, Berkeley, from www.researchconnections.org/location/ccrca3643.

SELECTED FURTHER READING

Adams, J. H., & Buell, M. (2002). Project CREATE: *Caregiver Recruitment, Education, and Training Enhancement.* Newark: University of Delaware, Center for Disabilities Studies. www.researchconnections.org/location/ccrca5913 Accessed April 2009.

Bradley, R. H., Caldwell, B. M., & Corwyn, R. F. (2003). The Child Care HOME Inventories: Assessing the quality of family child care homes. *Early Childhood Research Quarterly, 18*(3), 294–309. www.researchconnections.org/location/ccrca10292.

Bruenig, G. S., Brandon, R., & Maher, E. J. (2003, November). *Counting the child care workforce: A catalog of state data sources to quantify and describe child caregivers in the fifty states and the District of Columbia.* Seattle, WA: Human Services Policy Center, University of Washington. Accessed July 3, 2006 from hspc.org/publications/pdf/CCCW.pdf.

Burchinal, M., Howes, C., & Kontos, S. (2002). Structural predictors of child care quality in child care homes. *Early Childhood Research Quarterly, 17*(1), 87–105. www.researchconnections.org/location/ccrca1305 Accessed May 2009.

Caldwell, B. M., & Bradley, R. H. (2003). *Home observation for measurement of the environment early childhood (EC) home.* Little Rock, AR: University of Arkansas. www.researchconnections.org/location/ccrca5093.

Clarke-Stewart, K. A., Vandell, D. L., Burchinal, M., O'Brien, M., & McCartney, K. (2002). Do regulatable features of child-care homes affect children's development? *Early Childhood Research Quarterly, 17*(1), 52–86. www.researchconnections.org/location/ccrca365.

Hamm, K., Gault, B., & Jones-DeWeever, A. (2005). *In our own backyards: Local and state strategies to improve the quality of family child care.* Washington, DC: Institute for Women's Policy Research. www.researchconnections.org/location/ccrca6898.

Johnson, J. O. (2005, October). *Who's minding the kids? Child care arrangements: Winter 2002.* Washington, DC: U.S. Census Bureau. www.census.gov/prod/2005pubs/p70-101.pdf.

Layzer, J. I., & Goodson, B. D. (2006). *Care in the home: A description of family child care and the experiences of the families and children that use it.* National Study of Child Care for Low-Income Families, Wave I Report. Cambridge, MA: Abt Associates. www.researchconnections.org/location/ccrca11568.

National Association for Family Child Care (NAFCC). (2006, July). *Best practices for family child care union organizing.* A position statement of the National Association for Family Child Care. Salt Lake City, UT: NAFCC.

NICHD Early Child Care Research Network & Duncan, G. J. (2003). Modeling the impacts of child care quality on children's preschool cognitive development. *Child Development, 74*(5), 1454–1475. www.researchconnections.org/location/ccrca2820.

Raikes, H. A., Raikes, H. H., & Wilcox, B. (2005). Regulation, subsidy receipt, and provider characteristics: What predicts quality in child care homes? *Early Childhood Research Quarterly, 20*(2), 164–184. www.researchconnections.org/location/ccrca6437.

HELPFUL WEBSITES

Disclaimer: Links to Internet sites throughout this book are provided for your convenience and do not constitute an endorsement.

Council for Professional Recognition:	**http://www.cdacouncil.org**
National Child Care Association:	**http://www.nccanet.org**
State regulations and training requirements for child-care workers:	**http://www.resourcesforchildcaring.org**
Action Alliance for Children:	**http://www.4children.org**
National Child Care Information Center:	**http://nccic.acf.hhs.gov/pubs/cclicensingreq/cclr-famcare.html**
National Association for Family Child Care:	**http://www.NAFCC.org**
Red Leaf Press	**http://www.redleafpress.org**

For additional resources related to administration including videos, links to related sites for each chapter of the text, tutorial quizzes, glossary flashcards, and more, visit the Education CourseMate website for this book at www.cengage.com/login.

Cengage Learning

Setting Goals

Objectives

After reading this chapter, you should be able to:

- Tell what is meant by the philosophy of a school.
- Distinguish between goals and objectives.
- Discuss how goals are developed.
- List methods of evaluating program goals.

KEY TERMS

developmentally
appropriate practice

goal

objective

philosophy

A day in the life of . . .

A Director of a Church-Affiliated School

A Jewish family visited. They really liked our school but were worried about the conflict in religious beliefs. I told them their son would come home singing, "Jesus loves me." Seeing their reaction, I suggested that they enroll in a different program and listed several to visit.

In a few weeks, they returned saying, "We really like your school." After more visits and an agonizing decision, they enrolled their child.

We do not go to chapel before October so that students have a month to adjust to school before we add another transition. We had grown fond of the family, and I was afraid that they would remove their son from the program after he started talking about his experience at chapel. I heard him talking to his mother when she picked him up the first day after chapel. He exclaimed excitedly, "Mom, we went to chapel today!" When she asked him what he did in chapel, he replied, "We saw the Rabbi!" Our pastor was honored that the boy thought he was a Rabbi.

Every early childhood center has its own unique characteristics based on the ideas of the developers, refined by succeeding directors, and implemented by current staff members. A philosophy and a set of goals are at the core of these characteristics. They are used for planning and implementing all aspects of the school's operations: the facility design, hiring policies, equipment purchases, and activities offered. There is wide variation among schools, because there is no consensus regarding the best care for children. Ideas about what elements should be included change as research studies reveal more about how children learn, as social conditions change, as the needs of the children change, and even as political forces exert new pressures. The resulting changes are not always based on knowledge of the developmental needs of young children.

The National Association for the Education of Young Children (NAEYC) has been at the forefront of establishing guidelines for quality early childhood education. In 1984 a commission was created to develop a statement of appropriate educational practices for young children. The result of the commission's deliberations was first published in 1986, then expanded to book form edited by Sue Bredekamp in 1987, *Developmentally Appropriate Practice in Early Childhood Programs Serving Children from Birth Through Age 8*. The quality of early childhood programs is frequently measured on the basis of this book. Bredekamp and co-editor Carol Copple published a revised version in 2009 *Developmentally Appropriate Practice in Early Childhood Programs*.

They believed that the previous material was too narrow in scope and found that readers tended to interpret the information as being a prescription for correct practice. The latest edition clarifies what is meant by "developmentally appropriate practice." **Developmentally appropriate practice** results when professionals make decisions based on three areas of their knowledge about children. The first is knowledge about how children develop and learn—the predictable stages of children's development and an understanding of age-related skills and capabilities. The second is knowledge about children's "strengths, interests, and needs of the individual children in the group." This implies an ability of professionals to be responsive to children's differences as well as similarities. The third is knowledge about children's social and cultural environments. This last area ensures learning experiences that are meaningful for the children and their families and are respectful of their cultural background. Thus, developmental appropriateness has two dimensions: an understanding of the universal sequences of growth and change that occur in children and the recognition that each child is unique with an individual pattern and timing of growth.

It is the responsibility of the director of an early childhood program to see that the philosophy and goals of the center are implemented effectively. In an established program, someone else already has developed the philosophy and goals. These should be compatible with the director's own professional and personal beliefs and values. In a new facility, the director works with others to develop a philosophy statement and then a set of goals.

Philosophy

Formulation of a philosophy statement is intimidating to some directors and teachers; however, it should not be. A **philosophy** is a compilation of ideas, beliefs, and values held by a group or organization. There are three areas that are reflected in a philosophy statement: (1) assumptions about how children learn, (2) values held by program planners and parents of the children involved, and (3) ideas about education and about the function of a school. There will rarely be consensus, but discussions will engender valuable thought about the importance of each.

The process begins with an exploration of assumptions about how children learn:

- Some educators believe that children learn best when they are given extrinsic motivations in the form of rewards such as tokens or gold stars. This is called the environmental or behaviorist approach. What the child learns is determined by adults and can be observed or measured. The behaviorists Skinner (1953) and Watson (1924/1967) are associated with this approach.

- Others believe that there is an inner force that activates cognitive systems as children grow and mature. When children are developmentally ready, they will choose activities and experiences that they can accomplish. Their satisfaction at mastering tasks provides intrinsic rewards. Gesell (1940) and Erikson (1963) are most often associated with this approach.

- Another belief is that learning results from an interaction between children and their environment. Children construct their own knowledge through repeated interactions with people and objects. They experiment, consider their errors or misconceptions, and arrive at new conclusions, thereby constructing new knowledge. Piaget (1952) is associated with this approach.

- Finally, some believe that cognitive abilities develop from the interaction with more mature members of society. The social environment provides the intellectual support system that guides children in their development. Adults should structure learning experiences so that children gradually move from assisted performance to individual learning. This process is successful only when adults are sensitive to each child's level of competence. Vygotsky (1978) is associated with this approach.

The next step is to consider the values held by those involved in planning the program of the center: board members, administrative personnel, teaching staff, and parents. The underlying question is which development is more important for children: social/emotional or cognitive? The following questions should be asked:

- Which is more important, children's self-esteem or what they learn?
- Should children develop autonomy in order to enable them to participate fully in a free society, or should they learn to obey adults?
- Do children have a right to make their own choices, or should they accept adult decisions?
- Should families be more a part of school activities, or should school be the exclusive domain of professionals?

Nearly everyone has ideas about education and the function of schools. A thorough exploration of these ideas is a crucial part of developing a philosophy statement. For example, the planners may consider the following thoughts about education and a school:

- A school should have a nurturing and protective environment
- School should prepare children for life, not just for the next phase of education
- A school should leave the teaching of moral values to parents
- A school should provide an opportunity for students to retain their own cultural background

As the planners discuss these issues, they will probably discover more ideas and thoughts to include. One person should compile a list for each of the three areas of a philosophy statement. (Committee members can review the list and rate the importance of items. Discussion and negotiation will take place during this process period debate helps each member to clarify thinking and refine their own ideas. The dialogue will probably take weeks.

At the end of the process there should be a clear statement of philosophy. A set of goals can now be written. The following are examples of philosophy statements.

Example 1

The curriculum of the Child Learning Center is based on the belief that children learn best when they are rewarded for their accomplishments. For the youngest children, rewards are concrete and specific. As children grow, the emphasis shifts to encouraging children to take pride in their own accomplishments without expecting extrinsic rewards. The Child Learning Center also teaches children discipline and a respect for authority in preparation for later experiences in life. Staff members are expected to be positive role models for children.

Example 2

Each activity at Golden Preschool is carefully matched to coincide with universal stages in all areas of children's development: physical, cognitive, social/emotional, and creative. Therefore, when children move to new levels of ability, there are always experiences they can choose in order to gain new mastery. There are many opportunities for children to practice physical skills, learn problem solving, gain knowledge of their environment, and practice interacting more effectively with others. We also believe that parents are an important part of children's learning experiences and are partners in the education and care of the children.

Example 3

The recognition that children are continually learning, both in and out of school, is fundamental to the philosophy of the Green Oaks School. Children are given many opportunities to choose their own activities and to explore their own interests. All classroom experiences actively involve children in their own learning process.

We also believe that their educational development extends beyond the classroom and is influenced by occurrences in the home and neighborhood. Although the school has primary responsibility for the child's academic training, the support and cooperation of parents and others outside the school are necessary in creating an environment in which children can reach their full potential.

Example 4

Staff members at the Hanover House Preschool Program and After-School Child Care are committed to including all children and their families. We believe that all children have the right to live in a community where they are valued for their own special qualities. This means we accept children who have special needs or who come from a minority culture. Although we have an overall curriculum model, we are aware of individual children's needs, whether for educational experiences or for maintaining aspects of their culture. Our professional staff members are capable of assessing individual child characteristics and needs, planning educational and personal goals cooperatively with parents, and implementing appropriate learning activities and instructional techniques.

Formulating Goals

WHAT ARE THEY?

There must be a clear distinction between goals and objectives even though many people use these words interchangeably. Both a goal and an objective can be defined as a change at the end of a specified period of time. However, a **goal** indicates changes that take place over a long period of time. A month and a school year are the typical periods that are specified. When doing overall planning for a school, goals may even extend over several years. Use of the word **objective** is appropriate when referring to short-term changes. A day or a week may be the time period for the attainment of an objective. Teachers use objectives as the foundation for daily lesson plans. A director might set an objective of accomplishing a specific task during a particular week. A chart relating to goals and objectives is found in Figure 4-1.

When discussing goals, people frequently confuse which kind of goal is appropriate: overall, curriculum, or individual. Teachers sometimes make the mistake of thinking only in terms of overall school goals when planning a curriculum. A typical overall goal is "The Child Learning Center will provide a stimulating environment in which children are free to explore." That type of goal does not say anything about what happens to a child. A curriculum goal should reflect the expected change in the child. This is discussed in greater detail later in this chapter.

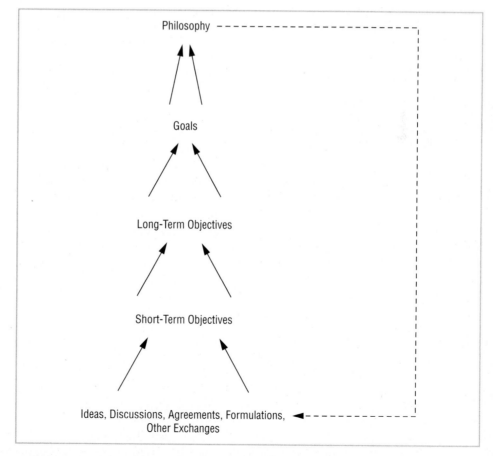

FIGURE 4-1   A chart for idea development.

FYI

As of 2005, 11,191 programs have received accreditation through NAEYC. These accredited centers serve 947,542 children. Many more programs are enrolled in self-study.

WHO SETS THEM?

Directors cannot always develop new goals for a program. They must often refine or renew existing goals when they assume leadership of an established entity. They are responsible for effective implementation and for regular evaluation. Therefore, every director must know how to develop and implement goals. Individuals or groups can develop goals. The process is largely determined by the type of school for which the goals are formulated. In a singly-owned program such as a proprietary school referred to in Chapter 2, the owner usually decides goals. In a corporate school, such as KinderCare, goals often come from the corporate office. However, even in that setting someone with an early childhood education degree needs to provide input.

As the preceding examples suggest, overall goal setting starts at the top of an administrative structure. One method for setting goals is to have one person determine a list of goals. School personnel are expected to use these goals to plan and implement the program. This method of goal formulation has the advantage that it is usually accomplished quickly. Its disadvantage is that those who are responsible for implementing the goals may not understand or be committed to them. At an extreme, teachers may be unaware of their existence.

A preferred method of setting overall goals uses a committee or group of people. The director, parents, teachers, and even community representatives may be involved. This method is often used by nonprofit schools such as cooperatives or church schools. The advantage in this method is that the goals are more likely to be implemented. With input comes an inducement to implement those goals. Conversely, the committee method may take longer to produce results. The diverse opinions of each member must be discussed and then negotiated until the final product satisfies all members. It is extremely important to include parents when this method of goal setting is undertaken. According to Gonzalez-Mena (2000), child-rearing practices and the beliefs, goals, and values behind them are deeply tied to culture. As long as parents can find people to care for their children who agree with them about child-rearing practice, there's no problem. Cross-cultural issues don't come into play when child-rearing practices are similar. Or if people choose to give their children a cross-cultural or multicultural experience, that's a different matter. However, a potential conflict exists when there is no element of choice, and a person of one culture cares for children of another culture whose value system is very different.

Therefore, the committee approach should include parents who are representative of the cultures within the center's student population in order to ensure some synchrony between the home and the school.

Directors can use a third method of setting overall goals. They can circulate a list of goals among staff and then gather opinions, changes, and further suggestions at staff meetings. From these, they can formulate a new list. That list, too, may be revised until all staff members are reasonably satisfied with the results.

A final method might be to use a set of existing goals from another source. Goals can be found in many books and pamphlets. One of the best sources is NAEYC. The association has developed a set of goals for high-quality early childhood programs to be used by schools and child-care centers as the basis for a voluntary accreditation system. A kit for self-study is available through the National Academy of Early Childhood Programs, 1509 16th Street, NW, Washington, DC 20009.

WRITING GOALS

Before writing goals, there are several issues to consider. First, it is better to have a few goals that can realistically be accomplished than to have a long list that can never be attained. Five to 10 goals is a reasonable number. Second, it may be helpful to categorize goals into the areas of a child's development: physical, social/emotional, and cognitive. Last, goals should be stated in terms of changes that will occur in children resulting from their school experiences.

Key words in the philosophy statement may be used as the foundation for writing goals. In Example 3 of the philosophy statements, key phrases might be the following:

1. Choose their own activities and explore their own interests.
2. Involve children actively in their own learning process.
3. Development is influenced by what happens in their home and neighborhood.
4. Environment in which children can reach their full potential.

Based on the first two statements, a goal might be the following: Children will choose their own learning experiences in order to stimulate their curiosity about the world and develop confidence in their own abilities as learners.

The third statement might refer to daily violence in children's neighborhoods. A goal for a school might be the following: Children will learn to resolve problems nonviolently and will acquire techniques for mediating disputes.

The fourth statement might yield the following goal: Children will learn to appreciate their own unique characteristics and abilities, and they will strive to reach their own level of excellence.

Goals can be categorized by the areas of children's development. Example 2 of the philosophy statements refers to children gaining mastery in all areas of their development. Those writing goals for this preschool might categorize them as follows:

Physical: Children will become competent in managing their bodies and acquire basic gross and fine motor skills.

Cognitive: Children will acquire cognitive skills to aid lifelong learning.

Social/emotional: Children will develop a positive self-concept and a genuine concern for others.

Creative: Children will develop an appreciation for artistic and cultural experiences.

As can be seen from the preceding examples, goals are merely statements of children's desired achievements that result from attending a preschool, school, or child-care center. Each facility will have unique goals. There are many variations, but each goal represents a commitment to help children reach their potentials.

Developing Objectives

FROM GOALS TO OBJECTIVES

Goals are broad statements, and it may seem difficult to determine daily activities of a school based on them. Actually, it is not too difficult. Objectives are paths or steps that lead to the goals. Many directions and different steps can be pursued before reaching the final goal.

It is helpful to write down the end behavior, attitudes, or abilities that will indicate the achievement of a goal. It is easier to describe this for goals that are about actions because actions are observable. It is usually possible to picture the kind of behavior that will indicate a child has achieved the ability to choose and carry through an activity.

It is more difficult to envision the behaviors that indicate a child has a positive self-image. An example will help to illustrate how to approach this task.

Example

GOAL: The child will be able to choose, carry through, and take pride in a variety of learning experiences.

What observable behavior would lead a teacher to decide that a particular child has achieved this objective? Many situations could be used, but a child's use of blocks is a good example. The teacher might observe the following incident:

> When free choice time is announced, John goes to the block shelf and takes a pile of long blocks. He places them in a square, returns to the shelf, and chooses four more blocks of the same size. He continues until he has a structure that is three blocks high. He searches for suitable materials for a roof. He decides against using blocks and chooses a square piece of plywood. It fits. John now tries to park some small cars on the roof. To drive the cars up to the roof, he attempts to build a long ramp with several inclines, using square blocks to lift the inclines to the right height. After several tries, he succeeds. After he drives the first cars up the ramp and parks them, he sits back with a look of pleasure on his face. He asks if his building can be saved to show his mother when she comes to pick him up.

John chose his own activity without help from the teacher. He solved the problems that arose as he completed his project. His pride in his accomplishment was indicated by his request to save it to show to his mother.

What steps were necessary to reach this result? There would have been many over a long period of time. A few will serve to illustrate the process. As you will see from the examples, a series of carefully planned challenges led John to achieve this goal.

Choosing

When the teacher suggests an activity, John willingly takes part.

When three activities are suggested, John chooses one.

When told that it is free-choice time, John chooses an activity without help from the teacher.

Carry Through

John completes a 15-piece puzzle with some help from the teacher.

John assembles a 20-piece puzzle by himself.

Take Pride

John complains that he cannot build a garage for his cars and wants some help. His teacher shows him how to start, and he continues to build.

John starts his building but gets frustrated when he cannot figure out how to make a ramp for the cars. He knocks down the building and goes to paint. His teacher suggests that next time he could ask for help in solving his problem rather than knocking down the whole building.

John builds the kind of structure he wants and asks to save it for his mother to see.

Each of these behaviors is a step toward the achievement of the goal. Similar steps might have been observed in art activities, outdoor play, or numerous other situations. They are all paths toward the goal's achievement. If teachers know the desired end behavior, they can observe it in many situations.

It is a little more difficult to describe the end behavior when the goal involves feelings or attitudes. For example, "The child will have a positive self-concept, valuing her- or himself as a unique individual." Each person will probably have different ideas about how a child will demonstrate those characteristics. Therefore, each teacher must decide what evidence suggests that a child has a positive self-concept. Consider some of the following attitudes and behaviors:

- The child is clear about being a boy or a girl
- The child walks with an appearance of self-confidence
- The child enters the room in the morning saying, "Well, here I am, Teacher"
- The child says, "I have brown hair, and my sister has blonde hair"
- The child often says, "I don't need any help. I can do it"

Many more attitudes and behaviors could be added to this list. Some may be specific to individual children. Each will constitute a step or path toward the attainment of the goal of a positive self-concept.

BEHAVIORAL OBJECTIVES

Behavioral objectives can be formulated after the steps toward the achievement of a goal have been outlined. Traditionally, this is done in the manner of the following outline:

- state the objective in terms of the child's behavior.
- specify the conditions for learning.
- verify that the behavior is observable.
- clarify the amount or extent of expected behavior.

Cengage Learning

Children learn as they play.

Certain words are helpful to clarify objectives. These are listed below.

To Describe Conditions for Learning
When asked . . .

When shown . . .

When completed . . .

Having used . . .

To Describe Observable Behavior
The child will select . . .

The child will place . . .

Behavioral Objectives
The child will express . . .

The child will return . . .

The child will identify . . .

The child will match . . .

Another example of a goal and the behavioral objectives leading to its attainment should help to clarify the process.

GOAL: The child will be able to attend to and appreciate music, poetry, and stories.

Behavioral Objectives:

- when reading a list of six words, the child will be able to say correctly a word that rhymes with three of them.
- when reading three lines of a four-line poem, the child will be able to state the final line.
- when hearing the sound of six hidden objects, the child will be able to identify five of them correctly.
- when hearing a recording of "Peter and the Wolf," the child will be able to name three of the instruments correctly.
- when alone with the teacher, the child will be able to attend to and identify 60 percent of the objects in a picture book.
- when participating in a group story time, the child will be able to listen to a short and simple storybook.

Each step reflects weekly objectives. Many more possible objectives exist. The teacher should carefully plan activities and experiences that the child needs throughout the school year. Daily, weekly, and monthly activities should not be haphazardly composed. Instead, they should be arranged in an organized manner. Figure 4-2 provides a sample plan for the goal and objectives that can be achieved during one week.

GOAL: The child will develop habits and attitudes that promote and maintain his or her physical health and well-being.					
Behavioral Objective: When presented with a new food, the child will taste it.					
Activity	Monday	Tuesday	Wednesday	Thursday	Friday
Learning Centers	Vegetable Lotto Game	Taped reading of Carrot Seed	Videocassette on food and nutrition	Categorize foods—cut and paste nutrition	Seed collage
Story	Carrot Seed		Stone Soup		
Play Activity	Prepare carrot and raisin salad for lunch		Cut up vegetables for lunch soup		
Lunch	Throughout the week, the children will set the table and serve their own portions from serving dishes.				
Outside	Throughout the week, the children will be preparing soil and then planting a vegetable garden.				

F I G U R E 4 – 2   Sample plan for a week.

Implementing Goals and Objectives

GENERAL PRINCIPLES

After objectives have been formulated for each goal, the teacher takes steps to implement them by following some general principles.

The child must have the proper environment. Implementing objectives begins with creating the environment. The teacher should organize the environment and structure the learning experiences to stimulate the desired reactions in the children. When implementing the goal of developing children's ability to make choices, the classroom must make this possible.

A variety of activities and materials should be available. Children should be free to choose whatever they wish.

The child must have opportunities to practice behaviors implied by the objective. Changes in behavior occur slowly. Therefore, children must have many experiences in which they can meet this objective. Often this means repeating the same activity. Young children will build a tower of blocks and knock it down repeatedly. Others will paint 10 pictures, each time experimenting with brush strokes or mixing colors. Each of these experiences provides an opportunity to practice a skill, leading eventually to the achievement of an objective.

The child must gain satisfaction from the desired behavior. Each learning experience should give the children satisfaction from having participated. Unpleasant experiences will cause children to avoid the same or similar experiences in the future.

Cengage Learning

Teacher preparing a child for kindergarten.

The child must be able to achieve the desired behavior. Teachers need solid knowledge of child development. With that knowledge, they are less likely to set unrealistic expectations for children. When a learning experience is designed to produce behavior in children that is far beyond their level of functioning, they become discouraged. If the experience is far below their level, they will not be challenged.

The child must have a choice of experiences that can result in the desired behavior. Any group of children will have numerous interests and abilities. Even individual children will vary across time. Choices will allow alternate ways of achieving an objective.

The child must utilize familiar activities in order to achieve the desired behavior. Every learning activity has many possible outcomes as children change.

At age three, children use clay to explore how it feels or how it changes under different conditions. They will cut it, roll it, pound it, and squeeze it. By age five, children use clay to express an idea. They may make a figure, a rocket ship, or an animal.

Many teachers get bored with the same activities or materials. With freedom to explore, children seldom get bored. At each age level, children find new uses for familiar materials.

OVERALL CURRICULUM DESIGN

It may be difficult for beginning teachers to apply all the guidelines outlined. At the start of their teaching career, many are unable to envision how a few goals and related objectives can be combined to form a curriculum for a semester or year. One method is to begin with one goal and the objectives that will lead to successful attainment of that goal. The teacher plans a variety of activities for each of the objectives. This may cover a period of days, weeks, or even several months. Next, the teacher keeps a log of the learning activities offered each day, including comments about how the children responded to the experiences and variations the children made themselves. The log should note suggestions for presenting the activity in another way, because a different arrangement of the activity may lead to earlier attainment of the goal.

After some months, the record of activities related to a particular goal will yield significant information that can aid in planning for additional goals.

Each of the developmental theories discussed earlier in this chapter includes general statements about how children learn. Curriculum designers should list their own beliefs and then decide which theory best matches those beliefs. Activities can then be planned that are commensurate with those beliefs and that are appropriate for the age level of the children involved. In practice, many teachers use an eclectic approach, taking methods from each of the theorists for different activities or age levels.

One possible approach, the environmental approach, is associated with behaviorists Skinner (1953), and Watson (1967). According to their ideas, children are like clay ready to be molded by adults. Activities are planned and controlled by adults through direct teaching of small units of learning broken down from larger tasks. Giving extrinsic motivations in the form of a special treat, such as a piece of candy, reinforces learning.

A teacher who uses this approach would determine what children need to learn and then outline a series of small steps leading to that outcome. Specifically, a long-term goal might be for children to acquire the skills needed for later academic achievement.

One of those skills is learning to read and therefore can be used to formulate a series of objectives. The first step may be helping children to recognize their own name. The teacher could start with flannelboard letters to teach them to identify the first letter of their name, then the last letter. When they can do that, they can distinguish the shape of their name. For example, Beth looks like this, but Elizabeth has a different configuration. Children are rewarded with a gold star, praise, or a treat as each step is achieved. Additional activities can lead to recognition of printed words.

The developmental approach described by Gesell (1940) and Erikson (1963) leads to a very different kind of curriculum. They believed behavioral changes result from physiological maturation along with environmental situations that encourage the achievement of developmental tasks. To stimulate changes, the teacher would provide a wide variety of materials suited to the general developmental level of the children. Children could choose those that suit their individual developmental level.

Learning activities can be designed in the form of units or broad themes founded on the children's interests. The children should be allowed freedom to sample activities. Motivation comes when children are praised for their efforts and when they feel pride in their own achievement.

An example of this approach to curriculum design is evident in the various activities that help three-year-olds develop the use of their fine motor coordination. The ability to use the fingers to hold small objects and to manipulate the objects is essential to the later ability to write. Therefore, in a classroom for three-year-olds there may be the following activities. At the art table there are many kinds of collage materials: small bits of fabric, beads, yarn, and buttons. Additionally, on the table are blunt-end scissors, some paper punches, and a stapler. At a math table, objects of different sizes can be handled, counted, and placed into numbered containers. Tweezers and tongs may also be included. A science table may contain small flower pots, packets of seeds, and planting mix. Children can put small seeds into a filled pot. These activities encourage children to use their thumb and fingers to manipulate small objects.

A Piagetian cognitive model is based on the belief that learning results from an interaction between the child and the environment. Piaget (1952) believed that children reorganize their learning as they reach each stage of development. Through constant interaction and experimentation they reach new levels of understanding. If teachers use this model, they would need a roomy environment that actively involves children. They should plan learning centers that contain multidimensional materials to encourage children to explore and problem solve in sequential steps.

Materials for the centers should be concrete so that children can use more than one sense to learn. Adults help children to conceptualize information, but are not involved in direct teaching. Motivation comes from the children's own joy of discovery and achievement.

A math center in a Piagetian classroom for four- and five-year-olds might include a simple activity for the younger children that involves matching a quantity of small objects to a number written on a heavy card. An activity in which the weight of an object is guessed, then the object is weighed, would challenge older children. Children doing this activity could also be asked to record their predicted weight, then compare it with the actual weight. This adds the dimension of having to write numbers. Other activities with varying degrees of difficulty could also be included. Children should choose the level for which they are ready.

The social cognitive approach associated with Vygotsky is based on the belief that cognitive abilities result from interactions between children and more mature members of their culture. Through carefully orchestrated instruction and specially designed play activities, children develop the capacity to manipulate and control symbol systems required by their particular culture. Interactions may be between adult and child or between children of differing competency and understanding.

Vygotsky envisioned a classroom as a community of individual learners who work cooperatively to develop understanding and acquire the skills expected of them by their society.

Activity centers that are part of a larger study unit are an integral part of a Vygotskian classroom. These are based on children's evolving interests and competencies rather than on long-term plans formulated by the teacher. Centers are designed to permit children to work together or with an adult on various culturally based projects leading to the achievement of individual and group goals. The teacher may have general goals for a specific unit to meet. The children give their input into selecting and organizing the tasks to meet those goals.

An example is a unit on the importance of plants in our environment for an after-school classroom that includes children ranging in age from six to 10. Two computers comprise one center where children can research rain forests. They may work together to map the areas where rain forests exist, list the animals that are endangered, or research the effect on global weather conditions. At another center, an adult may play 20 questions with the children. When presented with a box containing one vegetable, the children are encouraged to ask questions until they identify the vegetable in the box. A small group of children could work together in another area to plan a vegetable garden. They could refer to gardening books and discuss the kinds of vegetables that are their favorites. They have to make compromises because some favorites may not be adaptable to their particular region. They should list the vegetables, then draw a plot plan of the garden. A local farmer may meet with the children to discuss farming in their community. Some other philosophies may also inform educational thinking today and affect overall curriculum design. **Jean-Jacques Rousseau (Gauthier, 2006)** believed that in contrast to Christian doctrine of original sin, human nature is essentially good. He viewed the child as a child and not as an inadequate adult, believing that it had the potential within itself to develop almost unlimited talents.

Rousseau saw the role of the teacher not to restrain or indoctrinate but to arrange the child's environment so that it could learn for itself. He attacked the education of his time on the grounds of its "verbalism"; rote learning and textbooks were anathema to him. Children learned best from things that that they could experience. From observation and his intuitive sympathy for children he was led to conceive stages in their development toward adulthood, a notion Piaget later developed more scientifically.

The Swiss educator **Johann Heinrich Pestalozzi (Downs, 1975)** envisioned a science of education based on the psychology of child development. He laid the foundation of the modern primary school. His early experience with the life of poverty and degradation developed in him an acute sense of justice and a determination to help the underprivileged. Pestalozzi became a schoolmaster so he could fulfill his desire to improve society by helping the individual to help himself.

According to Pestalozzi, "the full and fruitful development" of the child according to his or her own nature is the goal of education. The school and teachers provide only the environment and guidance, most appropriate to free expression that allows the natural powers of the child to develop. Instruction should be adapted to each individual according to his particular changing, unfolding nature. Rather than from books, the child should learn by observing objects of the real world. Sense perceptions are of supreme importance in the development of the child's mind.

Friedrich Wilhelm Froebel (Ross, 1976) was a German educator and psychologist who was a pioneer of the kindergarten system and influenced the growth of the manual training movement in education. Froebel, like Rousseau, regarded man as essentially good and his pedagogy starts from perceptive observation of children's behavior. "Educators," he wrote, "must understand their impulse to make things and to be freely and personally active. They must encourage their desire to instruct themselves as they create, observe and experiment." The teacher was to guide the child in his self-discovery, not direct him. Each stage of development was critical and had to be fully experienced. Play was the young child's "spontaneous expression of thought and feeling" and was central to learning. For this reason, Froebel established the kindergarten which provided the activities and materials needed by the preschool child. He invented toys and exercises which became the basis of a pedagogic system whose formalism was curiously at odds with the permissiveness of his philosophy. He laid great emphasis on the relationship between teacher and pupil and on the need for continuity and connectedness in the school curriculum. At all times the school was to maintain close contact with family and community so it could remain relevant and vital.

John Dewey was a writer and philosopher whose theories had a profound influence on public education in the United States in the first half of the 20th century. Dewey was a strong supporter of what he called instrumentalism. His work as a psychologist and education thinker crystallized a reaction against the excessively formal and rigid education practices of the time. Dewey recognized that the child is an active, exploring, inquisitive creature, so the task of education is to foster experience-infused skills and knowledge. Dewey's enormous influence owed more to his skill at expounding the pragmatic, scientific, and democratic progressiveness of the America of his time than to accurate or technical philosophical argument.

The "progressive education" movement of the 1920s was an effort to implement Dewey's ideas. Because his educational theory emphasized the classroom as a place for students to encounter the "present" his interpreters tended to play down traditional curricular concerns with the "irrelevant" past or occupational future. His influence on American schools was so pervasive that many critics assailed his ideas as the cause of all that they found wrong with American education.

Maria Montessori (Standing, 1957) was best known as the founder of Montessori Schools. In 1894 she became the first woman physician in Italy. Her interest in children and education led her to open a children's school in 1907 in the slums of Rome. Montessori's view of the nature of the child is that children go through a series of "sensitive periods" with "creative moments' when they show spontaneous interest in learning. It is then that the children have the greatest ability to learn. These periods should be utilized to the fullest. Work, she believed, is its own reward to the child and there is no necessity for other rewards. Self-discipline emerges out of the learning environment that promotes independence.

She used what she termed a "prepared environment" to provide an atmosphere for learning, that is, small chairs and tables instead of rows of desks. The basic features of the method are development of the child's initiative through responsible individual freedom of behavior, improvement of sensory perception through training and development of bodily coordination games and exercise. The function of the teacher is to provide didactic material such as counting beads or geometric puzzles, and act as an adviser and guide, staying as much as possible in the background.

Dr. Montessori's method was basically at odds with behaviorism, Freudianism, and other major 20th-century trends. Thus at one time it was used only by a relatively few private schools. Since the early 1950s, however, her system has enjoyed a revival. Her works have been translated into at least 20 languages and training for Montessori teachers has been established in several nations.

Evaluating Outcomes

Goals must be evaluated continuously to determine whether they are being met. Evaluation of a director was discussed in Chapter 1, and evaluation of teachers appears in Chapter 8. The NAEYC accreditation process has its own method of evaluating the overall program of a school or child-care center. This section focuses on assessing curriculum goals.

EVALUATION PROCESS

If objectives are clearly stated, the process of evaluating outcomes will be easier. The objective should contain a statement of the expected behavior. Some examples are:

- the child completes a puzzle.
- the child shares a toy.
- the child unbuttons its sweater.
- the child returns the books to the shelf.

When the behavior is clear, standards should be established to judge an acceptable level of performance. Should the child always perform the expected behavior? Must the child be able to complete a series of tasks or only part of them? Some illustrations of this kind of statement are:

- shown five name cards, the child will correctly pick out his own name 75 percent of the time.
- shown the colors yellow, red, and blue, the child will correctly name each of them every time.

The evaluation process should also include a determination of where to look for evidence that the objective has been met. This is especially true of the social areas of the child's development. The teacher should look for these in situations where children are interacting, not during times when children are alone. Listing the possible situations in which the expected behavior might occur is helpful.

METHODS OF EVALUATION

Methods of evaluation are the ways in which the achievement of objectives is tested or judged. Regardless of the chosen method, evaluation will yield valuable information. As teachers focus on each child, they will become more aware of all children's abilities. The resulting information may force teachers to change their curriculum or their presentation of materials. Evaluation also helps teachers plan more effectively for individual children. When a particular child's strengths and weaknesses are known, teachers can plan to foster the former and help the child overcome the latter. Finally, if teachers thoroughly understand a child's capabilities, they can report more accurately to parents. Most parents want to know how their child is doing. Specific information is more helpful than generalities.

Although some methods of evaluation may be valuable, they may not be practical for daily use. Teachers simply may not have time for complex testing methods with each child. In this case, it is better not to do it at all because the results will not be accurate. The methods should suit the particular school and the staff available.

OBSERVATION

The most frequently used evaluation method in preschools is observation, or anecdotal record. Notes made by teachers as they observe children's behavior comprise the evaluation. Teachers often keep these records on index cards or in a log. Recorded items are what teachers deem to be important. They usually include what the child does and says. Sometimes teachers add their own conclusions about the behavior.

Many teachers choose to record information about each child on a weekly basis. Others find it is easier to focus on part of the group one week and the other the following week. In the conduct of a busy day, teachers often have little time to sit back, watch, and then record what is happening. Less frequent observations may still yield plenty of information. However, teachers must guard against coming to any conclusions about a child based on only one observation.

The difficulty with anecdotal records is that only a small portion of what the child is doing or saying can be recorded. Therefore, what teachers write may present a skewed picture of the child's behavior. Furthermore, two people looking at the same situation may see two entirely different actions. Still, with practice, teachers can learn to be more accurate in their reporting and can become better at choosing what is important.

The anecdotal record is only one form of observation that can help teachers. A video camera, tape recorder, or movie camera can provide more permanent records. These methods might be especially helpful when considering how to help a child who is having some difficulty. Rather than trying to simultaneously deal with and observe the child, teachers can later review what happened. Moreover, having additional people look at the record may yield further information.

COMMERCIAL TESTS

Tests exist that have been developed specifically for use in assessing young children's development. Those developed by experts usually have been tested with children of varying backgrounds. Choosing standardized tests only from reputable companies and following the directions for administration and interpretation are both essential to this approach.

Unfortunately, these tests have some drawbacks. First, administration can be time-consuming and inconvenient. Teachers seldom have the time to spend an hour alone with each child. Some of these tests require the administrator to have special training or to be a psychologist. Few schools have that type of person on staff or can afford to hire one.

An even more serious problem with commercial tests is the question of quality. Many tests are biased in favor of white, middle-class children. Therefore, they are inappropriate for certain situations. Children who come from poor families or who are bilingual will not be assessed accurately.

Before using commercial tests, the teacher should gather as much information as possible.

Personnel from another school that has used the test may be asked for opinions. Alternatively, the director can talk with college or university staff to learn about the particular test. If the teacher is part of a school district, the school psychologist can probably help.

NAEYC developed a position statement on standardized testing of young children in 1987. The developers have cautioned that standardized tests are possibly inappropriate because they seldom provide information beyond what teachers and parents already know. However, as some programs still choose to use this type of evaluation, the purpose of the position statement is to help educators make informed decisions. NAEYC believes that the most important issue in evaluating and using standardized testing is utility criterion. The purpose of testing must be to improve the services for children and to ensure that they benefit from educational experiences.

The following guidelines can be used to determine the appropriate use of testing.

- All standardized testing in early childhood programs must be reliable and valid according to the standards of test development set by the American Educational Research Association, American Psychological Association, and National Council on Management in Education (AERA, APA, NCME, 1985)

- Decisions that impact children (enrollment, retention, or assignment into classes) must never be based on a single test score

- Teachers and administrators are responsible for evaluating standardized tests critically to determine whether they achieve their intended purpose. They must also be knowledgeable about the testing and interpret the results accurately and cautiously to parents, school personnel, and the media

- Selection of standardized tests to evaluate a program must be based on the theory, philosophy, and objectives of the program

- Children must be tested by educators who are knowledgeable regarding testing and are sensitive to the developmental needs of young children. Additionally, these educators must be qualified to administer the tests

- Testing of young children must recognize and be sensitive to individual diversity

CHECKLISTS

Checklists are a quick and simple method to assess a child's capabilities. They can be constructed to cover almost any aspect of development. They can also be designed to match specific objectives. A checklist may have items that can be merely checked off, or it may include a rating scale indicating degree or frequency of accomplishment.

An example from one of the goals already discussed should help to clarify the process.

GOAL: The child will choose, carry through, and take pride in various learning experiences.

From the behavioral objectives listed for the attainment of the particular goal, the following checklist could be developed.

Children choose their own activities.

Activity	Usually	Sometimes	Never	No Opportunity to Observe
Chooses one of three activities				
Initiates own activity				
Completes 15–piece puzzle with help				
Completes 20–piece puzzle with no help				
Uses words to express pride				
Shows completed task to others				

Each school or center should develop its own checklist to suit its goals. Lists from other schools may provide helpful ideas, but each checklist should be specific for the program it is evaluating. Another word of caution: The checklist should not be so long that the evaluator begins to guess at items. It is easier to observe and check off a short list than to do a list of 30 or 40 items. Several short lists can be used during a school year to get an idea of a child's progress. An example of an evaluation sheet used at one center is shown in Figure 4-3.

PRESCHOOL EVALUATION SHEET

Name: _____   Date: _____/_____/_____

COLOR RECOGNITION

❑ red   ❑ blue
❑ yellow   ❑ green
❑ purple   ❑ orange
❑ black   ❑ brown

SHAPE RECOGNITION

❑ square   ❑ circle
❑ rectangle   ❑ triangle

LETTER RECOGNITION

❑ a ❑ n ❑ A ❑ N
❑ b ❑ o ❑ B ❑ O
❑ c ❑ p ❑ C ❑ P
❑ d ❑ q ❑ D ❑ Q
❑ e ❑ r ❑ E ❑ R
❑ f ❑ s ❑ F ❑ S
❑ g ❑ t ❑ G ❑ T
❑ h ❑ u ❑ H ❑ U
❑ i ❑ v ❑ I ❑ V
❑ j ❑ w ❑ J ❑ W
❑ k ❑ x ❑ K ❑ X
❑ l ❑ y ❑ L ❑ Y
❑ m ❑ z ❑ M ❑ Z

❑ writes name
❑ knows telephone number
❑ knows address
❑ fine motor activities
❑ gross motor activities
❑ listens attentively in groups
❑ participates in groups
❑ accepts and respects authority
❑ offers good suggestions
❑ follows directions
❑ makes good use of time
❑ listens while others speak
❑ speaks clearly and in sentences
❑ works and plays cooperatively
❑ takes good care of materials
❑ helps clean up

COUNTS TO: _____

Comments: _____

_____

_____

_____

Teacher: _____   Date: _____/_____/_____

FIGURE 4-3   Preschool evaluation sheet.

PARENT INFORMATION

Parents are an excellent source of information about children's progress and should be included in assessment procedures. Developing a questionnaire using a short list of questions that can be answered with "yes," "no," or a brief statement is helpful. The questions should be specific, such as "Can your child recognize his name?" or "Does your child speak clearly and in sentences? Give an example."

A face-to-face interview with a parent or guardian will provide even more information. During a conference, teachers have an opportunity to compare the way children function at home and at school. Children sometimes act differently in different situations, and the disparities can provide clues to their development that may not be evident only in the school setting. Even more importantly, an interview will allow parents to reinforce their goals for their children and to judge whether those goals are being met.

TIME SAMPLINGS

Sometimes, time-interval sampling of a behavior's presence is helpful in understanding a child. This is a record taken at periodic intervals. Behaviors that lend themselves to time-interval sampling are language development, interest span, and aggression. If teachers want to know how long a child remains with an activity, they can do a time sampling every five minutes, for a period such as half or three quarters of an hour. During that time, they will be able to see how often the child changes activities. It provides a better picture of the child's interest span than trying to record the number of minutes spent at each activity.

PORTFOLIOS

Elementary school teachers traditionally use homework and seatwork papers to judge how well children are doing. In preschools and child-care centers, a similar technique can be employed. Teachers can save children's artwork. As children develop and start to write their name or numbers, some of those efforts should be saved. Photos of their block buildings can be placed in a file. If a video camera is available, short vignettes of play situations can also be a valuable record.

ASSESSMENT INFORMATION SUMMARY

Once sufficient information about a child has been gathered, the teacher should organize it. This profile is a snapshot of the child's development. It should be organized according to the goals. If the goals have been categorized into the three areas—physical, cognitive, social/emotional—the organization of the profile may follow these guidelines. The teacher should summarize the information gathered from all sources that support the child's achievement of each goal or area. This information can then be used to plan further activities for each child.

Clear goals and objectives, along with an effective evaluation process, can make a school a model. However, neither goals nor objectives may be formulated or achieved in a short span of time. Both take thought, planning, and cooperation to reach worthwhile ends.

CASE STUDY

Wendy has been a teacher in several centers that are part of a large child-care corporation. Advertising for the chain highlights the "academic" approach, indicating that children who are enrolled in the program will begin to read as early as age two. Wendy has always agreed with this idea, but is beginning to believe there might be a better method to help children learn.

This is partly the result of a course she took at the local community college and also of attendance at several conferences on child care. Therefore, she decides to look for a new job.

Her first interview is with Ulma, the director of a private proprietary school. As they visit classrooms, Wendy observes that the children are all busy with what Ulma calls "hands-on experiences." She is introduced to a parent who is volunteering in a classroom. The mother tells Wendy about her son's excitement over coming to school and about how much he has learned. Wendy and Ulma talk about their differences in learning approaches, and Wendy becomes certain that she will not be hired.

1. Would you hire Wendy and hope that she could adjust to your philosophy of teaching?
2. What questions might you ask Wendy to determine whether she would fit into your school?
3. What would you do to help Wendy fit into your program?

SUMMARY

Every early childhood center has its own characteristics that are articulated in its philosophy and goals. A philosophy is a distillation of ideas, beliefs, and values held by an individual, a group, or an organization. The philosophy statement reflects three areas: (1) assumptions about how children learn, (2) values held by program planners and parents, and (3) ideas about education and the function of a school.

Although goal and objective are often used interchangeably, there is a difference. Goals indicate changes that occur over a long time—a month or even a year. Objectives describe changes that occur in a short time—a day or a week. Individuals or a committee may formulate goals. The process of writing goals begins by underlining key statements in the philosophy statement. These are each used as the basis for a goal that indicates changes in children's behavior resulting from their school experience.

Objectives are used by teachers to plan daily activities for children. Objectives can be thought of as steps or paths toward the achievement of goals. The teacher begins by writing down the end behavior and then lists all the steps that will lead to the goal. These become the objectives.

Once objectives are specified, the teacher can implement them by:

- organizing the environment in ways that stimulate the expected reaction.
- giving children ample opportunity to practice.
- allowing children to feel satisfaction.
- determining that the child is developmentally able to achieve the objective.
- providing a choice of experiences.
- allowing children to repeat familiar experiences.

Putting together an overall curriculum design is sometimes difficult for beginning teachers. One way is to start with one goal and the objectives that lead to it. Keeping a log and using it for later planning should be helpful.

Teachers should decide which of the developmental theorists is closest to their beliefs about how children learn. This information can be used to plan the curriculum.

An evaluation process is facilitated when a standard for judging achievement is established. Methods of evaluation include observation, commercial tests, checklists, parent interviews, time-interval samplings, and a collection of children's work.

Goal achievement for each child can be summarized by compiling a profile, a picture of the child's development at a particular time. This can be used for planning individualized instruction for each child.

STUDENT ACTIVITIES

1. Review Example 1 of the philosophy statement for the Child Learning Center. Write three curriculum goals for this school. Remember to state them in terms of what happens to children.

2. Write to, or visit, four different kinds of schools: a corporate school, a privately owned center, a Head Start unit, and a business-sponsored child-care center. Ask for a list of their goals and inquire how they were formulated. Are there similarities? What accounts for any differences?

3. State one goal for a group of four-year-olds. Write three behavioral objectives that would lead to achievement of that goal.

4. Use one objective to plan five activities that lead to its achievement.

5. Discuss your beliefs regarding parents' roles in setting goals for a school.

REVIEW

1. Define a philosophy of early childhood education.

2. How does a goal differ from an objective?

3. Three methods for setting goals were discussed in this chapter. What are they?

4. How many goals is a reasonable amount?

5. List the six general principles for implementing goals and objectives.

6. What is the most frequently used method of evaluating goal achievement?

7. State the drawbacks of using a commercial test to evaluate children's progress.

8. What kind of information about a child's progress can be obtained from a parent interview?

9. Describe time-interval sampling.

10. What is a profile? What information should be included?

REFERENCES

Bredekamp, S., & Copple, C. (Eds.). (2009). *Developmentally appropriate practice in early childhood programs* (Rev. ed.). Washington, DC: National Association for the Education of Young Children.

Downs, R. B. (1975). *Heinrich Pestalozzi, father of modern pedagogy,* Boston: Twayne Publishers.

Erikson, E. H. (1963). *Childhood and society* (2nd ed.). New York: Norton.

Gauthier, D. (2006). *Rousseau: The sentiment of existence.* Cambridge: Cambridge University Press.

Gesell, A. (1940). *The first five years of life: The preschool years.* New York: Harper & Row.

Gonzalez-Mena, J. (2000). High-maintenance parent or cultural differences? *Child Care Information Exchange, 134,* 40–42.

Piaget, J. (1952). *The origins of intelligence in children* (M. Cook, Trans.). New York: International Universities Press.

Ross, E. D. (1976). *The kindergarten crusade: The establishment of preschool education in the United States.* Athens, Ohio: University Press.

Skinner, B. F. (1953). *Science and human behavior.* New York: Macmillan.

Standing, E. M. (1957). *Maria Montessori: Her life and work,* Fresno, CA: Hollis & Garter Limited.

Vygotsky, L. S. (1978). *Mind in society: The development of higher psychological processes.* Cambridge, MA: Harvard University Press.

Watson, J. B. (1967). *Behaviorism* (Rev. ed.). Chicago: University of Chicago Press. (First edition published 1924).

SELECTED FURTHER READINGS

Carter, M. (2008). Assessing quality; What are we doing? Where are we going? *Exchange, 30*(6), 32–36.

Gestwicki, C. (1999). *Developmentally appropriate practice: Curriculum and development in early education* (2nd ed.). Clifton Park, NY: Cengage Learning.

Katz, L. G., & Chard, S. C. (2000). *Engaging children's minds: The project approach* (2nd ed.). Norwood, NJ: Ablex.

NAEYC, (2003). Where we stand on curriculum, assessment and program evaluation. Washington, D.C.: National Association for the Education of Young Children.

Williams, K. C. (1997). "What do you wonder?" Involving children in curriculum planning. *Young Children, 52*(6), 78–81.

HELPFUL WEBSITES

Disclaimer: Links to Internet sites throughout this book are provided for your convenience and do not constitute an endorsement.

ERIC Clearinghouse on Early Childhood Education and Parenting (ERIC/ECEP):	**http://ceep.crc.uiuc.edu**
Montessori:	**http://montessori.org**
Parents Action for Children:	**http://www.iamyourchild.org**
Reggio Emilia:	**http://www.reggiochildren.it**

For additional resources related to administration including videos, links to related sites for each chapter of the text, tutorial quizzes, glossary flashcards, and more, visit the Education CourseMate website for this book at www.cengage.com/login.

Cengage Learning

Planning: Infants and Toddlers

Objectives

After reading this chapter, you should be able to:

- Describe the steps in human development between birth and two years.
- State the components of a developmentally appropriate program for infants and toddlers.
- List and describe the essential areas to be included in an environment for infants and toddlers.
- Discuss the inclusion of children with special needs.
- State the characteristics of a caregiver for infants and toddlers.

KEY TERMS

attachment

developmentally
  appropriate
  infant–toddler program

psychosocial area

sensorimotor period

sensory diversity

synchrony

trust versus mistrust

A day in the life of . . .

A Director of an Employer-Sponsored Program

I had made a display of fall fruits, vegetables, and leaves in order to encourage an awareness of colors. At group time, one of the two–year–olds excitedly told me that the bumpkin was orange. To encourage appropriate language skills, I corrected him. I told him it was a pumpkin. He said, "Yeah, bumpkin."

I again said, "Pumpkin." He said, "I heard you. Bumpkin."

When his mother came to pick him up from her office next door, he excitedly ran to her and pulled her over to see the display. He said to her "Bumpkin, bumpkin." She answered "yes" she could see they was a pumpkin there.

An increasing number of parents place their infants and toddlers in child care while they work to support the family. Additionally, more single women and teenagers are having babies. The growing need for places that care for all young children is acute, and the supply is limited. Even scarcer are quality programs designed specifically to meet the needs of infants and toddlers rather than just adaptations of preschool practices. In order to add an infant-toddler program, planners must understand the characteristics of children under the age of two. This chapter will present an overview of developmental stages, then discuss appropriate programs.

Infant-Toddler Development

Most children predictably mature through universal patterns of development. Children crawl before they walk, and understand some words before they speak any. By understanding the pattern, it is possible to predict what a child will be doing in the future.

That does not mean that all children follow an exact pattern. They do not. Thus, along with understanding the universal characteristics, it is important to be aware of each child's uniqueness. Children have their own timing of growth; they go through the stages at different rates. They have different ways of approaching new experiences and different ways of interacting with others. Each may have special needs that must be addressed when planning a program.

The period between birth and age two is a time of startling change, more rapid than in any other stage of children's development. During these two years, children reach half their adult height and move from a state of helplessness to walking around freely. Completely dependent on others at birth, by age two they have learned to do things for themselves. They start to communicate their needs, thoughts, and feelings. Through exploration, they develop an understanding of the world around them. The following is an overview of developmental characteristics.

During infancy the brain has the greatest capacity to grow, developing synaptic connections that affect lifelong development. Research (Newberger, 1997) demonstrates that there are critical periods when certain kinds of learning take place. The neurons for vision are most active between two and eight months, while those for speech begin activity at about six months. At birth, children have extra neurons. When they experience positive interactions with adults, their brains are stimulated, causing the neural synapses to grow and connections to be strengthened. Continuously used synapses become permanent, while unused synapses are eliminated. If babies are given the proper stimulation, their ability to learn is enhanced.

Children younger than the age of two learn by experiencing their environment with all their senses. They taste, touch, look at, listen to, and smell whatever they contact. Piaget called this stage the **sensorimotor period**. Even infants, who cannot move around, use their senses to absorb the world around them. They stare at objects for long periods, attend to adult voices, and wave their arms to touch things within their reach. As they begin to crawl—somewhere between five and 12 months—their explorations become broader.

Mobile toddlers continue active exploration of their environment using their senses. However, they can also think symbolically. They can combine their sensory experiences and reach new conclusions about what they have learned. They remember some past events, can imitate previous experiences, and even think ahead to what will happen next. In this way, they begin to accumulate and organize information about their world.

Cengage Learning

Planners need to understand the characteristics of children younger than the age of two when adding an infant–toddler program.

Motor skills develop quickly and in an orderly sequence. In the first few months, babies are able to lift their heads, then roll over. Gradually they sit, then crawl. Most children take their first steps at about age one and can walk and run well by age two. Their ability to use their arms, fingers, and hands progresses through several steps as well. Initially, movement of their arms is random; then it can be controlled to touch an object. When they first grasp something, they do it awkwardly, using their whole hand. Later, they can use their fingers to manipulate or pick up small objects.

Infants are learning to trust themselves and others. Erik Erikson called this stage (from birth until approximately one year of age) in an infant's development **trust versus mistrust**. Erikson observed that through repeated experiences babies learn that adults will be there when needed, and that they will provide food, warmth, and comfort. This results in a feeling of trust in the world outside themselves. When adults are not always available or do not respond consistently to infants' needs, babies develop a sense of mistrust. They perceive that others are unreliable.

Along with developing trust in others, babies develop a secure sense of self. Having needs met can lead infants to realize they are worthy people. This is the beginning of later self-confidence and a positive self-image. As they move into the toddler stage, a secure sense of self allows them to act independently at times, but seek comfort from adults when they are tired or frightened.

Infants explore the world through their senses.

Infants and toddlers are developing strong attachments. Previously, people thought that babies could develop a strong relationship only with the mother. More recent research shows that babies are capable of forming strong attachments to several people.

The strongest attachments are to the parents. Attachment is a vital part of children's development. It provides them a safe haven from which to explore their environment. Those with the strongest attachments to parents or caregivers are the most comfortable in moving away from their caregiver, while still returning at intervals for reassurance.

At around nine months, many infants express some anxiety over separation from their parents. They cry and cling when they are left with the caregiver. During the next year or so, one of the primary tasks for caregivers is to manage separation anxiety.

Reaction to separation is not consistent. Sometimes infants or toddlers separate easily from their parents. A few weeks or a month later, they may cry or cling desperately when left. Eventually, by about age three, most children are able to manage separation more easily.

Along with separation from others comes an awakening awareness of themselves. They realize they are not a part of others but are separate with their own skills and capabilities. They learn the power that comes from being able to obtain responses. They gradually discover that they can do things on their own. The combination of these realizations forms their sense of self. This begins a lifelong process of developing and refining an identity.

Competence and independence are acquired during the first two years. As children's ability to control their bodies increases, they have a growing sense of mastery. The more they can do, the more competent they feel. Typically, toddlers go through a time of "I can do it myself." This is their way of saying they want to be capable and independent from others. They often become engrossed in perfecting their skills and resent any attempts to direct their energies elsewhere. Their striving toward independence includes learning to control body eliminations. During the second year, toddlers become more aware of their bodies; they begin anticipating the need to urinate or defecate. Soon, they are able to control their sphincter muscles long enough to reach the toilet. When they can do this, they usually have a tremendous feeling of power.

Language begins to appear during the second year and develops rapidly. Infants can communicate by crying or fussing. Parents and caregivers learn to interpret the cries, though some adults are more adept at this than others. However, the child's ability to tell others exactly what is needed does not develop until the second year. With the advent of words, children can begin to say what they mean. Simultaneously, they discover that words have tremendous power; they love to test the effect on others. One example is a toddler's frequent use of "No." With that one word, they can often control what happens to them and, sometimes, control the actions of others.

Infants and toddlers are learning how to get along with other children. Two babies on the floor together will look at each other intently. When they are mobile, they may move toward each other, then investigate with pokes and pats. It takes a long while for them to learn that the other object is another person who has feelings and can react. As they near the age of two, they begin to play together for brief periods of time. The abilities to share and to play cooperatively will not be fully developed for another year or so.

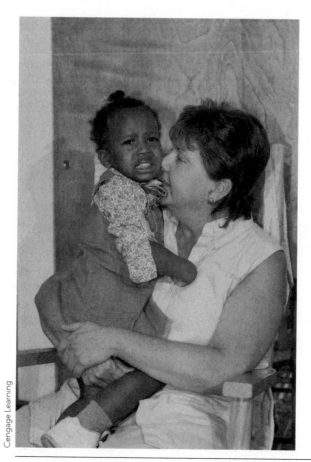

Cengage Learning

Infants express anxiety over separation from their parents.

FYI

A study published in the August 2000 issue of *Pediatrics* indicated that 20.4 percent of sudden infant death syndrome (SIDS) deaths occurred while infants were in the care of a nonparent. The deaths were more likely to occur between 8 A.M. and 4 P.M. to older, white infants with well-educated parents. Recently, efforts to have babies placed on their backs have resulted in an overall decrease in SIDS deaths, but babies in child-care settings are still likely to be sleeping on their stomachs. The study recommends that parents discuss with caregivers the importance of placing babies on their backs during naps.

SOURCE: American Academy of Pediatrics. Retrieved 2002 from http://www.aap.org

Characteristics of a Developmentally Appropriate Infant-Toddler Program

GOALS

A **developmentally appropriate infant-toddler program** is based on knowledge of the physical, emotional, social, and cognitive abilities of the children served. Program planners use this knowledge to develop goals that form the basis for planning for this age level. Goals are guidelines for choosing activities that allow children to explore their environment freely and to absorb information with all of their senses. Goals should imply the kinds of caregiver–child interactions that promote trust and attachment.

Goals should also address the development of language and learning to interact well with others. Guidelines for developing goals were discussed in Chapter 3. Some additional considerations that must be kept in mind when writing goals for an infant-toddler program are:

- do the goals reflect current research on infant-toddler development? New information is disseminated each year as more is learned about the earliest years.

- are the goals developmentally appropriate for this age level? Often, goals for infants and toddlers are a diluted version of preschool goals and thus may not be appropriate.

- do the goals take into account the unique ways that infants and toddlers learn? Goals should allow children to explore using all their senses and to develop their gross and fine motor skills.

INTERACTIONS WITH CAREGIVERS

A developmentally appropriate program for infants and toddlers should allow for maximum interactions between children and caregivers. During the early months of life, children are learning about themselves and others. They learn through their interactions with their caregivers. To allow time for this kind of interaction, the child/teacher ratio must be

Infants and toddlers are learning how to get along with other children.

kept low. The typical ratio is four children to one adult. Three children per caregiver, or even two to one, is a better ratio. This level of staffing adds to the expense of an infant-toddler program, but it ensures quality care.

Assigning primary responsibility for two or three children to each caregiver also helps. That person is the first to care for those children's needs. When the primary caregiver is occupied with feeding or diapering one child, other adults can share responsibility for the remaining members of the group. The pace of each day should be slow and based on the children's requirements, not the adults'. There should be time to hold babies and get to know each infant's way of expressing distress. A leisurely, flexible schedule will allow infants to explore their environment at their own pace. Additionally, there should be time for babies to adjust slowly to new situations and to learn gradually to anticipate the next step.

The way caregivers respond to infants is important. Sometimes the term **synchrony** is used to describe the coordination between infants and their caregivers. It signifies a bidirectional interaction that is responsive to the baby's needs. The baby coos; the adult responds. The adult tickles the baby; the baby laughs. The baby turns away; the adult waits quietly for a return of interest before responding again. From these kinds of play, babies learn about relationships—how to sustain them or how to withdraw if they become overwhelming. They also learn how they can get others to respond when they wish, and how they can respond themselves.

Toddlers develop feelings of competence and independence as their interactions with caregivers change. They move away from their caregivers at times to explore their environment, although they may return at intervals for comfort or encouragement. They test their new abilities by attempting tasks on their own, sometimes even angrily rejecting adult help. Frequently heard words or phrases during this period are "No" and "Do it myself." However, they also want the security of knowing that adults will "set limits" when their behavior overwhelms them or becomes dangerous.

● ● ● ● ● ● ROUTINES

Caregivers spend significant time on routines: changing diapers, washing, dressing, and feeding. Children need to have their own schedule, rather than one imposed by adults. Each routine activity should be perceived as an integral part of the curriculum, as it is just as important to infants and toddlers as examining a toy, building with blocks, or looking at a book. When caregivers give their undivided attention to children during routine functions, they are satisfying babies' needs for security, attention, and closeness. When adults talk to infants during diapering about what is happening, or what might happen next, they are teaching concepts of present and future. When caregivers quietly wait while one-year-old toddlers struggle to get food into their mouths, they are teaching the children to do things for themselves.

Sometimes caregivers' needs interfere with understanding babies' needs. While concentrating on their own needs for a response, caregivers may not recognize that babies are becoming overstimulated. Sometimes, caregivers want freedom from the demands of the children in their care and fail to recognize what the demands mean. A typical example is feeding a fussy baby because it is fretting when the baby really needs comforting. It helps if caregivers take time to listen, to look, and to try to feel what babies are communicating. This establishes two-way communication.

Routines can be used by caregivers to judge children's development. For instance, resistance to diapering or to using the toilet may be a sign of growth, a push toward

Caregivers should be sensitive to infants' ways of communicating.

independence. Children's ability to anticipate and cooperate in a routine can show the development of a cognitive ability. When children anticipate the next step, they are beginning a long process that eventually leads to logical thinking. Caregivers can facilitate this by talking about what is happening and encouraging cooperation. For example, "Lift your bottom so I can put your dry diaper on."

PARENT INVOLVEMENT

Parents need to be involved in order to manage their anxiety about placing their infant in child care. Some experience overwhelming feelings of guilt, whereas others are afraid their babies will become less attached to them. They also worry that others will not be as responsive to their babies' needs as they are. They frequently experience strong separation anxieties.

Parents are sometimes faced with other disturbing feelings. If their babies seem to get along well in child care and do not fuss when they are left, parents feel left out. If, conversely, the babies cry when left, parents feel equally terrible. There is a possibility for jealousy and competition with the caregiver. If left unrecognized, these feelings may turn into complaints and dissatisfactions.

Many of these problems can be prevented or alleviated when parents and caregivers work together. Good parent–caregiver relationships are based initially on an understanding of the importance of each in the child's life. Both must cooperate for the optimal development of the children. This happens when:

- caregivers recognize that parents are the most important people in children's lives.
- child-care staff create an open environment that welcomes and includes parents.
- caregivers and parents establish procedures for frequent communication through daily conversations, notes, telephone calls, conferences, or meetings.
- caregivers are sensitive to cultural differences in child-rearing practices.
- parents and staff members discuss and mutually determine ways to manage major changes in children's development, such as toilet training, weaning, and sleeping patterns, in order to avoid conflicts.

ATTACHMENT AND SEPARATION

A developmentally appropriate infant-toddler program should foster the development of **attachment** to caregivers and begin the resolution of separation problems. Developing attachment and managing separation are primary tasks of children during the first three years. Research by Mary Ainsworth (1973) points to the importance of the bond between a developing infant and an adult. She defined attachment as the affectional tie that binds one person to another and that endures over time. Infants want to be close to or maintain eye contact with the person to whom they are attached. Infants' first attachment is to their parents, but attachment can develop with a caregiver. In a child-care setting, this allows the infant to feel secure when separating from the parent.

Attachment develops when caregivers are deeply involved with the infants. This means significant touching, holding, interaction, and verbal responsiveness. The adult is truly with the child on the child's level. When stimulation is needed, the adult responds with appropriate suggestions or materials. When the infant needs comforting, the adult is there with hugging, holding, or stroking.

Attachment between infant and adult can occur only if there is daily consistency. Each child should have one or two caregivers who are there every day. As attachment strengthens, separation becomes easier but still may be difficult for the infant. Parents and caregivers can have trouble realizing that children who are expressing separation distress are behaving normally. When children cry or cling to the parent, they demonstrate attachment. When they can be comforted and transferred to the caregiver, they are developing attachment to the caregiver.

The following procedures will facilitate both parent and child adjustment:

- discuss the separation process with parents before the child enters the program.

- greet parent and child upon their arrival.

- encourage the parent to stay all or part of the first day and part of the next few days.

- allow the child to have a favorite object: teddy bear, blanket, or Mom's purse.

- be sensitive to the needs of each child. This may mean rocking a baby or allowing a toddler to play alone.

- maintain close communication with parents. Telephone at work during the day if necessary, or report on child's progress at the end of the day.

- be empathetic to parents' feelings about leaving their child.

- encourage friendships among the parents. Introduce them to each other, or plan social activities.

- remember that children's separation anxieties may be greater at nap time or when they are tired.

Attachment develops when there is a lot of touching, holding, interaction, and verbal responsiveness.

• • • • • RECORDS

Good record keeping is essential to an infant-toddler program. Daily notes kept by both parents and caregivers provide a record of children's development during this period of rapid change. Caregivers should record the routine activities of each child, as well as any pertinent comments about behavior or development. These should be kept in a specific place so they are accessible to each caregiver who shares responsibility for the child during the day. Protect confidentiality by ensuring these notes are not available to anyone who is not concerned with the child.

Consistent contact with parents is necessary so that caregivers know of any changes in the children that occur at home. Caregivers should know about babies' sleeping, eating, and eliminating patterns. Any changes in behavior such as fussiness or lassitude should also be shared with caregivers. Shared information should also include changes that indicate babies are reaching a new stage of development. Signs of greater acceptance of solid foods and drinking from a cup are examples. See Figure 5-1 for a sample daily information sheet to be completed by parents.

Caregivers should provide parents with a record of children's eating, sleeping, and eliminating behaviors during the day. Information for parents may also include new things

---

DAILY INFORMATION SHEET FOR CAREGIVERS

To Be Filled Out Each Day by Parents

Date_____

Child's Name_____

When was child last fed?_____ What was fed?_____

How much did child eat?_____

How long did child sleep last night?_____

When did child awaken this morning?_____

Did child sleep well?_____If not, what seemed to be the problem?_____

_____

Did child have a nap before arriving today? If so, please note the time.

From_____ To_____

Has child had a bowel movement today? Yes_____ No_____

What is child's general mood today?_____

_____

Is there any other information that will help us take better care of your child today?

_____

_____

FIGURE 5-1   Sample daily information sheet for caregivers.

that the children are learning. Caregivers should be cautious, though, about telling parents about important milestones such as first steps or first words. Sometimes it is best to let parents discover these things for themselves at home. See Figure 5-2 for a sample daily information sheet to be completed by caregivers.

With good records, parents and caregivers can plan better for each child. Decisions about when to introduce solid foods, when to start toilet training, or when to introduce new challenges to the children will have a stronger basis.

INFANT/TODDLER DAILY INFORMATION SHEET

Parent Report

Parent's Name _____

Child's Name _____   Date _____

Last fed: Time _____   What _____

Last slept From _____   To _____

Medication needed: Dosage _____   Time _____

Physician's note on file _____

Additional comments _____

_____

Staff Report

Your child slept   From _____   To _____

From _____   To _____

From _____   To _____

From _____   To _____

Your child ate: Amount/Type

_____   _____

_____   _____

_____   _____

Diaper changes: Time, BM or wet _____ _____ _____ _____

_____ _____ _____ _____

Needs: Diapers   Wipes   Clothing   Sheet   Blanket

Disposition/comments _____

Daily activities or special events _____

_____

Staff member reporting _____

FIGURE 5-2 Infant/toddler daily information sheet.

ENVIRONMENT

The environment of an infant-toddler program should be safe, while allowing the maximum possibility for exploration. There should be distinct and separate areas for the various activities that take place: diapering, eating, sleeping, and playing. The diapering area must have accessibility to running water. The table where the children eat should not have distracting toys, and the sleeping area should be quiet so that children will not be disturbed.

Vinyl tile and soft carpeting can provide a variety of surfaces for crawling babies. Ideally, the area should be large enough so that babies can explore freely and safely away from toddlers. Toys and activities should reflect children's interests and capabilities, being neither too simple nor too complicated. For example, at six months, babies can usually sit up and use their hands and arms to manage objects. They will enjoy having toys they can poke, bang, and shake. Manipulative boards, push toys, and pop-up toys are popular. Toys that make sounds are even better. At 15 months, most children are walking and love to push or pull toys as they wander around. At this age, children are also ready to climb simple structures. Vinyl-covered cubes or other shapes of different sizes can provide a safe climbing experience.

Outdoors should include areas and equipment that are appropriate for the age level. Babies need soft areas where they can explore freely and safely. Simple soft ramps allow them to use their large muscles. Hammocks, fabric swings, and tunnels offer additional possibilities. More active toddlers need to have separate places to play. Low fences can be used to provide areas where they can ride tricycles, run, and play ball. Low climbing equipment and a sandbox might also be in this area.

Within this environment there must be constant vigilance to maintain the health and safety of the children. Staff members must be able to anticipate and eliminate problems before any child is hurt. They must be able to see a tiny object on the floor that babies might put in their mouths or judge that a baby might get stuck in a certain space. They should be able to guess the kinds of explorations toddlers will make as they investigate their environment. Lowering oneself to the children's eye level and seeing the types of objects that might attract them helps. Potential dangers must be changed or removed.

PLAY

A developmentally appropriate infant-toddler program should allow for many kinds of play. Children should have choices of activities that are relevant to their age levels and interests. Caregivers should observe the children to determine their capabilities and desires. They can then provide toys or materials to foster interests. Consulting books or talking with other caregivers may generate ideas for play materials. However, constant variety is not necessary. Children enjoy familiar toys and often find many new uses for them.

Caregivers should encourage play interactions between children. If babies are placed on the floor near each other, they can look at, or maybe even touch, each other. Rather than always providing two of the same toy, caregivers should let two toddlers play together with one toy. This toy must lend itself to use by two children. A pegboard and large pegs and a shape box are examples.

Children need enough play materials so they can find those that meet their own particular interests. Include the current favorites of children in the group, but also add new things. Some children will use familiar toys to perfect new skills. Others will find new materials that provide an opportunity to develop additional skills. Balance between new and familiar situations should exist. Too much novelty causes some children to become frightened and withdraw. Not enough novelty means that they will be uninterested and will not learn.

Cengage Learning

The environment of an infant–toddler program should be safe to allow the maximum possibility for exploration.

LANGUAGE

A developmentally appropriate infant-toddler program should facilitate language development. From an early age infants use hand gestures to get their needs met. They point to a desired object, put up their arms to be picked up, and sometimes gaze intently at a toy or bottle. When adults respond to these ways of communicating they let children know they have been understood. At about three months infants begin to make babbling sounds using consonants ("da, ma, ba"). Adults imitate these sounds and begin to refine them into words such as "dada, mama, baba." The next step might be utterances that sound like words, but are not. This tells us that the infant is aware of the importance of using language. By the age of one year the infant will attach the words, "mama" or "dada" to the right person and will soon say a few real words that might be imbedded in gibberish. At this stage they also understand many more words than they use. By the age of 18 months they can name nouns (baby, ball) and respond to simple commands ("Go to the shelf and get your book."). At age two toddlers can combine two words to make simple sentences ("Mama go.") (Reese, 1998).

Toddlers often play on the floor.

Child-care settings should encourage children to use language skills. The first step is choosing caregivers who have good language skills themselves. They should not feel silly talking to babies or imitating baby babbling sounds. Toddlers need caregivers who will allow them to exercise the power of words without feeling threatened. "No" is a really powerful word and should be allowed in appropriate circumstances. Both infants and toddlers need caregivers who will listen when they attempt their newly acquired skills. Caregivers should model a balance between talking and listening so that children learn they need both skills.

Caregivers should be able to adjust their communication styles to suit the children in their care. Short, simple sentences are best to use with toddlers. Quiet children need caregivers who listen more than talk. Talkative children must learn to listen to others.

Activities during the day should provide children many opportunities to hear language and to try speaking. Caregivers should talk or sing to babies as they carry out routines.

Back and forth "conversations" in which the baby makes a sound and the caregiver responds encourage the development of language. Toddlers love to hear words in simple stories or finger plays.

Caregivers should foster children's language usage to solidify learning. Adults should use appropriate words to describe daily events and activities, serving as a model for the children.

Cengage Learning

Toddlers love to practice language.

Children should be encouraged to put ideas into words or to describe objects. Whenever possible, children should be motivated to relate past experiences or to explain concepts.

STAFF

The core of a developmentally appropriate infant-toddler program is an educated, stable staff. It takes special people to withstand the tremendous demands on infant-toddler caregivers. It is important to choose personnel carefully. Directors should look for people who are:

- physically healthy, with lots of energy.
- nurturing, providing comfort when needed.
- flexible to meet children's needs.
- patient and willing to wait while inept toddlers struggle to become competent.
- able to anticipate and plan for times a child may need extra attention or help.
- able to provide an interesting and varied environment.
- good listeners, who also will encourage language development.
- willing to continue learning about child development.

And staff members should be able to:

- help children learn to get along with others.
- include parents in decisions affecting their children.

Consistency of caregivers is especially important to infants and toddlers. Therefore, the director must do everything possible to retain staff. This includes being a strong advocate for adequate salaries, planning training sessions that help them improve their skills, and allowing them opportunities to discuss problems and voice frustrations. The director should encourage caregivers to see themselves as professionals who make an important contribution to the center and should include them in decisions that affect them.

Encouraging good relationships between the adults who work together in the infant-toddler room is essential. Caregivers should be chosen carefully. It is helpful if caregivers share common goals and do not have many conflicting ideas.

They should be encouraged to develop a mutually dependent relationship. There will be times when each will have to rely on another. While one diapers a baby, the other has to assume responsibility for the remaining children. They will have to plan activities together to meet the needs of all the children.

Program: Infant and Toddler Activities

The following are some suggested activities for planning a program for infants and toddlers. They are roughly arranged in developmental order. The first activities are appropriate for young infants; the later ones, for toddlers.

SENSORY ACTIVITIES

Touch

caregivers wearing different textured clothing

stroking, touching, holding

warm baths

container filled with different textured materials: rice, sand, spaghetti, plastic balls, cotton balls

assorted rattles, soft toys

nylon net balls, soft rubber balls, bean bags

textile books, textile cards

squish bags: resealable bags filled with Jell-O, whipped cream, shaving cream, small beans

finger-paints: starch and tempera paint, applesauce, shaving cream, chocolate pudding

sand and water play

Hearing

listening to music, singing

clapping patterns

making pretend sounds, imitating baby's sounds

recording baby's sounds, playing back

hide-and-seek with a squeaky toy

toys that make noise: bells, rattles, ball with bell inside

metal pans, objects to pound or drop into to make a sound

stories and finger games

experimenting with sounds shoes make on different surfaces

Seeing

caregivers wearing different-colored clothing

pictures at child's eye level

hanging a beach ball from the ceiling

opening and closing curtains

bright scarves

adding a fish tank and pets to room environment

changing objects in the room to add new colors: rug, vase and flowers, pillows on floor

adding toys with a variety of colors

unbreakable mirror at floor level

cloth or cardboard books

MOTOR ACTIVITIES

soft, low crawling ramp

placing a toy just beyond the reach of baby on the floor

putting baby on a large towel, pulling across the room

holding baby under stomach to encourage arm and leg movements

pull toys

large ball to encourage rolling and following

wagon, simple riding toys

providing containers into which balls, large pegs, spoons, or other objects can be dropped

stacking and nesting toys

simple puzzles, large pop beads, sorting box

cups, spoons, plastic glass, bowl

blocks, large

shape boxes

SOCIAL ACTIVITIES

imitating sounds baby makes

mirror

toy telephone

dress-up clothes, housekeeping equipment

dolls, small dishes, utensils

water play

Space: Infant-Toddler Environment

Some states may not have added regulations for infant and toddler programs to the guidelines for preschools and child-care centers. Directors should check to determine whether regulations exist and if they do exist, what they are.

Infant and toddler program guidelines usually have some general categories of requirements. One category may cover the sanitation of the building, playground, bedding, food areas, toys, and equipment. Requirements that all surfaces, including flooring, be washable may reflect health concerns. Specifications may stipulate that all toys be washable and free of small parts children might swallow. There may also be suggestions regarding cleaning and sanitation procedures for caregivers to follow.

Regulations will likely cover the arrangement of indoor space. Providing sleeping space separate from indoor activity space may be necessary. Requirements concerning safe places for babies to crawl and explore may exist. Guidelines may suggest that the environment contains pictures, books, and other objects that invite children to explore.

Regulations may also include requirements for outdoor space. Outdoor space should be fenced and safe from potential hazards. Specifications may require a shaded area and a sunny one. Crawling babies may need to be in an enclosed area safe from the more vigorous activities of the toddlers.

SAFETY

Caregivers must take extra precautions to ensure that the infant-toddler environment is safe. This age level involves active exploration, poking, pushing, and pulling on objects to discover what happens. Therefore, the elimination of all possible dangers is extremely important. Heavy pieces of furniture or equipment should be secured so they do not fall. All electrical outlets must be covered, and the sharp edges of furniture should be padded. Checking furniture to ensure there are no braces on legs that might entrap a baby's head is also important.

Babies must be protected from injury under the rockers of a rocking chair by keeping toddlers out of these chairs, because they may not notice crawling babies underneath.

Toddlers should have their own child-sized rockers. Another way to have rockers in the room, but protect the babies, is to place the rockers outside of the babies' crawling area or purchase glider rockers.

Gates or grates can close off any areas that might be hazardous to infants or toddlers. Securing stairways, air conditioning or heating vents, and kitchen areas is also imperative. Half-doors into the classroom may be a useful safety measure. The upper half can be left open so that anyone entering the room can see whether a small child is near the door before opening it. A telephone or intercom in the room will also allow help to be summoned in case of an emergency.

REST, SOLITUDE

The infant-toddler environment should provide areas where children can rest or where they can retreat to be alone. There should be a separate sleeping area for babies who nap frequently during the day. A walled-off area within the classroom will serve this purpose. By using clear Plexiglas™ for large areas of the wall, staff can view the babies, or babies can watch activities in the room if they wish.

Cengage Learning

Infants are curious about objects in their environment.

The National Association for the Education of Young Children has clarified accreditation criterion for supervision of sleeping infants. Attention to the following accreditation criterion will ensure that sleeping infants will be safe.

- Teachers must be capable of hearing and easily seeing all sleeping children. (If a full wall separates the infants, window openings must be large enough to allow a teacher to view all of the sleeping children)

- Teachers must visually check on the infants every five minutes

- Teachers must be able to respond to children quickly

- Sound monitors may be used in infant rooms to fulfill the auditory supervision. However, teachers who are actively engaged with babies that are awake must be aware of and able to attend to the sounds coming through the monitor

- Use of video monitors cannot replace visual checks by teachers

- Young infants must be placed to sleep on their backs unless parents sign a release

This information is available from the NAEYC Academy for Early Childhood Program Accreditation by e-mailing academy@naeyc.org to request receipt of the Accreditation E-Update.

To provide solitude, hiding areas can be provided behind low screens, under tables, or in large boxes. Crawling babies or walking toddlers can withdraw to these locations when group stress becomes too great. Outdoors, a sandbox, large packing boxes, tunnels, and

The sandbox encourages toddlers' play.

climbing structures can offer hiding areas. Providing privacy for children, either indoors or outdoors, also includes respecting their right to play by themselves. A toddler may want to play in the small sandbox alone or to be the only one in a large crate.

ETHNIC AND CULTURAL RELEVANCE

During the first three years of life, children lay the foundation for their sense of identity. Their cultural or ethnic heritage is an important part of "who they are." Therefore, the infant-toddler room should encourage and support the cultural background of each child's family. Parents should be consulted about the kinds of furniture or play objects the children might have at home. Where appropriate, those should be included in the infant-toddler room. Providing books and displaying pictures of babies and families from different backgrounds, decorating the room with colorful objects or fabrics that are culturally based, and playing ethnic music or singing folk songs are all helpful as well.

Additionally, using unbreakable mirrors in the infant-toddler room will foster children's self-image. These should be secured to the wall, at a crawling baby's eye level, and extend upward to a level that can be seen by standing toddlers. Some equipment-supply companies also feature a wall mirror that has a wooden bar across the center. This allows beginning walkers to watch their own progress while holding onto the wooden bar. Thus, they are able to see a new image of themselves as an upright person.

A display frame attached to the wall at floor level can exhibit pictures of families and children of different ethnic backgrounds. Crawling babies can see others like themselves or their own pictures. In choosing materials, it is also important to be aware of possible cultural biases about using food for play activities. Some parents would be unhappy to see their children using rice, beans, spaghetti, pudding, and so on as play media. If these concerns exist among your parents, be sensitive and find alternatives.

SENSORY INPUT

Infants and toddlers use all their senses to explore their environment and to organize information about the world around them. Therefore, they need an environment that is rich in **sensory diversity**. Items that they can look at, listen to, smell, feel, and taste should all be included.

Some ways to add sensory stimulation to the environment of these youngest children are the following:

For Looking

Provide windows so that children can see outside.

Provide skylights in the room for added brightness.

Choose light colors for walls of the classroom.

Add colorful curtains, objects, blankets, and toys.

Place pictures at the children's eye level.

Attach an unbreakable mirror to the wall at eye level.

Place an enclosed fish tank on a low shelf.

Hang a mobile over a crib; change at frequent intervals.

Include books with brightly colored pictures.

Hang a large ball, balloon, or mobile from the ceiling.

For Listening

Provide pieces of crumpled, heavy foil, parchment paper, tissue paper, and colored paper
    used for wrapping produce.

Play soft music at rest time.

Hang wind chimes near the door.

Include a music box or jack-in-the-box.

Include rattles and squeeze toys that squeak.

For Touching

Use both carpet and vinyl flooring.

Have grass or a wooden deck outside.

Place soft pillows in a corner.

Include cuddly toys.

Include large plastic beads or plastic keys.

Include a collection of fabric pieces with different textures and pieces of fur.

Provide a sensory enclosure large enough for a baby or toddler to sit in and fill with plastic
    or cotton balls.

Provide a large tub for holding cooked spaghetti or warm, soapy water.

For Tasting and Smelling

Serve foods with pleasing odors and tastes (avoid the strong odors and tastes that most
    children dislike).

Place fruit or flowers that have intense fragrances in the room.

Make sure the room always smells clean and fresh.

Choose cleaning and disinfectant materials that have a mild odor.

Cengage Learning

Pretending to drive a car like Daddy does.

FLEXIBILITY

Because infants and toddlers are growing and changing so rapidly, they need flexibility. Moveable partitions with Plexiglas windows can be used to change the configuration of the room as needed. All indoor equipment should be on large casters for easy movement. Large mats, cubes, and ramps can be used for building indoor climbing equipment. Tables that can be raised or lowered easily can be used as low as six inches off the floor for the babies and then raised to fit the toddler-sized chairs when needed.

Specific Areas

ROUTINES

Routines including feeding, sleeping, changing diapers, and toileting are an integral part of a daily infant-toddler room schedule. The areas for these activities must be planned so they can be both used and maintained easily by staff members, and also must meet the needs of the children.

Food Preparation and Eating

The eating area of an infant-toddler room has two parts: a place where food can be stored and prepared, and a place where babies can be fed and toddlers can feed themselves. Babies and toddlers seldom eat at regularly scheduled times, and therefore, staff must be able to provide nourishment quickly without waiting for food from a kitchen. Furthermore, many babies have their own formulas or special foods that parents bring from home. These need to be nearby.

The food storage and preparation area should include:

- a counter and sink.
- a refrigerator and microwave oven.
- utensils for preparing food (pans, spoons, tongs).
- unbreakable dishes, bottles, and nipples provided by parents.
- equipment used for washing and sterilizing dishes and area—these must be kept in a locked cupboard.
- a bulletin board for posting instructions for each child's food intake and schedule. It should also include a place for recording actual amounts each child consumes each day.

When babies and toddlers are eating, social interactions can occur. Children can see each other; adults and children can talk or listen. The eating area should foster as much interaction as possible. Some ways to do this are to:

- provide highchairs or low tables and chairs—chairs with curved backs are ideal for toddlers and babies who are able to sit up.
- arrange tables and/or highchairs so children can see each other.
- have rocking chairs so adults may nurture bottle-fed babies during feeding—add large, soft pillows for babies who attempt to hold their own bottle while being assisted by an adult.

Snack time can encourage social interaction.

Sleeping

The sleeping area should be separate from the play area. Staff members should be easily able to supervise it. The furniture should depend on the children's age. Checking licensing regulations for specifics regarding spacing or equipment is important. This area might include:

- bassinets for the youngest infants; cribs for older infants.
- cots or individual mats for toddlers—each child should have a separate sleeping place not shared with others.
- a rocking chair or other comfortable chair.
- at least one crib on wheels for transporting babies in case of an emergency.
- shades on windows so the room can be darkened.
- clean sheets and blankets for each crib (some centers may ask parents to supply and launder these).
- space of at least 24 inches between each of the cribs to protect against transmission of germs.

Diapering

A well-set-up diapering area will allow the task to be accomplished easily and will foster significant social play and interaction. The diapering area should be equipped with:

- a table that is a good height for the adults and has a barrier to prevent children from falling.
- a cupboard for the necessary supplies: lotion, ointment, wipes, paper covers for table, paper towels, and germicidal spray.
- a sink with a foot-operated faucet.
- a covered trashcan for used diapers.
- a mirror where babies can see themselves and the caregiver.
- mobiles hung from the ceiling.
- a sign reminding staff to wash hands.
- a step stool for older toddlers to get on the table, eliminating the need for staff to lift heavy children.

Toileting

During the second year, some toddlers begin to indicate they are ready to use the toilet. Facilities should be provided away from the play area for the children to develop independence in caring for their own needs. These facilities should include:

- low toilets, potty chairs, or toilet seat adapters (disinfect after each use).
- low sinks.
- steps for toilets or sinks if needed.
- soap dispensers and paper towel holder.
- a covered pail for used disposable diapers.
- a low mirror over the sinks.

Cengage Learning

Toddlers begin to indicate they are ready to use the toilet during the second year.

COGNITIVE AREA

A section of the room should provide a safe and interesting environment where both infants and toddlers can develop their cognitive abilities. The youngest babies must be in a protected area where they can see and hear activities in the room or explore a few simple toys. As they get older, they must be able to crawl about freely and explore wider sections of the room. Toddlers are mobile and need space to roam and to engage in social interactions. Therefore, depending on the age levels of the children, an infant-toddler room might have two cognitive areas.

For Infants to One Year

- a soft-sided pool for playing with plastic balls
- a space partially enclosed with low barriers and filled with textured pillows
- pictures at floor level
- texture boards, texture quilts, or wall quilts
- mobiles—some that make sounds, some that move—or balls hung from the ceiling
- unbreakable mirror mounted at floor level

- a few colorful, soft, washable toys—make sure there are no small parts that could come off and be swallowed
- cloth or cardboard books
- rattles, nesting toys, balls
- mechanical toys that make sounds: jack-in-the-box, pounding toys

For Toddlers

- vinyl flooring or large plastic sheets to cover the carpet
- low table and chairs
- large trays or tubs for floor activities
- low shelves containing a variety of manipulative materials: large beads, stacking cones, large Lagos, simple puzzles
- tubs to fill with dry rolled oats, rice, soapy water, and cooked spaghetti—add scoops, measuring cups, pans, sponges, or dolls as needed
- variety of mechanical toys that can be pounded, poked, or pushed
- kitchen sets, pots and pans, hats, purses for dramatic play

FINE MOTOR AREA

This area should include a variety of materials children can use to strengthen their fingers and hands. Many commercial materials are designed specifically for this purpose.

Many items that are found at home can also be used for infants and toddlers to manipulate. The following list contains items found in most households. Before these items are introduced to the classroom, they must be washed in a standard bleach solution and rinsed thoroughly. (The standard bleach solution can be made by mixing one-quarter cup bleach with one gallon of water.) Provide clear plastic boxes for storage and low shelves for easy accessibility.

- A selection of materials: large pop beads, nesting cups, small blocks, large Legos, simple puzzles, form boards, stacking toys, linking loops, large pegs and pegboard, form box, pounding toys, plastic lock box
- Large plastic curlers, plastic clothespins, plastic containers
- Large plastic or metal mixing bowls, wooden spoons
- Plastic bread baskets that can be used for putting things in and dumping them out

A low table may define the work area. If children prefer to work on the floor, large trays may be placed there. The children can take their materials to a tray and work. Alternatively, a mat or large piece of cloth may be placed nearby to indicate where to use the materials.

Looking at catalogs from companies that sell educational toys may be helpful. They contain a wide choice of materials.

LARGE MOTOR AREA

One of the main tasks for children during the first two years is to develop their large motor skills. They are eager to try new things and to repeat or practice things they have already learned. The large motor area will be a much-used part of both the indoor classroom and

Cengage Learning

Barriers should be low so children can see over or through them.

the outdoor play area of an infant-toddler program. Through large muscle play, children have an opportunity to develop their posture and balance. They gain a sense of security as they learn to control their own bodies. They can learn to integrate both sides of their body, sometimes using alternate sides for tasks.

There should be planned activities to maximize the safety of all the children in the room. Crawling infants must be protected from any equipment that might injure them, but they should be allowed access to any that is safe. For instance, if there is a rocking boat in the room or outside, infants should not be able to crawl nearby. Conversely, if large foam mats and cubes are used for a climbing activity, some babies may be able to manage safely.

Indoors, this area might include:

- large vinyl-covered mats, cubes, ramps, and foam tunnels.
- rocking boats, rocking chairs, a rocking horse, and rolling tricycles.
- low climbing structures with a low slide and steps.
- large pillows, bean bags, and buckets.

Outdoors, this area might include:

- low climbing structures.
- large boxes, either wooden or cardboard.

- buggies, wagons, bikes, sturdy tricycles, cars, and push toys.
- wide walking boards, steps, and ramps.
- bounce mattresses, barrels, and tunnels.
- large blocks and hollow blocks.
- rubber tires and inner tubes.
- a sandbox, shovels, pails, cups, pots, and pans.
- low sand/water tables.
- large balls.
- a wading pool or large tub for water.
- tire swings, and swings with safety belts.
- a variety of surfaces such as wood, grass, and sand.
- hilly and flat areas for walking, running, or rolling.
- low slides.

LANGUAGE AREA

By the end of the first year, infants can understand much of the language they hear. During the second year, they learn to use words themselves to express ideas, thoughts, and feelings. An infant-toddler program should encourage language skills as adults speak and listen to children. A language activity area can provide additional stimulus for language development.

The language area should:

- be in a secluded area, away from distractions (for example, an enclosed corner with shelves).
- have large, soft pillows or a low couch where children can sit.
- provide a collection of soft puppets.
- include a collection of cloth, cardboard, or plastic books that the children can look at and touch.
- include CD players.

PSYCHOSOCIAL AREA

A **psychosocial area** of an infant-toddler room should provide for interactions between adults and children, and among the children themselves. This area should allow children to learn about themselves and to develop relationships with adults and with their peers.

An area for learning about themselves might include:

- unbreakable mirrors attached to the wall at both crawling and standing height.
- small unbreakable mirrors that children can pick up and use.
- pictures of babies and children displayed at eye level.
- places for being alone—tunnels, enclosed areas, or large boxes.
- individual storage spaces for their belongings.

Cengage Learning

A language activity area can provide additional stimulus for language development.

An area for developing relationships with adults might include:

- comfortable, low places for adults to sit while observing or interacting with children.
- rocking chairs where an adult can comfort an infant, and soft chairs where an adult and toddler can sit together.
- low barriers—some made of Plexiglas—so adults and children can see each other.
- changing tables and feeding areas that are comfortable for adults and children thus fostering interaction.

An area for developing relationships with peers might:

- include low tables where toddlers can stand to play.
- provide enough duplicate toys so toddlers can play near each other with the same toy.
- have low barriers, shelves, or equipment so infants and toddlers can be together.
- provide padded areas where toddlers can jump and play together safely.
- provide safe places where babies can crawl together.
- provide a place for dramatic play—containing a table, chairs, a stove, dishes, pots, pans, dress-up clothes, dolls, and an unbreakable mirror.

Adaptations for Infants and Toddlers with Special Needs

Infants and toddlers with special needs can benefit from being mainstreamed into regular child development programs. Part-time participation will benefit these children, although some working parents may need all-day care. A quality program will include:

- albums with photos of the children and their families.
- pictures at the children's eye level.
- books that adults can read to or share with children.
- activities that these children need to optimize their development.

Furthermore, parents need help and support with the sometimes difficult task of caring for their children. When a decision is made to accept these infants or toddlers, the director should seek out community resources and consultation before planning an environment or program.

A basic need for all children during the first two years, and an especially important one for children with special needs, is the attainment of control over themselves and their environment.

In order to achieve mastery, the environment should:

- be appropriate for each child's capabilities.
- offer challenges while also ensuring some successes.
- be safe and free of any objects or obstacles that could be harmful.
- provide appropriate sensory stimulation for the infant with a visual disability.
- provide assortments of tactile materials for the child with a physical disability.
- provide auditory materials.
- include orthopedic chairs, a table, or other specially designed structures for making infants comfortable.

CASE STUDY

Lien and Chen Wang, twins, are enrolled in Emily's infant–toddler group. Chen goes to sleep fairly quickly in his crib at nap time, but Lien screams loudly. Emily rubs Lien's back, hoping that it will help her to relax. However, Lien persists and does not stop until she is finally so exhausted that she falls asleep. The other children grow increasingly agitated over the crying and some of them are unable to fall asleep.

Emily is distraught trying to determine what to do. She has tried all the things that help other children who are afraid to fall asleep in the child–care setting, but none have worked with Lien. She has spoken to Lien's mother, but Mrs. Wang has limited understanding of English and hasn't been able to help.

1. What do you think is the problem?
2. How could you find an answer to Emily's dilemma?
3. If you were the director of Emily's program, what would you suggest?

SUMMARY

Directors of infant-toddler programs need to understand the stages of children's development during the first two years. There are universal patterns of development that most children go through, although not at the same pace.

Children younger than the age of two experience their environment with all their senses. Piaget called this the sensorimotor period. During the stage that Erik Erikson called trust versus mistrust, most children learn that adults will provide food, warmth, or comfort as needed. Attachment to others develops during the first two years, but it also results in anxiety over separation from parents or caregivers. Language begins to appear during the second year, and toddlers learn the power of words to tell people what they mean or what they want. During this period, children also learn to get along with others, to share, and to play cooperatively.

Developmentally appropriate programs are based on a set of goals. Routines should be part of the curriculum. Developmentally appropriate programs also include interactions between adults and children, good record keeping, provision for many kinds of play experiences, and an educated and stable staff.

The environment should meet all licensing requirements and ensure the safety of the children. Infants and toddlers need places where they can rest and be alone, and where they can explore using all their senses. Materials should be representative of their cultural or ethnic background in order to lay the foundation for their identity.

Specific sections for an infant-toddler room should include spaces for each of the routines, cognitive activities, fine motor and large motor development, a language area, and a psychosocial area.

STUDENT ACTIVITIES

1. Make an appointment to visit a child development center that serves children from birth to school age. Spend time in a preschool classroom and then visit the infant-toddler room. Compare the kinds of toys and materials that are available in each. Are the materials in the infant room appropriate for the age level? If not, why not?

2. Interview a caregiver in an infant-toddler program. Find out what is most difficult about the work. What is most enjoyable? What are the most important characteristics for an effective infant-toddler caregiver?

3. Make a list of 10 pieces of equipment that might be included in an infant-toddler room. Defend each of your choices based on developmental appropriateness.

4. Observe a group of toddlers for at least one hour. List and describe any sensory activities they engaged in during this time.

REVIEW

1. Piaget called the period between birth and two years the sensorimotor period. What is meant by the term?

2. What is meant by the word synchrony in reference to infants and their caregivers?

3. It takes special adults to withstand the tremendous demands made on infant-toddler caregivers. List the characteristics a director should look for when choosing these personnel.

4. List five materials that will help infants or toddlers learn by using their sense of touch.

5. Describe three activities that will encourage babies to use their motor abilities.

6. Licensing requirements for infant-toddler programs have some specific areas of focus. What are they?

7. List some ways an environment can provide visual stimulation for an infant.

8. Describe a cognitive area suitable for infants up to one year of age.

9. List furniture and equipment that might be in a psychosocial area to promote development of relationships with peers.

10. In what ways can the environment support mastery in children with special needs?

REFERENCES

Ainsworth, M. D. S. (1973). The development of infant-mother attachment. In B. M. Caldwell & H. N. Riccuiti (Eds.). *Review of child development research* (Vol. 3). Chicago: University of Chicago Press.

Newberger, J. J. (1997). New brain development research—A wonderful window of opportunity to build public support for early childhood education. *Young Children, 52*(4), 4–9.

Reese, Debbie (1998). Speech development in the infant and toddler. http://www.kidsource.com.

SELECTED FURTHER READING

Bredekamp, S. (Ed.). (2009). *Developmentally appropriate practice in early childhood programs serving children from birth through age 8*. Washington, DC: National Association for the Education of Young Children.

Brickmeyer, J., Kennedy, A., & Stonehouse, A. (2009). Using stories effectively with infants and toddlers. *Young Children, 64*(1), 42–47.

Burman, L. (2008). *Are you listening?* St. Paul, MN: Redleaf Press.

Gallagher, K. C. (2005). Brain research and early childhood development. A primer for developmentally appropriate practice. *Young Children, 60*(4), 12–20.

Gonzalez-Mena, J. (2001). *Multicultural issues in child care* (3rd ed.). Mountain View, CA: Mayfield Publishing.

Gonzalez-Mena, J., & Eyer, D. (2001). *Infants, toddlers, and caregivers* (5th ed.). Mountain View, CA: Mayfield Publishing.

Miller, K. (2001). Sleep issues in infant and toddler programs. *Child Care Information Exchange, 140*, 50–61.

Robertson, C. (2003). *Safety, nutrition, and health in early childhood education* (2nd ed.). Clifton Park, NY: Delmar Learning.

Ross, H. W. (1992). Integrating infants with disabilities: Can "ordinary" caregivers do it? *Young Children, 47*(3), 65–71.

Torquatie, J, & Barber, J. (2005). Dancing with trees; Infants and toddlers in the garden. *Young Children, 60*(3), 40–46.

Yopp, H., & Yopp, R. (2009). Phonological awareness is child's play! *Young Children 64*(1), 12–18.

Zeavin, C. (1997). Toddlers at play: Environments at work. *Young Children, 52*(3), 72–77.

HELPFUL WEBSITES

Disclaimer: Links to Internet sites throughout this book are provided for your convenience and do not constitute an endorsement.

Baby Center (helpful information for parents about development and behavior management):	**http://www.babycenter.com**
Council for Exceptional Children:	**http://www.cec.sped.org**
Parents Place (resource for parents on development and health, plus a forum for sharing information):	**http://www.parentsplace.com**
Zero to Three (its mission is to support families, practitioners, and communities to promote the healthy development of infants and toddlers):	**http://www.zerotothree.org**

For additional resources related to administration including videos, links to related sites for each chapter of the text, tutorial quizzes, glossary flashcards, and more, visit the Education CourseMate website for this book at www.cengage.com/login.

Cengage Learning

Planning: Preschool-Age Children

Objectives

After reading this chapter, you should be able to:

- Describe the major developmental characteristics of three- and four-year-old children.
- State the components of developmentally appropriate practices in an early childhood program.
- List and discuss general considerations for organizing space.
- Describe adaptations of the environment for children with special needs.

KEY TERMS

aesthetic appeal

anti-bias curriculum

concrete materials

creativity

diversity

egocentric

multiculturalism

preschool period

scooter board

self-concept

A day in the life of . . .

A Director/Teacher of a For-Profit School

During our annual "Presidents' Day" discussion, I explained to the four-year-old class that the president of the United States lives in the White House. The lesson was going well and the children were interested. One little boy asked me, "If the president lives in the White House, who lives in the brown houses?"

The administrator of an early childhood center is responsible for helping staff to provide an optimum setting in which children can develop physically, socially, emotionally, and intellectually. The best preschool programs provide developmentally appropriate experiences for the children they serve. This means, simply, that learning experiences are based on knowledge of what most children are capable of doing and of where their interests lie. Therefore, this chapter provides an overview of the development of children in the preschool years, then some guidelines for planning a curriculum.

Note that when speaking of staff in this chapter and in other chapters in this text, two words are used: teacher and caregiver. The word teacher has long been understood by nearly everyone to designate a person who teaches or instructs. More recently, with the proliferation of child-care settings, the word caregiver has appeared in the vocabularies of early childhood professionals. It usually describes adults who care for infants and toddlers but may also designate an adult in after-school care. The use of this term implies nurturing and concern for the physical well-being of the children.

The two terms are sometimes used interchangeably because a teacher also cares for children and a caregiver also teaches children. A teacher should not be seen as more valuable than a caregiver. Each has an important function in furthering children's development. Educarer is a more recent term that has been proposed, but is not in wide use at this time.

Preschool Development

Preschool period designates the years before a child enters elementary school. Some people include children aged two to five; others term three- to six-year-olds as preschoolers. In the context of this chapter, preschooler means three- and four-year-olds. Two-year-olds are discussed in the previous chapter on infant-toddler development. Five-year-olds are usually in a prekindergarten or kindergarten program and, therefore, are not included.

Three- and four-year-olds each have distinct characteristics that must be considered when planning an appropriate program for them. The three-year-olds are no longer toddlers, but they often have some of the same characteristics. At other times, they show the motor skills and language abilities that are usually seen in four-year-olds. Similarly, four-year-olds sometimes function at the level of the previous age period. At other times, they display abilities to learn, think, and reason that would be expected of kindergarten children. Preschool teachers and caregivers must understand the continuum from toddlerhood to school age and must judge each child's development accordingly. Although the scope of this chapter cannot present a highly defined differentiation between these two age levels, where appropriate, the distinction will be made.

During the preschool years, physical growth slows down. By the age of two, most children have achieved adult body proportions. That is, the percentage of their height apportioned to the head, the torso, and the legs is similar to that of an adult. Two-year-olds look like children rather than round, roly-poly babies. This development continues in the preschool years, but the physical changes are less noticeable because they are slower.

If you had not seen a three-year-old for several months, you would probably not detect changes in physical appearance. This slowdown in growth is important because it means children need fewer calories per pound of body weight than they did in the previous years. Therefore, their appetites are noticeably smaller.

Along with changes in body height and weight, changes are occurring in the brain. By age five, most children have attained about 90 percent of their full brain weight. As the brain matures, specialization of function occurs. During this period, children must have the opportunity to maximize these functions as well as to increase the coordination between functions.

During the preschool period, children have an extremely high activity level. This is a period during which children are mastering their gross motor skills. They recklessly practice running, climbing, jumping, and so on. They test out what they can do and attempt to overcome fears of new activities. It can be a time when the accident rate is high unless preventive measures are taken.

Three- and four-year-olds are perfecting their fine motor skills as well. Three-year-olds have great difficulty managing complex tasks such as cutting with scissors or tying their shoelaces. They still tend to use their whole hands and cannot manipulate objects easily with their separate fingers. By age four, most children have mastered scissors, and many can tie their own shoes. Four-year-olds can use their fingers to pick up and manipulate small objects.

The difference between the physical development of boys and girls during this period is minimal. Boys may be slightly taller and more muscular. Girls may mature a little more rapidly. Their bone age may be ahead of boys, and they lose their baby teeth sooner. However, these physical differences do not seem to cause differences in abilities. The amount of practice children engage in has a greater impact on differences in abilities.

Children's play changes in the preschool years. During infancy and toddlerhood, play allows children to use all their senses and motor abilities to explore their environment. In the preschool period, children use play to master new skills. Block building provides an opportunity to learn how to control the hands while placing one block on top of another. Riding bicycles outdoors allows children to develop the ability to control their legs and arms.

Although three-year-old boys and girls often play together, by age four there is a decided preference for same-sex playmates and a difference in choice of play activities. Some researchers explain this by suggesting that the innate biological differences become more prevalent, causing this disparity (Powlishta, 1995). Others suggest that the explanation lies with the impact of how parents and culture shape children's gender identity, and therefore, their play preferences (Kallista, 2005). Whatever the cause, a decided shift to same-sex playmates at age four accompanies a corresponding preference for certain kinds of play activities.

Dramatic play becomes an important part of children's play during this period. In this kind of play, children act out familiar or fantasy scenes. Most children employ standard plots. Three-year-olds typically play out scenes reminiscent of home experiences. There may be a "mommy," a "daddy," and a "baby." The scenario includes all the experiences that are part of a child's day at home, from eating to going to bed, from administering punishment to giving rewards. On the other hand, four-year-olds branch out to characters and situations outside the home. They may play out scenes involving favorite TV people or people they see in their neighborhood. They become the current TV "monster," the neighborhood gas station attendant, or a firefighter.

Through dramatic play, children have an opportunity to test out what it might be like to be the person portrayed. This kind of play also provides them with an opportunity to perfect physical skills as they carry out the tasks assigned to each role. To be included in others' dramatic play, children must develop social skills and learn to cooperate to prolong the play. Finally, dramatic play allows children a chance to work out feelings they may have about their own experiences. Children who give "shots" with glee to other children during "doctor" play are reliving what it felt like to have an injection themselves.

Aggressive acts become more frequent during children's play in the preschool years. Two-year-olds often bite other children. This kind of aggression is not really directed toward the other child but is a way of expressing frustrations. During the preschool period, deliberate aggressive acts begin to appear. Sometimes these are poorly executed approaches to other children. They may not be meant as aggressive acts, but in their execution they

Preschool children are learning to work independently.

seem so to the child who is being approached. During this period children begin to hit when they are angry or to shove children who are in their way. This type of aggression should be seen as a healthy sign of developing assertiveness in the pursuit of their own goals. However, children need to learn to use language as a way to express their feelings and that physical acts of aggression are unacceptable. By the time children reach age four, aggressive acts begin to diminish.

Children are able to fantasize but may also develop fears during the preschool period. By age three, children are able to imagine but may still have difficulty knowing what is real. Some children develop elaborate constructions of a fantasy friend who is with them throughout the day. They talk to the friend, include the friend at the dinner table, and blame the friend for any transgressions. Other children develop fears. A typical example is fear of dogs, even though there has never been an unpleasant encounter with one. Some children have nightmares. Each of these developments comes from the ability to think about things that cannot be seen or may not have been experienced directly. Because children's understanding is still limited, some of their thoughts may frighten or overwhelm them. A fantasy friend, fears, and nightmares are normal for this age. With support from adults, most children manage to move beyond this stage.

During the preschool years, children are trying to define their self-concept. They begin to understand some of their own characteristics but have unrealistic ideas about others. They develop quite general and usually positive impressions of themselves.

However, they also have unrealistic ideas about what they are capable of doing. They may think they can build the biggest block building or can run faster than anybody else. This is vastly different from the elementary school child who says he is "good" in reading but is "terrible" in math.

Preschoolers are trying to solidify their understanding of gender. At about age three, most children become aware of differences. They are curious about other children's bodies and explore their own. Gradually, they begin to understand "I am a girl" or "I am a boy." However, not until close to the age of five do children know gender is irreversible—that they will always be the same. Until that time, they sometimes believe changing clothes or hairstyles will also change their gender.

Self-concept in the preschooler also depends on what Erik Erikson called "initiative." Because of higher activity levels, children are eager to initiate new experiences. Children enthusiastically enter into new play activities and try new things. When these efforts end in failure or criticism, children may feel guilt or that they are worthless. A certain amount of guilt is necessary to learn to control impulses and behaviors that interfere with others, but too much guilt paralyzes children's ability to function to their fullest.

As children develop their own sense of self, they also begin to have a greater awareness of others. This enables them to give up some of their strong attachment to their parents and to begin to move out into their wider environment. They begin to see that not everyone has the same needs, thoughts, and feelings that they and their families do. With help, they can learn to accept and appreciate those differences.

Children's thinking changes during the preschool years. The ability to imagine and think symbolically begins to emerge at about age two. Two-year-olds can pretend to play out scenes from their own experiences but require concrete objects to support their play. With a tiny cup in hand, they can feed their doll or teddy bear. By age three, children can pretend without props or can use any object to represent what they want. If a car is not at hand to add to their block play, they can pretend that a particular block is one. If they do not have an airplane, they use their hands and appropriate sounds to simulate a plane flying over their building.

Their ability to think has some limitations, however. They tend to be **egocentric**, being able to see things only from their own point of view. They cannot imagine reversing processes. As an example, children may understand that three plus one is four but will not be able to see that four minus one is three. This kind of thinking interferes with their ability to think through processes in a logical way.

Language develops rapidly during this preschool period. Some children will learn as many as 10 to 20 new words a day (Jones et al, 1991), usually following a predictable sequence. Nouns seem to be learned most easily by all children, often followed by verbs. It takes longer to add adjectives, adverbs, or interrogatives. Basic nouns such as "dog" come before categories such as "beagle." They may next learn to use interrogatives "what" and "where" in a sentence such as "Where dog?".

They seem to have some understanding of grammar, but often apply the rules incorrectly. For instance, children learn that adding an -s makes a noun plural. They may say "foots" until they learn the correct plural form. Similarly, they learn that adding -ed to verbs makes them past tense. They will say "he goed" instead of "he went." During this period, many children also try out the power of words. They learn that certain words bring intense responses from adults or other children particularly a forcefully uttered "no."

Differences in language skills are often evident during these preschool years. Girls, firstborns, and singleborns tend to be more proficient in language than boys, laterborns, and twins. Middle-class children often have more advanced communication skills than lower-class children. Family communication patterns also affect children's language skills. Parents who talk to their children, listen to their communications, and encourage further conversation produce children with greater ability in language skills. In addition, reading books and talking about the pictures or story help children to increase their vocabulary (Morgan, 2007).

A developmentally appropriate child-care center can foster optimum growth in all areas of children's development. Environment, activities, and adult–child interactions must be based on a firm knowledge of what children are like at this stage of their development. Additionally, adults must understand the characteristics of a good program, then adapt these ideas to fit the needs of their particular school.

Characteristics of a Developmentally Appropriate Program

• • • • • GROUPING CHILDREN

Imagine being a child in a classroom full of other children, materials, and strange adults. Moreover, imagine a lot of noise, confusion, and people moving around. All but the most independent child might be overwhelmed. In order to facilitate each child's adjustment to a group setting, group sizes must be manageable. The National Association for the Education of Young Children (NAEYC) recommends that a group for three- and four-year-olds be no larger than 16, and should be staffed by two adults. When staff members are highly qualified, groups can contain up to 20 children with a teacher/child ratio of 1:10. However, group size and teacher/child ratio are also affected by other factors.

Licensing requirements usually specify the number of children allowed in a particular physical space. The regulations typically state that there must be 35 to 50 square feet per child indoor space. So the size of the classrooms will determine how many children can be accommodated there. The classroom may have fewer children, but it cannot exceed that limit.

The philosophy and goals of a program may also dictate the number of children in each group. Some people believe that children do best when they have the opportunity to develop close, interactive relationships with adults. This requires a small group of children so that teachers or caregivers can develop a close bond with children. Others believe that children do best when they work independently of adults. In this kind of situation, a larger group of children can be managed.

The needs of children may dictate the best group size. When a group contains children who have special needs, consideration should be given to limiting the total number of children and increasing the number of teachers . Children who have any of the disabilities discussed later in this chapter may require additional time and attention. In some situations, this can best be accomplished in smaller groups.

Directors must also decide which age groups to put together in each room. The most frequent grouping puts children who are close in age in the same group. This is called peer or chronological grouping. Many directors and teachers feel this configuration allows for better programming. They can plan materials and activities more easily when children are close together in age. An alternate way of grouping children is in "family groups." Here, children may differ in age by as much as two or three years.

A typical group might have a few two-year-olds, some three- and four-year-olds, and possibly even some five-year-olds. Rationale for this kind of group is that children can help each other and can learn from each other. Another argument cites the closer resemblance to a family.

Children with disabilities require additional time and attention.

Licensing or other program requirements may set the ratio of children to the number of adults in a group. Staff qualifications may also determine the size of preschool groups. When staff members are highly qualified and have had experience planning and implementing programs, they can usually manage the maximum number of children in a group. Preprofessionals who are learning to be qualified teachers should either be under the supervision of experienced teachers or be assigned to a limited number of children. (Specific staff qualifications are discussed extensively in later chapters.)

SCHEDULE

The daily schedule should allow alternating periods of quiet and active experiences. There should be a pattern that minimizes the possibility that children will become overstimulated or overtired. If quiet times are interspersed with times that allow children to move around vigorously, children will not become exhausted.

The schedule should provide what is best for the group as well as for the needs of individual children. Many children benefit from the stimulation of group activities. Others cannot stay with a group for long periods and should be allowed to do something else. Some children get engrossed in an activity and deeply resent having to do something else. They want to spend a longer time at a particular activity, and, whenever possible, should be allowed to do so.

Child-initiated activities should be balanced with teacher-directed ones. Children need large blocks of time in which they can choose from various activities or even do nothing if they wish. At other times, there should be group learning activities led by the teacher. Children need to develop abilities both to be self-directed and to function in a teacher-structured situation.

The schedule of a day should provide for both indoor and outdoor play. Some schools have an open indoor/outdoor program in which children can move freely from one to the other. This requires an adequate number of staff to supervise, and a mild climate.

Other schools set times when all children in a group move outdoors and then back inside again. This is the more usual approach as it allows more than one group of children to use the outdoor space. In areas where winter weather prevents children from being outside, they will need plenty of opportunities to engage in active play. Indoor climbing equipment, active games, or music activities can substitute for outdoor play.

GOALS

Goals provide the framework for designing a developmentally appropriate preschool program. In its publication *Accreditation Criteria & Procedures*, NAEYC recommends that staff provide activities and materials that help to achieve the following goals:

- Foster positive self-concept.
- Develop social skills.
- Encourage children to think, reason, question, and experiment.
- Encourage language development.
- Enhance physical development and skills.
- Encourage and demonstrate sound health, safety, and nutritional practices.
- Encourage creative expression and appreciation for the arts.
- Respect cultural diversity.

ASSESSMENT

A program for three- and four-year-olds should be realistic, that is, based on an assessment of what children are capable of doing. The most frequently used assessment tool is observation—watching the children to find out what they can do. Simple tests can also be used to evaluate children's abilities. Games that require physical agility can become tests for those abilities. Checklists are an easy way to assess other abilities. Discovering individual or group interests is possible by listening to the questions children ask or what they talk about. This will provide clues to their interests.

Developmentally appropriate learning experiences should be designed based on children's capabilities and interests. Materials and learning activities should fit the age of the children. Some should be easy for most of the children so they will have a feeling of competence. Including some experiences that will challenge children is important to help them move to a new level of functioning.

Activities should be planned to fit the needs and interests of the gender makeup of the group. As indicated in the overview of development at the beginning of this chapter, a group of three-year-olds seldom divides along gender lines. However, by age four children show decided sex preferences in playmates and play activities. Teachers and caregivers should provide for those differences and encourage children to cross strict gender lines in their play.

VARIETY

Children should be provided with a wide variety of materials and activities so they can select their own experiences. This fosters the development of initiative and also allows children to choose what is best for them. Some classrooms have a selection of materials available on shelves at all times. There may be puzzles, manipulatable materials, art materials, construction kits, and block accessories. Children are free to take down what they want, use it, and then replace it before moving on to another area. In other classrooms, teachers select a variety of materials to put out each day and allow children to move between them. The first method allows children a wider choice, but requires a lot of storage space for the materials. Another drawback is that occasionally teachers fail to change or add to the selection, and the children become bored. The second method allows children a smaller number of choices each day, but may offer more choices in the long run.

COGNITIVE DEVELOPMENT

The preschool program should be designed to foster children's cognitive development through the use of **concrete materials** that children can touch, taste, smell, hear, and see. There should be blocks, cars, trucks, and planes for building; dolls, dishes, and dress-up clothes for dramatic play; puzzles, Legos, and other small manipulative materials; and real tools for real tasks such as cooking. Children can manage knives for cutting food and blenders or frying pans for preparing food when they are closely supervised. All materials should be relevant to the children's own lives, things they either know about or have previously experienced. In this way, each new experience builds on the base of previous experiences.

Materials and activities should foster children's self-confidence and independence. One typical way in which this is accomplished is through learning centers. In specific areas of the room, teachers set up materials that children can explore either with a few friends or by themselves. The activity must be designed so children can participate with a minimum of help and supervision from adults. The best learning centers are set up so that children can immediately see what might be done there and can proceed entirely on their own.

Cognitive activities should encourage children to think, question, and experiment. Open-ended activities that have multiple answers do this. An example is a collection of spoons for children to categorize. The collection should include small and large spoons; silver, plastic, and wooden ones; and soup ladles, stirring spoons, and teaspoons. Children can categorize this collection according to size, material used to make the spoon, and use for the spoon. There may even be additional categories such as color, kind of decorations on the spoons, and slotted or unslotted.

Cognitive activities should encourage children's language skills. Children should be able to add new words to their vocabularies through their play activities. They should have many opportunities to practice language by explaining what they have learned, by asking questions, or by solving problems. Gradually, the development of language skills may include the ability to recognize some written words. Children learn to recognize their own names during the preschool period, some as early as age three. A few children learn to read other words during this period.

Cognitive activities should emphasize the development of physical skills. There should be ample opportunities to enhance both large- and small-muscle development. Scissors, paintbrushes, collage materials, and puzzles are some examples of materials that require small-muscle coordination. Music, movement activities, and outdoor play

Cengage Learning

Play is work for children and their way to construct knowledge.

encourage children to use their large muscles. Both are necessary for the development of preschool children.

CREATIVITY

The preschool program should provide children opportunities to be creative. In the context of this chapter, **creativity** means a unique way of reacting to a situation, not just imitating what others have done. Unique ways of reacting call for behaviors that include intuition, originality, divergent thinking, and flexibility.

Opportunities for creativity can be provided in many of the activities of the preschool. Art is often thought of first. Children should be given materials to use as they wish. Patterns and prepared models stifle creativity. There should be selections of paint, paper, brushes, collage materials, scissors, marking pens, and so on. From these tools, children can use their imaginations to produce whatever they want.

Creativity can also be fostered in the dramatic play area of a classroom. The kind and variety of props available to the children will dictate the subject for their play activities. They will enjoy a selection of clothes, jewelry, hats, shoes, brushes, combs, hair curlers, razors (without blades), and so on. Anything children may have in their own homes will encourage play in this area.

DIVERSITY

Early childhood professionals stress the importance of including concepts concerning **diversity** in the early childhood curriculum. Two terms are used to describe these ideas. **Multiculturalism** is the most widely used, and its focus is on introducing children to the similarities and differences among different cultures and ethnicities. The goal of a

FYI

Statistics concerning America's children are disheartening. There are still many children whose needs are not being met, although the number has decreased in several states.

Children represent 25 percent of the US population. Yet, 41 percent of all children live in low-income families and nearly one in every five live in poor families. There are more than 25 million children under age 6 in the United States. However young children under age 6 appear to be particularly vulnerable with 44 percent—11.1 million live in low-income and 22 percent—5.5 million live in poor families.

Black, American Indian, and Hispanic children under age 6 are disproportionately low income, with children of Hispanic origin comprising the largest group of low-income and poor young children.

The following is a 2009 breakdown of children under 6 by race who live in low-income families:

30 percent of white children—3.9 million

64 percent of black children—2.2 million

28 percent of Asian children—0.3 million

69 percent of American Indian children under age 6—0.1 million

43 percent of children under age 6 of some other race—0.4 million

64 percent of Hispanic children under age 6—4.1 million

SOURCE: National Center For Children in Poverty (NCCP), November 2009

Cengage Learning

Children learn many concepts during the process of block building.

multicultural program is to provide opportunities for children to develop a positive self-concept, including an acceptance of their own differences, and the differences of others. **Anti–bias curriculum** is the term used to describe a broader approach that includes not only cultural aspects, but also gender and physical ability differences. Those using this approach stress the importance of freeing children from gender stereotyping, and preventing the development of biased attitudes toward people who are differently abled. The additional goal of an anti-bias curriculum is to encourage children to develop critical thinking skills that will enable them to counteract injustices directed toward themselves or others.

Whichever approach one chooses, all activities should be part of an integrated curriculum, not just added on to the existing curriculum. Too often, an attempt to introduce diversity into an early childhood program becomes what Louise Derman-Sparks (1989) labeled the "tourist" curriculum. Cultural concepts are introduced through holiday celebrations such as Chinese New Year or Cinco de Mayo. This method causes children to learn only about the more exotic aspects of a culture. She recommends that children learn about the everyday aspects of life in other countries starting with those cultures represented in their neighborhood.

She also suggests that children should "be free to ask questions about any subject, to engage in real dialogue with adults, to make choices, and to have some say in their daily school life. If we are to facilitate children's sense of self-esteem, critical thinking, and ability to 'stand up' for themselves, then our methodology must allow them to experience their intelligence and power as having a constructive effect on their world" (2006).

The following materials can be used to create an environment that supports appreciation of diversity:

- Images of people of different color, women and men doing work in the home or outside the home, elderly people, differently abled people, different family configurations.

Cengage Learning

Friendship develops early.

- Books that show a diversity of gender roles, people from different cultures or backgrounds doing ordinary tasks, various families.
- Dramatic play materials that reflect various gender roles, including everyday objects used in different cultures, tools and equipment used by people with special needs (crutches, canes, and so forth).
- Art materials that include various skin-tone colors, papers and fabrics that suggest different cultures, paintings or sculptures done by artists from different backgrounds.
- CDs that reflect various cultures, opportunities for children to sing or dance to ethnic music.
- Dolls that represent ethnic groups, both male and female dolls, dolls that reflect different kinds of disabilities.
- Foods of different cultures.

STAFF

Staff interactions with children should convey warmth and acceptance of each child's worth and uniqueness. Teachers and caregivers do this by touching children, holding them, and speaking to them at eye level. This is especially important at the beginning of the day, when children may feel anxious about separation from their parents. A warm good-bye at the end of the day will also help to bridge the gap to the following day.

Staff should use positive management tools that empower children to resolve their own problems. When these techniques are used, children learn to take control of their own actions and feel good about themselves (Nelson, Lott, & Glenn, 1993). One method is to anticipate problems and make suggestions for alternative behaviors from which the child can choose. An example is: "Evan, your freeway is about to get in the way of Kathy's house. Can you make an off-ramp or change the direction so that it won't knock down her building?" Another method is to ask questions and let the children decide how to resolve the problem. An example is: Two girls want to wear the same costume from the dress-up box. The teacher can help them resolve the conflict by saying, "I can see you both want to wear that pink dress. What can you do so that both of you can have fun playing in the dramatic play area?"

Staff interactions with children should foster the development of self-esteem. According to Eaton (1997), "The goal in using discipline is to guide children's behavior in such a way that they will internalize expectations and develop the self-control that they need to function securely in life." Young children do not have the cognitive skills to understand why they should consider others when trying to satisfy their own needs. Management strategies should help them to problem solve while taking control of their own actions. The first step is to calm the children and help them focus on the problem. The next step is to give each party to the conflict an opportunity to relate what happened. It helps to clarify the problem by restating what the children have said. Finally, the adult can encourage the children to find a resolution that will satisfy all those involved. Certain behaviors in children such as messiness, crying, resistance, and aggression are part of normal development. Adults should accept these behaviors as indications of the child's developmental stage while guiding them to more acceptable behaviors. Adults must never respond to children in ways that will destroy or decrease their self-esteem. This includes yelling in anger, blaming, teasing, accusing, insulting, threatening, or humiliating children.

Staff should encourage children to be as independent as they are capable of being at each stage of their development. Three-year-olds can work with an adult to put away some of their toys and to wipe up spills at snack time. A reminder will encourage them to care for their personal belongings and wash their hands after toileting. Four-year-olds will probably be able to do some of these tasks without reminders and adult help. Four-year-olds take pride in getting out their own materials and in putting them away at the end of a play period. They can participate in preparing snacks, serving them, and then cleaning up afterward. Four-year-olds are pretty independent in caring for their own personal needs. They can manage their clothes in the bathroom and put on their own jackets.

Staff should be responsive to children. They should be ready to listen as children communicate their ideas, thoughts, and feelings. They should encourage children to share their experiences. All adults should allow children to put their feelings into words and to talk about things that make them angry or frightened. Each communication from children to adults should be treated with respect. Children's thoughts and feelings should not be belittled or ignored as unimportant. In this way, children learn to understand themselves better and to accept their own feelings.

PARENTS

Children learn more effectively when parents participate in the school. A good preschool program includes parents whenever possible. Parent involvement begins with an orientation process in which parents learn about the goals of the school and its operating procedures. Pre-enrollment visits may be scheduled for parents and children. It is helpful to ask parents to stay with their child during the first few days of school. Parents should be involved in plans for bringing about separation from their child.

Once separation has taken place, the teacher should keep parents informed about their child's progress. Frequent informal reports as well as parent conferences let parents know what is happening at school. Daily written communications are an established procedure in many schools. Newsletters, telephone calls, and bulletin boards also keep parents informed.

The teacher should encourage parents to visit whenever possible. In some situations, parents can have lunch with their child or visit briefly at the beginning of naptime. Some parents can volunteer time in the classroom. If parents cannot be involved because of working hours, other family members should be encouraged to be a part of the school activities. Grandparents or older siblings may participate for parents.

PEER RELATIONSHIPS

A quality preschool should foster the development of friendships between children. The group makeup should allow most children to find someone on their own level with whom they can talk and play. This usually means having a mix of ages, genders, and abilities. A group of 14 boys and one girl will not work as well as one in which gender is more evenly distributed. A group of 15 three-year-olds may not offer a counterpart for a capable four-year-old.

Activities should be designed to encourage social interactions among children. When some learning stations are set up, they should accommodate more than one child working there at a time. Double-sided easels allow two children to work in close proximity, possibly encouraging interaction. Activities set out on tables should accommodate several children simultaneously so that they can talk about what they are doing.

Cengage Learning

Children enjoy preparing their own snacks.

Staff interactions with children should foster relationships and cooperation. Children should be encouraged to play together and to talk to each other. They should be allowed to work out their own problems whenever possible without undue adult interference. When adults do step in, it should be to help children find their own solutions.

Program: General Considerations

When planning an early childhood education program, it is important to keep in mind two other considerations. One is the addition of computers to the classroom materials. Today's generation of children will probably need skills to manage many kinds of technology when they become working adults. Therefore, perhaps it is appropriate to begin children's technological education early. The second consideration is how best to incorporate children with special needs into the regular activities of an early childhood environment. The answers are not easy to find and cannot be thoroughly explored within the scope of this text. A brief discussion follows, but it will be necessary to do additional research and reading, and to discuss theories before making program decisions.

COMPUTERS

The use of computers in early childhood classrooms is still the topic of significant controversy. Although they are becoming more common, many professionals question the appropriateness of including computer activities in the early childhood curriculum. They point to the belief that children learn best by hands-on experiences with concrete objects. They ask, "if children learn best what a square is by handling a square object, can they really learn the same concept by drawing one on a computer screen?" The answer that seems to be emerging from research is that it depends on the type of software programs used. Open-ended programs do help children to make significant gains in several areas: intelligence, nonverbal skills, structural knowledge, long-term memory, complex manual dexterity, and self-esteem (Haugland, 1992).

There are some specific areas in which computers are particularly effective. When preschool children have plenty of time to practice, computers can aid them in increasing prereading or reading skills. This requires the use of an easy-to-use word processor program, not just sight-reading practice programs. In order to integrate computer work into a whole-language approach, children should be encouraged to work together to plan stories, revise them as needed, discuss how the story is presented, and consider the spelling of words before using the spell-checker. Children can take risks when putting their thoughts into words because the text can be so easily revised on the computer.

Open-ended programs such as Logo™ can also increase children's problem-solving skills. Research studies show that preschool and primary grade children can use Logo to perform some higher-level thinking tasks (Clements, Nastasi, & Swaminathan, 1993). They can plan an approach to a problem; break the solution into small, understandable tasks; write a set of instructions to perform each task; construct a program to perform all the tasks in the right order; and evaluate the program.

Logo is easily used for developing mathematical concepts, but can also fit into other areas of the curriculum. The Logo Website: (http://www.terrapinlogo.com) (2006) reports the following uses of the program:

- "First graders in New Hampshire use a single-stroke version of Logo™ to move the turtle and explore shapes and lines."

- "Fourth graders in California program a miniature golf game in Logo™."
- "Fifth graders in Massachusetts learn the geography of their state by drawing a map in Logo™."
- "Paralyzed students in Pennsylvania use a single-switch device with Logo™ to move the turtle and create designs."

In 1996, NAEYC developed a position statement on computer use in early childhood programs. This was in response to the growing use of technology throughout society, in homes, schools, and businesses. Research points to the benefits of technology on children's learning and development. Clements (1993) found that computers are most often used to supplement rather than replace the usual early childhood activities and materials. Shade and Watson (1990) learned that although computers can be used in developmentally appropriate ways, they can also be misused. NAEYC cautioned that educators must use care and knowledge when evaluating the introduction of computers into early childhood classrooms. The NAEYC *Position Statement on Technology and Young Children—Ages 3 Through 8*, lists the following criteria. The complete statement can be found at www.naeyc.org.

1. It is up to the teacher to use professional judgment to determine if a specific use of technology is developmentally appropriate.
2. When used according to principles of developmental appropriateness, technology can increase children's cognitive and social abilities.
3. Computers or other technical equipment should be integrated into the total learning environment and should supplement other learning experiences.
4. There should be equitable access to computers for all children and their families, including children with special needs.

Cengage Learning

In 1996, the increase in technology led the NAEYC to develop a position statement on computer use in early childhood programs.

5. Software programs or other related materials must be free of stereotyping of any group and of violence as a problem-solving method.

6. Technology should be recognized as an important tool for professional development and continuing education.

CHILDREN WITH SPECIAL NEEDS

With the passage of PL 101–476, the Individuals with Disabilities Education Amendment of 1990, the question for early childhood administrators is no longer whether to accept children with special needs. The question now is: "How can we best meet the needs of these children in our program?" The law requires that an individual education plan (IEP) be prepared for each child. In most cases, a multidimensional assessment is done by a team consisting of physicians, psychologists, teachers, child-care workers, parents or guardians, and the child. This should provide information needed to develop a comprehensive intervention plan. General goals for including children with special needs should be to support families and promote children's mastery and independence. Additionally, children should be encouraged to develop skills that will allow them to have normalized life experiences. Lastly, goals should be established that prevent the emergence of future problems or disabilities (Wolery & Wilbers, 1994).

Attention Deficit Disorder

Description. Attention deficit disorder is a condition characterized by an inability to sustain attention, lack of perseverance, impulsivity, inability to suppress inappropriate behavior, overactivity, and excessive talking.

Teaching methods. Children with this impediment do best in a loosely structured environment in which they can be actively involved. Providing materials and activities that are developmentally appropriate is also important. Behavioral treatment should include giving rewards for appropriate behavior, providing brief and specific directions, and being consistent in methods of discipline.

Developmental Delay

Description. Levels of delay are often determined by testing, but teachers should use their own observational abilities to further assess children's abilities. They should look at motor, language, and social abilities; notice how much help is required from adults or how much the children can do themselves; and note attention span and comprehension of concepts.

Teaching methods. Low child/staff ratios will provide maximum individualized attention that will be needed. Tasks should be broken down into small components and should allow for many repetitions. Teachers should use a lot of positive reinforcement and should be consistent in routines and presentation of experiences.

Physical Disabilities

Description. Physical disabilities may range from poor coordination to severe limitations of mobility. Some children show difficulty when attempting tasks that require fine motor skills and become easily frustrated. Other children have trouble climbing, riding bikes, or doing other large-muscle activities.

Teaching methods. There should be easy access ramps in all areas of the physical environment. Children should be encouraged to participate in various activities requiring physical skills. Teachers should investigate innovative materials that will enhance physical skills and offer positive reinforcement for successes.

Hearing Disabilities

Description. Limited communication is a frequently observed result of a hearing disability. Additionally, these children often do not understand or respond when others talk to them. They may be inattentive at group times.

Teaching methods. The teacher should face children with hearing disabilities when talking to them and should articulate clearly. In group times, these children should be seated close to the adult. The teacher should talk to these children to provide language stimulation and should use tapes for additional listening opportunities.

Speech and Language Disabilities

Description. Many children exhibit articulation problems as they develop language. Some children continue to have difficulties beyond the expected period of time. They may omit, substitute, and distort sounds of words and letters. Other children exhibit language problems by using gestures or only single words when you might expect them to use sentences.

Teaching methods. Teachers and caregivers can assist children in developing language by using simple phrases or short sentences. Additionally, daily activities that include singing, talking, and word games provide help. Listening activities such as stories read by the adult or on a tape or CD allow children to hear the use of correct language. Above all, adults should listen and respond to children's attempts at communication.

Aggressive Behavior

Description. In preschools, teachers often see overly aggressive children who are competitive, hostile, defiant of authority, and combative. They react to situations by hitting, pushing, and kicking. These children strike out at others because of frustration or because of interference from another child. They may also be reacting to tensions in their outside environment which they cannot understand and are unable to talk about. Some children react to the increasing amount of violence portrayed on television or in films.

Teaching methods. Before deciding upon a strategy for dealing with these behaviors, it is important for the teacher to observe and document the incidents including what led up to the behavior. Interpretation of the behavior should be done only after a series of documentations. It may then be decided that these children will benefit from individual attention, especially help in verbalizing their feelings. It may also help to make accommodations to the environment allowing more space for activities or providing for individual learning styles. Mary Louise Hemmeter (2007) suggests that a behavior might get worse before it gets better causing teachers to abandon their intervention plan. Hemmeter suggests that consistently implementing a plan will eventually bring about the desired changes. During this time it is important for the directors of a program to support the staff.

Visual Disability

Description. Children who have been diagnosed as having a visual disability may be categorized as either partially sighted or blind. Children who have visual problems may be observed rubbing their eyes, squinting, and blinking. They may also hold objects far away or too close. Their heads may tilt when they try to focus. A few will complain of headaches or dizziness.

Teaching methods. The teacher should provide a variety of materials and activities that require the use of other senses. Children's independent movement in the classroom is fostered by orienting them to where things are and then keeping the arrangement constant. Sometimes other children can be encouraged to help by offering guidance when needed and by stimulating social interactions.

The most important task of a director is to provide a quality, developmentally appropriate program for the children enrolled. It benefits the children by allowing for maximum development and is a good business practice. The school will build a reputation for being a good place for children and their families. That makes it easier to fill the enrollment. Furthermore, staff will probably take greater pride in their jobs, and there will be less staff turnover. All of these advantages are worth the time and effort it takes to work with staff to create a good program.

Space: General Considerations

REALITY

Every director and probably most teachers have a picture of the ideal school. It has lots of open space with rooms that are clean and bright. Each room has a bathroom and sinks with hot and cold running water. Spaces exist where teachers can relax and prepare materials. Other space is available to provide privacy for parents and staff to talk. For most, that is just a dream.

The reality is that most directors and staff find themselves in a space that has either been planned by someone else or that has been used for another purpose. That space has to be adapted to fit their school's requirements. In an existing school, the kinds of changes that can be made may be limited. Renovating a residence or commercial building may be costly. So the ideal school always has to be weighed against what is possible and the demands of the budget.

Drastic changes in an existing school, where rooms and supporting space have already been designated, may be impossible. However, changes within rooms or using rooms for new purposes may be feasible. The director should start by asking the teachers to make detailed plans of their indoor and outdoor space. The plans should locate indoor electrical outlets, doors, windows, and any fixed objects. Outdoors, they should include placement of trees, walkways, and gates. In a series of meetings, the staff can consider ways their space can be changed, keeping in mind the considerations listed in the following sections.

A director who is starting a school in a space that has been used for another purpose will have to visualize how the space can be divided. Adding or removing walls, bathrooms, or doors may be possible. To minimize the cost, it is important to get as much information as possible before deciding on a final plan. The director should visit other schools to see how they utilize space, talk to other directors, refer to child-development textbooks that deal with planning space, and consult an architect.

REGULATIONS

The director should check licensing requirements for any regulations that might affect plans for the environment of the program. There will probably be statements regarding the amount of space per child, the number of bathrooms, space for isolating sick children, and areas for adults. There may also be specifications for outdoor fences and the kinds of surfacing used.

City departments may also have regulations governing child-care facilities. Building codes may specify the kinds of changes that can be made to indoor space. Health departments may have requirements for storage of food or cleaning supplies. The fire department may require firewalls and doors.

GOALS AND OBJECTIVES

Both indoor and outdoor space should reflect the goals of the school. The director and staff should examine the basic educational purposes of the program and consider ways in which they can be furthered through a planned environment.

As an example, one of the goals of a program may be to encourage children to take responsibility for themselves and their belongings. There are many ways this can be accomplished, such as the following:

- Cubbies for each child's belongings.
- Areas for performing real tasks such as woodworking and cooking.
- Child-sized tables and chairs.
- Learning centers that require no assistance from adults.
- Faucets and drinking fountains at children's level.

One of the goals might be to encourage children's social skills. If so, space might be provided for the following:

- An area where children work together on a common project.
- A block area that will accommodate a group of children.
- A housekeeping center.
- An art area where several children can work together.
- An outdoor dramatic play area (playhouse, store equipment, gas pumps, and signs).

PROGRAM TYPE

The type of program will have an impact on the overall design of space. An all-day center must provide areas for the physical-care activities that are less important in a half-day school. There must be space for children to eat their meals, take a nap, and care for their physical needs. Few centers have the luxury of a separate room for naps or meals. These functions must be carried out in the same classroom where all other activities take place. If meals are served, there must be enough space to seat each child comfortably. Having additional small tables so that children can serve themselves buffet style or clean up their dishes when finished is helpful. Cots must be stored in a manner that makes it easy to take them out when needed. Bathrooms need places for children's toothbrushes and washcloths.

An all-day school should plan areas where children can be alone. The stimulation of being in a group for long hours during a day can be stressful for some children. They need a quiet place where they can be by themselves or where they can work individually.

A parent cooperative or a laboratory school must consider a place for adults as well as for children. Rooms have to be large enough to accommodate the adults who participate during the course of the day. A laboratory school will be enhanced by the addition of an observation room and a place where students and instructors can meet.

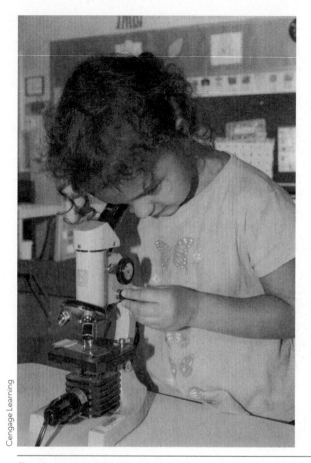

Cengage Learning

The environment is planned for independence.

AGE APPROPRIATENESS

Environments should be appropriate to the age level of the children who will use them. Very young children have different requirements than do older children. For instance, two-year-olds seem to feel more secure if their indoor and outdoor space is not too large or does not have too much equipment. On the other hand, four-year-olds need lots of space for strenuous physical activities. They need places to ride their tricycles, climb, and run.

If the age level is mixed, the problem is a little more difficult. The environment must provide challenges for the oldest children while still being safe for the youngest. In this kind of setting, equipment should be changeable and movable. Indoors, there should be enclosed spaces with partitions for some of the youngest children. Children need places to play on the floor rather than always at tables. Outdoors, the use of movable barriers will allow some children more active play while protecting the younger ones. Equipment such as boxes, boards, tires, and inner tubes can be used by many different age groups.

TRAFFIC FLOW

When planning space, the director should consider traffic flow. This includes examining where doors are placed and imagining the ways children and adults are likely to move through the room to enter and exit. Next, the director must decide whether to allow direct access or to divert the flow somewhat. Large pieces of furniture or equipment will change the way people move from one place to another.

Furniture can be placed so that activities are not interrupted by children moving about the room. A reading corner can provide a cozy place for quiet contemplation if others are not tramping through it. A block area will be used more extensively if buildings that the children make are protected from traffic paths.

The director must consider the safety of children when planning the placement of outdoor equipment. Children are more active outside, running or riding their bikes. They can be oblivious to possible safety hazards, so swings and climbing equipment should be placed away from the traffic flow. It is important to check licensing regulations because some states prohibit swings in child-care centers. Interesting walkways will invite children to explore their environment on foot or on bikes. A path with a slight incline or a bridge is much more enticing than a straight, flat one.

NOISE LEVEL

A room full of preschoolers can get pretty noisy at times, causing tension and irritation to both adults and children. When planning space, the noise levels of different activities must be considered. It is best not to have two adjacent noisy activities. Block play and dramatic play are examples. They should be separated into different areas of the room. Sound-absorbing materials such as carpeting, drapery, and acoustical tiles will help to modify sound level.

Noisy activities should be separate from those that require the children to pay attention and concentrate. Science activities should take place in a quiet area of the room. A reading or music area may be enclosed with shelves or cupboards. A quiet area might also be designed into a structure within the room. For instance, some schools build a loft

Cengage Learning

Learning centers allow children to explore.

structure inside. In the upper level, children can play without interruption from activities below. In the lower level, there might be cozy spots where children can be alone.

Outdoors, children need areas where they can run vigorously, jump, or climb. Other areas should accommodate more quiet play with sand, dolls, and materials that can be manipulated. Hills, plants, large boxes, and pieces of equipment can be used to separate these areas.

STORAGE

Adequate storage should be provided in all areas of the school. A central storage area is essential. It should allow for storage of supplies such as paper, paint, and glue. Additionally, there should be room for teaching materials that can be shared by more than one classroom. Boxes that contain special science or math projects can also be placed here. Extra props for dramatic play may also be included. This should be a place where teachers can come to find new materials to enrich their daily classroom activities.

Outdoors, there should be a place to store bikes, sand toys, and other movable equipment at the end of the day. A large outdoor shed, where dramatic play and art materials can be kept, will be a tremendous asset to any school.

Each classroom should have space for curriculum materials. Teachers should have closed cupboards where they can store materials that they take out as needed. Open shelves can be used for materials that children are allowed to get out for themselves. These should be placed close to where the materials will be used. Children will not carry a puzzle across the room to a table. If there is no table nearby, they will use the floor. Often the result is that puzzle pieces get lost.

HARD AND SOFT AREAS

The preschool classroom should include both hard and soft spaces. Children respond to tactile stimuli, so the classroom should have some objects that are soft and pliable to the touch. Rugs, pillows, soft furniture, fingerpaints, and clay are some examples. Kritchevsky, Prescott, and Walling (1977) of Pacific Oaks College studied the effect of both soft and hard environments on children and concluded that soft objects "provide experiences where the environment responds to the child." Children can roll around on a rug, pound clay, and spread fingerpaint. Each object does what the child wants it to do.

In contrast, hard surfaces provide a different kind of experience. Tiled floors, wooden furniture, and asphalt playgrounds tell children that they must do what the environment requires of them. Prescott and her co-authors feel that young children are not ready to abide by that message for long periods of time during the day. She says that, especially in a full-day program, inhibiting children's behavior through a hard environment is fatiguing and will lead to tension.

There should be hard and soft areas outdoors as well. Children need soft areas for playing in sand and water, digging in the dirt, or gardening. Wood chips and grass are another way to provide soft play areas. Cement or asphalt areas are hard surfaces where children can ride bikes, build with blocks, or play ball.

AESTHETIC APPEAL

Play areas for young children should have **aesthetic appeal**. Children may not comment on the appearance of a room, but they do react to a pleasant environment. Soft colors should be used in the classrooms, with well-designed basic furniture. The environment

Cengage Learning

Play areas should be designed with children in mind. Bright colors, eye-level bulletin boards, and low furniture will capture children's attention.

should be simple and uncluttered. Children's eye level is much lower than adults' eye level. Therefore, furniture lines should be low so that children can see over them. Bulletin boards should be at the children's level so that they can see them.

In outdoor play areas, trees, shrubs, and flowers add to the pleasure children get from their environment. Natural woods used in play equipment add another dimension. Surfaces such as grass, dirt, redwood chips, and sand add to the interest of outdoor areas (Wilson, 2002).

DIVERSITY

Earlier in this chapter, the importance of diversity in the early childhood curriculum was discussed. One goal is to introduce children to differences and similarities of ethnic and cultural groups. The second goal is to stress the importance of freeing children from gender stereotyping and preventing the development of biased attitudes toward persons who are differently abled. Activities and materials are suggested to create a diverse curriculum. In addition to the materials, the total environment of an early childhood classroom should reflect an attitude of acceptance of diversity, as well as provide spaces for activities.

Furnishings and equipment in the classroom should include articles from different cultures. Examples are the following:

- A child's chair from Mexico.
- A bedspread from India.
- Tatami mats from Japan.
- A Chinese wok.
- Baskets from Guatemala.

Cengage Learning

Furnishings and equipment in the classroom should include articles from different cultures.

Pictures displayed at activity areas should show the following:

- Persons of different ethnic/racial groups doing everyday tasks.
- A balance of men and women doing jobs both inside and outside the home.
- Images of elderly persons of various backgrounds doing different activities.
- Images of children and their families, showing a variety of configurations and backgrounds.
- Images of differently abled persons from different backgrounds doing work or in recreational activities.

Artwork displayed in the classroom should reflect the culture of the artist.

- Sculpture, wood carvings.
- Woven textiles.
- Ceramics.
- Paintings or prints.
- Folk art objects.

Diversity should be considered in the planning of outdoor areas as well.

FLEXIBILITY

An environment for young children should be flexible, not set in one pattern. Periodically, staff must assess what is happening within that environment and decide whether to change it.

The director should ask the staff to consider how the environment either fosters or deters goals. They might ask themselves the following questions:

- Are children using the environment in ways that are achieving my goals?
- Are children using the environment in ways I had not thought of?
- Are there other ways I can arrange materials or equipment to further my goals?

Teachers can include children in a discussion of the environment. They can talk about the ways the space is being used and any problems that occur, and they can question whether any changes are possible. Some brave teachers have even taken all the furniture out of a room and then asked the children to bring it back in and arrange it. It is certainly worth trying to stimulate new ways of looking at physical space.

Specific Areas

Aside from the general considerations used when planning space, the director and teachers might wish to consider ways to plan for specific activities. Most schools for young children have specific areas for blocks, dramatic play, creative activities, learning, music, and reading. The goals of each school may call for the inclusion of some additional areas.

DRAMATIC PLAY

The dramatic play area is often called the housekeeping center because the first play usually focuses on activities that the children have experienced at home. They cook, put babies to sleep, clean the house, go off to work, and discipline the children. They may talk to each other on the telephone or visit for meals. It is an area where children can role-play being an adult or a baby. They can use small-muscle skills to prepare meals or do cleaning chores. They also have many chances to increase their social skills and language abilities.

As children get older, dramatic play areas may include a doctor's office or hospital. Sometimes a restaurant, fire station, or gas station appears. This kind of play gives them additional opportunities to role-play jobs and situations they have witnessed. Some of the play in these areas mimics situations they have seen on television.

To make dramatic play as satisfying as possible for children, they must have an appropriate setting and adequate props. The teacher should select props to put out at various times to further play already in progress or to stimulate new play.

The setting should:

- be in a place free of traffic interference.
- have enough space for several children.
- include convenient storage space.
- allow some privacy but also allow for adequate supervision.
- be near related activity areas or be large enough so that the play can accommodate more than one dramatic theme (inside and outside the house, bike riding and gas station, cooking and sleeping).

Props for dramatic play can include the following:

For Housekeeping
child-sized furniture (stove, sink, refrigerator, table, chairs, beds, mirror)
dishes, pots and pans, utensils

dolls representing a variety of ethnic groups: African-American, Latino, Asian-Pacific, Native American, Caucasian (dolls can be homemade or bought, but should be reasonably authentic looking)

dolls that are both male and female, with an assortment of appropriate clothing articles

dolls with different kinds of disabilities (bought or homemade)

empty food containers, including some that are typical of specific ethnic groups

food models (plastic fruit or vegetables, meats, breads, eggs)

dress-up clothes for both males and females, and representing both work and play activities

costume jewelry

cleaning equipment (broom, mop, sponge, bucket)

tools that are used outside the house (rake, wrench, wooden hammer, flashlight)

unbreakable mirror at children's eye level

two telephones

tools and equipment used by people with special needs (canes, braces, heavy glasses, crutches, wheelchair, hearing aid)

For Doctor or Hospital

- cot or doll bed, blankets, small pillow.
- stethoscopes.
- white jackets, surgical masks.
- Band-Aids, pill bottles (use small cereal for pills).
- cotton balls, elastic bandages.

For Gas Station

- gas pumps, short hose lengths.
- signs.
- ramp for repair area.
- tools and toolbox (wrench, screwdriver, flashlight).

For Fire Station

- short fire hose lengths (one half–inch hose).
- firefighters' hats.
- firefighters' jackets.
- firefighting tools (plastic hatchet, flashlight).

For Hairdresser

- curlers, hair clips.
- combs, brushes, hand mirror.
- makeup (face powder, lipstick, eyebrow pencil).
- soft whisk.
- electric trimmer (remove cord).
- razor (remove blade).
- cloths for shoulder covers.

The possibilities for dramatic play props are almost endless. Materials should be available as children's interests call for some new accessories to their play. These can be stored in the school's central storage area and shared by all the classrooms.

BLOCK AREA

Teachers often feel that if they had a limited budget to spend on equipment, they would still include a good set of unit blocks. This is because of the versatility of blocks. They can be used in many different ways and by widely divergent age groups. Blocks allow children to develop their fine and gross motor skills while working out problems of replicating their own experiences. Block play encourages the use of social skills as children work toward a common goal. They can learn mathematical concepts as well as increase their understanding of balance, spatial relations, size, and shape.

The setting should include:

- a large enough set of wooden unit blocks to accommodate several children at the same time; arcs, ramps, and cylinders should be included in this set
- shelves that are wide enough to accommodate the largest blocks
- cars, trucks, boats, planes, trains, road signs, and rubber or wooden animals (as needed by children)
- various hats

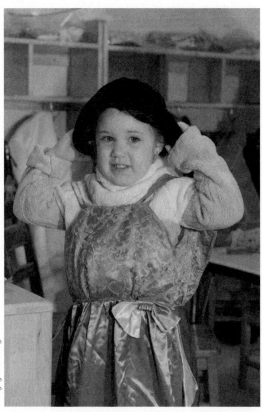

Dramatic play needs the right clothes.

- flat boards, hollow blocks, colored blocks, trees, rocks, and pieces of driftwood
- people, both male and female, from different ethnic groups
- pictures of buildings, freeways, train tracks, boat docks, airports, farms, forests with wild animals, and men and women working at a variety of jobs in order to stimulate ideas
- dollhouse furniture

ART CENTER

The freedom to explore and experiment in an art area affords children an opportunity to develop a variety of skills. Children can acquire fine motor skills as they manipulate paint-brushes, cut with scissors, use a paper punch, or paste small pieces on a collage. They use their whole arms when playing with clay, fingerpaints, or easel paints. This develops large motor skills. Art materials allow children to feel successful at an activity of their own choice and thereby increase their self-image. An art area can be set up so that children work together strengthening their social skills. Some children use creative activities to express their feelings about themselves, their experiences, and their environment. Art experiences help children to develop an appreciation for color and form or, perhaps in a broader sense, beauty.

The setting should include:

- easels and brushes of different sizes
- paints, including tan, brown, and black paint
- crayons that include skin-tone colors
- mirrors so children can look at their own appearance
- paper of different colors, textures, and sizes
- scissors, rulers, paper punch, stapler, tape, and glue
- felt pens and chalk
- collage materials: fabric scraps, ribbons, glitter, beads, wood pieces, wrapping paper, and so on
- Styrofoam™ pieces and toothpicks
- textured materials—sandpaper, rubber, and plastic
- sewing equipment—burlap, tapestry needles, buttons, embroidery hoops, and yarn
- magazine pages, wallpaper pieces, and tissue paper

The teacher should add any other materials of interest to the children. The variety is endless.

MATH AND SCIENCE CENTER

This area should provide children many opportunities to explore and to test their own knowledge or skills. They should be able to increase their vocabulary of mathematical and scientific words. They can learn to count, sort, and classify objects. Children can judge and understand size, shape, and texture of objects. They should be able to learn about their physical environment, about matter and energy, and about living things. Activities in this area should provide many opportunities for children to use all their senses to consolidate their learning.

Cengage Learning

A child explores with art materials.

A math and science center can be set up in two ways. It can be arranged at a table so that several children can work at the same time on separate projects or together on a single project. It can also be placed in an area where children can work alone. Either way, it is important to place this center in a place where the children will not be distracted by noisy or active play from others. Some science projects may require the use of electricity, which further dictates where the center should be located.

The teacher should plan carefully how a science table or individual workplace will be set up. The use of large trays is one way to delineate each work space. If the setup is attractive, children will be motivated to explore this area. The arrangement should tell children what to do with the materials.

The setting should include:

- materials for counting, sorting, weighing, and measuring (beads, beans, small blocks, wood shapes, pegs and pegboard, empty egg cartons, measuring cups)
- scales, a magnifying glass, color paddles, a thermometer, a prism, and magnets
- growing plants and animals
- large numbers and letters of varied textures (sandpaper, cardboard, felt)
- collections of birds' nests, eggs, insects, feathers, shells, rocks, and crystals
- small pets such as a fish, hamster, or gerbil
- pictures and books on science-related topics
- books that require counting objects

As with each of the areas described here, the variety of materials that can be included are not limited to those listed here. Many different kinds of materials can be used for counting, weighing, and measuring. The physical world provides countless objects and ideas for exploration.

Cengage Learning

Carefully planned math and science tables will motivate children to learn.

READING AND WRITING CENTER

This area should provide opportunities for children to acquire skills they will need to read and write. That includes an appreciation of books, the development of language skills, and the improvement of fine motor skills. Activities in this area should also help children to develop the ability to put events in proper order and to relate a story from beginning to end.

The setting should include a selection of storybooks that:

- reflect diversity of racial and cultural backgrounds, ages, gender roles, and physical abilities
- show people of all groups working at daily tasks
- show different lifestyles based on income level or family configurations
- reflect different languages (alphabet books, stories in different spoken languages, stories in Braille, or stories in sign language)

The setting should also include:

- large picture-card stories reflecting diversity
- a puppet stage and puppets (both male and female, of different ethnic groups, and some with special needs)
- a tape recorder or CD player and recorded stories (earphones for individual listening are recommended)
- soft places to sit as well as a small table and chair for writing
- writing materials (pencils, felt pens, and paper of different sizes and colors)
- feltboard stories and a feltboard

MUSIC AND LISTENING CENTER

The purpose of this center is to encourage children to listen for information and for enjoyment. Activities should increase their language skills as well. Children should have opportunities to create rhythms and their own dance movements.

The setting should include:

- a CD player and CDs, including music that reflects different cultures
- musical instruments, both homemade and commercial, including some that are typical of different cultures
- pictures of instruments and musical games

CIRCLE AND GAME CENTER

There are times during each day when most teachers schedule an activity involving all the children. Conversations can take place and children can share experiences. Group lessons can be given or plans can be made for future activities.

This setting should include:

- a quiet comfortable area, large enough for all the children
- carpet or another soft surface for sitting
- a bulletin board and flannelboards
- freedom from other distracting materials

COOKING CENTER

Cooking can be seen as a science activity, but it also incorporates many other learning opportunities; therefore, it is treated here as a separate center. Young children enjoy the real tasks involved in preparing their own snacks or meals. While doing so, they have an opportunity to use real tools, playing a role they have observed many times. Additionally, cooking gives them a chance to see how matter changes under different circumstances. Social skills develop as children wait their turn or share tasks with others. Cooking activities can also provide children with some basic information about where food comes from and about nutrition.

This center should include:

- a table—the number of children at this center can be limited by the size of the table
- an electrical outlet—the table should be placed so that children will not trip on the cord
- a portable oven, frying pan, ice-cream maker, popcorn popper, blender, mixer, and food processor
- mixing bowls, spoons, measuring cups, and knives—children can safely use short serrated knives with rounded ends
- large trays, cutting boards, and baking pans
- recipe picture books, flip-card recipes, and pictures of food and food products
- sponges, buckets, and soap for cleaning up
- aprons for children—for especially messy projects

COMPUTER CENTER

Computers can be used as another learning center in a preschool classroom. They should not replace the concrete, hands-on kinds of experiences, but they can supplement and reinforce learning activities. The key is in choosing appropriate software to achieve the goal the teacher has in mind. Some programs allow a great deal of creativity and imagination, while others are designed to teach specific, limited skills.

Certain computer tasks may be appropriate for preschoolers. They can use the direction keys, joysticks, or a mouse to move objects right, left, up, and down to solidify their sense of direction. They can compare and match objects or discriminate between them. They can create shapes and then change them. Some programs require problem-solving skills or memory. They can play games that test their hand–eye coordination or the speed of their reactions. Programs like Logo allow children to assemble their own figures on the screen, then move them in any direction.

Aside from the physical and cognitive skills that computer use can develop, there are some emotional and social benefits. Children will often stay at a computer center for long periods of time, exhibiting a high level of motivation. They obviously enjoy the sense of control over this adult tool. Computers can become a drawing point for social interaction among children. This social interaction leads to acquisition of new words and increases in language ability almost as a by-product.

This setting should:

- be in an area away from light sources that will reflect off the monitor screen
- be in an area away from heat, dust, and magnetic fields created by television monitors, telephone, and vacuums
- be placed on a static-resistant mat if the area is carpeted
- contain a child-sized table with at least two chairs
- include a central processing unit, a monitor, and either a keyboard, mouse, or joystick
- be near an electrical outlet and include a power strip (a multi-outlet strip that includes a surge suppressor to protect from surges of electrical power)
- be placed so that the on/off switch is easily reached
- have pictorial labels on switches and disk drives showing the sequence of actions to be followed. (Including a chart of the sequence of steps may be helpful.)
- include a place to store and display software conveniently (Software programs should be labeled with a picture for children who cannot read the name.)

OUTDOOR SPACE

Outdoor space should be planned as carefully as indoor areas. Outdoor time should allow children to explore freely and to experience the sights, sounds, and smells of the outdoors. They should be able to run, jump, climb, swing, and ride bikes. Additionally, the outdoors can stimulate new kinds of dramatic play incorporating widely separated areas. The drama can move between the playhouse, the bike-riding area, and the sandbox. Some educators (Henniger, 1994) even believe that outdoor play should allow children to take healthy risks as they try to master progressively more difficult physical tasks.

Most playgrounds typically include permanent equipment such as swings, slides, a jungle gym, and a sandbox. These are certainly well used by children, but children lose interest in them after awhile, or their play themes may remain static. They also do not provide children with new challenges to their physical abilities. The following list contains suggestions for making the playground an exciting place for children to play. The setting should include:

- pathways for running or bike riding
- clearly defined areas for each activity
- different surfaces: sand, grass, cement, dirt, and wood chips
- shaded and sunny areas
- hilly areas and flat surfaces
- natural areas for trees, bushes, and plants
- large boulders or logs for climbing on
- an easily accessible source of water and a drinking fountain
- a sandbox with storage for sand toys
- spaces for woodworking, art activities, and dramatic play

Equipment should include:

- a multilevel climbing structure
- accessories for the climbing structure: boards with cleats, a rigid ladder, a rope ladder, and a pulley
- innovative additions to basic equipment: tires, inner tubes, plastic-covered pillows, planks, sawhorses, large boxes, and a hammock

Cengage Learning

Outdoor time should allow children to explore freely and to experience the sights, sounds, and smells of the outdoors.

- items that can be used for dramatic play: hoses, signs, hats, tools, and house-keeping furniture
- prop sets collected in crates or boxes: gardening tools, house painting materials, and transportation toys
- a collection of different sizes and kinds of balls
- tricycles, wagons, and scooters
- storage areas for outdoor equipment

Adaptations for Children with Special Needs

Many early childhood centers now incorporate children with special needs into regular classrooms. More will do so in the future. Some adaptations to the environment must be made to accommodate these children. The safety of the children should be of primary concern to those planning an environment that includes children with special needs. There should also be every attempt to remove any barriers that prevent the children from participating as fully as possible in all the school's activities. The following list provides some ideas. Refer to the reading list at the end of this chapter if you wish to obtain further information.

Indoor Adaptations
Build ramps into the room and out to the playground.

Widen doors to 32 inches or install offset hinges.

Remove any barriers to free movement around the room, especially for children in wheelchairs.

Install grab bars beside toilets.

Provide easy access to cubbies from a wheelchair—position them at proper height for a seated child.

Install a smoke alarm with a flashing light.

Store materials where they can be easily seen or reached.

Label areas in Braille, with different textures of fabric, or with pictures.

Set up areas in such a way that children easily recognize the routine—place bright aprons at the entrance to the art area to remind children to put them on before painting.

Provide easels, tables, and a water table that can accommodate a child in a wheelchair.

Purchase wheeled equipment (**scooter boards,** wagons) for children who navigate by crawling.

Provide adaptive equipment that assists children to stand.

Display books on slanted shelves or hanging in clear plastic pockets—more easily read by children with visual disabilities.

Build a low platform or use futons or low couches in the reading area—children on scooter boards or in motorized carts can easily move to them for comfortable reading.

Provide tabletop easels for children who wish to read seated in their wheelchair.

Secure any loose rugs or use carpet and nonskid floor covering.

Purchase an overhead projector for enlarging pictures.

Outdoor Adaptations

Provide wheelchair-accessible pathways from one area to another.

Build a table-high sandbox.

Place extra railings and handles on climbing equipment.

Provide bucket seats with safety belts on swings.

Include grassy areas where children who use wheelchairs can be out of their chairs and feel the grass.

Include plants that have a fragrance and bamboo or trees that make sounds in the wind.

Delineate pathways with low-growing plants that have interesting textures.

Include plants that attract butterflies or birds.

Use planter boxes or containers for vegetable gardens.

The environment "tells" both children and adults how to behave there. To have a well-functioning, effective program with reasonably content inhabitants, it is important to start with a well-planned physical plant. Directors should assess it periodically to determine whether it continues to meet expectations. If not, it should be changed.

The physical space, equipment, and materials of the school are the most important assets. Visitors notice and assess the environment long before they understand the intricacies of the curriculum or the skill of the staff. An environment that is as attractive as possible will help to convey what the program is about.

Cengage Learning

Children enjoy playing on swings.

CASE STUDY

Maria teaches in a new center that is part of a corporate child-care chain. She is assigned to a classroom of 11 three-year-olds. The children seem to be particularly interested in the new outside play equipment.

Maria enjoys watching the children explore their new environment, but is experiencing some anxiety about the almost daily accidents on the large, colorful, twisting slide. The most recent occurred when Miguel started down before Mary was finished. They bumped together but were not hurt. A more serious accident occurred when Aimee fell from the top and landed on the wood chips covering the ground below. The director of the program purchased the slide from a large child care–equipment distributor, and it was very costly. She justified the expense feeling that it would clearly be a selling feature for parents and it could be used in the after–school program in the late afternoon.

1.　How can directors and teachers determine whether equipment is age appropriate?
2.　How should Maria communicate to the director her concerns about the slide?
3.　What can Maria do to see that the equipment is safe for the children in her group?

SUMMARY

The best early childhood centers provide developmentally appropriate experiences that are based on knowledge of the capabilities and interests of most children. Several changes take place in children during the preschool years. The body changes size and shape, and the brain reaches 90 percent of its full weight. Play changes as children choose playmates and develop their interests. Children also try to define their self-concept, and they change the ways they think.

There are 11 components of a developmentally appropriate program, ranging from group size to parent involvement. The ideal environment for an early childhood center is one in which children feel calm, competent, and cooperative. Physical space in most facilities is subject to licensing regulations, but also must be commensurate with the goals of the program. Additional considerations when planning space include providing various areas and surfaces and setting aside special areas for some activities. Outdoor space should be planned as carefully as indoor space. It should include pathways, water, areas for specific activities, hilly and flat sections, basic equipment, and storage facilities.

If children with special needs are included in a program, adaptations to the environment must be made. Safety of the children is of primary concern and every attempt should be made to allow them to participate as fully as possible in all of the school's activities, both indoors and outdoors.

STUDENT ACTIVITIES

1.　Visit a preschool. Observe a play area for at least half an hour. Observe the activities of two boys and two girls. Guess their ages as either three or four and write down what they do. Try to find a common thread of behavior. Confirm their ages with the teacher.
2.　Collect several lesson plans. Analyze each to find whether they agree with the developmental level of the children for whom they are written.
3.　Plan a playground for a group of three-year-olds. Draw the plans, placing all equipment in appropriate places. Indicate any movable or changeable equipment.

4. Examine the outdoor environment of a center. List the ways it would have to be changed to meet the needs of children who use wheelchairs or children who are blind.

REVIEW

1. What is meant by the term developmentally appropriate practice?
2. Unless preventive measures are taken, the accident rate among preschool children can be high. Why?
3. As children develop language skills, they sometimes apply rules of grammar incorrectly. Indicate how children might handle the following tasks:
   a. change go to past tense
   b. make goose plural
4. What is the maximum group size for preschool children recommended by NAEYC?
5. NAEYC recommends that staff provide materials and activities that help children achieve specific goals. List the goals.
6. What factors affect achievement of an ideal physical setting for young children?
7. How are space requirements of an all-day program different from one that is in session only four hours each day?
8. Give some examples of how pictures can be used in the environment to convey attitudes toward diversity.
9. List props that can be added to a dramatic play area to expand children's awareness and acceptance of diversity.
10. Describe a cooking center for a group of three-year-olds.

REFERENCES

Clements, D. H. (1993). The uniqueness of the computer as a learning tool: Insights from research and practice. In J. L. Wright & D. D. Shak (Eds.). *Young children: Active learners in a technological age,* (pp. 31–50). Washington, DC: National Association for the Education of Young Children.

Clements, D. H., Nastasi, B. K., & Swaminathan, S. (1993). Young children and computers: Crossroads and directions from research. *Young Children, 48*(2), 56–64.

Demmeter, M. L. (2007). We are all in this together: Supporting children's social emotional development and addressing challenging behavior. *Exchange,* November 2007, 32–35.

Derman-Sparks, L. (1989). *Anti-bias curriculum tools for empowering young children.* Washington, DC: National Association for the Education of Young Children.

Eaton, M. (1997). Positive discipline: Fostering self-esteem of young children. *Young Children, 53*(6), 43–46.

Haugland, S. W. (1992). The effect of computer software on preschool children's developmental gains. *Journal of Computing in Childhood Education, 3*(1), 15–30.

Henniger, M. L. (1994). Planning for outdoor play. *Young Children, 49*(4), 10–15.

Jones, S., Smith, L., & Landau, B. (1991). Object properties and knowledge in early lexical learning. *Child Development, 62,* 499–516.

Kallista, M. (2005). *Play culture in a changing world.* McGraw-Hill, Open University Press.

Kritchevsky, S., Prescott, E., & Walling, L. (1977). *Planning environments for young children: Physical space* (2nd ed.). Washington, DC: National Association for the Education of Young Children.

Morgan, N. (2007). *Successful language development strategies in the early childhood classroom.* St. Paul, MN: Redleaf Press.

Nelson, J., Lott, L., & Glenn, S. (1993). *Positive discipline: A to Z.* Rocklin, CA: Prima.

Powlishta, K. (1995). Research in review: Gender segregation among children. *Young Children, 50*(4), 61–69.

Shade, D. D., & Watson, J. A. (1990). Computers in early education: Issues put to rest, theoretical links to sound practice, and the potential contribution of microworlds. *Journal of Educational Computing Research, 6*(4), 375–92.

Wilson, R. (2002). Nature and young children: Encouraging creative play & learning in natural environments. NY: Routledge.

Wight, V. R., & Chau, M., (2009). *Basic Facts About Low Income Children,* New York, Columbia University, National Center for Children In Poverty.

Wolery, M., & Wilbers, J. S. (Eds.). (1994). *Including children with special needs in early childhood programs.* Washington, DC: National Association for the Education of Young Children.

SELECTED FURTHER READING

Bunnett, R., & Kroll, D. (2000). Transforming spaces: Rethinking the possibilities. *Child Care Information Exchange, 131,* 26–19.

Caesar, B. (2001). Give children a place to explore. *Child Care Information Exchange, 138,* 76–80.

Curtis, D., & Carter, M. (2005). Rethinking early childhood environments to enhance learning. *Young Children, 60*(3), 34–38.

Delaney, E. (2001). The administrator's role in making inclusion work. *Childhood Education, 56*(5), 66–70.

Frawley, R. (2005). Gender bias in the classroom. *Childhood Education, 81*(4), 221–227.

Geist, E., & Baum, A. C. (2005). Yeah, but's that keep teachers from embracing an active curriculum. Overcoming the resistance. *Young Children, 60*(4), 28–36.

Haugen, K. (1997). Using your senses to adapt environments: Checklist for an accessible environment. In Beginnings Workshop, "Environments for Special Needs." *Child Care Information Exchange, 3,* 50–56.

Louv, R. (2005). *The last child in the woods; Saving our children from nature-deficit disorder.* Chapel Hill, NC: Algonquin Books.

Nabhan, G. P., & Trimble, S. (1994). *The geography of childhood. Why children need wild places.* Boston: Beacon Press.

NAEYC. (1993). *A position statement on violence in the lives of children.* Washington, DC: National Association for the Education of Young Children.

Rivkin, M. S. (1995). *The great outdoors: Restoring children's right to play outside.* Washington, DC: National Association for the Education of Young Children.

Schoen, T. M., Auen, J., & Arvantis, M. (1997). Children blossom in general education integration plan: A private child care center and a public school collaborate. *Young Children, 52*(2), 58–63.

Stoecklin, V. L. (2005). Creating environments that sustain children, staff, and our planet. *Child Care Information Exchange, 164,* 39–49.

HELPFUL WEBSITES

Disclaimer: Links to Internet sites throughout this book are provided for your convenience and do not constitute an endorsement.

American Academy of Pediatrics (data for optimal physical, mental, and social health of all children):	**http://www.aap.org**
National Network for Child Care (publications and resources relating to child care, support, and assistance from experts):	**http://www.nncc.org**

For additional resources related to administration including videos, links to related sites for each chapter of the text, tutorial quizzes, glossary flashcards, and more, visit the Education CourseMate website for this book at www.cengage.com/login.

Cengage Learning

Planning: School–Age Children

Objectives

After reading this chapter, you should be able to:

- Describe children's development between the ages of 5 and 12.
- List the components of a developmentally appropriate program for older children.
- Describe the characteristics of a **caregiver** for school-age children.

KEY TERMS

adventure play areas

caregiver

clique

code–switching

industry versus inferiority

multipurpose equipment

peers

A day in the life of . . .

A Director of a Church-Affiliated School

We recently added a terrarium containing three newts to our science center. The teachers and children debated a long time before coming up with the names: Sir Isaac Newt, Wayne Newt, and Fig Newt.

Parents and professionals sometimes refer to the middle childhood years as a period of relative quiet between the difficulties of the early years and the storms of adolescence. Changes take place, but they seem to proceed more smoothly than during earlier or later times. Physical growth slows down, cognitive development helps children to learn quickly, and social development allows them to relate easily to their peers and teachers. However, some children have problems as they pass through this stage.

Those who lack physical skills, those who are not successful in school, or those who have difficulty making friends may pass into adolescence with feelings of inferiority or rejection that will affect them the rest of their lives. Before- and after-school programs can help children meet the challenges they face during middle childhood, but this requires knowledge of the developmental stages during that time span. This chapter gives an overview of development during the years between 5 and 12, which can be used as a guide for planning a program for school-age children.

School-Age Children

In contrast to the rapid growth spurts of the preschool period, growth in middle childhood children occurs more slowly. The next rapid change does not take place until the approach of adolescence. However, observe children on any elementary school playground and there are wide variations in height and weight. Heredity accounts for some of the differences, but nutrition is also a factor. The different growth rates between boys and girls also cause variation. Girls grow faster and are often noticeably taller than boys during part of this stage. However, girls stop growing earlier than boys, and by adolescence the boys catch up and soon surpass the girls.

Motor abilities develop rapidly during middle childhood, and both boys and girls are usually equal at most tasks. However, there are some differences. Girls develop small-muscle control earlier than boys and, thus, are more adept at writing tasks. Boys have greater forearm strength and may do better at sports like baseball. Girls seem to excel at gymnastics. However, neither sex nor body size is as important as experience. These children need to be active, and both boys and girls benefit from practice. When they have ample opportunities to perfect their skills, differences between the genders lessen.

During middle childhood, children's cognitive development allows them to be much more aware of others than during the previous years. Therefore, any differences in appearance are noted as they judge themselves and others. Children who are obese often are teased or rejected. Early- or late-maturing youngsters may feel they do not belong. Many sixth-grade girls already have maturing breasts, and some even begin their menstrual cycles. These girls may suffer because they contrast themselves to their peers and are embarrassed by menstruation. Late-maturing boys also have difficulty. They compare themselves with boys who are beginning to show signs of puberty, such as facial or pubic hair and greater height. They worry that they will never catch up to their peers in appearance.

LANGUAGE

During the preschool years, children's vocabulary, grammar, and pragmatic language skills develop rapidly. By the time they reach middle childhood, they are ready to use language in new ways. They enjoy experimenting with words and use them as the subject of jokes, changing words around or playing with the ambiguity of words. They test the power that certain words have to evoke reactions in others by using slang or profanity. Groups of children coin their own words. Those who use the words are accepted as part of the group, and those who do not are excluded. During this period, children also learn to use words to achieve more positive ends. They learn to express feelings and to resolve conflicts through discussions.

Middle childhood youngsters are adept at changing between forms of speech, a process called **code-switching**. When they talk to their parents, for instance, they omit profanity or the words used by their peer group. The most obvious example of code-switching occurs when children use one form of speech in the classroom and another when they are on the playground with their friends. When addressing the teacher, they use complete sentences, attempt to speak grammatically, and eliminate slang. On the playground they lapse into "street" talk, "Black English," or include words specific to their own native languages.

FYI

Children in kindergarten through eighth grade are in the following group child-care settings:

61 percent in school- or center-based programs at a public school

9 percent in a church or other place of worship

10 percent in private schools

8 percent in community centers

SOURCE: National Center for Education Statistics. Retrieved from http://nces.ed.gov/pubs 2006/no newer information available afterschool/01.asp. December 2006.

THINKING

Children's cognitive abilities change dramatically during the period between ages five and seven. They have a good memory for concrete ideas and can remember facts and events. They are able to sustain interest in an activity over a long period of time, enabling them to plan ahead and postpone the achievement of a goal until a future time. They are sometimes able to apply logic to practical situations and can give thought and judgment to decisions or problems. They weigh cause and effect, consider alternatives, and choose appropriate actions or solutions.

One change that is particularly important in a child-care setting is children's increasing ability to understand and abide by rules. At age five or six, they begin to accept that rules are for everyone, that rules are guidelines for play, and that rules must be followed. This comprehension allows them to engage in organized sports and games, activities that were difficult or impossible a year or so earlier. However, not all five- or six-year-olds will be ready to play by the rules. Some will still need flexibility when they engage in organized activities.

INDEPENDENCE

Middle childhood brings about children's greater independence from their families. They spend a large portion of their days outside the home, either at school, in child care, in neighborhood parks, or on the streets. In doing so, they broaden their horizons, encountering new people and new ways of life. They form clubs, **cliques,** or "gangs" to strengthen bonds with their peers and to free themselves from adult supervision. They feel more secure as part of a group while they learn how to find their own way in the world outside their families.

However, the groups often impose their own rigid standards on their members. Each group has its own social codes, its own games, and its distinct manner of dress. To be a member of the "in" group, members must adhere strictly to the rules. Those who follow the group rules have a sense of belonging. Others are left out and subsequently suffer. The group influence is powerful and can induce children to engage in behaviors they would not attempt by themselves. This can be a positive influence, encouraging children to develop new skills and gain new experiences. However, sometimes the behaviors encouraged by the group are socially unacceptable ones such as shoplifting, smoking, or drinking. In the case of gangs, encouraged behaviors may include some that are more dangerous.

PEERS

Friends are extremely important to school-age children. Although they still depend on parents for some kinds of support, they begin to rely more heavily on their **peers**. Their self-esteem is closely related to how their peers perceive them. If other children like them and seek them out, they feel good about themselves. Friends also provide a sounding board for weighing parental values, deciding which to keep and which to discard. A good friend can help with the emotional ups and downs of development. Being able to talk to a friend about one's worries and fears is comforting, as is finding that others have similar feelings.

Children tend to seek out friends who are like themselves in regard to age, sex, race, socioeconomic status, and interests. Friendships are intense and usually last for many years. Many children, especially girls, acquire one "best friend" on whom they depend a great deal while they negotiate new experiences and environments. Temporary setbacks in the friendship, or its dissolution, may cause severe suffering in some children.

SKILLS

Erik Erikson called middle childhood the stage of **industry versus inferiority.** During this period, children acquire the skills they will need as adults in their particular environment or culture. Children acquire many of these skills in school, so curriculum planners try to predict what children will need as future workers. Consequently, today's children not only learn to read, write, and compute; they also learn about complex technology. In addition to work-related skills, children need to learn practical, everyday skills: how to use tools, how to build and repair objects, how to cook, and how to care for babies or animals. Previously, parents taught children to perform these tasks. Currently, as more children spend their out-of-school hours in child care, those kinds of experiences need to be included in group programs.

Children also need to develop social skills such as helping, cooperating, negotiating, and talking to others to resolve problems. Group settings are ideal situations to learn new ways of interacting with others. Caregivers can help children through difficult encounters with individuals or can plan specific activities to enhance social skills.

SELF-ESTEEM

The most important key to success and happiness is a positive self-concept. As children pass the preschool period, they begin to develop theories about who they are. These ideas change based on a combination of past experiences, the opinion of others, and, as yet, untested assumptions about themselves. Past experiences with success contribute to a positive self-image, while failures can add to a lack of self-worth. Children who perform well in school or are competent at other activities such as sports, music, or art feel good about themselves. When peers, parents, or teachers praise or reward them for their achievements, their esteem is boosted. Moreover, children test their assumptions about themselves. They look at themselves with greater cognitive awareness and become more accurate in assessing which assumptions are true. As an example, some children will say, "I know I am not very good at math, but I'm getting pretty good at music."

Children look to role models to help them shape their own identity. During the preschool period, children model their behavior after the people closest to them, their immediate family members. In middle childhood, they can choose from a broader circle of role models. Although they continue to imitate some of the behaviors they see at home,

Cengage Learning

Children need time and a place to do homework.

they can now take on the characteristics of friends, teachers, or caregivers. They may also admire and try to emulate the people they see on television or in films. Sometimes family cultural values conflict with the other role models in children's environments.

Characteristics of a Developmentally Appropriate Program

GOALS

The National Association for the Education of Young Children (NAEYC) has developed guidelines for appropriate practices in primary grades (Bredekamp & Copple, 1997). Although those guidelines are written as curriculum goals for academic programs, they are still pertinent to before- and after-school programs. They state that appropriate practices should be:

- designed to develop children's knowledge and skills in all developmental areas—physical, social, emotional, and cognitive.
- designed to develop children's self-esteem, sense of competence, and positive feelings toward learning.
- responsive to individual differences in ability and interests.

Bredekamp (1987) discussed two components of developmental appropriateness: age appropriateness and individual appropriateness. The first refers to knowledge of universal, predictable growth and changes in all children. For example, all children go through predictable changes in their motor skills. Similarly, during middle childhood children predictably strive to achieve independence.

The second component, individual appropriateness, describes each child's unique patterns and timing of growth. Although all children go through similar changes, each may do so at very disparate times. Two children of the same age can vary tremendously in appearance, abilities, use of language, and thinking processes. Two school-age children can look very different. One might be tall, having already gone through a growth spurt. Another may be much smaller, still having the appearance of a much younger child. Children may vary in their ability to think through problems logically. One child may be able to resolve a problem by imagining the solution, while another is still dependent upon concrete objects. A developmentally appropriate program must address both components to meet the needs of all children.

Albrecht and Plantz (2008) provided guidelines for developmentally appropriate practice in school-age programs. They were guided by input from child-care experts and also reviewed research studies on the development of school-age children. They recommend that the child-care schedule offer a change of pace from the school day. Each day should have some structured time in which the whole group meets together. Project Home Safe guidelines also suggest that schedules be flexible and that required participation in activities or experiences is limited.

Developmentally appropriate programs should offer children many different ways to enhance their ability to function independently. They also need many opportunities to develop cognitive and physical skills. Friends are important to school-age children, so an after-school program should have times when children can be with one or two special friends. There should also be times when they can enlarge their circle of friends by participating in a group project or in group games. Parents should be kept informed of their child's progress and should be included in special events.

Cengage Learning

Best friends are important during school ages.

PACE

An after-school child-care program for older children must offer a change of pace from the day at school. Children spend long periods of the school day sitting down. They need an opportunity to work off some of their pent-up energies. They should be allowed to actively participate in games or sports or to use outdoor equipment. Each day should have some structured time in which the whole group meets together. Typically, this is at the beginning of the afternoon session. This is a time for discussions, planning, reading a story, or singing together. After the group time, children should be free to choose among the activities that are available.

Some children may want quiet time by themselves, away from the pressure of group activities. They should have places where they can work on an individual project, read, or "just do nothing" for awhile. Some children need a short rest period, occasionally falling asleep. Other children look for an adult to help them make the shift from school to child care. A brief period of time talking with a caregiver allows these children to move into more active participation.

INDEPENDENCE

After-school programs should offer children many different ways to develop their need for independence. A wide variety of materials should always be available so that they can initiate their own activities. Materials for creative activities should be easily accessible. Different kinds of paint, paper, collage materials, fabric, and the like will encourage children to devise interesting art projects. Materials for dressing up can encourage impromptu dramatic play or more planned and structured productions. A CD player, tape player, or various instruments can lead to experimentation with music. Some adults are successful in getting children to do some creative writing.

Participation in planning and decision making also increases children's feelings of independence. For example, children can plan and prepare their own snacks. The director may allow them to decide on snacks for a week, let them make a shopping list, then send them with a caregiver to purchase the supplies. Simple cooking activities can be part of each day's program.

Children should also have opportunities to plan their own program, including special events. They should be able to decide what kinds of activities will be scheduled next week or next month. Children really get involved when they set out to plan a special day for parents or a trip to the zoo or park.

It is important to foster independence by allowing children to resolve their own problems. This means that caregivers should not step in quickly when two children are involved in an altercation unless there is danger that one will get hurt. Encourage children to work out their differences in ways that are satisfying to each of them. When a group has a common problem, caregivers can encourage independence by leading a discussion. The children should clarify the problem, offer solutions, and institute a plan of action.

SKILLS

A developmentally appropriate program will allow many opportunities for the development of skills. Various activities should encourage children to think, reason, experiment, and question. Participating in science activities, classifying collections, and performing magic tricks all further the development of skills. Many games require reading and math. Time should be set aside for children to do homework, with tutors provided as needed.

Activities should fit the age level.

Both individual physical activities and organized sports offer additional ways to develop skills. Some children just want to practice shooting a basketball, for instance, while others need the competition of a game. Some children want to improve their skills by using gymnastics equipment, while others want organized competitions. Opportunities and equipment for both individual and group activities should be present.

Children can develop needed skills when they are involved in planning and maintenance of their play areas. They can learn how to do simple repairs using real tools. They can learn that materials must be put away after use so that they will be available when needed at another time. Sometimes, they will also have to use their problem-solving skills as they perform these tasks. Children should be encouraged to see these as real jobs that they take responsibility for, not just something to occupy their time. Thus, they will increase their sense of independence as they learn the skills involved.

FRIENDS

A quality child-care setting will provide opportunities for children to make friends. Time should be provided when children can choose to participate in an activity with one or two best friends. Children should not use this time to exclude others, rather they should use it to solidify friendships.

There should also be times when caregivers encourage children to include a larger circle of peers in a play activity. These times can be used to emphasize accepting differences and learning to compromise. Activities such as producing a newspaper or putting on a play can draw on the talents of many children. These joint efforts can benefit from the diversity. Group sports are another time when a larger number of children can be included. Those children who feel inadequate at sports may need help to find a place in the game. However, if some children do not want to be involved in competitive sports, their wishes should be respected.

Children should have opportunities to develop friendships with their caregivers. There should be times when adult and child can sit and talk, or times when they can work together at a needed task. Some children miss the comfort that a parent traditionally provided at the end of a school day, and they need to find that same kind of comfort in their child-care worker.

PARENTS

By the time children reach middle childhood, parents do not need to be as closely involved in their child's school and child-care center as in earlier years. However, parents should be kept informed about the child's progress. They need to know that the transition from school to the child-care setting is occurring smoothly. They certainly want to know about the kinds of activities in which their child participates. They want to be included in special events. They also need to know about any signs of illness the child might show during the day.

Program: Activities

The following are some activities most children between 5 and 12 seem to enjoy. Many more activities can be found in curriculum books. Teachers can add their own ideas or ask the children to suggest activities.

Creative Activities

- painting with brushes, hands, string, marbles, sponges.
- clay, play dough, papier-mâché.
- collages from leaves, flowers, fabrics, buttons, ribbons.
- crayon etchings, chalk drawing, textile painting.
- basket making, sewing, knitting, crocheting.
- tie-dyeing, batik.
- puppets, puppet shows.
- making and playing musical instruments.
- painting to music.
- writing a play, making costumes, producing the play.
- dancing to popular, classical, or ethnic music.

Games

- Mother may I?, Simon says, charades.
- tic-tac-toe, memory games, card games, dice games.
- gossip, 20 questions, guess the number.
- jump rope, hopscotch, leapfrog race, obstacle race.

Field Trips

- beach or zoo.
- print shop, computerized office, newspaper.
- local radio or television station.
- artist's studio.
- museum, children's museum.

Science and Math Activities

- care for animals such as fish, bird, gerbil, guinea pig, hamster, kitten, rabbit, snake, lizard, tortoise (Some areas may prohibit one or more animals on this list.).
- cultivate a garden outdoors, keep potted plants indoors.
- collect shells, rocks, fossils.
- experiment with magic.
- chart the weather, make predictions.
- weigh various objects, weigh themselves.
- play table games that require counting.
- cook a snack using a recipe that requires measuring.

Characteristics of Teacher/Caregiver

The adults who care for children in before- and after-school programs have various titles: aides, teachers, assistants, caregivers, leaders, guides, and recreational supervisors. This text uses the term **caregiver** because it implies an essential function of these adults: the ability to provide a caring, nurturing environment for children who must spend their out-of-school hours away from home. Whatever the director chooses to call the staff members hired for the school-age program, they should have certain characteristics. The director should look for people who:

- like being with school-age children.
- are good role models for children to emulate.
- have many interests they can share with children.
- can allow children freedom to be independent, while also setting limits.
- have good communication skills, including the ability to listen.
- enjoy physical activity such as active games or sports.
- care about families and can accept each family's uniqueness.
- understand a caregiver's role: a blending of teacher and parent.
- can work with other staff members as a team.

Beyond these personal characteristics, there are two broad areas of education and experience usually required in school-age child care. Some directors want adults who have completed courses in early childhood education, including human development and curriculum planning. Other directors lean more heavily toward people who have backgrounds in recreation. Those staff members will have taken courses in physical education and may have had experience in supervising playgrounds or working in summer camps. The ideal staff member for a school-age program would have both, but there is an alternative. The staff can be balanced, containing some members with an early childhood education background and others with recreation experience. Including both men and women achieves further balance and provides the children with additional role models.

Space: General Considerations

LICENSING

Just as with infant programs, regulations in some areas may not have caught up with the trend toward adding school-age child care to existing preschools. It is important to check with the state licensing agency to find out whether guidelines exist.

Where school-age regulations have been adopted, several categories may be covered. One may require the separation of older children from younger ones within the preschool setting. Outdoors, this can be accomplished by using low fences, establishing a separate play area, or scheduling use of outdoor space at different times. Indoors, older children should be separated from preschoolers for unstructured play activities. Movable walls and partitions can be used to create separate areas for older and younger children. Each group can use a room at different times. During structured activities, older children and preschoolers can often work together effectively.

Regulations will probably specify toilets with separate stalls for individual privacy, or even separate bathrooms for boys and for girls.

Even in areas where regulations for school-age child care have been adopted, they are likely to be less stringent than for younger children. Older children are less vulnerable to physical hazards than infants and preschoolers. This does not mean that a director should not be concerned. Regulations are minimum standards only, and every center should provide the best possible setting for the children it serves.

GOALS

Goals are the basis for planning all aspects of a facility for young children. School goals must be reviewed before deciding how to plan space in the school-age section. Although the overall goals for the school may include statements that can be applied to the school-age program, there will probably need to be others specific to that age group. Some examples will help to illustrate. Children should be able to:

- sustain cooperative efforts and involvement in activities over a long period of time.
- gain greater control over their bodies through participation in individual activities and organized games.
- develop independence in caring for themselves.

SAFE YET CHALLENGING ENVIRONMENT

The school-age period is a time when children are rapidly developing their physical skills. They are capable of performing almost any motor skill and can challenge themselves and each other to reach higher levels of mastery. Some of this testing can put them into dangerous situations. Picture an eight-year-old walking along the top of a narrow, high wall to test his balance, or an 11-year-old plunging off a ramp on his skateboard. The physical skill that allows children to perform these feats is present; the judgment to assess the danger may be lacking.

Children should be able to test their physical abilities as far as possible in after-school programs, but they should be protected from serious injury while doing so. The child-care center should provide space only for those activities that the children are developmentally capable of performing. Areas for active play should be separated in distance from quieter pursuits. All playground areas and equipment should be inspected and maintained periodically. Children must be taught ways to use equipment safely and must always be closely supervised. Space and opportunity for sewing, knitting, painting, or preparing food should also exist.

HOMELIKE ATMOSPHERE

The setting for after-school child care should be quite different from the typical schoolroom environment. At school, children have to sit on hard chairs at desks or tables. The environment tells them how to behave. In child care, they should be able to sit in soft chairs, lie on a couch, or sprawl on the floor. Therefore, the child-care environment for older children should be more like home than school.

A homelike atmosphere can be accomplished by including some of the following:

- couches or soft, easy chairs
- large pillows, beanbag chairs, soft mats
- appropriately sized tables and chairs
- places to store children's school books, lunch boxes, and jackets
- places to store children's ongoing projects such as stamp collections or woodworking projects
- places to store games children bring from home
- places to be alone—boxes, lofts, tents, screening
- broom, dustpan, bucket, mop, and sponges for cleanup

Cengage Learning

School–age children build on skills.

FLEXIBILITY

Space for school-age children should be flexible and easily modified. Children change over a period of time, so what was suitable in September may not fit their needs in May. Furthermore, the age span in an after-school program may be from 5 to 12 years. Physical space must accommodate the different interests of children at these widely diverse ages. There are many ways to make space flexible such as:

- providing various spaces—large open ones, or small ones designed for specific functions.
- having mobile dividers to create work spaces.
- having plenty of things that can be moved around to create spaces the children can design themselves—boards, crates, large building blocks, ladders, platforms, blankets, tires, and ropes.
- providing various surfaces that can be used for different activities—blacktop, grass, sand, hills, and dirt.
- allowing access to water for sprinkling on hot days, playing in water, gardening, and playing in the sandbox.
- creating spaces for privacy for individuals or small groups—loft, tree house, hammock, or rocking chair.

SIZE

School-age children need furniture and equipment that is appropriate for their size. If they must use a classroom that is used by preschoolers at other times of the day,

Both preschoolers and older children can use this playground.

there should be at least one larger table with proper-sized chairs. Older children can use the table for working on projects, doing homework, or eating snacks. Some areas can be used by both age levels. The preschool classroom may have large pillows or beanbag chairs in a reading area. Older children can use this area as well. Additions for the older children might include a workbench for woodworking and an adjustable easel for painting. Trays or mats can designate places for games or other activities to be done on the floor.

Outdoor equipment should allow for the kinds of activities older children enjoy. Examples include trees to climb, swings, a high jungle gym, and a horizontal ladder. A blacktop area will provide space for organized games.

AESTHETICALLY PLEASING SPACE

Space for all ages should be pleasing to the eye. The color of the walls or furniture, pictures, and interesting objects will make the environment cheerful. Children's artwork should be framed and displayed.

The children will be able to suggest ways to make the environment cheerful. They may wish to paint posters, put up signs, or bring objects from home to add interest and beauty. Where it is possible, they should be allowed to paint a mural on a wall. The most important thing is that the environment should be pleasing to the children.

STORAGE

If storage of equipment is convenient, children will have more time to spend at activities and play. Ample space should exist for the ongoing projects school-age children enjoy. At this age, children have the attention span to work on long-term projects. They like to collect stamps, insects, rocks, shells, and so on. They may start a woodworking project that will take a week or two to finish. They must have safe places to store these materials over days. If they share space with younger children, these cupboards should be secured from interference.

These children should also have a place to put their school belongings—their books, lunch boxes, and jackets.

Specific Areas

QUIET CORNER

After a long day at school, many children need to have a quiet time to "unwind" before being involved again in group activities. Some may want to rest, read, or just sit by them-selves. Others may want to sit quietly and do their homework. Some children will use this space for meetings of "secret clubs" or as a place to talk to a special friend.

This kind of area can be created by providing:

- a corner enclosed by shelves or dividers: furnished with rugs, large pillows, bean-bag chairs, or a sofa.
- an extra space for being alone such as stairways, closets, or offices.
- a book corner with a selection of appropriate books.
- a music corner where a child can listen to music with earphones.
- a properly lit, comfortable table or desks where children can do their homework.

CREATIVE AREAS

Creative materials can provide children with a release from some of the tensions left over after a school day. A variety of materials, along with an adequate place to work, should be available. This area can be furnished with some of the following:

- paint: fingerpaint, tempera, watercolors, brushes of all sizes.
- wide variety of paper: colored, parchment, oatmeal, and so on.
- play dough, clay, papier-mâché.
- crayons, chalk, marking pens.
- colored sand, glue.
- scissors, paper punches, staplers.
- popsicle sticks, coffee stirrers, Styrofoam pieces.
- weaving materials, small looms.
- yarn, knitting needles, crochet hooks, tapestry canvas.
- tissue paper, struts for kite making.
- fabric and materials for tie-dyeing, batik.
- collections of collage materials: wood pieces, fabric, ribbons, beads, shells, rocks.
- fabric markers, puff pens.
- large pieces of fabric for making costumes.

GAMES AND MANIPULATIVES

School-age children enjoy the challenges provided by games, puzzles, and other kinds of manipulative materials. Many of the materials used in the preschool can also be fun for this age level. These activities can take place either at a table or on the floor. Children can get the materials from a shelf and return them when finished. Some things to include in this area are:

- playing cards for games such as concentration, go-fish, war, rummy, hearts, and solitaire.
- board games such as Monopoly™, Scrabble™, Life®, Clue®, checkers, Chinese checkers, jackstraws, bingo, tic-tac-toe, and dominoes.
- marbles and jacks.
- magnetic marbles, magnetic building sets, magnetic designers, and magnetic mazes.
- Legos and Lego™ accessories.
- parquetry-design blocks, and design cards.
- large jigsaw puzzles and small 100- to 500-piece jigsaw puzzles.
- plastic building sets and Tinker Toys™.

WOODWORKING, COOKING

School-age children enjoy the independence that comes from being able to use real tools to perform real tasks. These activities should be set up in an area free from traffic flow and away from any quiet areas. Safety precautions must be taken to ensure that children do not trip on electrical cords or get burned by hot appliances. An adult must explain to the children safety rules for the use of woodworking tools.

A woodworking area should be equipped with:

- a sturdy workbench.
- safety goggles.
- saws, hammers, screwdrivers, drills, pliers, clamps, level, and tape measure.
- a variety of sandpapers, nails, screws, nuts, and bolt.
- sheets of wood, small wood pieces, wooden spools, and wheels.
- varnish, paint, and brushes.

A cooking area should be equipped with:

- a table to work on, either at sitting or standing height.
- pot holders and aprons.
- water and cleaning supplies nearby.
- a variety of cooking tools: mixing and measuring spoons, measuring cups, cookie cutters, graters, and rolling pins.
- a cutting board and knives.
- several sizes of pans and mixing bowls.
- cookie sheets, muffin tins, baking pans, and pots.
- a hand or electric mixer and a blender.
- a popcorn popper, electric frying pan, ice cream maker, small oven, waffle iron, and toaster.
- cookbooks written for children or other cookbooks containing easy-to-prepare recipes.
- a fire extinguisher.

DRAMATIC PLAY

Through dramatic play, children can imitate adult role models, play out their fantasies, or relive childhood experiences. Some children will use dramatic play to relieve stresses they encounter at school or at home. As children in this age range get a little older, they use dramatic play materials for producing their own plays or skits.

A dramatic play area should be equipped with:

- a full-length mirror.
- clothes for dress up and an assortment of hats.
- washable face paint or makeup.
- scarves, jewelry, and plastic or silk flowers.
- a puppet theater and an assortment of puppets.
- a stethoscope, gauze, splints, and Band-Aids™.
- a tool carrier, tools, old shirts, and flashlight.
- theatrical or Halloween costumes and wigs.

BLOCK BUILDING

Children at widely different age levels can use blocks. If the after-school program is housed in a preschool classroom, the children can use the blocks that are already there. The block area should be placed where buildings will not be toppled by other children moving around the room. Having a hard surface to build on is ideal, but children can also build on a carpeted floor. The children can be encouraged to add to the basic materials to create their own play activities.

Some of the things that might be in a block area are:

- wide shelves to hold the blocks: shelves on casters can be moved if needed.
- containers for accessory materials such as dolls, cars, trucks, boats, trains, airplanes, and animals.
- colored blocks, sheets of Masonite™, or thin plywood.
- large hollow blocks and large cardboard blocks.
- giant lock bricks, waffle blocks, and giant Legos.

DISCOVERY CENTER

A discovery center for school-age children should supplement the kinds of learning children are exposed to at school. However, activities should be presented in such a way that children do not feel pressured to participate, but can follow their own interests. This area can promote children's natural curiosity and ability to pursue topics over a period of time.

The discovery area should be equipped with:

- magnets and an electromagnetic kit.
- a simple microscope and a collection of prepared slides.
- magnifying glasses and insect collections.
- an aquarium and books on tropical fish.
- an ant farm.
- a bug house, bug-catching containers, and a butterfly net.
- collections of shells, rocks, and fossils.
- sun-sensitive paper.
- prisms, gyroscopes, and color wheels.
- small animals, cages, and an incubator for hatching eggs.
- seeds, potting soil, and small pots.
- binoculars and bird books.
- a selection of books with project ideas and science information.
- objects to disassemble: clocks, small appliances.

LANGUAGE CENTER

Even though language development is a significant part of the elementary classroom, children can also enjoy participating in this kind of activity in the child-care center. As with the discovery center, there should be no pressure to participate, and the activities should be fun.

Cengage Learning

School-age children can create elaborate block structures.

The language area might include:

- a table and chairs or soft pillows and beanbag chairs
- a selection of books
- stamp pads with letters—both uppercase and lowercase
- poster boards of different colors
- word puzzles, crosswords, and word games such as Scrabble™
- word-matching games, word lotto, and letter dice
- individual chalkboards, chalk, a wipe-off board, and marking pens
- paper, pencils, and pens
- a typewriter

HIGH-TECH CENTER

School-age children enjoy the challenge of operating equipment that is part of contemporary society. They get excited when they can master a computer, use a calculator, or type on a typewriter.

This center could include:

- a table and chairs at a comfortable height
- a computer, a rack for software, bulletin board or manuals with instructions for use, and a printer

- a calculator, paper, and pencils
- a typewriter and paper
- a filmstrip projector and filmstrips

CLUBROOM

During the school-age period, children develop strong relationships with their peers and begin to group themselves according to shared interests. These friendships and interests are fostered through the formation of clubs, allowing groups to pursue topics in depth or sustain an interest over a period of time. Typical topics that appeal to children are photography, calligraphy, ceramics, computers, cooking, magic, collecting (rocks, shells, stamps), dance, drama, ecology, stitchery, space, sports, and woodworking.

A clubroom might include:

- a table and chairs or beanbag chairs and soft pillows
- shelves or a cabinet for storing materials
- a sign and decorations made by the children
- a bulletin board for posting rules, outlining plans, or presenting a display
- specific materials or equipment needed for special interests

SHARING INDOOR SPACE

Not every school has the luxury of having a separate room for school-age children. This group may be required to share space with another age level, or to use space that was designed for another purpose. With a bit of imagination, creating an environment that fits their needs is possible. The following are suggestions for the director and staff:

- Set up interest centers each day. Store all the materials necessary for an activity in large boxes, shoe boxes, baskets, or five-gallon ice cream pails.
- Label each container, and list the materials contained in each.
- Put large casters or wheels on cupboards, bulletin boards, or dividers that can be used to designate activity areas. Label the cupboards according to contents and apply locks.
- Choose furniture with multiple uses. Examples are cupboards with doors that can also be used as bulletin boards or chalkboards.
- Attach hooks to the side of cupboards so that a screen or divider can be attached to create an enclosed space.
- Use large pegboards, framed and mounted on casters, for hanging woodworking tools, art supplies, or cooking equipment.
- Have large pillows or beanbag chairs to create a quiet corner.
- Involve the children in setting up the environment each day or in finding new ways to use the area. They are the ones who will use the space and often have creative ideas about ways to adapt it to their own needs.
- Purchase adjustable equipment that can be raised when used by older children: tables and easels are examples.

- Utilize extra space such as hallways or special rooms for small group projects.

- Place stackable containers on a wheeled platform for use as individual cubbies for the children.

- Provide carpet squares or mats for designating areas for floor activities.

- Use large corkboards or foam boards mounted on wheels to display children's artwork or project displays.

- Most important, encourage all staff members who share space to work together to make the arrangement mutually satisfying. It will take patience, flexibility, and time to develop ways to share space without problems.

- Before the program begins, meet together to plan.

OUTDOOR ENVIRONMENT

After being confined in the elementary school classroom all day, children need the opportunity to be outside, engaging in active play. Additionally, they are rapidly developing physically during the middle childhood years. They are able to run rapidly, throw a ball fairly accurately, and climb more easily than they did at an earlier age.

Cengage Learning

A jungle gym stimulates a wide variety of play activities.

They want to be competent at any of the physical activities they try, and they need to have places and opportunities to practice their skills. While the outdoor environment should be safe, it should also offer some challenges. Adding new equipment when children reach higher levels of agility can accomplish this objective. Most school-age children can swing themselves, climb a jungle gym, go up a ladder, and slide down a slide. It takes greater agility to cross a swinging bridge strung between two structures or to traverse a horizontal ladder. An outdoor environment for older children should include the following:

- single-purpose equipment: swings, parallel bars, ladder, slide, climbing rope, swinging bridge
- **multipurpose equipment**: sandbox, large boxes, jungle gym with different levels
- an **adventure play area** where children can build their own structures using large blocks, cartons, cables, and spools, sawhorses, tires, inner tubes, logs, pieces of wood or cardboard
- areas where children can talk with friends or be alone: a playhouse, park bench, tree house, or a secluded corner under a tree
- space for special activities: hard surfaces for skateboarding or roller-skating; covered areas for creative activities; blacktop for dodgeball, kickball, or jump rope; basketball court; baseball diamond or soccer field; swimming pool
- different levels for climbing or hiding: hilly area, ladder, tents, benches, large pipes, low tree branches, a fallen log
- shaded area for resting or reading: a large tree in a grassy area, a hammock, large plastic-covered pillows
- area where children can learn about and gain respect for their natural environment: unmanicured grass, bushes, plants, some rocks, a birdbath or feeder, plants that attract butterflies or birds, a garden for planting flowers or vegetables
- storage area for additional equipment as needed: balls, racquets, hoops, hockey sticks, jump ropes, tumbling mats, horseshoes, yo-yos, batons

SHARING OUTDOOR SPACE

It is often difficult for staff members in school-age programs to plan shared outdoor space with younger children. Many directors solve the problem by scheduling groups to use the play areas at separate times, but that does not completely address the needs of children at disparate age levels. The following suggestions may help:

- Provide adequate supervision of the entire playground.
- Establish clear rules so that older children know what they may do when younger children are present.
- Encourage older children to help younger children.
- Use movable equipment (see suggestions in the previous section) that can be brought out when younger children are not present.
- Set aside some areas for the exclusive use of older children using movable barriers or fences.
- Schedule times when older children can use community facilities such as a park, a baseball diamond, a basketball court, or a swimming pool.
- Plan joint activities with another school-age program that has its own outdoor area.

Parallel bars are an example of single-purpose equipment.

CASE STUDY

Ignacio is the site supervisor of a school-age program and has experienced a high turnover in staff. In an attempt to discover the reason, he distributed a supervisor review form for the staff to complete. Among other things, he has learned that the employees are unhappy with his management style and programming skills. The employees do not feel valued and are not included when important decisions have to be made. He sends them written directives about what to include in their program without considering their interests and abilities or the interests of the children.

1. What can Ignacio do to improve morale in this program?
2. How do you feel about staff reviews of supervisors?
3. How would you react if your staff had these complaints about you?

SUMMARY

Middle childhood is often referred to as a period of quiet as changes occur more slowly and smoothly than in early childhood. Physical growth slows, while cognitive growth rapidly develops. Children become independent from their families and form strong bonds with their peers.

NAEYC drafted a statement of characteristics of developmentally appropriate programs for children during middle childhood. They include the following:

- Opportunities for children to develop skills in all developmental areas.
- A program designed to enhance children's self-esteem.
- A responsiveness to individual differences in ability and interests.

Project Home Safe redrafted the NAEYC guidelines to fit the needs of after-school programs. Space for school-age children, both indoors and outdoors, should be designed specifically for their needs. Ideally, this means having "dedicated" space, not shared by other parts of a program. General considerations for planning space for older children are similar to those used for younger children, but they are implemented differently. Guidelines for planning space include the following:

- Safe yet challenging.
- Homelike atmosphere.
- Flexibility.
- Appropriate size.
- Aesthetically pleasing.
- Storage.

Specific areas are listed as well as suggestions for how to share space with other programs.

STUDENT ACTIVITIES

1. Observe a group of school-age children on a playground or in your child-care group. Are there some children who are much taller or much smaller than the others? How do they seem to get along in the group? Are there children who are excluded? Why do you think they have difficulty joining the activities?

2. Obtain several catalogs from companies that supply materials for school-age children. Choose three items each that you would use indoors and outdoors for a group of 18 children ranging in age from five to 11. Defend your choices in terms of what you learned from reading this chapter.

3. Plan and conduct one indoor and one outdoor activity for a group of six eight-year-olds. Evaluate the success of the activities. How long did the children stay involved? What comments did they make? Would you change either the materials you provided or the way in which the activity was conducted? If so, in what ways?

4. Write several paragraphs describing the kinds of play activities you enjoyed during middle childhood. Which of the interests inherent in these experiences do you continue to pursue?

REVIEW

1. What changes take place in children's thinking during the period between ages five and seven?

2. During middle childhood, children form clubs, cliques, or gangs. What are the purposes of these alliances?

3. What are the bases for children's self-concept?

4. How can caregivers provide opportunities for children to make friends?

5. List three field trips and three games that would be of interest to school-age children.

6. State one goal that is applicable to a school-age program.

7. How do licensing requirements for school-age programs differ from those for younger children?

8. List several ways to make space flexible.

9. State six ways to adapt indoor space when it must be shared with younger children.

10. Describe ways that outdoor space can be successfully shared with other groups.

REFERENCES

Albrecht, K. M., & Plantz, M. C. (2008). *Developmentally appropriate practices for school-age children (5–12 years)*. Dubuque, IA: Kendall/Hunt.

Bredekamp, S. Ed. (1987). *Developmentally appropriate practice in early childhood programs serving children from birth through age 8*. Washington, DC: National Association for the Education of Young Children.

Bredekamp, S., & Copple, C., Eds. (2009). *Developmentally appropriate practice in early childhood programs, revised edition*. Washington, DC: National Association for the Education of Young Children.

SELECTED FURTHER READING

Clemens, J. B. (1996). Gardening with children. *Young Children, 51*(4), 22–27.

Click, P., & Parker, J. (2002). *Caring for school-age children* (3rd ed.). Clifton Park, NY: Cengage Learning.

French, M. A. (1999–2000). Building relational practices in out-of-school environments. *The Wellesley Centers for Women Research Report, 20*(1), 8.

Katz, L. G., Evangelou, D., & Hartman, J. A. (1990). *The case for mixed-age grouping in early childhood education*. Washington, DC: National Association for the Education of Young Children.

Starbuck, S., & Olthof, M. R. (2008). Involving families and community through gardening. *Young Children 63*(5): 74–79.

HELPFUL WEBSITES

Disclaimer: Links to Internet sites throughout this book are provided for your convenience and do not constitute an endorsement.

Afterschool.gov:	**http://www.afterschool.gov**
National Institute on Out-of-School-Time (NIOST):	**http://www.niost.org**
National SAFEKIDS Campaign:	**http://www.safekids.org**
National School Age Care Alliance:	**http://www.nsaca.org**

For additional resources related to administration including videos, links to related sites for each chapter of the text, tutorial quizzes, glossary flashcards, and more, visit the Education CourseMate website for this book at www.cengage.com/login.

PART III
Staff Administration

Staff Selection/Personnel Policies

Objectives

After reading this chapter, you should be able to:

- State the procedures for finding qualified staff.
- Plan the steps in recruiting employees.
- Describe the process of selecting a staff member from qualified applicants.
- List the kinds of information contained in a personnel policy statement.

KEY TERMS

contract

knowledge

probationary period

skill

statement of personnel
     policies

A day in the life of . . .

The Director of a Child-care Learning Center

Our center recently experienced some staff turnover because several employees returned to college. I felt stressed because of the changes, the parent complaints, and the realization that the applicants did not meet my expectations. I interviewed 20 candidates and would have considered only a few of them for a position. I was becoming depressed. It seemed as though all the wonderful teachers were now leaving the field of early childhood education and as though the people applying had no ambition to work with children.

I always have my staff participate in evaluating any applicant I am considering for a position, because they must work together daily. It is important that I receive their input. During these interviews my staff members were also getting depressed because they too did not care for the people who were applying.

A dedicated employee who has worked with me since the center opened walked into my office after spending the day with three applicants. She patted me on the back and said, "Don't worry Karen, you can count on some of us." She then offered help with anything I needed or wanted her to do.

Staff Turnover

Many directors in early childhood programs know that personnel turnover is unavoidable. Despite this knowledge, the dreaded departure of a valuable employee produces anxiety. The average turnover rate is 30 percent for all teaching staff, so most directors experience the frantic feeling of suddenly having to find a new employee (Center for Child Care Workforce, 2001).

Several factors contribute to turnover and make it difficult for directors to maintain the overall quality of a program. The most important factor is the extremely low compensation for early childhood teachers. Preschool teachers nationwide earn only $9.05 per hour, or no more than $21,000 a year (payscale.com, 2009). Salaries have not changed over the past decade, and highly qualified female preschool teachers earn half as much as women with comparable education, while males earn less than one-third as much as men with the same education. In addition to the low salary, few early education teachers receive benefits. These teachers are without health insurance, sick leave, or paid vacations.

Another contributing factor is the low professional status of child-care personnel. Preschool teaching often is seen as women's work, comparable to babysitting. Consequently, college and university students do not view early education teaching as a career, but merely as a step toward a position in an elementary school or toward other professions. Low status combined with low salaries makes teaching in an early childhood program very unattractive.

Recruitment and hiring is often done too quickly and without proper planning. The ratio of adults to children must be maintained in order to meet licensing requirements, creating an urgent need to fill a vacancy as quickly as possible. Often, teachers are hired only for the director to find that they do not fit the goals or requirements of the program. That leads to more turnover and necessitates the process of recruitment and hiring once again.

The need for child care far outweighs the number of teachers prepared to fill positions in child-care centers. The Center for Child Care Workforce (2001) reports that there are 2.3 million teachers and caregivers for children ages birth to five. This number includes center-based settings, family child-care providers, and paid or nonpaid relatives. However, the National Association for the Education of Young Children (2003) estimates that another two million teachers are needed. Faced with this lack of supply, every early childhood education program director must develop a plan and effective processes for finding and keeping qualified staff.

Staff Qualifications

The first step in a recruiting process is understanding what makes an excellent teacher. Researchers have been interested in whether teachers with higher levels of education are better in their interactions with children or in their ability to provide a learning environment, particularly because many teachers in early childhood programs begin with little or no specialized education. Whitebook, Howes, and Phillips (1990) found that education was a good predictor of sensitive, caring interactions with children. More recently, a study done by the National Institute of Child Health and Human Development (1996) found no relationship between the teachers' educational level and their positive caregiving interactions. Both of these studies looked at general educational level. However, specialized education experiences, apparently affect teacher effectiveness. A follow-up of the Whitebook et al. 1990 study by the same researchers (1992) showed that specialized education at the college level was an important factor, particularly with infants and toddlers.

Several studies have shown that there is a relationship between teacher education and the quality of the learning environment as measured by the Early Childhood Environment Rating Scale (ECERS) (Harms & Clifford, 1980). Whitebook, Howes, and Phillips (1990) found that there is a positive correlation between "appropriate caregiving," a category of the ECERS, and overall classroom quality. Epstein (1993) found general education of caregivers was associated with higher scores on the Harms scale and the Infant and Toddler Environmental Rating Scale (ITERS) (Harms, Cryer, & Clifford, 1990). However, a higher level of education does not guarantee that caregivers will design a better learning environment. Educational level is a starting point for investigating caregiver qualifications.

EDUCATION

Check your state's licensing requirements for the academic background of teachers of young children. Specifications are usually minimal. The educational requirement may be as low as 12 postsecondary semester units in early childhood education or child development. A teacher in an infant-toddler room is sometimes required to complete an additional course in infant studies. Teachers in a before- and after-school program for older children might be able to substitute credits in recreation, physical education, and elementary teaching for early childhood education courses. The director should set standards for the school as high above the minimum as possible.

Publicly funded programs have different requirements for teachers. In public school early childhood education programs, teachers must have teaching certificates for the primary grades. They must also meet any other requirements set by the local school board. Head Start has made efforts to improve the quality of its programs by encouraging teachers to continue their education. A survey in 2001–2002 indicated that only 29 percent of Head Start teachers had a B.A. or higher degree, 23 percent had A.A. degrees, 35 percent had a C.D.A. or State Credential, and 13 percent had neither degree nor C.D.A. (National Institute for Early Education Research, 2003).

Nonteaching staff in a school also must meet minimum licensing standards. They must be in good physical health and free of diseases that could be transmitted to children. A background check should indicate that they have not been convicted of any crime except a minor traffic violation.

EXPERIENCE

The director decides the experience staff members should have. Licensing guidelines in each state will specify a minimum amount, but the director can decide to require more. In some states, teachers are only required to have one year of classroom experience with children, whereas assistant teachers need none. In a new school, it is best to look for experienced teachers who will be able to function without initial training or supervision. The first year of operation will be smoother, and that is probably worth the increased percentage of the budget allocated to salaries.

PERSONAL CHARACTERISTICS

The success of a school depends on the employees and the relationships they establish with each other and with the children. Therefore, staff members must be chosen carefully, based on a clear image of the necessary characteristics. Experienced directors cite the following important characteristics most often. They say they look for staff members who:

- like being with children (some adults prefer being with infants while others prefer preschool or older children).
- are nurturing (especially important for infants and toddlers).
- are flexible.
- are patient while children accomplish tasks themselves.
- are good role models for children.
- have good communication skills, including the abilities to write and listen well.
- can allow children to independently resolve their own problems.
- can accept individual differences in both children and adults.
- are able to work as a team with colleagues and with parents.
- are healthy, energetic, and enjoy physical activity.
- have many interests that can be shared with children and adults.
- are willing to continue learning.

REQUIRED SKILLS

The director should list the skills that a position requires. According to the dictionary, a **skill** is an ability that comes from knowledge, practice, or aptitude. It is the ability to

The success of a school depends largely on the adults who work there and the relationships they establish with each other and the children.

perform certain tasks as part of a job. A common synonym is competency. This task is applicable to all positions.

Teachers must be capable of doing various tasks as part of their job. The choice of which skills to include in job requirements depends on the type of school. The following list is a compilation of skills that might fit several settings. It is a guide for developing a more specific list.

A teacher should be able to:

- set up an environment that motivates children to participate.

- design activities that stimulate children to think, solve problems, and make choices.

- encourage children to use language by listening and by responding to their communications.

- promote children's physical development.

- help children feel successful.

- create an environment that helps children accept ethnic differences.

- assess and measure children's achievement.

NAEYC has published a statement titled "Where we Stand" (2003) on what teachers should know and be able to do. The following are the five statements found in that pamphlet.

1. Promoting child development and learning.

    Well-prepared early childhood professionals understand what young children are like; understand what influences their development; and use this understanding to create environments where all children can thrive.

2. Building family and community relationships.

    Well-prepared early childhood professionals understand and value children's families and communities; create respectful, reciprocal relationships; and involve all families in their children's development and learning.

3. Observing, documenting, and assessing.

    Well-prepared professionals understand the purposes of assessment; use effective assessment strategies; and use assessment responsibly to positively influence children's development and learning.

4. Teaching and learning.

    Well-prepared professionals build close relationships with children and families; use developmentally effective teaching and learning strategies; understand the content areas and academic subjects; and use their knowledge to give all children the experiences that promote comprehensive development and learning.

5. Becoming a professional.

    Well-prepared early childhood professional identify themselves with the early childhood profession; use ethical, professional standards; demonstrate self-motivated, ongoing learning; collaborate; think reflectively and critically; and advocate for children, families, and the profession.

The entire statement can be found on the Internet at http://www.naeyc.org/about/positions.asp.

KNOWLEDGE

Knowledge is a familiarity with a particular subject or branch of learning. It also means an acquaintance with facts, truths, or principles. Knowledge provides the information that allows workers to do their jobs. Should the teacher have knowledge of child development? Should the cook need to know something about nutrition in order to plan meals? Will the secretary need to know public relations techniques?

To make these decisions, the director must know the functions and needs of each job and then must consider the knowledge necessary to perform those functions.

Some examples of what teachers need to know are:

- stages of development, with special emphasis on cognitive, language, physical, social, and emotional development.
- atypical development.
- how young children learn.
- positive guidance strategies.
- ways to present materials and activities to motivate children to get involved.
- how the family influences the child's development.
- ways to form a partnership with parents for the education and care of the child.
- communication and conference techniques.

Some examples of what a secretary needs to know are:

- how to type or use a computer.
- how to set up and maintain a filing system or computer database.
- how to perform bookkeeping tasks either manually or on a computer.
- how to set up and maintain a schedule.

A food preparation person may need to know:

- the food guide pyramid.
- recommended serving sizes for children.
- methods to prepare and store food for maximum health and safety.
- the foods that most children enjoy.
- how to present food in appealing ways.
- health regulations.

Staff Recruitment

The search for qualified personnel can begin after the formulation of desired qualifications for each job. A concise announcement should be prepared for each position. As shown in Figures 8-1 and 8-2, the following information should be included:

- name of school.
- address of school.
- job title and brief description.
- contract period (September to June or the calendar year).
- salary range.
- brief statement of qualifications.
- name and phone number of person to contact.

RECRUITING NOTICE

The Village Child Care Center at 8126 West 8th Street is seeking a Head Teacher for a group of 18 four-year-olds. Responsibilities include planning and conducting the program for the group, working with parents, and participating in staff planning and decision making.

The applicant selected will be given a one-year contract with a salary ranging from $18,000 to $24,000. The school is in session all year, with each staff member entitled to 15 days paid leave each year. Starting date for this position is August 1. Deadline for applying is July 1.

Applicants should have a B.A. degree in child development or related fields and have had at least two years' experience in a preschool program. We are an Equal Opportunity Employer.

An application, résumé, and three letters of reference are required. The application form may be requested by calling:

Mary Anton

555-8659

F I G U R E 8 - 1   Sample recruiting notice for a head teacher.

- application process.
- deadline for applying.
- affirmative action statement.
- starting date of position.

This notice does not have to be fancy or expensive. With a computer, it is easy to put together an attractive notice by varying the type font, using bold letters, or adding a border. With a typewriter, capital letters and underlining create emphasis. Brevity is the key. Most people will not read a lengthy notice with wordy sentences.

Job information should be distributed as widely as possible. If more people see it, there is a greater probability of finding the right person. If there are several positions to fill, there may be many applicants. In that case, it may be better to eliminate the telephone number from this information, and instead request that applicants write for application materials.

ASSISTANT TEACHER WANTED

Teacher Assistant for infant-toddler room in a church-sponsored school. Responsibilities include all aspects of daily child care, planning appropriate activities, and maintaining children's records. Must have at least 15 college units in Early Childhood Education including a course on infant-toddler development. Experience preferred. Job available immediately. Send résumé to P.O. Box 1320, Thousand Oaks, CA 91359 or FAX to 815-222-3487. We are an Equal Opportunity Employer.

F I G U R E 8 - 2   Sample newspaper advertisement for an assistant teacher.

If the school is already in operation and there is only one position to fill, the director should notify current staff members. An assistant teacher may feel ready to apply for a position as teacher. A secretary who has taken some early childhood courses may be ready to seek an assistant's job.

Further distribution sources are:

- public and private schools
- unemployment service offices
- college and university placement offices
- civic groups, clubs, and special interest groups
- professional organizations
- churches

The director can also place an advertisement in local newspapers. The advertisement needs to be shorter than the recruitment notice. It should be only a few lines long and contain the following information:

- name of school
- position being filled
- required background and experience
- contact—address or telephone

Many directors find the search for qualified staff a difficult and frustrating part of their job, and high turnover in early childhood centers causes the search to be a constant one. Although turnover of employees cannot be eliminated, it may be significantly decreased by creating a climate in which staff members feel valued. This will help to retain staff. A good personnel policy statement is also important, as you will read later in this chapter.

Application Information

The director should develop an application form to use repeatedly. There may be one basic form for all jobs or one for teachers and one for other categories. Forms should be simple and short. Questions should be clear and related to the job.

The application form might include the following:

- date the application is completed by the applicant
- name of the applicant
- address of the applicant
- telephone number of the applicant
- Social Security number of the applicant
- position applied for by the applicant
- applicant's job or volunteer experience (include dates and type of work)
- applicant's educational background
- applicant's hobbies or special interests
- applicant's references (include name, address, and telephone)

Additionally, the application for a teaching position may include the following:

- credentials and/or academic degrees
- professional affiliations
- published works

Some applicants may need help in completing an application form. Language differences, inexperience with forms, or limited education should not deter a potentially qualified person from applying. The secretary or another staff member should be available to help.

Additional information can be obtained by observing an applicant's response to children. With the teacher's permission, the director should ask the applicant to sit in on an activity, participate in a snack time, or read a story to the children. How does the applicant interact with the children? Are the applicant's responses appropriate for the age level of the children? Does the applicant ask to see lesson plans or resource materials? Some center directors ask the top three candidates to spend half a day in the classroom. However, it may be unrealistic to expect that a candidate can perform as well as they would if they were familiar with the children and the children were familiar with them. Nonetheless, observing a candidate's interactions with children should yield useful information to add to the verbal interview information.

Selection Process

SCREENING

After the application deadline has passed, the screening process begins. An advisory committee member or a teacher may be asked to help. Although the director or the board of trustees will make the final choice, others can make recommendations. When staff members participate in this process, they have a chance to learn some new skills. Having influence in choosing their colleagues can promote staff solidarity as well.

The director should look through each of the applications and sort them into three groups. The first will be for those who meet all the minimum requirements, usually including academic background, experience, and credentials or licenses. The second will be for those who meet some of the minimum requirements. The last will be for those who meet none. The last group can be eliminated immediately. It is important to check references. A reference can be in the form of a letter submitted along with the application, or it can be the name of a person to contact.

The director should read written recommendations carefully or telephone the personal contacts. It helps to have some specific questions to ask. "What are X's greatest strengths working with children?" "In what areas do you think X needs additional knowledge or experience?" "Would you hire X to work with a group of three-year-olds?"

Once the director narrows the field of applicants to a few candidates, they can schedule interviews. Usually three to five applicants who meet all the requirements will yield one satisfactory new hire.

INTERVIEWING

The interview portion of the application process is the most difficult, but it can be the most valuable. When meeting with a prospective staff member, there is an opportunity to explore the fit of the person to the school. This is a two-way process. The applicant needs

Cengage Learning

The interview should be preceded by a tour of the school, if time permits.

to find out whether the school is appropriate for their beliefs, and the director needs to determine whether the applicant will suit the program.

Minimally, one-half hour should be allowed for the actual interview, with 10 or 15 minutes between candidates for jotting notes about each person. It is best not to rely on memory. When several consecutive interviews have been conducted, the applicants will begin to blur together. Notes will refresh one's memory when trying to make a final decision.

The interview should be preceded with a tour of the school if time permits. This will allow the applicant to obtain information about the school. It will also provide a chance to see how the person responds to children. Comments or questions during the tour can provide important insights about the applicant.

Sometimes, several people will compose an interview committee. The director, a board member, a parent, a supervisor, or a teacher may be included, depending on the school. If several people will be involved, some directors schedule separate interviews for an applicant with each committee member. Others conduct interviews as a group, with one applicant meeting the committee. However, too large a committee may overwhelm some candidates.

For purposes of later evaluation, the interview should have some structure. This applies whether one person interviews candidates or a committee is involved. Each applicant should be asked similar questions, which have been written out before all the interviews. Consequently, there is less likely to be a question of preferential or prejudicial practice.

In a committee, one person should be designated to lead. To avoid repetition of information, each member should choose an area to question. For example, one might ask about curriculum skills, while another asks about previous experience. The procedure is still the same if committee members conduct separate interviews. The group should agree

---

INTERVIEW QUESTIONS

Name of Applicant   Date of Interview

Position Applying for

Interviewer

1. Briefly state your teaching philosophy.
2. What are your strengths as a teacher of young children?
3. What are your weaknesses?
4. You have a child in your toddler class who is biting other children. How would you respond?
5. What would you do if a child kicked you?
6. A parent tells you she is very upset over an incident that happened the day before. What would your first response be? What else would you do to help that parent?
7. Briefly describe three activities that would be age appropriate for three-year-olds.
8. What would be your primary focus as a teacher in an infant program?

Signature of Interviewer

Rate applicant on a scale of 1 to 10, 10 being an outstanding applicant and 1 being someone you would not consider for this position.

Rating

FIGURE 8 - 3   Sample interview question form.

ahead of time about the questions to ask. Each may pursue particular areas, or they may all ask similar questions. For a sample interview questions worksheet, see Figure 8-3.

Questions that require only a one-word answer should be avoided because they provide very little information. "Did you decide to become a preschool teacher because you like children?" is an example. Questions that already imply an expected answer should also be avoided. "What kind of punishment would you use for a child who hits others?" Here the implication is that punishment is the only way to handle that kind of behavior.

The interview should be conducted in a quiet place, free from interruptions. It is important to ensure the applicant will be comfortable. The applicant should not be asked to sit facing a row of committee members or an interviewer who is barricaded behind a desk. A circle configuration is the most effective.

Each committee member will need time to review the application material and to familiarize themselves with the applicant's academic background and previous experience. This will save time by eliminating direct questions about that kind of information in the interview.

The director should begin the interview by introducing themselves, and others, if more than one person is participating. If the applicant has not had a tour of the school, the director can describe the school briefly and talk about the specific class in which there is an opening.

It is best to ask an easily answered question first, mainly to help the applicant start talking. For example, "I see by your application that you have worked at. . . . Tell us what you liked best about the job," or ". . . Describe any aspects of that job that might be applicable to the position here." Questions should begin with words like the following:

- Tell me . . .
- Describe . . .
- List . . .
- Outline . . .

To learn about personal qualifications, it is helpful to pose a question that might show the person's feelings or attitudes.

- Enthusiasm for teaching: "What do you like best about working with young children?"
- Attitudes toward differences in people: "Suppose you had a child in your class who was blind. What are some things you would do to integrate that child into the classroom activities?"
- Ability to manage problem situations with children: "You have a child in your class who refuses to participate in any of the group activities you plan. She either won't come to the group area, or if she does, she never says anything. What would you do?"

To get information about specific skills, the director might ask the applicant to plan a specific learning activity for a particular age group; for example,

- "Describe one science activity that would be appropriate for a group of four-year-olds."
- "List three things you might do to encourage parents to get involved in the education of their children."
- "Plan a cooking activity that would be appropriate for a group of children in an after-school program."

To find out the applicant's knowledge of child development, ask one of the following questions:

- "Briefly describe how you would design an indoor environment for a group of four infants and six toddlers."
- "Name three art activities that most two-year-olds should be able to do successfully. Name three that might be a little difficult."

To elicit unstructured information, applicants should be encouraged to talk freely about themselves.

- "What else would you like to tell us about yourself that might be important as we consider you for this position?"
- "Tell us what you feel your strengths are. What are the kinds of things you would like to do?"
- "What kind of job do you expect to be doing 10 years from now?"

Some areas of inquiry should be avoided, and some information should not be requested either in an interview or on an application. The following are some guidelines:

- The interviewer can ask for place of residence, but not whether the person owns or rents their residence.
- It is legal to require applicants to provide proof that they meet a minimum age requirement, but it is illegal to seek any information that identifies someone as older than 40.
- The interviewer can ask the name and address of a parent or guardian of a minor, but cannot ask questions that indicate applicant's marital status, number and ages of children, or provisions for child care.
- It is illegal to ask any questions regarding the applicant's race; complexion; or color of skin, eyes, or hair.
- It is acceptable to state that employment is contingent on passing a physical exam and ask whether there is any physical condition that would limit the applicant's ability to perform the job. It is unacceptable to inquire about the applicant's general physical and mental health.
- A prospective employer can require references, but may not directly ask those people questions about the applicant's race, religion, national origin, medical condition, marital status, or sex.

The interview is an opportunity to observe the applicant. Depending on what is important, the director might look for the following:

- Ability to communicate: How clear are the answers?
- Organizational ability: Does the applicant organize answers logically and in a way that is easy to understand?
- Sense of humor: Does the applicant see some difficult situations from a humorous viewpoint?
- Tense or relaxed: Does the applicant's body language communicate extreme tenseness or relaxation?:

The applicant should have an opportunity to ask questions at the end of the interview. The questions asked will give valuable clues to the person's understanding of the job. They may also provide insight into the person's particular interests or even biases.

This interview format can be used for employees other than teaching staff. The same kinds of questions can be asked; however, the content should be modified to match each specific job. The following are some examples:

- Find out how the maintenance person will react to children: "The children have been playing in the sandbox with water from the drinking fountain. You arrive just in time to see a child using a very sandy bucket to get some more water. What would you say?"
- Find out whether the cook can plan nutritious meals that children will like: "What would a typical lunch for a group of four-year-olds consist of?"
- Find out whether the secretary has good public relations skills: "Some irate parents tell you there is a mistake on their bill and that you have overcharged them. You know the bill was correct and that a payment was missed. What would you say?"

The interviewers should record their information and impressions as soon as the interview is concluded. They should not talk to their co-interviewers first. (Caution: The interviewer should not write notes during the interview. The applicant may worry about what the interviewer has chosen to write down, presenting an inaccurate picture of the person's abilities.) Some situations may require rating each candidate on a numerical scale. This should be done following the interview. The interviewers' notes should include a recommendation for whether the applicant should be hired.

EVALUATING

Evaluation of applicants is the final step of the selection process and is sometimes the hardest. The evaluation will be based on several sources of information: the applicant's educational background, experience, responses to questions, and image. It is important to be as objective as possible.

It is generally easy to evaluate an applicant's background and experience. If a specific degree or credential is required, it will appear on the application. The applicant's experience will also be listed there. However, the only way to judge the quality of a person's background or experience is in an interview. For example, someone can take a course in human development, but not really have an understanding of the stages of development. Someone else may have many years of teaching experience, but it may have been in a very different program. Evaluating answers to questions posed in the interview sometimes seems an almost impossible task, but if interviewers have a clear understanding of what they are looking for, the task is manageable.

Some well-qualified applicants may not perform well in an interview. The opposite is also true. Someone who interviews well may be a poor choice for the school. However, there is a way to give an applicant a further chance to display his or her abilities and give oneself a further chance to choose the most appropriate candidate.

The finalists can be asked to spend a half-day working in a classroom. They should be paid the going salary rate for their time. This procedure will provide additional information for making the final choice. It will allow the director to observe how the candidate relates to both children and adults. What is their body language telling you? Do they seem comfortable or anxious in this environment? What is their tone with the children? How do they relate to the adults in the classroom? Are there conversations with the teacher? Do they ask questions, or is there an apparent lack of involvement? And finally, what does the candidate say about the time in the classroom?

Finally, there is not a perfect method for finding the perfect employee. It is necessary to listen, watch, and evaluate each candidate. The more often directors go through this process, the more accurate they become in choosing the best staff.

Notification of Employment or Nonselection

When a new staff member has been selected, most directors are eager to finalize the process. One way is to telephone the person, then follow that with a letter. The letter should give the starting date of employment and the salary offered. If the center uses a contract, that should also be included.

The successful candidate should be given a deadline to return the contract or to come to the school to complete the process. This deadline may also be for submitting the required credentials or transcripts and completing payroll and personnel forms.

VILLAGE CHILD CARE CENTER

(Date)

Dear: _____:

Thank you for your interest in Village Child Care Center and your desire to become a member of our staff. We wish to inform you that we have made a different selection from the applicants for the recent opening.

Your application will be kept on file, and should an additional opening become available, you will be notified. If you are still interested in working with us, we hope that you will reapply.

Sincerely,

(Signature)

Mary Anton, Director

FIGURE 8-4   Notification of nonselection.

When the hiring process is completed, the director should send information about the new employee to any interested people. This may include board members, advisory committee members, or existing staff. The director should also tell parents about the new staff member. The children, too, need to know who their new teacher will be.

Those who were interviewed and not hired should be informed. This is never a pleasant task, but they should not be left wondering. If possible, the director should telephone the people who were interviewed, thank them for their time, and tell them the position has been filled. The director may wish to ask whether they can be called for substitute jobs, or if future openings become available. If necessary, it is acceptable to send a letter like that in Figure 8-4 to these people. Additionally, a simple note to each person who sent in an application would be both courteous and professional (see Figure 8-5).

VILLAGE CHILD CARE CENTER

(Date)

Dear: _____:

Because of the large number of responses to our recent recruiting efforts, we were unable to interview all applicants. However, we wanted to notify you that the position has been filled. Your application will be kept on file, and you will be notified when we have other openings.

Sincerely,

(Signature)

Mary Anton, Director

FIGURE 8-5   Notification of applicants who were not interviewed.

Personnel Practices

In some preschools and child-care centers, staff members stay for years. In others, turnover occurs frequently. What accounts for the difference? Sometimes people leave a job looking for higher pay. Others stay in a job despite low salaries. Teachers who stay in a school when they could earn more elsewhere often give a reason such as "It's a good place to work." Directors can make their school that type of positive workplace by treating the staff as professionals, providing job security, developing fair personnel practices, paying the best salary possible for each job, supporting fringe benefits and retirement plans, and offering employees a contract.

CONTRACT

A **contract** or personnel agreement is a written commitment between employer and employee that promotes job security. A contract states that during a specified period of time, each has an obligation to the other. The employer agrees to employ the person for that period at a designated pay level. The staff member agrees to carry out the job's functions (see Figure 8-6).

A contract is essential for high morale in any teaching staff. Young children need to have the security of teachers or caregivers who are continuously present. It is hard for a child to learn to trust that school is a good place if adults disappear frequently, never to be seen again. Parents, too, feel better if they know the adult who cares for their child. Learning to trust their child's caregiver takes time. Teachers need time, too, to learn to cooperate. Teachers sometimes say that working together in a classroom is like a marriage. It takes "working at" and does not happen overnight.

The contract should be a statement of all the conditions of employment. The following points should be included:

- time period of the contract: the date when the contract goes into effect and the termination date
- **probationary period**: the time before the full contract goes into effect, usually from one to three months
- salary: pay for the period covered by the contract
- fringe benefits: the number of days of vacation and sick leave, and the medical and retirement benefits
- termination: conditions for termination of the contract (would include termination by either the employer or employee)

PERSONNEL AGREEMENT

Employee: Name: _____

            Address: _____

            _____

            Phone: _____

JOB TITLE: Head Teacher

JOB DESCRIPTION:

I. Basic Functions: The head teacher is responsible for supervising the development and implementation of a daily program that will promote the children's physical, cognitive, social, and emotional growth.

II. Responsibilities:
    1. Reports to the executive director of child-care center.
    2. Ensures that written class plans are prepared in a timely fashion and posted prominently.
    3. Provides ongoing direction to staff as needed.
    4. Confers with director about changes, programming, and/or problems.
    5. Refers individual children who may need services from outside agencies to the director.
    6. Provides opportunities for staff to develop.
    7. Shares pertinent information or concerns about individual children with assigned staff.
    8. Confers with staff on a weekly basis to discuss planning, individual children, and concerns of individual staff.
    9. Prepares performance appraisals of staff according to policy.
    10. Ensures communication between staff and parents through daily informal contact and semiannual scheduled conferences with written progress reports.
    11. Arranges conferences with parents whenever deemed necessary.
    12. Ensures a physically safe environment.
    13. Ensures daily attendance and maintains health logs.
    14. Approves break time.
    15. Assumes responsibility for continued professional growth in the areas of early childhood education.
    16. Substitutes for the director during periods of director's absence.
    17. Complies with personnel policies.

III. Conditions of employment:
    1. Salary: $24,000 for a 12-month calendar year.
    2. Health insurance program when permanent status is achieved.
    3. Paid holidays: New Year's Day, Memorial Day, Fourth of July, Labor Day, Thanksgiving Day, and Christmas Day.
    4. Paid annual vacation days, 10 (5 after 6 months, 5 additional after 1 year).
    5. Paid annual sick days: 6.
    6. There is a probation period of three (3) months after which the full contract is in effect. This agreement may be terminated after due process if it is determined that you have not fulfilled the responsibilities of the position as described above. Termination by either party must be preceded by a notification period of thirty (30) days.

Approved by: _____   Employee: _____

Dated: _____

FIGURE 8-6   Sample personnel agreement.

ORIENTATION OF NEW EMPLOYEES

The center director is responsible for ensuring that each new employee receives the information necessary for a smooth introduction to the work environment, including the specifics of the job. All staff members, including supporting staff, need to be given a statement of personnel policies as soon as they are hired. This is a written document, described in the following section, detailing all facets of the employee–employer relationship. Employees should be told to read it and to ask for clarification of any items they do not understand.

New employees should be given a tour of the entire physical plant and introduced to all staff members during their first day of work. They should be shown where materials are stored, where the adult restrooms are located, and where their personal belongings can be safely kept. Teachers should be introduced to the parents as soon as possible. Some directors notify families of staff changes by mail; others post notices on the parent bulletin board or include the information in a newsletter. Ideally, however, parents should have a personal introduction when they bring their child to school. The director must be available at arrival time to introduce the teacher and parents to each other. When the timing can be synchronized, a new teacher can be introduced to parents at a meeting. During the first weeks of employment, the director must check with the new employee frequently to answer any questions, help with problems, and build a supportive relationship. During this time, the new employee should become familiar with the performance standards the director expects. Sometimes it is not possible for the director to spend enough time with each new employee. In this circumstance, a senior staff member should be available to support the new employee until they feel comfortable. The director should still find time to meet with the new employee or visit the classroom during the early weeks. It is important to establish the kind of relationship that lets the new staff member know the director is available to give support and help when needed.

In addition to the statement of personnel policies, some directors provide handbooks for new staff members. This document contains guidelines ranging from capacity limits for outdoor structures to responsibilities for daily cleaning. A handbook should include any rules that govern conduct in the classroom or ensure safety on the playground. A staff handbook may include these items:

- philosophy of the center
- statement of goals
- bylaws of the board (where applicable)
- classroom procedures
- playground rules and restrictions
- suggestions for interacting with children
- copies of forms used for children's records
- information about the community the center serves
- directory of staff members

When this information is available to all staff members, they have a common reference point. If questions arise, they can refer to the written information.

One final method for orienting new employees is a training session. This is especially effective if multiple staff members have been hired at the same time. General information can be distributed, questions can be answered, and confusions can be clarified. This is also a good opportunity for senior staff members to meet new members and to begin sharing useful strategies or materials.

New teachers should be introduced to parents as soon as possible.

STATEMENT OF PERSONNEL POLICIES

A **statement of personnel policies** is a written document covering employer–employee relations. It elucidates the conditions of employment. Given to new employees, this kind of document will convey information about the job in a concise manner. Even though some employees may not read the entire document, the information is there for reference. It will not eliminate problems, but when they do arise, the statement may provide a solution or prevent misunderstandings. If employees are required to read the entire document, they may be asked to sign a statement indicating they have done so.

A written statement of personnel policies should be:

- short and to the point
- clear
- organized into logical sections

Many directors say they do not have a written policy statement because conditions change each year. Some conditions change, but many remain the same. It is generally easy to redo a few pages to meet any changing circumstances in a school. Information can easily be inserted or deleted with a computer. The pages can be photocopied and put together into a loose-leaf booklet.

The director must decide what to include in the school's statement of personnel policies. An overview of the sections to include is presented in the following paragraphs.

Details of Employment

One section should be devoted to the details of employment: the number of hours per day, holidays, and vacations. A calendar showing holidays and starting dates of the school year would be helpful. The length of the probationary period and events during that period could be outlined.

Example

The probationary period is three months. During that time you will be observed by the director at least once a month. A conference will be scheduled at the end of that time to evaluate your performance. If performance has been satisfactory, the full contract will go into effect. Once the contract is in effect, each employee will be evaluated once a year. The observation and conference will be scheduled at a mutually agreed upon time between the director and the employee.

New employees should know the lines of responsibility in a school. When problems arise, they should know whom to go to first. They should also know who will be directly responsible for supervising them. An organizational chart included in the personnel policies manual will show these personnel relationships.

If the school provides payment for—or requires—continuing professional training, that information should be included. Some schools pay for conferences and professional dues. Some offer full or partial tuition payments for staff to attend classes.

Physical Environment

A personnel policies statement may include a section on managing the physical environment. Staff members might need to know where to get keys to the classroom or where to park. Parking may not be an issue in some areas, but in crowded urban settings it could create problems. Assigned spaces help to alleviate hassle and possible expense. Personnel also need to know if there is a safe place for them to leave their belongings. Many centers forget this while concentrating on making the environment appropriate for children. There could also be a statement concerning teachers' responsibilities for maintaining their classrooms and equipment. Although there may be a regular cleaning service, teachers usually must do a certain amount of cleaning and straightening in their own classrooms.

Health and Safety Matters

Every employee should be fingerprinted for use in completing a background check. Records will show whether this person has ever been convicted of a crime that would be detrimental to the safety of the children. Health examinations should be required, including a tuberculosis test. The director should also consider requiring that staff members be immunized for hepatitis B or receive booster measles immunizations. Another issue to clarify is whether the employee must pay for the health exam.

The statement of personnel policies should outline procedures for reporting employee accidents. If a form is required, an example should be included with instructions for where it can be obtained. There must be clear procedures for dealing with disasters such as fires, earthquakes, or tornadoes.

Employees will need details about the fringe benefits the school offers. If a medical plan is included, it is important to explain the procedures for enrolling and the services covered.

Some programs offer free or reduced-cost child care for employees' children. Some offer a broad family benefit package that allows choices such as child care, elder care, maternity leave, or family leave. Similarly, employees should be informed about how many "sick leave" days each of them have. Can the days be carried over from one year to another? What are the conditions under which employees will be excused from work due to illness? If there is a retirement plan or if the center pays into Social Security, that information should be included. Other types of benefits, such as group life insurance, unemployment insurance, and workers' compensation, should be outlined.

Information about employee relief periods is appropriate for this section. Each staff member should have at least 10 minutes of relief during every four-hour period. If a staff member works more than four hours, a 30-minute break should be scheduled for rest and lunch away from the children. Some schools allow staff members an hour while children are napping, if they stay on the premises. Thus, they are available if an emergency arises.

Termination of Employment

The personnel policies statement should include procedures for terminating employment. How much notice is required when the employer or the staff member ends employment? It is customary to provide a two-week notification. The causes for termination should be clearly stated.

It is important to have a grievance process that can be followed when problems arise. Such a procedure might prevent termination of employment, increase staff morale, and decrease turnover. One church school has the following statement:

> In the event of disagreements between members of the teaching staff, the Director will make the final decision. When there is a disagreement on procedure between members of the teaching staff and the Director, the Director may ask the Vice-President, Education, to arbitrate. Both parties, Director and staff member, will abide by the decision.

This statement provides for the settlement of most disputes by working through the chain of command from staff member to director to church board. Another method should also exist for cases when staff members have serious disagreements with a director. It may be necessary to designate some person within the school organization whom staff members can contact when problems cannot be resolved by going through the usual channels.

Job Description

A job description should be included for each position. This is a list of duties and responsibilities. A teacher's job description should include all activities related to teaching, communicating with parents, and attending staff meetings. The job description should include minimum legal and local qualifications for the position as well (see Figure 8-7).

Job descriptions for personnel other than teachers will have information related to the particular position. As an example, a cook's job description may include statements about planning menus, preparing food, purchasing food items, storing food, and maintaining kitchen cleanliness (see Figure 8-8).

Advancement Opportunities

The school may offer opportunities for staff to advance to higher pay levels or to other positions. If so, that information should be included in a personnel policies manual. Conditions for advancement should be stated, whether they are further education or time of service. A salary scale showing the steps, the requirements for each step, and the salary at each level is an excellent method to furnish this information.

CREATING AN EFFECTIVE PERSONNEL MANUAL

"What is our policy on sick days?" "Do we get Martin Luther King Day off?" "Does our insurance cover orthodontists?" The answers to these questions and many more should be carefully explained in an employee handbook, also known as a Personnel Manual. Such manuals can improve employee morale, prevent disagreements, and even keep the center out of court. One of the most important reasons to create a personnel manual is to document the employer's expectations. A good manual will describe expected performance and clarify the employer's requirements regarding work hours, dress, disciplinary action, sick and vacation leaves, and other topics.

The process of creating a manual also helps employers improve their leadership—first by considering useful and practical policies, and after concrete policies are established, by helping to better manage employees because objectives for each position have been examined, benefits have been considered and perhaps retooled, and personnel policies have been established before contentious issues arise.

JOB DESCRIPTION: CLASSROOM TEACHER

The person in this position is responsible for the general management of a group of 15 children between the ages of two and five.

QUALIFICATIONS

The person selected for this position must have successfully completed at least 12 postsecondary units in early childhood courses. Additionally, this person must have had two years' experience as a teacher in a preschool classroom. Personal qualifications for this position include the abilities to interact effectively with children and parents, to work cooperatively with other staff members, and to be flexible. Good health would be beneficial.

RESPONSIBILITIES

The teacher will be responsible for planning and conducting a program for a group of children and all activities relating to that program. Duties will include, but are not limited to:

- planning and conducting daily experiences for the children based on the goals of the school.
- preparing all materials required to implement the program.
- planning and maintaining a physical environment that meets the goals of the school, is safe and free of health hazards, and is attractive.
- planning for the needs of individual children in regard to their interests, special needs, pace, and style of learning.
- including materials and experiences in the classroom that foster children's cultural or ethnic identity and awareness.
- attending and participating in staff meetings, training sessions, and planning activities.
- participating in recommended courses, conferences, or other activities for professional growth.
- participating in ongoing assessments of children's development and progress.
- planning and participating in activities designed to include parents in the education of their children.
- conducting ongoing parent contacts and conferences to notify parents of their children's progress.
- assisting in public relations events sponsored by the school.

FIGURE 8–7   Sample job description for a teacher.

JOB DESCRIPTION: COOK

The person in this position will be responsible for the general planning and implementation of all food services of the school.

QUALIFICATIONS

This person must have had experience in quantity cooking and have shown an ability to plan for economical purchases of foods. This person should be able to plan, prepare, and serve nutritious and appetizing meals under the supervision of the school's nutritionist. This person should have good personal cleanliness habits and should be able to maintain an orderly and hygienic kitchen. Lastly, this person should like being in an environment with young children and be able to work well with other adults.

RESPONSIBILITIES

- using menus planned by the nutritionist, purchase, prepare, and serve two meals and two snacks each day to all the children
- reviewing the food service periodically with the nutritionist and the director
- coordinating food services with other activities of the school
- incorporating foods for special celebrations into the regular menus
- maintaining a clean and orderly kitchen and storage area
- storing foods properly to minimize waste
- participating in periodic training sessions with other staff members to increase knowledge of child development
- attending training sessions as required to upgrade knowledge of nutrition and food preparation

FIGURE 8–8   Sample job description for a cook.

Loosely defined policies can hurt an employer. Courts generally view both written and verbal policies as a contract. Verbal policies can be implied or given by someone with no authority to make promises. A written document is specific and reduces the chance of a court case in which the owner's word is judged against that of an employee.

Although it is important to legally protect yourself by having a personnel manual, most programs view their staff as members of the same team, working toward shared goals. Therefore, the employee handbook should be an effective tool for promoting growth, improving morale, and aligning employee behavior with personnel policies.

The tone of the manual should be positive. The introduction can set this tone by stating the philosophy, mission, and objectives of the program. One aid in writing a manual is content of those used by other programs. Tailor the content to reflect your own policies, procedures, and type of center. The organization of your manual can also be found in such manuals, including proper wording and general policies on subjects ranging from substance abuse to safety and security, absenteeism, and vacation.

Another possibly helpful source for creating your manual is computer software that outlines the major items to be included in a personnel policy handbook. (See Helpful Websites for Jian Tools for Sales, Inc. and other sites with helpful information.) Do not forget that employees may also have useful information. Solicit input from all personnel so that your manual addresses a wide range of concerns.

Once you have a manual, update it regularly. Change your written policies to conform to actual practice or changes in the law. Reserve the right to change, add, or terminate policies at any time. Remember to state that "all new policies override previous ones, both verbal and written."

Key components of a personnel manual

Keep in mind when developing your manual not to include unnecessary information; shorter is usually better. Experts consider the following subjects to be the most essential ones to cover:

- **Program overview:** Introduce your program with a few paragraphs about its history, mission, goals, ethics, and philosophy.
- **Equal opportunity statement:** State that an employee's religion, age, sex, or race will have nothing to do with hiring, promotion, pay, or benefits.
- **Job descriptions:** List qualifications, responsibilities, and to whom the position reports.
- **Work schedule:** Part-time, full-time, and workdays.
- **Pay and performance issues:** General information on paychecks; promotions and wage increases; classification of employees (part-time, full-time, on-call); and policies on leaves without pay, overtime, and other pay irregularities.
- **Information at a glance:** For ease of use, include a section outlining your insurance benefits packages. Include important numbers (such as group insurance numbers or the company code) and phone numbers of benefit representatives.
- **Pension plans:** Discuss how employees become eligible, whether an employee contribution is permitted or required, and when employees become vested.
- **Standards of conduct:** Detail desired behavior (such as dress and timeliness), as well as your policies on sexual harassment; racial and sexual discrimination; use of alcohol, drugs, and tobacco in the workplace; and disciplinary procedures.
- **Resignation and termination procedure:** List the just causes for which you will fire an employee, including criminal activity, poor performance, child abuse, absenteeism, and so forth. Include rules requiring immediate discharge.

- **Staff training and development:** Kinds of training, frequency of training, and whether training is required or optional.
- **General information:** This section should be geared toward new hires. Consider including such items as area maps, a parking pass, an organizational chart, phone lists, and a statement regarding the confidential nature of your business.
- **Forms:** Have blank forms attached to the policies regarding sick leaves, vacations, seminar attendance, grievance filing, travel reimbursement, performance reviews, and accident reports.
- **Reader acknowledgment:** Protect your liability and encourage employees to read the handbook by having them sign a receipt that goes in the personnel file. One copy stays in the personnel file, and the employee gets a copy.

Personnel Records

Licensing guidelines usually require each school to maintain updated records on each employee. Thus, it is important to complete each file as soon as possible after hiring and to update it as necessary. The contents of the file may vary among schools, but generally they will contain similar kinds of information. The following paragraphs describe the categories of records in a personnel file.

APPLICATION MATERIALS

Each file should contain an application form that is completed even before the person is hired. The form should have a place to record the employee's name, address, Social Security number, and an emergency contact.

Application records may also contain:

- records of education and relevant experience
- transcripts and/or credentials
- reference letters or forms

HEALTH

Health records should be maintained on each employee. If the school requires a pre-employment physical examination, a summary of that exam should be placed in the file. Many states require periodic tuberculosis testing for preschool and child-care personnel. The test results should be in the file. Immunization against hepatitis B is recommended. The health record should be included in each personnel file.

Any injuries incurred while working should be recorded in the employee's file. The record should include the treatment and the outcome. Figure 8-9 provides a sample staff injury report. It is also important to keep a record of each person's absences due to illness. Frequent illness may indicate that some measure needs to be taken to ensure better health in that employee.

EMPLOYMENT RECORD

An employment record form should be included in each file. This should show the starting date, any leaves that may have been granted, and the final date of employment.

It should also allow space for salary levels during the time of employment and include any promotions or transfers to another school within the organization.

STAFF INJURY REPORT

Name   Position

Address   Phone Number

Date of Injury   Time

Location Where Injury Occurred

How Injury Happened

Description of the Injury

Witnesses

Physician's Name   Phone Number

Type of Treatment Required

FIGURE 8-9   Sample staff injury report.

Staff should be allowed to add to their own files if they wish. Special awards or commendations are examples of additional information to add to an employment record.

EVALUATION

If the school has a system of evaluation, the record of each rating should be placed in the employee's file. A series of assessments over a period of time will provide a useful record of each individual's job performance. A periodic review of evaluations may indicate the need to provide more, or different kinds of, in-service training.

CONFERENCES

The director should record any conferences scheduled with staff members and place the information in each employee's file. This will include routine conferences that follow each evaluation. It should also include conferences that the director or the employee requests to discuss a problem. The record should be brief and to the point. It is enough to state the problem discussed and to describe any resolution.

TERMINATION OF EMPLOYMENT

When an employee leaves a job or is fired, the director should place a record in their file. A brief note stating the reason should be enough. It must be objective and factual.

RECOMMENDATIONS

Employees who leave a center may later ask for a reference letter for a new job. If the director cannot write a positive letter, the employee should be told so. If the director does write a reference letter, a copy should be placed in the employee's file. Future requests can be filled easily by copying the first letter unless specific new information is requested. The file should include a record of the dates and of to whom copies have been sent.

The creation of a professionally oriented atmosphere in a center is a challenge. It often means a delicate balance between economic pressures and personnel requirements. The center should offer the best salaries that can be managed within the budget and include some fringe benefits. Beyond that, personnel policies that convey to staff members that they are important will go a long way toward making any center a good place to work. These efforts should result in less employee turnover and greater harmony among staff.

Classroom Substitute Personnel

Careful planning for substitute staff will help ensure program quality and integrity. It is easy to forget the importance of this responsibility. However, careful planning will help ensure continuity. Substitute staff should have the same personal and professional qualifications as the staff they are replacing. Past job applicants who interviewed well yet were not chosen might be willing to become part of a substitute pool. Successful substitutes also can be attractive candidates when there are future staff openings. It is recommended that potential substitutes visit the classrooms and get to know the program, the staff, and the children. Children should also be prepared for the fact that there will be a substitute teacher when one of their teachers is out.

Detailed written plans and procedures for the substitute should be placed in a file folder, manila envelope, or notebook in an easily recognizable place in each classroom. The substitute guide should include:

- professional-looking blank nametags for the substitute so that he or she can be easily identified.
- a list of children in the class and nametags for each so that they can be easily recognized. Felt circles with safety pins can easily become nametags and be placed on the child's shirt. In the absence of cloth or felt, masking tape will work as makeshift nametag materials.
- a list of children who have allergies and other special needs; specific direction for their care and where support is available if necessary.
- the chain of command at the center and the easiest way to contact the director.
- a note indicating where the first-aid kit is located and a list of its contents.
- a list of reasons for the child to be excluded from the class (for example, fever or vomiting).

- a list of the children's parents or primary caregivers and emergency contacts.
- a list of staff members, including their names, their job titles, and their schedules (including breaks).
- a daily class schedule with a list of routine activities for each block of time.
- routine transition activities (for example, a "clean-up song" or dimming the lights to get the children's attention).
- a staff manual outlining daily procedures including:
- arrival and greeting.
- pick up and drop off.
- daily health check.
- lunch, toileting, and snack routines.
- administrative procedures (injury reports, daily notes, attendance count).
- a job description outlining the responsibilities of the substitute (locking or unlocking gates, preparing snacks, feeding fish, and so forth).
- two or three days worth of lesson plans and a list of where related materials are located. A diagram of where the mats or cots are placed for nap time.
- a map of the facility including locations of emergency exits, fire extinguishers, phones, bathrooms, the playground, and storage.
- evacuation procedures.

The substitute should be encouraged to introduce himself or herself to the parents, children, and other staff and to ask any questions that may arise. The director should remember to get the emergency contact information for each substitute in case of an accident or illness.

CASE STUDY

Angela Suarez is a first-year director of a large child-care center. The beginning of the school year was approaching, and she had several teaching positions to fill. She placed ads in the local paper, notified the job placement office of the nearby college, and told as many people as she could that she was looking for staff members. Several teachers applied and she interviewed each of them. Finally, she made some decisions, checked references, and offered jobs to several people. During the first day of employment, Angela distributed the necessary personnel paperwork and then mailed the required information on her new hires to the Department of Justice (DOJ). She was pleased that the new school year was off to a great start.

Four weeks into the semester, Angela received a notice from the DOJ that a new employee, Amanda Anniston, had a criminal record. The information she received was limited, but after gathering further information, she discovered that Amanda had a history of alcohol abuse, including one DUI conviction. The children and parents seem to like Amanda, and her teaching performance is satisfactory.

1. What would you do in this situation?
2. What would you say to Amanda?
3. Are there laws or regulations covering this kind of situation? If so, what are they?
4. Is there a way that Angela could have avoided this problem?

SUMMARY

The director of a child-care center should develop and follow systematic procedures when seeking new staff members. Important factors to look for are education, experience, personal characteristics, skills, and knowledge.

A statement listing full requirements for each specific position can be used to advertise for positions both inside and outside the school.

The selection process should be standardized. The first step is to screen applications for minimum requirements, check references, and note special talents.

Next, the director prepares an interview schedule. This includes setting up the interviews and notifying the interviewing committee. A chairperson designates uniform question areas to be covered. Everyone on the committee should record impressions of each candidate immediately after the interview.

The director should notify the person selected as soon as possible and also inform those not selected. Personnel selection is not an easy process, but careful procedures pay big dividends.

Once the personnel are hired, they should be inducted into fair and consistent employee practices. A written contract is one of the best ways to do this. Procedures explained in a policy statement should include those regarding physical environment, health and safety conditions, terms of employment, job description, and advancement opportunities.

Personnel records are vital and often required by law. A permanent file should include the original application, health records, dates of employment and duties involved, evaluations and conferences, and date and reason for termination (if needed).

Open, frank, and reasonable personnel practices lead to happier employees and reduced turnover.

STUDENT ACTIVITIES

1. Write a statement for recruiting an applicant for a job vacancy you have.

2. Get application forms from three different schools. Note the different kinds of information each asks. What does this tell about the school?

3. Role-play an interview with a prospective teacher. Alternate the roles of teacher and director. Ask for subjective feelings involved in each role. What insights does this give in this process?

4. Write a job description for child-care assistant.

5. Invite several teachers and directors to discuss salaries and fringe benefits with your class.

REVIEW

1. List five sources for recruiting teacher applicants.

2. This chapter listed characteristics most directors look for when recruiting staff members. How many can you recall?

3. List the skills teachers need in order to fulfill their job responsibilities.

4. What information should be included in a recruitment statement?

5. Describe the process for screening applicants for a staff position.

6. Who should be included in the screening process for new staff members?

7. Formulate questions to be used in an interview to obtain the following kinds of information:

   a. attitudes toward differences in people

   b. specific skills

   c. knowledge of child development

8. What points should be covered in a contract?

9. List the kinds of information that are contained in a statement of personnel policies.

10. What kinds of information should be included in a personnel file?

REFERENCES

Center for the Child Care Workforce. (2001). *Current data on child care salaries and benefits in the United States.* Washington, DC: Author.

Epstein, A. S. (1993). *Training for quality: Improving early childhood programs through systematic inservice training.* Ypsilanti, MI: Highscope Press.

Harms, T., & Clifford, R. (1980). *Early childhood environment rating scale.* New York: Teachers College Press.

Harms, T., Cryer, D., & Clifford, R. (1990). *Infant/toddler environment rating scale.* New York: Teachers College Press.

Howes, C., Whitebook, M., & Phillips, D. (1992). Teacher characteristics and effective teaching in child care: Findings from the national child care staffing study. *Child and Youth Forum, 21,* 399–414.

Mean hourly wages of child care educators. (2009). Retrieved from Internet, April 2009. http://www.payscale.com/research/US/indu.

National Institute of Child Health and Human Development. (1996). Characteristics of infant child care: Factors contributing to positive caregiving. *Early Childhood Research Quarterly, 11,* 299–306.

U.S. Bureau of Labor Statistics. (2001). *Survey output.* Washington, DC: U.S. Government Printing Office.

Whitebook, M., Howes, C., & Phillips, D. (1990). *Who cares: Child care teachers and the quality of care in America. Final report of the national child care staffing study.* Oakland, CA: Child Care Employee Project.

SELECTED FURTHER READING

Blood, P. J. (1993). But I'm worth more than that! *Young Children, 48*(3), 65–68.

Bloom, P. (1988). *A great place to work: Improving conditions for staff in young children's programs.* Washington, DC: National Association for the Education of Young Children.

Bredekamp, S., & Willer, B. (1993). Professionalizing the field of early childhood education: Pros and cons. *Young Children, 48*(3), 82–84.

Epstein, A. S. (2002). Early childhood professions: current status and projected needs. *Child Care Information Exchange, 143,* 45–48.

Heng, A. C. (2001). Hiring the right person. *Child Care Information Exchange, 141,* 10–12.

Klinner, J., Riley, D., & Roach, M. (2005). Organizational climate as a tool for child care staff retention. *Young Children*, *60*(6), 90–95.

Manfred-Petitt, L. (1993). Child care: It's more than the sum of its tasks. *Young Children*, *49*(1), 40–42.

Manning, D., Rubin, S. E., Perdigo, H. G., Gonzalez, R. G., & Schindler, P. (1996). A "worry doctor" for preschool directors and teachers: A collaborative model. *Young Children*, *51*(5), 68–73.

National Association for the Education of Young Children. (1990). NAEYC position statement on guidelines for compensation of early childhood professionals. *Young Children*, *46*(1), 30–32.

Phillips, C. (1990). The child development associate program: Entering a new era. *Young Children*, *45*(2), 24–27.

HELPFUL WEBSITES

Disclaimer: Links to Internet sites throughout this book are provided for your convenience and do not constitute an endorsement.

Center for the Child Care Workforce:	**http://www.ccw.org**
JIAN Tools for Sales, Inc.:	**http://www.fundaccountingsoftware.com**
Bureau of Labor Statistics:	**http://www.bls.gov**
National Institute for Early Education Research:	**http://nieer.org**
Sample employee handbook information:	**http://www.employeehandbookstore.com**
Sample employee handbook information:	**http://sampleemployeehandbook.com**
Council for Early Childhood Recognition:	**http://www.cdacouncil.org**
Center for Child Care Workforce:	**http://www.ccw.org**

For additional resources related to administration including videos, links to related sites for each chapter of the text, tutorial quizzes, glossary flashcards, and more, visit the Education CourseMate website for this book at www.cengage.com/login.

Cengage Learning

CHAPTER

9

Staff Supervision and Training

Objectives

After reading this chapter, you should be able to:

- Discuss the components of effective supervision.
- List the steps in an evaluation process.
- Cite methods and sources for staff training.
- Discuss strategies for preventing burnout among employees.

KEY TERMS

critical job elements

evaluation

mentor

supervision

A day in the life of . . .

A Director of a Child-care Learning Center

A four-year-old child walked into my office one morning concerned about what we would be serving for lunch. I informed her and her mother that it was spaghetti and meatball day. Her little face lit up and she said, "Yes, I love the way Miss Linda makes her meatballs. I don't like the way my mommy makes hers. I am going to ask Miss Linda to teach my mommy right now. Come on Mom, let's go to the kitchen."

Staff members in early childhood programs come from various backgrounds. Typically, those who become teachers or caregivers take one of three paths: (1) the traditional path of academic preparation, (2) the parental path of firsthand experience, or (3) the accidental path beginning with an unrelated job. The first group consists of people who set out to prepare for an already chosen profession in early childhood education. They attend college and perform supervised teaching. The second group

234 PART III | Staff Administration

consists of people who learn from firsthand experience of caring for their own children. They may gain additional experience through becoming home-based child-care providers or participating in Head Start. The third group consists of people who prepare for a career unrelated to teaching but by luck or chance find themselves in a setting where there are children. They find the work rewarding, and they decide to change careers.

Almost every child-development center or child-care center will have staff members who fit the three categories. The reality is that directors cannot afford to recruit only people with extensive academic preparation in early childhood education to fill the positions in their school or center. The extremely limited supply of such people is one reason that untrained staff are desperately needed to care for all the children who are in group settings. The important need to staff early childhood centers with people who reflect the backgrounds of the children enrolled is another reason. The children need teachers who come from their own communities, who understand their culture, and who speak their language. Some of these adults may not have extensive academic backgrounds.

Directors who view individual differences of staff members as an asset will value every staff member regardless of their training or credentials. These directors will also help each to continue to grow professionally. Effective and fair methods of supervision and evaluation, followed by training activities that motivate staff members to increase their skills can accomplish this. The Council for Early Childhood Professional Recognition is addressing differences in staff education and training on a national level through its Child Development Associate (CDA) program. The program is administered by the CDA National Credentialing Program in Washington, DC. Teachers in Head Start, early childhood centers, and child-care programs can participate. To qualify for a CDA credential, teachers must show evidence that they are competent to do the following:

- plan and set up a safe and healthy learning environment
- cultivate physical and intellectual competence
- support social and emotional development
- ensure positive participation of children and adults in the learning environment
- establish and maintain close coordination between school and families
- sustain a commitment to professionalism

Participants in the CDA program go through three steps before the credential is awarded. They do field work, take courses, and are evaluated by a person appointed by the council. There are approximately 41,000 CDAs in the United States, with the largest percentage in Head Start. About 15 percent are in private sector early childhood centers. To receive a copy of CDA Competency Standards, write to: Council for Early Childhood Professional Recognition, 2460 16th Street, NW, Washington, DC 20009-3575, or telephone 800-424-4310. Additional information can be found at http://www.cdacouncil.org.

The director of an early childhood center will probably be responsible for supervising all employees, although in Head Start or in large corporate organizations, another employee may fulfill this function. In its narrowest sense, **supervision** means overseeing staff members during the performance of their jobs. However, from a broader perspective, supervision is a constantly changing relationship between employer and employee that is based on mutual respect. Daily contact with employees and the many hours spent talking together facilitate that kind of relationship. This is the basis of an essential support system in which employees can try out new ways of fulfilling job responsibilities.

States differ in requirements for prekindergarten teachers in state-funded programs. As of 2005, nationally

49.4 percent of teachers have a bachelor's degree

23.6 percent have a master's degree or higher

22.8 percent hold a CDA credential

SOURCE: Gilliam, W. S., Marchessault, C. M. (2005). From capitols to classrooms, policies to practice: State-Funded prekindergarten at the classroom level. New Haven, CT: Yale University Child Study Center.

The director establishes rapport with each staff member by being available as often as possible. A good place to start is greeting staff members when they arrive and planning to be free for a short chat. Some directors do relief teaching for short periods while a teacher takes a break, prepares materials, or meets with a parent.

They also help out in classrooms when there is an emergency such as a sick or injured child. Staff members may need the director to be available at the end of the day as well. This is a time when teachers are often tired or discouraged and a willingness to listen may relieve some of the negative feelings. These strategies will be effective in developing a relationship of mutual trust only if the director's attitude expresses genuine caring and a willingness to help.

An important part of supervision involves ensuring compliance with policies and procedures. Sometimes, administrators issue directives and expect their staff to comply. Safety rules, health procedures, schedules, and methods for ordering materials are all examples. Clearly communicating expectations to every employee is essential, as is subsequently checking that employees meet these expectations. Are the teachers in the infant room following the health procedures when they change diapers? Is the cook following guidelines for ensuring the safety of food while cooking and serving? Other times, differences in interpretation of guidelines are acceptable. Curriculum goals are a prime example. Each teacher will implement a school's goals somewhat differently. Here, supervision involves assessing whether each teacher's method of implementation follows the guidelines closely enough, or if a change is needed. The director will need to spend time observing each teacher in their job setting and then discussing these observations.

When an employee must change, the director's job becomes one of helping to bring about that change. This is one of the most difficult aspects of being a director, because it demands significant time and extensive expertise in communication.

The director becomes a coach, providing ideas, encouragement, and feedback. Sometimes, it means observing; at other times, it calls for modeling behavior. Inexperienced teachers will need more time and coaching. Teachers who have a lot of experience require less time, but still benefit from support. They need constructive criticism at certain times and positive reinforcement at others. As staff members become more accomplished and learn to work within the framework of a particular setting, there is another way in which administrators provide supervision. Directors can help these staff members to evaluate their own performance and to discover ways of performing their jobs more effectively. Furthermore, directors can help these employees develop the necessary skills to take responsibility for supervising aides, assistants, student teachers, or volunteers.

Evaluation of Staff Performance

Evaluation is a process that determines whether the goals of an early childhood center are being met. Teachers are evaluated on their ability to implement the educational goals of the center. Support-staff members are assessed on their ability to perform their jobs in ways that supplement the center's educational function. In most education settings, all staff members are evaluated at least once a year. Teachers will often welcome and benefit from more frequent reviews.

Although most teachers and directors see evaluation as a means of professional growth and the basis for improving performance, evaluation has some inherent problems.

First, the process creates anxiety in both the person to be evaluated and the evaluator. Few teachers are completely comfortable having someone judge their performance, and many directors are uneasy about judging their staff members.

Second, two different levels of performance can be evaluated. On one level are obvious factors—performance that can be seen and sometimes measured or counted. The secretary types 10 letters a day with great accuracy or only eight with numerous errors. The teacher keeps the room orderly or leaves it messy. On the other level are factors that cannot be seen, touched, or heard. How does the director evaluate the ability of a teacher to encourage decision making in children or the secretary's ability to create an accepting atmosphere for visitors? If only one performance level is used, it may result in an incomplete or skewed picture of the staff member's ability.

Third, someone must decide who is responsible for evaluation. The final responsibility is that of the director. The actual rating may be done by any number of people in a school. Sometimes evaluations are more meaningful when more than one person is involved, each one having a specific part in the procedure.

In a small school, the director will probably evaluate all the employees. Staff and director develop the procedures cooperatively, and the director executes them. In a larger school, the director may work within a more complex organization for evaluating performance of employees. Staff members at different levels may be responsible for those under their immediate authority. The head teacher evaluates the assistant teacher, and the head cook evaluates the assistant cook, for example.

In a very large system or organization, one person may evaluate all employees. This evaluator works with the director and possibly a few other staff members to design and facilitate the process. Sometimes, people on a specific job level might evaluate others on the same level. As an example, one teacher might evaluate another teacher. This is peer evaluation.

Some evaluation systems may include self-evaluation by the employee. This would not replace other evaluations but would supplement them.

The director usually decides whether all employees should be evaluated, or if only those in certain job categories should be rated. If a school wants to create an atmosphere in which children can grow and change, no staff member can remain static. All employees must be aware of their own strengths and weaknesses and must be helped to find ways to improve. If the school encourages real learning, the dynamics must apply to every staff member.

Evaluations determine whether the goals of an early childhood center are being met.

THE EVALUATION PROCESS

Obviously, evaluation cannot focus in great detail on all areas. An overall evaluation in some specific areas may be enough at certain times. Whatever the focal point, the decision of when and what to evaluate should be a cooperative one between the evaluator and the person to be evaluated. No employee should be formally rated without advance notice.

Objectives

The procedure for evaluation should begin with an agreement between the director and the staff member concerning what is to be accomplished during a stated period of time. These expectations should flow from the statement of goals for the entire school or from the job description for that position. For example, one of the school's goals might be the development of decision-making skills in children. The director and the teacher may list as many ways as possible this can be done. The evaluation will determine how effectively the teacher implemented these.

Standards

The director and the staff member should also agree on the standards for judging achievement. The staff member should know what will be considered a satisfactory level. In the example just given, the teacher should know whether implementation of only a certain percentage of all possible methods for developing decision-making skills will be acceptable. A refinement of this is the establishment of various levels of achievement: outstanding, superior, average, below average, and inferior, or similar terms. Each of these should be defined as precisely as possible if they are used. A "pass" and "fail" standard is easier to understand, but it is sometimes more difficult to use.

Teachers have their own styles of implementing learning activities.

The director and the staff member should decide when the rating will occur. A written understanding that the evaluation will be done at a certain time and will cover a specified period should probably be made. For instance, the rating will be done on March 8, and will cover the period from September 1 to March 8.

Both the evaluator and the person to be rated should agree on the form of the evaluation. Each one should understand that a checklist will be used, or that there will be two observations on certain dates (October 11 and March 8), followed by a conference. If the evaluator will observe the staff member, that person should know the evaluator's objectives. If the director will use a checklist, a copy should be given to the teacher well in advance of the first visit.

METHODS OF EVALUATION

In an earlier chapter, methods of evaluating curriculum were listed and examined. Similar procedures are used for evaluating staff members. Figure 9-1 contains a sample rating form for evaluations.

Tests

Tests are primarily an entry-level screening device. However, they can be used to gauge staff development, especially in subject matter areas. Colleges and universities offering teacher-training programs are a good source for locating appropriate test materials. Educational testing services are another source for prepared tests.

Knowledge of child development, curriculum construction, main points of nutrition, and first aid are topics that lend themselves to a prepared test. Professional organizations and universities are trying to develop teacher competency tests, but in general, tests are not substitutes for direct observation.

RATING SHEET

Date _____

Name _____   Rated by _____

PERFORMANCE CHARACTERISTICS	Often	Sometimes	Never
Personal Qualities			
Has a sense of humor			
Is friendly, cheerful			
Assuming Responsibilities			
Is independent in assuming responsibilities			
Initiates solutions to problems			
Working with Children			
Determines and plans for each child's needs			
Creates a stimulating learning environment			
Working with Adults			
Cooperates with other staff members			
Includes parents in plans for their children			

Specific strengths _____

_____

Areas for improvements _____

_____

I have read this evaluation.

Signed: _____

(Employee and Title)

Further comments by either employee or supervisor _____

_____

FIGURE 9–1   Sample rating form.

Performance Elements

A newer approach to evaluation begins with listing the most important elements in the total job of teaching. This is a joint effort initiated by the director and executed by the teacher. From this list, both choose a number of (usually three to five) **critical job elements**: things that, if they were not done, would seriously impede the total teaching practice. Alternatively, both can agree to elements that this particular teacher wishes (or needs) to focus on for the next period. These elements would form the basis of evaluation for the next rating cycle. These elements will very likely be unique to each teacher. When these are agreed upon and written down, the director and teacher may try to agree on a rating scale of, again, three to five points (outstanding through unsatisfactory). The scale is far less important than is agreement on the major critical elements.

The performance elements methodology is an ongoing process. It probably should be for rather limited time periods and a restricted number of elements. One benefit of this method is that the director gets to know each teacher much more intimately than would be possible using almost any other rating method.

Observations

Once the staff member and director have agreed on objectives to be met, it is time to schedule observation visits to each classroom or work site. The staff member should know when the visit is scheduled. The director should plan to spend an adequate amount of time. Recording the visit as accurately as possible is essential. (The director should use abbreviated words in order to record more information.)

Some staff members may be open to the use of videotapes or a tape recording, but many will feel intimidated. Unless the person is comfortable with taping the visit, this is not a good idea because it will not be an accurate record of performance anyway.

The director should plan multiple observations at different times of the day or several over a period of a month. The director should record examples to substantiate the ratings, thereby making an evaluation more objective.

Sampling of Behaviors

Another method of evaluating teacher performance is to record samples of specific kinds of behavior. For example, a teacher might decide that one objective or critical element would be to encourage language development. One way to measure success in meeting this objective would be to count the number of words spoken by the teacher and by the children at a particular time. This count would be repeated at intervals. Analysis of the results would show whether the children were encouraged to talk. The evaluator can also make samplings of other behavior at specified intervals.

Collecting the children's work is another way to evaluate performance. An increase in the number or changes in the quality would determine whether an objective or critical element had been achieved. For example, if a teacher's objective was to develop more extensive use of art materials, a comparison of the number and quality of paintings at the beginning and the end of the semester would yield some information.

Questionnaire or Checklist

The evaluator may complete questionnaires or checklists privately or in the presence of the teacher in a colleague-like way. Self-designed lists may be constructed to be answered by a simple "yes" or "no," but these are often overly simplistic. Lists requiring longer answers or multiple responses are usually preferred. An example might be, "Does this teacher encourage the children to take care of their own physical needs?" The question may be answered yes or no, but it may also be answered on a scale such as often, sometimes, or never.

• • • • • USE OF EVALUATIONS

Every evaluation should be followed by a conference between the evaluator and the staff member. The evaluator should focus first on the strengths exhibited by that person during the assessment process. It is important to be specific, pointing out the ways in which teacher behaviors support the goals of the school. If there are areas that need improvement, the evaluator should be objective, relate all observations in a nonjudgmental manner, and then ask the staff member whether their perception is the same. If it is not the same, the evaluator should ask how it is different. Good questions to ask are "Why did you do it that way?" or "What was your reason for doing it that way?" The evaluator can learn much by listening carefully to responses. A "right way" seldom exists in any teaching environment. A teacher's actions should reflect sound educational practices, and there are many ways to do that.

The director should make a permanent record of evaluation results, regardless of the method, or combination of methods, used for evaluation. The personnel file of each staff member should contain the periodic evaluations. Each staff member may then see the total picture of development, and the evaluator has a record of past performance.

A written copy of the evaluation should be given to each person evaluated. This can be a written copy of the rating or a summation of notes of the conference. No doubt should exist about the outcome of the evaluation or the areas of recommended improvement. Rewarding excellent performance with due praise is equally important. The employee should sign the evaluation form after reading it.

When a staff member gets an unsatisfactory or borderline rating, the director should make a great effort to bring about improvement. The director and employee must agree as to the specific steps to be undertaken. Few things are as discouraging as being rated unsatisfactory without being told how to improve. Lists of things to do with milestone dates are sometimes helpful. Simple encouragement often works. Most importantly, every attempt should be made to end on an optimistic note.

As will be seen later in this chapter, the evaluation process can reveal strengths and weaknesses in the teaching staff. A good many of these weaknesses, insofar as they involve lack of knowledge, may be remedied by various means of staff training.

Evaluation is an effective and powerful tool to be used with great care and sensitivity. It can be an instrument for change and self-growth. It can also produce profound discouragement if not done well. The following are suggestions for the evaluator:

- Be objective: Describe specific incidents to illustrate behavior being discussed. (Count them, if possible.) "I observed three times that you failed to respond to Anthony at story time when he was trying to ask a question."

- Be gentle: Discuss the positive things you have observed before going on to the negative.

- Establish a climate for discussion: Let staff members know what you are criticizing, but allow time to listen to their points of view. Try to look at the behavior from the teacher's view.

- Be constructive: Help teachers or other staff to find alternatives. Provide resources for further information where applicable. Offer help and continued support.

- Be professional: Do not discuss evaluations with other staff members unless they share evaluation responsibilities.

Staff Development

Staff development is a broad term that refers to all the processes that encourage personal growth in employees in any work environment. In an early childhood setting, it usually refers to procedures that help the teaching staff achieve greater professionalism. This chapter has already discussed the supportive relationship between a director and staff members that enables staff to try new ways of carrying out the various functions of their jobs. Additionally, changes in teacher behaviors can be brought about through specific training activities.

PLANNING STAFF DEVELOPMENT

All personnel in an early childhood facility begin the job with a certain level of skill and knowledge. Training activities should help them move to new levels of effectiveness in carrying out their jobs. Some beginning teachers, for instance, are at a "survival level." They just try to get through the difficulties of each day. In-service instruction can help them interact with children in ways that not only minimize their frustration, but also increase their enjoyment.

Experienced teachers sometimes feel "stale" and in need of new ideas or challenges. Training can give these people curriculum ideas that will spark a new enthusiasm for teaching.

Another purpose of staff training is to help those who want to move to new job categories. Assistant teachers may dream of having their own class. A teacher may feel ready to assume some administrative tasks. A secretary may want to assist in the classroom. Training activities can give these employees opportunities to gain the skills necessary to move to those new positions.

Another important purpose of staff training is to develop professional identity. Teachers sometimes have difficulty defining who they are and relating the importance of what they do. Consequently, others also regard early childhood education as less important than other levels of schooling. As teachers gain knowledge and add to their skills, they will be able to take pride in their work and project a more professional image.

An additional reason for promoting staff development is that parents are much more demanding of their child's caregivers than they were in the past. Parents know more about child development and what their children should be learning. They ask teachers questions about their child's stage of growth. They want to know about the school's curriculum and to discuss issues of child rearing. Teachers must have the background to respond knowledgeably.

Stress and burnout are often a fact of life for those who staff all-day, year-round centers. Working with children is exhausting at best. People with minimal skills can have even more difficulty in dealing with the problems that arise. Staff training can furnish some new strategies that minimize stress and decrease burnout.

The director may want to offer staff training but not know how to get started. So much new information is always available. Research studies and pilot programs constantly reveal more information about children's development, curriculum effects, and family influences. By attending conferences or meeting with other professionals, directors gain new insights. Choosing from the many different training topics is difficult. Thus, the director must identify the training areas that the staff needs at a particular time. There are several ways to do this.

Cengage Learning

Staff training provides information for those who want to change positions within the child–care center.

Staff-Needs Assessment

Establishing an open-door policy is one of the simplest ways to find out the areas in which staff members need additional training. This means being available to listen to both staff members and parents, encouraging suggestions and discussion of issues, and being receptive to questions and ideas for change. In this kind of atmosphere, there is an opportunity to hear the areas where teachers feel they need help or what parents want stressed in the curriculum.

Teachers can also be asked to do a self-evaluation. A rating scale or question-naire are the simplest forms, but an evaluation can be as simple as asking staff members to indicate the areas in which they feel the need or the desire for additional training. Evaluation should be seen as an instrument for growth, not as a means for criticism.

Observations of staff members, both teaching and nonteaching, as they perform their jobs will also provide some ideas about training needs. In order to do this, the evaluator needs to have a good knowledge of each job. What are the basic tasks a person in this job must be able to do? Moreover, what constitutes an "acceptable" performance and an "out-standing" one?

Information from professional sources will also provide data to use when planning staff training. Organizations such as the National Association for the Education of Young Children (NAEYC) have lists of competencies that teachers should acquire. College and university child development programs may also have compiled information about teaching skills.

The director should get regular feedback from employees about their own prog-ress. Are they using information from previous training sessions? If not, what is standing in their way? Perhaps they were not ready to use that information, instead needing to "fill in some gaps" in knowledge before doing so. Giving positive feedback is important when they are striving to be more capable.

The director should also make a list of topics individuals have indicated are training needs and circulate the list among all staff members. Nonteaching staff should be included because they, too, may want to know more about child development or how to manage child behaviors. The employees should rank the topics in order of importance. Figure 9-2 is an example of a staff-interests survey.

A staff-needs survey often highlights the fact that staff members have different lev-els of needs. Some people want only to add to the very basic information that all peo-ple who interact with children need to know. Others want practical information such as planning a more exciting and challenging curriculum. Still others may be ready to explore theoretical issues such as learning theory or the influence of environment on children's development.

Size of Groups

Next, the director decides whether staff training will be for all personnel at once or for multiple small groups at different times. When staff members are extremely diversified in their levels of knowledge, it sometimes is more feasible to divide them or even to pro-vide individualized training for some. Nonetheless, people learn from others. Therefore, sometimes a group with mixed abilities allows for learning from peers.

If the number of employees is large, meetings for the entire staff may be unwieldy for certain kinds of training activities. A discussion is difficult if there are more than 10 people. A workshop can accommodate as many as the space allows. Conversely, a small group sometimes needs outside stimulation and ideas. When the number of employees is small, the director might consider using films, lectures, or field trips.

STAFF–INTERESTS SURVEY

I need information concerning topics for upcoming staff training sessions. The following is a list of some suggestions that have been made in discussions with staff members. Choose six and rank them in importance to you with "1" being the highest priority.

_____ Enhancing children's language development

_____ Using computers in our classrooms

_____ Stimulating more creative outdoor play

_____ Involving children in snack preparations

_____ Suggesting individualized music activities

_____ Rearranging our environments to achieve our goals

_____ Learning carpentry skills

_____ Developing science activities that are easy to plan and implement

_____ Stimulating dramatic play using kits

_____ Understanding what babies are really learning

_____ Conducting more effective parent conferences

_____ Avoiding burnout

Suggestions or comments: _____

_____

_____

_____

Please return your form to me by the end of the month so that I can begin to plan upcoming sessions.

Thanks,

Betty Beaumont
Director of Country Day School

FIGURE 9-2　Staff interests survey.

Time

Finding the time for staff training is very difficult in an all-day school. Many schools resolve this problem by scheduling meetings while the children are napping. Teachers can rotate nap room duty, allowing the others to attend. The director should not make the mistake of always assigning one person to nap room duty, thus excluding that person from training sessions.

Another alternative is to schedule training meetings before or after school hours. A small group meeting could be held early in the morning before the children arrive. Holding meetings right after the last child leaves in the evening is another possibility. The staff could have a potluck dinner and have the meeting while they eat. This serves two purposes.

It provides staff social time, and it avoids the fatigue that comes when staff must return later in the evening. When people are actively involved in discussion or an interesting workshop, they tend to overcome any fatigue they may have felt at the beginning. If the activities are exciting, staff will be "recharged" rather than tired out at the end. Schedules for meetings should be set at regular intervals, preferably covering at least a six-month period. Thus, all staff members can plan their schedules to be available.

Place

The director must select an appropriate setting for the chosen kind of training activity. For a workshop, there must be enough space for everyone to work. Teachers who sit on child-size chairs all day will appreciate comfortable tables and chairs. For a discussion, including everyone is important. There should be no "back row sitters," because they will not really feel a part of the proceedings. For a sample staff meeting agenda, see Figure 9-3.

Attendance

A question many directors ask is whether attendance at training sessions should be mandatory. Staff will be there "in body" if it is required as a condition of employment, but they cannot be forced to learn. However, a purely voluntary training policy may result in avoidance by the people who need it most. It is probably best to require staff to attend and to make the training provocative and practical. Staff should be paid for the extra time.

Skills Application

When a training session has been completed, staff will need to practice their new skills as soon as possible. The director should provide them with the materials they will need and allow them time to plan and prepare lessons. Following a science workshop, for instance, it is important to see that teachers have the kinds of equipment they need to put their new ideas into effect. Many teachers feel really anxious about offering science

---

STAFF MEETING AGENDA

Thursday, February 19
7:00 P.M. Teachers' Lounge

I. Discussion of individual children
Patty will discuss Jerrod
Suggestions

II. Discussion of individual children
Annemarie will discuss Emily
Suggestions

III. New children who have entered or will be entering
Donna will give brief background information on each child

IV. Report on recent professional conference attended by Donna and several teachers
Display new materials and resources
Discuss new ideas

V. Adjournment

FIGURE 9-3 Sample staff meeting agenda.

lessons and need a lot of encouragement. If they have the right equipment, they may feel a bit more secure.

Learning Styles

Just as children learn in very different ways, so do adults. Some people can learn by seeing or hearing information. Others need to be actively involved in doing before they learn. The director should ask staff members how they learn best and then choose training activities to meet those needs. For some, a workshop will be the best way to help them learn. For others, films, discussions, or even reading will be the most effective.

POPULAR TRAINING METHODS

Orientation

Training begins as soon as a new employee is hired. The director should start by giving the new worker the employee handbook and then sit down with that person to answer any questions. Next, the person should be taken to the work site (the classroom or the kitchen, for instance), shown where materials are and how to operate the equipment, and introduced to other staff members.

Orientation for teachers has some added dimensions from those of other employees. Teachers can read the philosophy and goals in the handbook, but they may need to understand how to implement them in the classroom. Therefore, the director should spend extra time with all new teachers during the early weeks of employment.

Briefly visiting their classrooms and getting to know their teaching styles is helpful. (Visits too frequent or too lengthy may overwhelm or frighten some new teachers.) The director will need to meet more frequently with new teachers than with experienced staff. These can be brief meetings before or after school to answer questions or clarify problems. Additional effort in the beginning will often prevent later difficulties. Refer also to Chapter 7 for more extensive information on orientation.

Mentoring

A mentor program is one way to help new teachers or to upgrade the skills of more experienced teachers. In the context of education, a **mentor** is one who serves as a trusted counselor helping a teacher to perform more effectively. Program developers have identified requirements for mentors (Whitebook, Hnatiuk, & Bellm, 1994; Bellm, Hnatiuk, & Whitebook, 1996). A mentor should have a solid background in early childhood education and have spent time in a classroom or in family child care. Personal qualifications include good interpersonal skills, the ability to develop a supportive and trusting relationship with others, and experience or education in working with adults. They should also have a willingness to continue their own learning, because many mentors say they learn as much from their trainees as they teach them because they are forced to reevaluate their own methods. The mentor must also be committed to helping adults and have the time to devote to the process. The mentor certainly should be paid for the time. This responsibility should not simply be added to other duties without extra compensation.

A mentoring relationship differs from supervision. A supervisor has responsibility for evaluating the trainee; a mentor guides, supports, and encourages without being judgmental. Establishing trust through confidentiality is essential in this relationship. The trainee must feel secure that whatever is discussed within the working relationship will not be shared with others. An important exception would be if the protégé's actions in some way jeopardize the safety of the children.

Professionals who adopt this kind of training use a variety of methods that seem to have positive results. They:

- establish a relationship of trust with the protégé.

- observe for a whole day, then consider what changes can be accomplished.

- model behavior.

- start an activity with children and ask the trainee to finish.

- give frequent and immediate feedback.

- ask questions that lead to thoughtful discussion. "What gave you the most difficulty today?" "What would have made it easier?" They discuss the responses.

- provide resources for information or materials as needed.

- are sensitive to the fact that adults, like children, have different styles and rates of learning.

Mentoring has proved an effective method of improving the quality of educational settings for children.

Those interested in starting a mentoring program can contact the National Center for the Early Childhood Work Force (NCECW) to receive training materials for mentors. Write to: National Center for the Early Childhood Work Force (NCECW), 733 15th Street, NW, Suite 1037, Washington, DC 20005–2112. Telephone 202-737-7700; fax 202-737-0370.

Team Teaching

Another way to provide informal and ongoing training is to set up a partnership style of training. In this method, two teachers work closely together as equal partners. They function as a team, with common aims. Each learns from the other, as they come to recognize their own strengths and weaknesses. To make this kind of relationship work, they must be able to overcome the competitiveness many teachers feel. They also have to spend time talking with each other, planning, learning, and resolving problems. The director should meet with them periodically to assess their progress and perhaps suggest resources for learning.

College and University Classes

Colleges and universities offer another source for training staff. Well-qualified professors with wide experience teaching the classes can be an advantage of using this resource. Additionally, other students from varied backgrounds offer stimuli for learning. The campus setting often offers facilities such as a laboratory school, a library, and even remedial help for those with learning or language difficulties.

Considering the disadvantages of college courses for staff training is important before choosing this method. The philosophy of an instructor may differ markedly from that of a particular director. Disruptions occur when staff members return to the school and want to carry out ideas that differ from the goals of their employer. The cost of tuition may be prohibitive for the student and more than a school can support. An additional difficulty is that many college courses are scheduled during the day. Teachers who work all day cannot attend.

Staff Meetings

Staff meetings are a time for all staff members to communicate with one another, perhaps the only time during their busy days with children. This can be a fruitful time to clarify issues and brainstorm solutions to problems. In order to be effective, the director must

Staff meetings are a time for all staff members to communicate with one another.

create a climate in which each person's ideas and opinions are valued and where it is safe to express feelings. A skilled director who can accomplish this will foster a collegial climate as was discussed in the beginning of this text. They will also serve as a model for other staff members to emulate in their dealings with one another, with children, and with parents.

Each meeting should be planned to consider concerns, needs, or questions of the director and staff members. The director should write an agenda and distribute it to staff members minimally a week before the meeting, should add any information that needs to be read before the meeting, and should post the schedule or place a copy in staff mailboxes (see Figure 9-3). The biggest mistake many directors make is trying to do too much at one meeting. Setting limited objectives is best so that there can be more thorough coverage. Whatever the topics, staff meetings should be opportunities for everyone involved to learn. A meeting might be devoted entirely to discussing several children who are creating problems for staff members. The primary teachers can present information about the children, with additional information from any other teachers who have contact with them. Another meeting might be devoted to some new curriculum ideas along with an opportunity to look at actual materials. Another kind of meeting might be one in which a major decision has to be made, for instance the purchase of some new playground equipment. The director can distribute information about the options, then the staff can discuss the pros and cons of each choice, culminating with a decision.

Portfolio

Writing a portfolio can be a meaningful way for teachers to evaluate their own abilities and to upgrade their skills. A portfolio is a written documentation of what teachers do, why they do it, and how it relates to competency as a professional. Portfolios are used as a self-study vehicle and as the basis of discussions between teachers and supervisors. They are the primary means for assessing competency of Head Start teachers who are candidates for the CDA credential. However, portfolio writing is an effective instrument for staff development in any early childhood setting. An important benefit teachers will gain from portfolio writing is practice describing the teaching processes in their own words. As they learn to refine and clarify their writing, they will be able to view differently what they do. They will gain insight into their own strengths and weaknesses, as well as an awareness of where changes need to be made.

Directors should schedule time to discuss portfolio entries with teachers. This can be a time to focus on teachers' strengths and show genuine interest in their progress. A dialogue about recorded incidents will also provide a greater understanding of how each teacher functions in the classroom. Sometimes, directors will need to answer questions or be a resource for finding information.

Portfolio entries can be supplemented by videotapes of teachers as they work in the classrooms or on the playground. Obviously, one needs to have a good camera and someone with time to operate it. Introduction of this device as a method of training needs to be done with extensive sensitivity for people's feelings. Many people do not like to see themselves portrayed in photographs, and a video is even more revealing. The staff member to be taped must be included in the decision to do so and allowed to decide when and where the taping will be done. Following the taping session there must be time for the staff member to view the tape and to discuss it with the person responsible for training. The discussion should include ways to change or improve performance. If done carefully, videotaping can be a powerful tool for increasing staff competencies and self-esteem.

Workshops

A workshop is sometimes called a "hands-on experience." Participants get actively involved in doing or in making something to broaden their practical skills. In a workshop, teachers can learn songs, make curriculum materials, and practice reading or telling stories. A workshop can be planned for other job categories as well. Cooks from several schools could get together to try out new recipes that children might like.

Again, planning is the key to a workshop's success. Providing a comfortable setting is important, as is making sure that the task is accomplishable in the time allotted. The director should have enough materials for everyone to use, distribute copies of directions or any information needed to complete the task, and be available to offer help or give encouragement as participants work.

Group Discussions

The format of a group discussion can range from open discussion during an entire meeting to a short interchange following a presentation. Group discussion is one of the most effective ways to help adults learn. One of the tremendous advantages of this format is that often the whole staff can be included, not just teachers. Some of the same problems are encountered whether a staff member works in the kitchen, drives the bus, or manages a classroom. Each frequently has the same kinds of reactions to children's behaviors and needs to have an outlet for expressing those feelings.

Group discussions are an effective way to pursue a specific topic. For example, discipline is a commonly requested topic for discussion. Ask any group of adults who are around children all day, and they will reveal that discipline is their biggest problem. Simply giving them a list of techniques to manage difficult children is possible. However, a more effective way of helping them is to encourage a discussion of their own feelings about children's behavior. They may find that their own reactions contribute to the trouble. Once they have gained that kind of insight, they will be more open to trying new techniques for managing children's behavior.

Role-Playing

Role-playing is a drama in which the participants put themselves into a designated situation. It is an informal type of meeting that can be adapted to many kinds of problems.

Role-playing is an excellent tool for resolving interaction problems between adults. Several participants act out the problem or situation. The audience watches, listens, and then discusses what happened. The "actors" can contribute how they felt as the play progressed. The final result may be a discovery of alternate ways of behaving, or just the insight gained from understanding the feelings involved. When two staff members are having a problem, asking them to role-play, with their parts reversed from reality, helps. When each is asked to "assume the role" of the other, the situation may look quite different.

Exchange Observations

Exchanging observations between teachers within a school is another way of encouraging new ideas. By mutual agreement, two teachers observe each other in the classroom. After the visits, they meet to discuss their observations.

Obviously, this kind of staff training can work only when teachers trust and respect each other. It is not appropriate at the beginning of a school year, or with new or insecure teachers.

Films, Slides, and Tapes

Audiovisual materials add other dimensions to training sessions. Public libraries have many free materials. Some schools allow money in the yearly budget for renting or purchasing materials. Watching the local television schedule for useful programs is also helpful. (Nonprofit educational institutions are allowed to use recorded material for instructional purposes, but copyright laws forbid keeping taped materials longer than 45 days.) If the director or a staff member owns a video camera, the school can make its own tapes. Slides or tapes are frequently available at professional conferences. NAEYC is an excellent resource for training materials. Some of their videos that can be used for staff training include the following:

- *Building Bridges to Kindergarten: Transition Planning for Children*
- *Child Care Administration: Tying It All Together*
- *Culture and Education of Young Children*
- *Appropriate Curriculum for Young Children: The Role of the Teacher*
- *Designing Developmentally Appropriate Days*
- *Daily Dilemmas: Coping with Challenges*
- *Painting a Positive Picture: Proactive Behavior Management*
- *Partnerships with Parents*
- *Child Care and Children with Special Needs*

This is only a partial list of videos available through NAEYC. Call 866-623-9248, fax 770-442-9742, or visit their website, http://www.naeyc.org, to receive their latest catalog.

Field Trips

Field trips are another way to broaden staff members' learning. Some visits can be made as a group in the evening or on weekends. Others will have to be made by individuals when they can be relieved from duties at school. Visits to other schools usually give teachers new ideas for curriculum or arranging their environment.

Often, just the opportunity to talk to other teachers in different settings renews enthusiasm for teaching. On a weekend, the group could visit a supplier of learning materials. Many of these places have employees who are knowledgeable about children and who can offer new ideas for learning activities.

Guest Speakers

It is often helpful to invite guest speakers to attend training meetings. The director should provide the speaker with information to use in determining the focus of the presentation and share any questions or interests staff members have communicated. The speaker should also know how much time is to be allowed and whether there will be time for questions and discussion following the talk. Staff members should be provided with reading material if appropriate and asked to come prepared with questions they might want answered. After a meeting of this type, it is the director's responsibility to follow up with staff members to help them implement any new ideas they have gained from the session. See Figure 9-4 for a sample staff meeting agenda, which includes a guest speaker.

Professional Meetings

Staff should be encouraged to attend meetings and conferences of professional organizations. Chapters of NAEYC are found in many areas of the United States. Everyone on staff will benefit from membership. Meetings and conferences offer various speakers, workshops, and displays from which teachers can learn. Publications are also available through the organization.

Reading

It is worthwhile to provide employees with books, pamphlets, and magazines that will help them develop their skills. The director can encourage them to use the materials by

---

STAFF MEETING AGENDA

Thursday, May 28
7:00 P.M. Teachers' Lounge

I. New enrollments
    Background information and assignment of new children

II. Introduction of guest speaker
    Dr. Martha Emrin, Pediatrician
    She will discuss the inclusion of a child with AIDS.
    Ample time will be allowed for discussion and questions.

III. Adjournment

You will find an article on pediatric AIDS in your mailbox. Please read it in preparation for this meeting.

FIGURE 9-4   Sample staff meeting agenda that includes a guest speaker.

bringing some to a staff meeting and pointing out some of the interesting articles or parts of a book that they might want to read. The collection should be expanded as often as possible. If the budget is limited and does not allow for the purchase of books, the director can make a list of what is available in the public library and distribute copies to the staff.

FORMAT FOR TRAINING SESSIONS

Knowing some general principles for effective training sessions that can be used for several different methods may be helpful. They can be varied to fit each method of training. The following are some guidelines:

- Arrange the setting for the purpose of the session.
- Provide participants with an agenda, including objective.
- Prepare the setting ahead of time.
  - **a.** Put out materials, arrange chairs, provide coffee or other beverages.
  - **b.** Check any audiovisual equipment being used.
- Carry out the procedure as planned.
  - **a.** Begin and end at the time planned.
  - **b.** Stay as close as possible to the objective.
- Ask participants to evaluate the meeting.
- Follow through.
  - **a.** Provide materials so participants can practice new skills.
  - **b.** Get feedback after staff put new ideas into practice.

Staff Relationships

A discussion of staff development would not be complete without considering how the people in a school get along with each other. They spend long hours together each day. Nerves become frayed with the constant demands that young children make on their patience and energy. Bickering, competitiveness, or burnout may result. The director is the key person in changing destructive patterns of interaction into ones that are positive and cooperative.

COMMUNICATION

The director should start by helping the staff to develop good communication skills. One way is to plan a workshop on effective communication using Thomas Gordon's "I" messages. The staff is asked to practice stating problems or concerns by starting a sentence with phrases such as "I feel sad," "I get upset," or "I am discouraged." The group discusses how the listener might react when this approach is used. It is important to consider nonverbal communication as well. What type of message is conveyed by a clenched jaw, tightly folded arms, lack of eye contact, or raised eyebrows? This discussion can be followed with a role-play. The participants should be asked to note whether "I" messages were used and whether the verbal message was congruent with the body language.

After this kind of workshop, staff members should be encouraged to resolve some of their own problems. Rather than having them expect intervention each time a difference arises, the director should send them back to talk to each other. They will probably find they like the feeling of competence that comes from dealing with difficulties themselves. They will also develop closer rapport with one another.

At staff meetings, it is important for each member to participate. In any group of people, some speak out even if they have nothing meaningful to say. Others seldom say anything. The director should limit the participation of the "big talkers" and encourage the nonparticipants to contribute.

Goal:

DECISION MAKING

Goal:

When there is a democratic atmosphere in a school, staff will feel included in important decisions that affect them. Effective directors will encourage this kind of participation. The purchase of expensive pieces of playground equipment is an example. Some staff members will request one kind, while others will want another. If the director chooses, part of the staff will be happy, and the other part will be disgruntled. Having the staff go through a decision-making process and make the choice themselves is better. They will learn from the process and will probably be more satisfied with the result.

To decide which playground equipment to purchase, the staff could go through the following steps:

1. Gather information: They should find out as much as they can about the possible choices. What do the pieces look like, and how long are they expected to last? What is the cost of each piece? What possible uses can children make of each? Is there a good place on the playground to put all the pieces?

2. Set priorities: The next step is to list their priorities based on the goals of the school. One piece may lend itself to imaginative play, whereas the other will develop children's physical abilities. Which will more closely fit the school's goals?

3. Make a choice: A consensus should be reached among staff about which one to choose.

4. Decide how to implement the choice: Should the equipment be purchased immediately? Will it be installed during school hours so the children can watch, or on a weekend so that the children can be surprised?

5. Evaluate the choice: For future learning, the staff should evaluate the decision after a period of time to determine whether the choice was a good one. Are the children using the equipment as expected? Are there other ways it is used that were not expected? Should a different choice have been made?

This process of decision making has been described in terms of a concrete object, the piece of equipment. The same steps can be adapted to other kinds of decisions.

Burnout

Stress and burnout are problems that plague many people who work in jobs that require a lot of emotional energy. The very character of early childhood programs contributes to the likelihood of staff burnout. Several causes of burnout can be identified.

CAUSES

- Lack of recognition as a professional is one cause that teachers often list. Their low status is reflected in the minimal salaries that many schools pay their staff. Along with low pay, few have fringe benefits such as a medical or retirement plan. Low status is also seen in the reaction of some parents to early childhood teachers and caregivers. They may comment "You only play with the children all day," or they refer to the child-care center teacher as their child's "babysitter." Few parents have a real idea of the curriculum of their child's school and, thus, little appreciation of what is being taught. All these factors contribute to teachers feeling that they are not valuable.

• Time pressures also lead to fatigue and burnout. Child-care teachers spend six to eight hours a day with children. During that time, children's demands leave little opportunity for any planning or preparation. Few schools pay teachers for time away from the children. Any work they might do to enhance classroom activities must be done at the end of a long day. Consequently, planning may be haphazard, further contributing to dissatisfaction with their job.

• An unrealistic view of their role may be another cause of burnout in teachers. In their book, *Planning and Administering Early Childhood Programs,* Decker and Decker (2001) write that teachers are "unable to maintain a detached concern" because they see themselves as surrogate parents. These authors also feel that teachers are so indoctrinated with the importance of the early years that they are let down if they do not meet their own expectations. Preschool teachers often feel personally responsible for the development of the children in their care. Any achievements the children make confirm their own value as teachers. Any failures to move forward are considered evidence of the teachers' failures.

• Classroom management problems sometimes cause extreme stress, and then teacher burnout. One difficult child in a group can create chaos for all the others if the behavior is not curbed. Inexperienced teachers who have not developed ways of managing these children have an especially difficult time. More experienced teachers, who still have difficulty being firm, may also find this kind of child "trying."

• Administrative incompetence and insensitivity should certainly be mentioned in a discussion of burnout. This refers to directors who fail to take into account the needs or feelings of employees. Sometimes this happens when directors make decisions that affect staff without consulting them. Other times, directors are unaware of how teachers feel. When asked, teachers will describe various behaviors that fall into this category. "I came in one morning to find that I had two new children in my group." "I was told that I couldn't take the time off to go to my daughter's school play because they couldn't pay a substitute." "My director does not really understand how much that one child disrupts my group. She says I should be able to control him." All these examples are indications that the directors did not take the time to consider their employees' feelings. The result could be built-up resentment and burnout.

PREVENTION

Various sources offer suggestions for alleviating stress and preventing burnout. The following have been culled from several of these sources. For more in-depth reading, look to the Selected Further Reading at the end of this chapter. Among the items on the following list, there are some that the director can facilitate. The others can be passed on to employees as suggestions to help themselves.

- Deal with problems as they occur. Do not let them build up. Discuss problems in a nonconfrontational manner.
- Find an outlet for tension that works for you. Try walking, gardening, games, crossword puzzles, and so on. Stay away from the things that work for only a short time, such as eating or drinking too much.

- Learn more about child development. When you know what to expect of children at different age levels, you will be neither surprised when some behaviors appear, nor disappointed when others do not appear.
- Be prepared each day with lesson plans, but be flexible and willing to adapt or change those plans as needed.
- Keep records on children so that you can really see they have made some progress.
- Try to detach yourself from situations that cannot be changed. There will always be some children you cannot change or some families you cannot help. Learn to accept this.
- Keep in good physical health. Get enough sleep; eat a balanced diet.
- Get away from the children for brief periods during the day. A 10-minute break can definitely help.
- Try to avoid getting caught up in the daily "gripe sessions" with fellow employees. They do little good and only make you feel worse.
- Become an advocate for recognition of early childhood education as a profession with adequate and competitive compensation.

Facilitate bathroom breaks

The challenge as a director of a school for young children is to help the staff become the very best they possibly can be. This is admittedly more formidable than trying to help children change. Adults are less malleable and are more set in their ways. They resist any change with reactions of anger or anxiety. However, when the director begins to see the results of a quality staff-training program, it will be clear that all the efforts have been worthwhile.

CASE STUDY

Eva has been a preschool teacher for the last 15 years. Over these years she has worked in toddler, two-, and four-year-old programs. Generally speaking, she works well with children, families, and staff. Lately, she seems to be in a "slump." Her lesson plans have been lacking creativity, and she has been impatient with the children and other staff members.

Late one evening, the director of the center received a complaint from one of the children's mothers. According to Mrs. Guirreza, Eva was angry with Angelita because she had refused to participate in an activity and was poking other children during circle time. Eva yelled at the child and Angelita began to cry. Mrs. Guirreza is concerned because her daughter does not want to return to the center. She did not like the way Eva handled the situation and feels that perhaps Eva should not continue working with children.

1. How should the director respond to Mrs. Guirreza? What is appropriate information to share with her about "burnout" in the child-care industry?
2. What can the director do to help Eva and other staff members to prevent or overcome burnout?
3. How could the director plan a staff development day to further educate and rejuvenate the staff members?

SUMMARY

Staff members in early childhood programs usually take three different paths to become teachers: (1) the traditional path of academic preparation, (2) the parental path of experience, and (3) the accidental path beginning with an unrelated job. All are needed to care for the children who are in group settings.

Directors who value individual differences will be faced with the task of helping each type of staff member to grow as professionals. This can be accomplished through fair and effective methods of supervision and evaluation, followed by training activities.

Another way that teachers can become more professional is to participate in the Child Development Associate credential program.

Supervision means overseeing staff members during the performance of their jobs. It is also a constantly changing relationship between director and employees.

Evaluation is a process to determine whether the goals of an early childhood center are being met. The evaluation process should begin with an agreement on goals to be reached during the time period being assessed and include standards of measurement. Methods of evaluation may be a combination of tests, observations, samplings of behavior, questionnaires, and checklists. A record of evaluation results should be placed in personnel files and a written copy given to the teacher. Every evaluation should be followed by a conference between the director and the staff member.

Staff development is a broad term that refers to all the processes that encourage personal growth in employees in any work environment. In an early childhood setting, it refers to procedures that help teaching staff achieve greater professionalism. Staff-training needs are revealed during supervision and evaluation activities. Other sources of information include staff self-evaluation and information from professional sources.

The director should plan training activities by grouping staff appropriately, finding a time that fits staff schedules, choosing a place that fits the activity, and deciding whether attendance is mandatory. When a training session is completed, staff should be encouraged to practice their new skills.

Popular training methods are orientations, mentor relationships, team teaching, college classes, staff meetings, portfolio writing, workshops, group discussions, role-playing, exchange observations, audiovisual materials, field trips, guest speakers, professional meetings, and reading.

Staff development must include helping staff get along with one another. They will benefit from practice in communication and decision making.

Burnout may occur among people who work in early childhood settings. Identifying the cause and providing staff with suggestions for preventing or alleviating stress is important.

STUDENT ACTIVITIES

1. With permission of the director, survey the staff members of a child-care center. Ask the following questions:

    a. How long have you been a teacher/caregiver?

    b. Where did you work before your present position?

    c. What kinds of academic preparation or experience qualified you for this job?

    Summarize your findings. Compare the profiles of staff members at this center with the three paths leading to a teaching profession that are described in this chapter.

2. Interview a director of a child-care center. Ask about the methods used to evaluate teachers. Are support staff evaluated as well? If so, what methods are used?

3. Plan a staff training workshop. State specifically what will be accomplished, materials needed, and room arrangement. If possible, implement your plan at the school where you work. How successful was the session? Are there things you should have done differently?

REVIEW

1. There are three different paths that lead to becoming teachers or caregivers. What are they?

2. Teachers must show evidence that they are competent in six areas in order to qualify for a Child Development Associate credential. List the six competencies.

3. Define the words supervision and evaluation.

4. Briefly describe the following methods of evaluation and the ways they are used:
    a. tests
    b. performance elements
    c. samplings of behaviors
    d. observations
    e. questionnaires or checklists

5. State two purposes of staff training.

6. Finding time for staff training is often difficult in an all-day school. What suggestions were made in this chapter?

7. List seven popular training methods.

8. Discuss the use of portfolio writing as a staff training method.

9. Describe the steps in setting up a training session.

10. List the steps in a democratic decision-making process.

11. What are the causes of professional burnout?

12. List the suggestions for preventing burnout.

REFERENCES

Bellm, D., Hnatiuk, P., & Whitebook, M. (1996). *The early childhood mentoring curriculum: A trainer's guide and mentor handbook.* Washington, DC: National Center for Early Childhood. Work Force.

Decker, C. A., & Decker, J. R. (2001). *Planning and administering early childhood programs* (7th ed.). New York: Prentice Hall.

Whitebook, M., Hnatiuk, P., & Bellm, D. (1994). *Mentoring in early care and education: Refining an emerging career path.* Washington, DC: National Center for Early Childhood Work Force.

SELECTED FURTHER READING

Abbot-Shim, M. (1990). In-service training: A means to quality care. *Young Children,* *45*(2), 14–18.

Albrecht, K., & Engel, B. (2007). Moving away from a quick-fix mentality to systematic professional development. *Young Children, 62*(4), 18–25.

Carter, Marge, (2008). Assessing quality. *Exchange, 30*(6), 32–36.

Epstein, A. (2002). Early childhood professionals: Current status and projected needs. *Child Care Information Exchange, 243,* 45–48.

Feeney, S., & Freeman, N. K. (2002). Early childhood education as an emerging profession: Ongoing conversations. *Child Care Information Exchange, 143,* 38–41.

Forrest, R., & McCrea, N. (2002). How do I relate and share professionally? *Child Care Information Exchange, 143,* 49–52.

Hansen, J. K., & Gable, S. (2007). Challenges and rewards: Developing an entry-level early childhood training program. *Young Children 62*(4), 46–52.

Hildebrand, V. (2003). *Management of child development centers* (5th ed.). New York: Merrill.

Nolan, M. (2007). *Mentor coaching and leadership in early care and education.* Clifton Park, NY: Cengage Learning.

Washington, V. (1996). Professional development in context: Leadership at the borders of our democratic, pluralistic society. *Young Children, 51*(6), 30–34.

Waxman, S. (1998). Legacy of a mentor. *Young Children, 53*(6), 62–63.

HELPFUL WEBSITES

Disclaimer: Links to Internet sites throughout this book are provided for your convenience and do not constitute an endorsement.

Council for Early Childhood Professional Recognition:	**http://www.cdacouncil.org**
Center for Child Care Workforce:	**http://www.ccw.org**

For additional resources related to administration including videos, links to related sites for each chapter of the text, tutorial quizzes, glossary flashcards, and more, visit the Education CourseMate website for this book at www.cengage.com/login.

PART IV
Management

CHAPTER 10

Budget

Objectives

After reading this chapter, you should be able to:

- Define a budget.
- List the major categories of expenses.
- List the sources of income.
- Describe a budget process.

Cengage Learning

KEY TERMS

budget

budget calendar

fixed expenses

fringe benefits

variable expenses

A day in the life of . . .

A Director of a Church-Affiliated School

One day a mother of one of our preschoolers poked her head into my office and said, "Just thought you'd like to know, my son refers to you as Mrs. Office."

The budget is one of the most important written documents a center has. Those who choose to start child-care programs do so because they want to make a difference in the lives of children, not because they want to operate a business. However, the success of a child-care center is related to both knowledge of children and responsible fiscal management. Directors must employ effective financial management skills in order to maximize the resources of the center. Unfortunately, few directors receive training in fiscal management prior to taking the position.

The 1995 Report of the Cost and Quality Outcomes Team suggests that fiscal tasks take about 50 percent of a director's time. A director without effective fiscal management skills is at a distinct disadvantage and may even put the future of the center at risk. The financial status of the program affects both the range of program services and their quality (Peisner-Feinberg, 1995).

A **budget** is a statement of goals for one year stated in financial terms. The first budget will be the most difficult to establish, with each one following being a little easier, but just as important.

Planning should include everyone involved with the program because the budget influences all aspects of it. The board of trustees, director, assistant director, teachers, families, secretaries, cooks, and maintenance personnel can contribute to the budget design. By doing so, each will have a stake in its success and fulfillment.

The budget must be viewed both seriously and realistically. A child-care center is a small business, with all the strengths, vulnerabilities, and challenges of this kind of enterprise. It cannot lose money and continue to function.

Development of the Budget

Because budgets are based on the program goals, special objectives to be reached during a particular year should be listed in order of their priority. As the budget process continues, it may be necessary to eliminate some items from the list, and all those concerned with the program should agree on what these will be.

It is wise to seek the help of an accountant when preparing the first budget. Although accounting and legal fees are costly, they are well worth the price to ensure that all necessary expenses are covered and the year will end without a deficit. Occasionally, a center has the luxury of having an accountant or attorney on the board of trustees who can perform this service.

Time is an important consideration in planning any budget. Most organizations have a budget cycle. When one budget is finished, planning for the next year begins.

If you are a "for-profit" center, your fiscal year should end when you have the least money left in your budget. Traditionally, programs have the least money in August because of the amount of staff taking vacations, limiting cash flow. Therefore, it is recommended that you consider running your fiscal year September through August.

A standing committee of the board, or of the staff, may have responsibility for providing input on the budget. The process consists of gathering reasonable requests for new equipment or additional programs from all concerned. Guidance is needed to assist staff in defining "reasonable" in achievable terms. Experience is helpful in this process. The director is responsible for keeping the budget process moving forward.

The next step, after (re)stating goals and objectives, is to prepare a **budget calendar**. This will consist of dates that are deadlines. This document should be circulated to all concerned: director, assistant director, board of trustees, teachers, secretaries, cooks, and maintenance personnel. Establishing a "tickler" file that will be a reminder of specific budget milestones is also important. The director should hold meetings and make decisions as the process unfolds.

A justification must accompany budget requests from various areas of the program. The justification must be linked to a program goal or objective and should be clear to everyone participating in the budget process. Once all budget requests have been accumulated, the next step is to put together a working budget.

A computer and a data management software program make the budget process much simpler. (Appendix A lists several that are designed specifically for early childhood centers.) If a computer is not available, the director must decide on a form for the budget at this point. Corporate- or government-sponsored schools often have a predetermined budget form. The director of a for-profit center will have a line-item cash flow budget. Figure 10-1 shows one example. There are two major sections in a budget: income and expenses.

SAMPLE BUDGET FORM

Number of Weeks of Operation	52
Number of children: 12 infants, 12 toddlers, 40 preschoolers	64
Tuition: Infants ~$230 per child per week = $143,520 per year	
Toddlers ~$185, per child per week = $115,440	$518,960
Preschool ~$125 per child per week = $260,000	
INCOME	**AMOUNT**

Fees From Tuition
- As a general rule, calculate approximately 75% of total enrollment for the first year.
- Decide whether you will charge a flat weekly rate per child or charge by the hour?
- Decide whether you will charge more for a three-hour block (often for preschool enrichment versus child care)
- Will you charge parents for holidays, sick days, special staff training, and development days and vacation?
- Will you offer a second-child discount for siblings?
- Will you have a sliding fee scale?

$519,200

Registration Fees
- Will you charge an enrollment fee per child? How often?
- Will that fee be deducted from tuition charges?
- Will that fee be per child or per family?

At $50 per child per year
$3,200

Transportation Fees
- Will you charge for providing transportation for children to and from their home or school to your center? If so, calculate the cost of gas, oil, tires, repairs, and additional insurance into the fee determination for this service.

At $50 per child per week × 12 children = 12 × 52 × $50 = $31,200

USDA Food Program Reimbursement
- If you choose to participate, your potential USDA income will vary depending upon the income levels of the families you will serve.

Fund-raising and Contributions
- Design a plan to solicit contributions, gifts/donations.
- How much fund-raising is realistically possible?

$ 6,000

Grants

$ 5,000

Total Yearly Income

$564,600

EXPENSES	**AMOUNT**

Personnel Considerations:
- Determine your staff/child ratio based on the ages of your children.
- Determine salaries for each position based on the going rate in your area.
- Decide whether you offer higher-than-average salaries to attract candidates with higher qualifications.
- Will you offer paid breaks and lunch periods, paid set-up and closing times, and paid planning time per week?

FIGURE 10-1 Sample budget form.

- Will you need substitutes for staff illness and/or vacation?
- Will you need to hire staff for meal preparation, building maintenance, transportation, landscaping, and/or snow removal?
- Include cost of hiring substitutes for 20 days per year.

Salary Detail

Director's Annual Salary FT	$ 35,000
Head Teacher's Annual Salary FT	$ 28,000
Assistant Teacher's Annual Salary FT	$ 24,000
Aide's Annual Salary FT	$ 15,000
Secretary's Salary—50% time, 20 hours per week	$ 15,000
Substitutes—$15/hour × 8 hours/day for 20 days/year	$ 2,400

PERSONNEL EXPENSES

1 Director	$ 35,000
4 Head Teachers	$ 112,000
4 Assistant Teachers	$ 96,000
4 Teacher's Aides	$ 60,000
Personnel Sub-Total	$303,000

Fringe Benefits
- Calculate:
  - FICA
  - Unemployment compensation
  - Workers' compensation
- Determine whether you will offer such additional benefits as:
  - Health insurance
  - Tax deferred annuities
  - Child care
  - Paid sick time
  - Paid holidays/vacations
  - Cafeteria plan

Approximately 25% of
Total = $75,750

Approximate Cost of Fringe Benefits	
Personnel Total	$378,750

OPERATING EXPENSES

Activities—Based on $25 per child per year	$ 1,600

Advertising
- Business cards
- Advertising
- Distribute flyers and/or brochures

$ 1,500

Audit	$ 1,200
Books and Subscriptions	$ 600
Contingency Fund—recommend no less than 3% of operating budget	$ 14,000
Dues and memberships	$ 250

Equipment—Major (Equipment lasting longer than two years, $500 or more, anything you can depreciate)

F I G U R E   1 0 - 1   Sample budget form *(continued)*.

- Kitchen—equipment for meal preparation (stove, refrigerator)
- Housekeeping—vacuum
- Office—computer, desk, copier, file cabinet
- Educational $ 6,000
  - Additional furniture for the children
  - Additional toys/manipulatives for:
    - Large and small motor activities
    - Dramatic play
    - Language development
    - Intellectual stimulation

Equipment—Minor
- CD players
- Microwave $ 3,500
- Camera
- Meal cart

Fees—Licensing fee, fingerprinting costs, and so on $ 1,500

Food—Meals and snacks
- The current national average is approximately $1.52 per day. Formula for calculating the $25,293
  cost of food is $1.52 × the # of days × the # of children

Garbage—calculate per month cost × the # of mos. of operation $ 600

Insurance
  - Liability
  - Building and premises $ 5,000
  - Personal property
  - Professional liability
  - Auto

Interest $ 1,000
Legal/Accounting/Consultation $ 1,500
Maintenance/Repairs—(plumbing, lawn care, snow removal, repair, maintenance of
heating/air condition, and so on)—calculate per week cost × the # of mos. of operation $ 3,200
Postage—Mail brochures or packets to prospective parents, newsletters $ 600
Printing $ 800
Rent/Mortgage $15,000
Repairs—calculate per month cost × the # of mos. of operation $ 500
Office Expenses and supplies—calculate per week cost × the # of mos. $ 600
Supplies—Housekeeping, kitchen, and classroom consumable supplies $ 4,000
Telephone $ 720
Travel and transportation
- Staff Travel—Pay staff travel for conference attendance, and so on $10,500
- Auto Expenses—Lease/purchase a van and related auto costs
Utilities—Water, electricity, heat, air conditioning—Project 5% increase per year $ 3,600

TOTAL EXPENSES $491,113

FIGURE 10-1   Sample budget form *(continued)*.

BUDGET FOR A SINGLE FOR-PROFIT SCHOOL

INCOME

Tuitions		
Infants: 6@700/mo.	50,400	
Toddlers: 8@650/mo.	62,400	
Preschool: 50@550/mo.	330,000	
School-age: 25@300/mo.	90,000	
		532,800
Vacancy: 5%	<26,640>	506,160
Registration fees: 89@50	4,450	
TOTAL INCOME		510,610

EXPENSES: PERSONNEL

Director	26,500	
Teachers: 4@17,800	71,200	
Teachers: 4@16,000	64,000	
Teachers: 4 PT@10,000	40,000	
Assistants: 5@8,000	40,000	
Substitutes	4,000	
Secretary	17,500	
Cook: PT	8,000	
		271,200
Benefits (FICA, workers' compensation, unemployment, medical): 13%	35,256	
Total Personnel		306,456

EXPENSES: VARIABLE

Equipment		
Educational	4,000	
Supplies & materials		
Educational	5,500	
Office	1,500	
Housekeeping	1,000	
Food	27,000	
Staff development	4,000	
Advertising	3,500	
Petty cash	1,800	
Total Variable		48,300

EXPENSES: FIXED

Building lease	60,000	
Utilities	12,000	
Insurance	10,000	
Taxes	800	
Other	500	
Total Fixed		83,300
TOTAL EXPENSES		438,056
Cost per child (89 children)	4,921	
NET (income minus expenses)		72,554

FIGURE 10-2   Budget for a single for-profit school.

Expenses—Personnel

STAFF SALARIES

Salaries comprise the largest proportion of a budget—on average 65 percent, but in some schools as high as 75 to 80 percent. This budget category includes administrative personnel (director and assistant director), teaching staff (teachers, assistants, substitutes), and nonteaching staff (secretary, cook, janitor, bus driver, maintenance person). Decisions concerning salary levels for all employees will be influenced by several factors. The first is the education and experience of the teaching staff. Teachers with bachelor's or master's degrees and previous experience will command higher salaries than those without degrees. A second consideration is the current rate of pay in the local area of the country. Salaries tend to be the highest in the northeastern states and lowest in southern states. Third, employers must comply with minimum wage and tax laws.

One last factor may affect the salaries of employees. Staff who are members of a union have a standardized pay scale. The center may also be part of another entity, a public school or community agency. Each of these will also have a predetermined pay scale. (Download a printable version of this form from http://www.cengage.com/login.)

Historically, salaries for child-care personnel tend to be low. The sample budget shown in Figure 10-1 reflects a realistic budget based on current salary levels. Chapter 15 contains a discussion of the Worthy Wage Campaign undertaken by the National Center for the Early Childhood Work Force in 1994. The chapter also includes an editorial that appeared in the National Association for the Education of Young Children (NAEYC) publication *Young Children* suggesting ways directors can improve staff compensation and quality.

Personnel costs include taxes that must be paid to various governmental agencies and the fringe benefits offered to employees. Required payments include the percentage of an employee's salary for Social Security, workers' compensation, and unemployment insurance. A growing trend in early childhood centers is to offer **fringe benefits** as a means of retaining qualified staff. Benefits correlate with a reduction in staff turnover, lessening the cost of recruiting and training new staff. Fringe benefits most often include health insurance, personal leave, sick leave, vacation pay, and retirement plans. When considering such options as reduced cost child care, it is important to remember that the monetary value of any benefit that you offer to one staff member, by law, must be offered to all staff.

Fringe benefits may add an additional 30 percent to the total salary amount. When doing an initial budget estimate, that figure can be used as a guideline. A computerized budget form will facilitate budget formation, allowing the director to calculate fringe benefit costs accurately and ensuring that no essential items have been left out.

Expenses—Variable

Variable expenses are those over which the director has some measure of control. They will vary depending on how much is spent for supplies and equipment, which services are used, and how much is spent for food or transportation.

CONSULTANT OR CONTRACT SERVICES

Not all schools will require the services of a consultant or someone who contracts for a service. In this category are people who perform specific services on an as-needed basis.

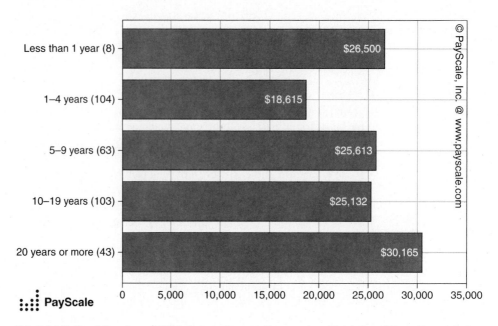

F I G U R E   1 0 - 3 a   2009 Salary Survey Report for Child Care/Day Care Worker (United States), Median Salary by Years Experience.

Updated: 7 Apr 2009 | Individuals reporting: 321.

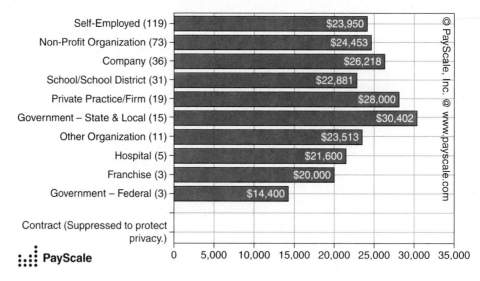

F I G U R E   1 0 - 3 b   2009 Salary Survey Report for Child Care/Day Care Worker (United States), Median Salary by Employer.

Updated: 7 Apr 2009 | Individuals reporting: 321.

Included are educational consultants, accountants, lawyers, dentists, doctors, nurses, social workers, psychologists, and nutritionists. In public school systems or in large organizations, they may be considered regular employees rather than occasional consultants. Usually, consultants work for a fee, agreeing to provide specific contracted services. Fees for consultants are usually paid on a per diem basis, including any expenses they incur while working under their contracts. The rate may include food, transportation, and lodging if the consultant is not local.

EQUIPMENT

Equipment Major is most often defined as nonexpendable items that are not replaced in a short period of time. Three to five years is the usual time allocation. Tricycles, computers, copy machines, refrigerators, and desks are all examples. Equipment Minor is defined as nonexpendable small items used in the classroom. This includes educational puzzles, a CD player, and a woodworking bench. The director should keep a chart of the state of repair of each major item and schedule replacement at regular intervals. Each item usually has a "period of obsolescence." If this can be ascertained, funds for replacement of each item should be allocated well ahead of time.

SUPPLIES AND OTHER MATERIALS

Consumable supplies are all necessary, daily-use items that need to be replaced on a regular basis (e.g., classroom, office, maintenance, and kitchen supplies). Food is considered separately.

TRANSPORTATION

Transportation or van service is expensive and customarily includes the cost of gas, maintenance on the vehicle, and insurance. The transportation line item in the budget should include any planned field trips, journeys to other schools, conferences, and workshops if the school vehicle will be used to transport children or staff members.

FOOD

This item includes all meals and snacks served at the school. Expenditures of $1.52 per child per day is now the national average. This item will vary based on the nutrition program offered by the center. A small margin should be added each year for inflation.

MARKETING

For an initial budget, overestimating slightly is best when considering money allocated to marketing. Every business needs to be marketed to the particular client community in which it is situated. Potential clients need to know about its existence and about the product it offers. In the case of a child-care center, the product is its unique educational program. Marketing should be done through various means, including advertising. Common marketing strategies include newspaper and telephone book ads, brochures, flyers, and local radio or TV spots. Some centers design an easily recognized logo that is used on signs, T-shirts, coffee mugs, stationery, and business cards. Additionally, marketing can be done through websites that offer various information about the program.

A marketing budget for a center that is just being established should be larger than for one that has been in existence for a long time. Even then, marketing should be an ongoing process that keeps the public aware of the presence of the center and knowledgeable about what it offers.

Expenses—Fixed

Fixed expenses are those that either do not vary, or change very little over long periods of time. The director has limited or no control over them.

SPACE COSTS

Space costs cover rent or mortgage payments on a building. In either case, this cost must be analyzed carefully, because this may be a long-term commitment. The amount of income generated from the total square footage is limited because most state licensing regulations specify the maximum number of children that a particular space can accommodate.

The income that can be generated from tuitions must be enough to cover this cost.

UTILITIES

Utilities include water, gas, electricity, telephones, and trash removal. In some areas it may also be necessary to include sewer charges. If these costs are included in rent payments, they should not be duplicated here.

INSURANCE

In recent years, liability insurance has become an increasingly high-expense item. Directors should get multiple quotes for insurance before committing to an amount in the budget, and they should try to get the best coverage for the least money. Fire insurance and necessary incidental coverage can be purchased simultaneously. A reduction in rate may be given if all insurance is purchased as a package.

TAXES

Tax implications vary according to the type of center. Not-for-profit schools have significant tax advantages over profit-making ones. Make direct inquiries regarding nonprofit status to a certified public accountant or to a local, state, or federal tax authority.

A yearly audit by an independent auditor is a necessary part of operating any business.

AUDIT

An audit is performed to oversee the general accounting practices, and it protects the financial personnel by ensuring that the job is done according to procedures. It also provides assurance to a board or an agency that funds are being utilized as intended.

OTHER COSTS

It is essential to include a reserve or contingency fund here. This will allow a margin for expenses that may not have been anticipated.

Income

TUITION

The first operating budget must estimate income from all sources. Tuition will be a major source. The director must contrast and compare local tuition rates for comparable early care and education services to determine the fees that the center will charge. Tuition has to be high enough to cover expected expenses in order for a school to stay in operation. Therefore, a director must carefully think through tuition decisions.

Once the tuition rate has been determined, it would seem straightforward to multiply the fee by the number of children the center can be licensed to enroll. In practice, however, it is not that simple. First, many schools do not want to enroll the maximum number of children they are allowed or cannot attain full enrollment. To fill enrollment and to accommodate parents, many schools accept children two or three days a week. Additionally, some schools have children who attend only before they leave for elementary school and then again after school. All these charges must be figured in the estimated income for the year.

SOME OTHER SOURCES

Generally, any fees charged beyond tuition are meant only to cover expenses. Most schools are now charging an annual, nonrefundable registration fee. This fee may range from $25 to $75 and is most often payable each year before school begins. Fee payment is included in the process of enrolling a new child or reenrolling a child. Because traditionally this fee is nonrefundable, it is a method of partially ensuring enrollment for a future period, and it also helps to defray the cost of handling enrollment paperwork.

A materials fee is levied when special curriculum materials or books are required. It should include the cost of the articles plus handling and storage charges.

A fee for transporting children to and from the program may be charged. Some centers include this in the tuition. It is important to include transportation in your budget if the center is providing this service, because transportation can become very expensive.

Some schools charge a fee to cover the cost of food. Many schools today find it too costly to serve school-prepared meals, preferring to confine their food service to snacks and perhaps milk at lunch. In this case, children bring their own lunches from home. Many centers serve a meal as a convenience to parents and often receive funding through the United States Department of Agriculture (USDA) Food Program. Without this funding it may be necessary to charge an extra fee for this service. Including the costs of your nutrition program in your tuition is preferable because most parents object to many isolated fees. Special activities such as dance and swimming are expensive; these activities should be charged separately. In fact, any activity that only a few children require should be examined for its fiscal implications.

Fund-raising and contributions vary tremendously as sources of income. Very few centers start with an "endowment," or a gift of investment capital. However, as time goes on and the school prospers and gains in reputation, the possibility of a fund-raiser or a request for contributions should be considered in the planning. Annual dinners, picnics, parents' days, award banquets, or any festive occasion may be converted into a fund-raiser. And if the school is certified as nonprofit by the Internal Revenue Service (IRS), contributions may be tax deductible.

FEDERAL, STATE, AND LOCAL ITEMS

There are other sources of income, occasionally of great value, that are not covered in detail in this text, including federal, state, and local foundation grants. Generally, a school must be IRS-certified nonprofit (have 501-C3 status) to qualify, although there are exceptions. The Catalog of Federal Domestic Assistance is issued yearly by the Government Printing Office in Washington, DC. However, the bulk of government aid is allocated through the State Departments of Education (SDE), located in the various state capitals. Directors should write to their SDE for pertinent information.

The techniques and procedures of application, and of being eligible, for all types of grants are quite complex. The whole field is often referred to as "grantsmanship" and is one that requires special study.

Often as fruitful in a search for funds, especially when launching special projects, are the County Foundation for your area, Rotary Clubs, the United Way, other service groups, private donors, and even the department of social services, which are sometimes interested in centers that benefit the community. The local library and a consultation with the librarian may unearth unexpected resources. Today's grant writers should utilize the Foundation Center, an online resource that offers an array of valuable information including available grants. (See Helpful Websites at the end of this chapter.)

SOME INTANGIBLES

When computing income for the first operating budget, one of the most uncertain areas of income is estimation of the "shrinkage," or vacancy and dropout factors.

These may vary widely according to school location, economic factors, tuition cost, and many other factors. Experience is a reliable guide here. The school year will not end with exactly the same number of children with which it started. Therefore, tuition estimates should allow for less than full enrollment.

A final caution is to provide for uncollected or uncollectable tuitions. For various reasons, such as when families move or are unemployed, it may be impossible to collect some money that is owed. An efficient secretary can be helpful in keeping this amount at a minimum by reminding parents when tuitions are overdue.

Some centers charge fees for overdue payments and/or require payment of tuition before services are rendered. Parents pay at the beginning of a month rather than at the end.

HOW TO CALCULATE YOUR BREAK-EVEN POINT

The break-even point is the number of children that must be served in a program in order to generate enough income to cover costs, in other words the point at which income equals expenses. There is no profit made or loss incurred at the break-even point but it is a starting point for calculating anticipated profit. This figure is important for anyone who manages a business. The break-even point can be calculated using the following method.

Example:

One year's profit	$26,000
Divided by one child's tuition	$ 6,500 = 4
If the licensed capacity is 64, the break-even point is 64 minus 4 = 60	
Tuition has been set at	$6,500 per year
Yearly expenses have been calculated	$390,000 per year
The yearly expense divided by the tuition equals	60
The break-even point requires enrollment of 60 children.	
When enrollment is full with 64 children, the profit will be	$26,000

Trial Budget

When all Income and Expenditure items have been assembled, the hardest part of budget making begins. The trustees, corporate headquarters, or other higher authority should be told of the results. A special meeting of the board of directors may be solely devoted to budget, the budget committee of the board may meet, or the data may go to corporate headquarters.

Naturally, the budget balance must not be a deficit. Ensuring a small surplus balance is necessary upfront, either for reserve funding or for unexpected additions before the budget is finalized. If the center is a for-profit business, now is the time to calculate the amount of that profit.

The director should hold a staff meeting where everyone concerned may make comments on items submitted. Almost without fail, some entries must be curtailed or eliminated. This is painful. However, throughout the budget process, keeping everyone informed who is involved with finances is important. The watchword is "no secrets!" The staff should be able to agree on trade-offs, substitutions, and the establishment of priorities that extend over years.

Next, the director should set a date for the accomplishment of the publication or summary budget, solicit final input, and again send the budget for final approval to the next level of administration (if any).

Finally, by the last day of the fiscal year on the budget calendar (or preferably before), the final budget should be completed. This is the working financial outline for the coming year. Beyond this date, the budget cannot be altered. Some changing among categories of expenditure may be made, but this practice is not recommended.

After a year or so in operation, enough data should have been collected to ascertain at what particular month of the year specific expenditures should most advantageously be made. For example, while equipment rental and parent communications do not vary during the year, spending for educational supplies and maintenance change to fit the calendar. Maintenance projects are often done before the heavy enrollment in September, during Christmas (billed in January), and at the close of the fiscal year in September. With a computer, it is possible to compare current expenditures in a timely manner on a monthly basis. The computer compares actual versus allocated values and imposes tighter budget controls in a timely way.

Summary of Budget Cycle

The following are suggestions for the director who is planning a budget.

1. Begin a new budget when the current one is completed—the process is cyclical.
2. Start with your goals for the year. List them.
3. Seek outside help if necessary on a first budget.
4. Assign one person as the central authority for the budget.
5. Publish budget deadlines and expectations of each staff member.
6. Try to include as many people as possible in planning.
7. Ask for written budget requests on a standard form.
8. Ask for a justification for each major request.
9. Assemble a trial budget and establish priorities.
10. Be sure a positive budget balance, or profit, is calculated.
11. Consider using computerized methods.
12. Publish the trial (preliminary) budget and circulate it for written comments.
13. Keep major divisions of Income and Expenditures.
14. Get committee approval at board, staff, or other levels.
15. Submit final budget for approval by higher authority after incorporating last comments and discussion.
16. Publish final budget.
17. Begin new budget.

Of course, this list is an idealized schedule. It does not include the traumas and drama of any real budget. However, having an agenda and sticking with it is important.

Budget Analysis

Before the budget is finalized, the director should ensure every item is included and that this document will support the program goals that have been set for the year. Keeping notes in a budget folder is a valuable practice as the year progresses. "Running out of money" before the end of a fiscal year is a rather frightening experience. Good planning and ongoing analysis will help to eliminate this.

The review process ensures inclusion of every vital factor. The following are a few questions to ask when analyzing the budget.

- Is every item necessary for meeting the goals of the school included?
- Have obsolete goals been abolished and new ones provided for?
- Has every cost been included?
- Are there significant differences between this budget and last year's budget? If so, what has changed? Are the changes necessary? Have changes been fully justified?
- Has any single item shown a significant increase or decrease? If so, have objectives changed? Marked increases may signal the need for cost-control measures.
- Was there great difficulty in reconciling differences between Income and Expenditures? If so, the purchase of what major equipment, maintenance, or other items may have to be delayed?

Implementing the Final Budget

The approved paper budget is only the road map; a skilled driver is necessary to arrive safely at the destination. That person is the director. The director implements the budget during the year by using skillful management techniques.

- Only one person should have purchasing authority. Requests for budget expenditures must be submitted in writing.
- One person has the responsibility for disbursing money. The bank should honor the signature of only one (or at most two) authorized person.
- Each person involved with the budget should have an overview copy as well as a detailed subsection for particular expenditures.

FYI

According to the Children's Defense Fund 2006, median wages for child-care workers range from $13,970 in Louisiana to more than $21,00 in Massachusetts, New York, and the District of Columbia. They make less that half the elementary teachers in New York.

- Monthly progress reports of budget income/expenditure should be issued to all concerned. This is especially easy to do with a computer.
- Overspending should be curtailed early. Underspending should be investigated at the end of the year. Some "corrective" factors may be necessary if this is a first budget.

Keeping Budget Records

Future budget preparation is easier if accurate records are kept. Budget tracking information for each month is shown in Figure 10-4. Minimally, the following are included as permanent file entries.

- Current cost of all budget items
- Budget forms used by school or other agencies

MONTHLY FINANCIAL REPORT FOR BUDGET TRACKING

Period covered: From _____   To _____

INCOME	This month	Year to Date
Tuition		
Fees		
Donations		
Total Income		
EXPENSES		
Salaries and wages		
Taxes and benefits		
Staff training		
Lease payment		
Food purchases		
Utilities		
Supplies		
Equipment		
Insurance		
Advertising		
Total Expenses		
Previous Balance		
Income for (month)		
Expenses for (month)		
CURRENT BALANCE		

FIGURE 10-4   Monthly financial report for budget tracking.

VARIABLE EXPENSES	OCT	NOV	DEC	JAN	FEB	MAR	APR	MAY	JUN	JUL	AUG	SEP	TOTAL
Educational supplies	484	484	1,166	497	506	870	524	510	1,155	494	494	1,176	8,360
Equipment rental	123	123	123	123	123	123	123	123	123	123	123	123	1,476
Maintenance	2,500	800	875	1,350	875	1,125	800	850	875	900	875	1,250	13,075
Parent communications	150	150	150	150	150	150	150	150	150	150	150	150	1,800

FIGURE 10-5   Sample budget detail, month by month.

- Copies of taxes, insurance, licenses, and assessments
- Copies of budgets for last three years
- Copies of cost-control practices used
- Budget correspondence
- Minutes of budget review meetings
- Copies of the annual report for three previous years

CASE STUDY

Twelve parents at a center have been laid off from a local retailer due to a mild recession in the area. Eleven of the 12 families withdrew from the program with little or no notice. All contracts require a two-week written notice, but under the circumstances, these families could not comply.

The director developed her budget based on 95 percent enrollment of the center, which has a capacity of 70 full-time enrollments. She is now expecting approximately $4,700 less per month than planned. Additionally, she is staffed for these 11 children, all in different programs because their ages range from two through three and a half.

1. How could the director attempt to reconcile the budget?
2. How could the director avoid layoffs in her own staff? Is that possible?
3. Do you think the director's aim of 95 percent enrollment is realistic? Why?
4. What could you learn from this case study?

SUMMARY

A budget is the statement of goals for one year given in financial terms. The director should begin to compile it with lists of services to be provided, programs to be included, and goals to be reached.

The following items are included as major headings of budget expenditures.

- Staff salaries
- Fringe benefits
- Consultant services
- Equipment
- Supplies and materials
- Transportation
- Insurance
- Cost of space
- Utilities
- Food
- Taxes (if any)
- Other costs

The following are customarily listed as major income line items.

- Tuition
- Materials fee
- Transportation fee
- Nutrition fee
- Special activities fee
- Fund-raising and contributions
- Possible federal, state, or private sources (Foundation or other funding streams)

The budget should allow for decreased enrollment and for uncollected tuitions.

A budget calendar includes deadlines for meeting each milestone in budget development. The director is responsible for estimating Income and reconciling Expenditures.

Once a trial budget is outlined, it is important to request further input. The budget should be analyzed for omissions and deletion of unneeded items. The final steps include making compromises, reconciling the budget income with expenditures to establish profit, achieving final approval, and issuing the final budget.

Authority for budget administration should be centralized. The director must examine the budget continually and work to keep a balanced budget. Good recordkeeping will assist with the preparation of future budgets.

STUDENT ACTIVITIES

1. Contact several child-care directors. Ask for an estimate of their cost per child per year. How does it compare with the amount shown in Figure 10-2? What accounts for the difference?

2. Prepare a questionnaire to distribute to your fellow students. Tell them their answers will be anonymous. Ask the following:

   a. Are you currently teaching in an early childhood center?

   b. How many hours a week do you work?

c. What is your weekly pay?

d. Do you receive any benefits other than those required by law? If so, please list them.

Summarize your findings and report to the class regarding working conditions for early childhood teachers.

REVIEW

1. Define a budget.
2. List at least six items of expenditure in a budget.
3. What should one of your first actions be in beginning a budget?
4. Who has responsibility for budget preparation?
5. What single item constitutes the largest budget expenditure?
6. What are some of the major steps in the budget cycle?
7. What is a reasonable percent of profit for a preschool? Defend your statement.
8. Specify some methods of budget review.
9. Tell how a budget can be controlled. Why is this important?
10. What items should be included in budget records as an aid to planning?
11. Where would you go to receive assistance in writing, maintaining, and/or balancing a budget?

REFERENCE

Peisner-Feinberg, E. S. (1995). *The cost, quality and child outcomes in child care centers study.* Denver, CO: Center for Research on Economic and Social Policy.

SELECTED FURTHER READING

Bush, J. (2001). *Dollars & sense: Planning for profit in your child care business.* Clifton Park, NY; Delmar Learning.

Campbell, N. D., Appelbaum, J. C., Martinson, K., & Martin, E. (2000). *Be all that we can be: Lessons from the military for improving our nation's child care system.* Washington, DC: National Women's Law Center.

Cantrella, G. (Ed.). (1999). *National guide to funding for children, youth, and families* (5th ed.). New York: The Foundation Center.

Geever, J. C., & McNeill, P. (1997). *The Foundation Center's guide to proposal writing* (Rev. ed.). New York: The Foundation Center.

Jack, G. (2005). *The business of child care: Management and financial strategies.* Clifton Park, NY: Delmar Learning.

Mitchell, B., Stoney, A. L., & Dichter, H. (2002). *Financing child care in the United States: An expanded catalog of current strategies.* (2nd ed.). Kansas City, MO: Ewing Marion Kaufman Foundation.

National Association for the Education of Young Children. (2001). Financing child care facilities. *Young Children, 56*(2), 56.

HELPFUL WEBSITES

Disclaimer: Links to Internet sites throughout this book are provided for your convenience and do not constitute an endorsement.

Bureau of Labor Statistics:	**http://www.bls.gov**
Families and Work Institute:	**http://www.familiesandworkinst.org**
Federal Grant Sites and the Catalog of Federal Domestic Assistance:	**http://www.dhhs.gov/progorg/grantsnet**
United States Small Business Administration:	**http://www.sba.gov**
Wisconsin Childcare Improvement Project:	**http://www.wccip.org**
Foundation Center:	**http://www.fndcenter.org**
County Foundation:	**http://www.countyfoundation.org**
United Way:	**http://unitedway.org**

For additional resources related to administration including videos, links to related sites for each chapter of the text, tutorial quizzes, glossary flashcards, and more, visit the Education CourseMate website for this book at www.cengage.com/login.

CHAPTER 11

Maintenance, Health, and Safety

Objectives

After reading this chapter, you should be able to:

- Differentiate between maintenance and operations activities.
- Tell how maintenance, cleanliness, and safety are related.
- Discuss the components of a safe environment.
- Describe how to deal with an emergency.
- State goals for a health plan in a childhood center.
- Discuss ways to implement health goals.

KEY TERMS

AIDS

disaster plan

maintenance

operations

A day in the life of . . .

A Director of a Church-Affiliated School

There can be anxious days in the life of a director. One day Patrick's mother arrived to pick him up from "lunch bunch," and we could not find him. He had been with two teachers and a group of children on the playground. One minute he was there, and the next he was gone. Our playground is fenced but has one gate that can be opened by the students. A teacher is always near the gate to supervise children who may have to go to the bathrooms. We checked the bathrooms first, then every classroom, then the parking lot.

By now my heart was racing, and Patrick's mother started to panic. I will never forget the look on her face as long as I live. We were close to calling 911. I kept thinking how hard it would be for a child to leave our playground or school without being noticed, so I decided to check the playground one more time. I looked in the bushes and the playhouse. I walked around the sand area where we have a large tractor tire. I spot-ted Patrick curled up inside the cozy, warm curve of the tire, sound asleep! Whew! Patrick had been "missing" no more than 10 minutes, the longest 10 minutes of this director's life.

When so much emphasis is put on other aspects of an early childhood program, it is easy to overlook the physical environment. This can be a costly error both psychologically and financially. Teachers and children spend their day either in pleasant and safe surroundings or in a mess. Order and safety have logical connections, and a regard for healthful conditions is both a legal and parental concern. The director is responsible for ensuring orderliness and security in the school.

A safe and healthy environment requires careful and continuous maintenance. In an unkempt environment there is the possibility that either children or teachers may be injured or become ill. Orderly, clean rooms create an atmosphere that is more pleasant and conducive to learning than one that is constantly disordered. Natural hazards exist in a play yard, as well as the possibility of injury on play equipment. However, with a well-managed schedule of maintenance, injuries can be kept to minor ones.

Maintenance or Operations?

Many schools distinguish between maintenance and operations. **Maintenance** consists of major repairs and projects such as repainting exteriors and interiors, repaving, and reroofing. **Operations**, however, are daily housekeeping tasks such as sweeping, dusting, cleaning, emptying, and other seemingly endless tasks that go into making a tidy and attractive school. The difference may be especially important at budget time. Most maintenance efforts are scheduled at yearly (sometimes longer) intervals. Maintenance tasks are often costly, and money must be set aside each year to cover the expense when it finally occurs. Operations take place each day and are essentially short range. This kind of expense must be part of each month's expenditures.

MAINTENANCE

Aside from high cost, a major problem with maintenance projects is scheduling. Repainting is very difficult to do when school is in session. Weekends are a possibility, but a better solution is to group all major maintenance for times when children are not present for at least a few days. Although there are increasingly more year-round schools, there are sometimes a few days or a week during the year when rooms are vacant. It helps to plan a year or so ahead for this and keep a log of when major maintenance tasks are due.

In addition to charting due dates of all projects, the director should keep a list of local maintenance services and make notes about their cost and reliability. Such services as plumbing and electrical work are sometimes needed in an emergency. Figure 11-1 shows a suggested format for keeping a record of phone numbers and comparative prices.

Proper maintenance may also include periodic replacement of some furniture or equipment. A child-care center, open 10 or 12 hours daily, will need a larger budget for maintenance and operations than one that is in session only a few hours each day. Active, young children are physically demanding on their environment. Anticipate that things will wear out rapidly and plan accordingly. Figures 11-2 and 11-3 show ways of recording when maintenance, repairs, and replacement have been performed or need to occur.

REPAIR AND MAINTENANCE SERVICES				
Name	**Address**	**Telephone**	**Rate**	**Comments**
Plumbing				
Carpentry				
Painting				
Paving				
Roofing				
Electrical				
Gardening				
General Repairs				
Other				

F I G U R E   1 1 - 1   Sample repair and maintenance service form.

EQUIPMENT MAINTENANCE RECORD

Item _____ Date Purchased _____ Price _____

Purchased from _____

Warranty No. _____ Manufacturer _____

Warranty Expiration Date _____

Maintenance Record _____

Service Date	Description	By Whom	Charge

F I G U R E   1 1 - 2   Sample equipment maintenance record.

REPAIR AND REPLACEMENT RECORD					
Item	Repair	Replace	Repaint	Date Requested	Date Completed
Classrooms					
Tables					
Chairs					
Shelves					
Book cabinet					
Hollow blocks					
Floor blocks					
CD player					
Sand table					
Play Yard					
Swings					
Sandbox					
Sand					
Wheel toys					
Planks					
Boxes					
Jungle gym					
Playhouse					
Storage					
Office					
Typewriter					
Duplicator					
Adding machine					
Paper cutter					
Desk					
Computer					
Printer					
Grounds					
Driveway					
Parking lot					
Walks					
Garden					
Lawn					
Other					

FIGURE 11-3   Sample repair and replacement services form.

OPERATIONS

Seldom can a child-care center afford an in-house custodial staff. Some corporate schools have crews that clean and repair, but this is not the norm at most preschools. Another means of routine cleaning must exist. The aim should be the maximum health and safety of the children. For optimum results, an outside cleaning service, hired on a part-time basis, is about the only solution economically possible.

There are many such cleaning services, and they perform at all levels of efficiency. The director should prepare a list of essential tasks that must be done before beginning negotiations with any of them. One way is to list specifications and ask for bids. The next step is to examine the two or three lowest bidders and interview the owners or managers. Pertinent questions to ask are who they employ, how long they have been in business, what hours they will work, their cost per hour, and how long their contract will run. They must be available on a schedule that fits the school's needs.

Figure 11-4 provides some suggestions as to frequency of cleaning and general house-keeping. The initial contract for services should be short so that the performance of the cleaning service can be assessed.

The director must be especially alert when adding new programs. In addition to the cost of the room and equipment, there must be sufficient money to provide a safe, clean, and comfortable environment. Although this is especially true when adding an infant-toddler room to a school, it is important to any addition. The staff, parents, and children will notice the difference. In some surveys, cleanliness (in rather broad terms) is the most requested and looked-for item when parents are seeking child care.

Teachers question the degree to which they should be involved in routine cleanup procedures. Undoubtedly, if teachers keep their rooms tidy during the day, cleaning needs will be significantly less. However, during the day teachers should not feel that their first duty is orderliness in the classroom. A short cleanup period at the end of the day or the lesson helps. (A discussion of the special requirements in an infant-toddler room is found later in this chapter.) Children should participate in putting away materials. Learning to store objects in their proper places is part of the maturing process. Extreme disorder is conducive to neither learning nor pleasure for most children and teachers.

Inventory

The director should prepare an inventory of all physical equipment in the school over a specified dollar value. This list should be created when the school begins and should be updated yearly. Recordkeeping of this type is necessary minimally for tax purposes. Each piece of equipment should be depreciated on a fixed basis. A tax adviser can recommend the precise time span. Computer inventory programs can be used, or this information can be tracked on note cards as shown in Figure 11-5. These cards should be kept permanently in a safe place.

Safety

ENVIRONMENT

Creating a safe environment should be a top priority in any setting for groups of children. As children proceed through various stages of development, they test their physical skills, sometimes doing things that may be potentially harmful or dangerous. All equipment and materials both indoors and outdoors should allow children to develop their skills without

HOUSEKEEPING SCHEDULE					
Task	Daily	Weekly	Twice Weekly	Monthly	Comments
Bathrooms					
Toilets sanitized	X				
Washbowls cleaned	X				
Floor mopped	X				
Mirrors cleaned		X			
Towels refilled					As needed
Walls wiped				X	
Classrooms					
Floors wet mopped	X				
Floors waxed				X	
Carpets vacuumed			X		
Tables and chairs cleaned	X				
Cots and mats sanitized	X				
Wastebaskets					
Emptied	X				
Washed			X		
Windows washed				X	
Shelves dusted		X			
Stove cleaned				X	
Refrigerator					
Cleaned			X		
Defrosted				X	
Hallways					
Vacuumed		X			
Offices					
Vacuumed		X			
Dusted		X			

FIGURE 11-4 Sample housekeeping schedule.

EQUIPMENT INVENTORY RECORD			
Item _____ Date Purchased _____ Price _____			
Dates Inventoried	Accumulated Depreciation	Depreciation Current Year	Insurance Value

FIGURE 11-5   Sample equipment inventory record form.

risk of injury. Acknowledgment of potential hazards is necessary, as is constant vigilance to prevent deterioration of the environment. The director should have a thorough knowledge of how to create a safe environment. Additionally, teachers must be alert to potential hazards and know how to prevent injuries to children.

Prevention measures should begin with a weekly check of both the classrooms and the playground. Teachers should check a classroom other than their own. They may notice something overlooked in the day-to-day functioning in the area. The director should look for places in the school where young children may be hurt, arrange for repair of any equipment, as needed, and remove any that cannot be repaired. Developing a checklist for the particular environment is helpful, so that nothing is overlooked during a walk-through. Figure 11-6 is a suggested checklist for assessing the safety of the environment.

FIRST AID

Every school should have at least one major, well-stocked, and freshly renewed first-aid kit. There should also be at least one adult who has taken the American Red Cross First Aid course including cardiopulmonary resuscitation (CPR) and how to recognize and care for breathing or cardiac problems with infants or very young children. If possible, smaller first-aid kits should be stored in each classroom, with antiseptic and adhesive bandages as minimal contents.

A list of emergency telephone numbers for fire, police, and utilities should be permanently affixed near the first-aid kit and in each room as needed. The school physician's (or nurse's) phone number should be readily available. The number of the nearest emergency room, hospital, or paramedic unit should also be posted. All other information should be centralized so that staff can deal with emergencies expeditiously.

The central first-aid kit should be stocked with items such as:

adhesive tape (1/4" and 1")	hot water bottle	splints
alcohol	ice pack	thermometer
adhesive bandages	tongue blade	blades
blanket	safety pins	towels
cotton balls	scissors, blunt	triangle bandage
flashlight	soap, liquid	tweezers
gauze pads, assorted	spirits of ammonia	petroleum jelly

SAFETY CHECKLIST

Classrooms

_____ Furniture is free of sharp corners.

_____ All furniture is an appropriate size for the children using it and has been tested for safety.

_____ Safety devices are on all electrical outlets.

_____ Childproof locks are on cupboards containing cleaning supplies.

_____ Hot water heater is set at 120°F.

_____ All toys less than $1\frac{1}{2}$ inches in diameter have been removed. Staff has been trained to use the " choke tube" measuring tool.

_____ No small objects such as pins, thumbtacks, nails, or staples are accessible to children.

_____ All broken toys or parts of toys have been removed.

_____ Art supplies are free of toxic ingredients.

_____ There are no loose or torn carpet areas.

_____ Vinyl flooring is not slippery.

_____ Each classroom has a working smoke detector.

_____ An emergency evacuation plan is posted in a visible place in each classroom.

_____ Directions for emergency shutoff of gas, electricity, and water are posted in a visible place.

_____ The infant-toddler room has one clearly marked crib on wheels for quick evacuation of nonwalking children.

Outdoors

_____ All equipment has an adequate fall zone with safety-certified ground cover.

_____ All moving parts on equipment have been checked for defects.

_____ All equipment meets licensing requirements.

_____ There is adequate spacing between pieces of equipment.

_____ Platforms have sturdy guardrails.

_____ Play equipment is sturdy and free of sharp edges or splinters.

_____ There are no loose nuts or bolts on equipment.

_____ Play equipment is anchored securely to the ground.

_____ There are no tripping hazards such as raised concrete on walkways or warped surfaces on climbing equipment.

_____ Grass has been cut; walkways are free of debris.

_____ The playground is free of broken toys, glass, or any objects that may have been thrown into the area.

_____ All fences are at least four feet high and have securely latched gates.

_____ Sandboxes are clean and have been raked at least once a week.

_____ Riding toys have a low center of gravity and are well balanced.

_____ The riding area for wheel toys is separate from other play areas and away from traffic patterns.

_____ The riding area for wheel toys is smooth and not slippery.

_____ Children and staff members are aware of the rules regarding use of equipment.

FIGURE 11-6   A sample safety checklist.

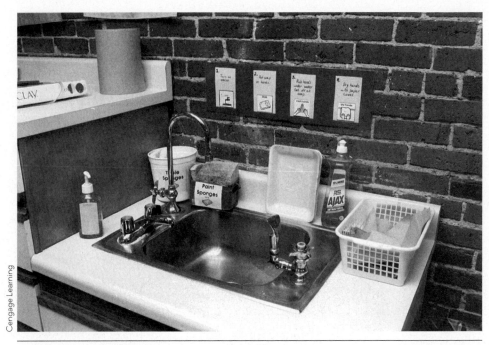

A clean and organized classroom.

ACCIDENT MANAGEMENT

Every school or child-care center needs a standard procedure for managing any accidents that happen at school or when children are in transit. The following are some recommendations for the director.

- Each child's file should contain a form signed by the parents authorizing emergency medical treatment.
- Have a standard form printed in triplicate on which pertinent accident information can be recorded. Complete it as soon as possible after the accident (see Figure 11-7).
- Call paramedics or take the child to the nearest emergency room as required by the nature of the accident.
- Telephone the parents as soon as possible. If the child will be taken out of the school, ask that the parents go directly to the hospital.
- If the injury seems minor and does not require emergency care, the parents should still be notified. A joint decision can be made whether the child should stay at school or be taken home.
- If the child stays at school, make sure that teachers watch for any further signs of difficulty during the day.
- Answer any questions the other children may have as completely and honestly as possible. Reassure them that the injured child is receiving care.

DISASTER PLANS

Your state's licensing regulations may require a **disaster plan**. Even if not mandated, preparation for disasters such as fires, floods, hurricanes, tornadoes, and earthquakes should be made

Outdoor equipment must be sturdy and solid.

before any children enter a child-care facility. There may also be a need to plan for disasters such as a bomb scare or a shooting. Building emergencies such as electrical blackouts, gas leaks, and noxious fumes from a chemical spill can also happen. Every staff member must be familiar with procedures for evacuating children or moving them to safe places in the building, and each should be assigned to specific duties when an emergency occurs. An evacuation route diagram should be displayed prominently in each room and at the entrance of the school. Fire alarms, fire extinguishers, and emergency-exit lights should be clearly visible and checked regularly. Drills should be scheduled frequently so that children have a chance to practice and staff have an opportunity to evaluate whether the plan needs any changes. Parents must be aware of disaster plans, including alternative shelters where children might be taken.

One staff person should be designated to summon emergency help and to ensure that the building has been completely emptied. That person will also contact parents.

A final check of the building should be made to turn off any equipment, shut off gas lines (important in earthquakes), and take any other necessary measures in a particular facility. A kit with tools needed to accomplish these tasks should be easily available and include—a crescent or pipe wrench, a shovel, and slotted and Phillips screwdrivers.

Emergency supplies for evacuation of children and adults should be packed in easily movable containers so that staff can take them to the alternative shelter when necessary. This emergency kit should include:

- fire extinguisher
- first-aid supplies
- blankets
- diapers and wipes
- shoes or boots for children and adults
- extra clothing for children

ACCIDENT REPORT FORM

Name of School _____ Date of Report _____

Child's Name _____ Sex M F   Birth Date _____

Parent Name _____ Phone Number _____

Home Address _____

Date of Injury _____ Time _____ AM PM

Location Where Injury Occurred _____

Teacher in Charge _____

Present at the Time of Accident _____

Type of Equipment Involved _____

Description of How Accident Happened _____

_____

_____

Action Taken: _____

First–Aid Treatment _____
                        (Name of person administering)

Taken to Doctor _____
                        (Name of doctor)

Taken to Hospital _____
                        (Name of hospital)

Refused Treatment _____
                        (Name of person refusing treatment)

Parent Notification:

Was Parent Notified?   Yes   No   Time of Notification _____

How Was Parent Notified? _____

Comments from Parent _____

_____

_____

_____

Witnesses to Accident _____

_____

Director's Signature _____

FIGURE 11-7 Accident report form.

- water, at least one day's supply
- essential medications needed for children with special needs (for example, inhaler for asthmatics)
- nonperishable food such as juice boxes, energy bars, canned foods
- manual can opener
- flashlights and extra batteries
- battery-operated radio
- cell phone
- parent phone list and any alternative contacts
- children's books, games, crayons, paper, and small toys
- bottles of antibacterial hand wash
- large plastic bags for trash and waste
- whistle to signal for help

HELPING CHILDREN AFTER A DISASTER

NAEYC brochure #533 addresses ways to help children who have experienced a natural disaster or violence in their communities either directly or through coverage by the news media (Farish, 2006). The following strategies can show families and child-care personnel how to provide support.

- Offer reassurance by being physically close: Give hugs, hold hands, or smile. Tell them there is someone who will keep them safe and who will take care of them.
- Maintain routines and structure: Consistency and security are important to children when their world is unpredictable. Let each day be the same with familiar routines for all activities.
- Respond when children want to talk about the disaster: Talking with an understanding adult can clarify their worries and feelings. Do not pressure children to talk, but let them know you are ready to listen when they are ready to talk. You may tell them that you too are concerned or anxious, but let them know how you manage those feelings.
- Provide experiences that help children release tension: Allow children to relax while playing with water, clay, sand, or play dough. Some children will play out their anxieties through dramatic play. Provide opportunities for physical activities outdoors.
- Watch for any changes in behavior: Some children may revert to an earlier stage of development, including thumb sucking or bed-wetting. Some show changes in sleep patterns. Others may isolate themselves from other children or become irritable or aggressive.
- Allowing time to take care of your own feelings is important.

TRANSPORTATION

A discussion of safety would not be complete without considering measures to be observed when transporting children by car or bus. This is especially important today when many child-care centers or preschools provide a pickup service. Even schools that do not offer that convenience occasionally take children on field trips.

The driver of any vehicle must be properly licensed. The person should also be responsible and able to manage a group of children. Some training may be necessary to provide that capability. Parents should know the person who transports their children to school in order to feel more confident. A written permission form should be on file at school.

Sometimes teachers may be used as substitute drivers. The director must be particularly sure in such cases that the teacher has had the same training and has the same license as the regular vehicle driver. People operating in a different environment are often susceptible to accidents.

All vehicles used to transport children should be equipped with restraints appropriate for the age of each child and approved for the make of the vehicle. Infants should be placed in rear-facing seats. Preschoolers who are at least two years old and weigh at least 20 pounds can use front-facing seats with a full harness restraint (lap and shoulder belt). When children reach the top weight for their car seat or if their ears reach the top of the seat, they can use a booster with lap and shoulder belts. A few cars and vans are equipped with built-in seats and may be used by preschoolers. Each child must be buckled in for every trip, no matter how short.

Maintenance of all vehicles used for children is extremely important. Periodic inspections should be followed by any necessary repair work. A fire extinguisher should be placed near the driver so that it is easily available when needed. Adequate liability insurance must be purchased to cover the vehicle, driver, and the maximum number of passengers.

In some schools, parents transport children on field trips. Precautions are necessary to ensure children's safety at these times as well. A safe place for cars to park when loading and unloading children must be present. Parents may need to be reminded to use restraints and to watch when closing doors. Although the school is not liable when parents transport their own children, it may be liable when they carry other children on a field trip. The director should make certain that insurance will cover such an eventuality. A last precaution is to use parents for field trip transportation as infrequently as possible. It is risky.

Health

The U.S. Department of Health and Human Services' Child Care Bureau and Maternal and Child Health Bureau have launched a campaign to promote healthy children. The campaign revolves around a Blueprint for Action encompassing 10 steps. Communities can use existing resources, or they can create new services to assess child-care and health-care resources and to implement the goals.

The 10 steps were outlined in a January 1996 issue of *Young Children*.

1. Promote safe, healthy, and developmentally appropriate child-care environments for all families.

2. Increase immunization rates and preventive services for children in child-care settings.

3. Assist families in accessing key public and private health and social service programs.

4. Promote and increase comprehensive access to health screenings.

5. Conduct health and safety education and promotion programs for children, families, and child-care providers.

6. Strengthen and improve nutrition services in child care.

In a child center, children brush their teeth.

7. Provide training for and ongoing consultation with child-care providers and families in the areas of social and emotional health.

8. Expand and provide ongoing support to child-care providers and families caring for children with special health needs.

9. Use child-care health consultants to help develop and maintain healthy child care.

10. Assess and promote the health, training, and work environment of child-care providers.

A more complete description of the campaign and information about implementation can be obtained from: The National Center for Education in Maternal and Child Health, 2000 15th Street North, Suite 701, Arlington, VA 22201-2617; phone 703-524-7802; fax 703-524-9335; or visit http://www.ncemch.org.

Health Goals

The Healthy Child Care Campaign is an effective way to make families and child-care providers aware of the importance of promoting child health. Each child-care center should have a set of health goals and methods for implementing those goals. The result will be healthier children with fewer illnesses. That should be a bonus for working parents who will miss fewer work days because their children are ill. If the policy also includes health and safety education for families, the impact of the program will extend even further to all family members.

The following are some sample goals.

- Assess the child's current health status and recommend treatment of existing problems.
- Suggest treatment for conditions that are progressive.
- Identify and suggest treatment for conditions that may interfere with how the child functions in school.
- Institute practices that prevent future illnesses.

ASSESSING CURRENT HEALTH STATUS

When a child first enters a school, knowing the status of the child's health is important, particularly whether the child should be restricted from participating in some of the school's activities. Most schools require a pre-enrollment physical examination. The physician's report will certify that the child is free of communicable diseases, describe any abnormal conditions, and include a record of immunizations.

Further assessment may include a discussion with the child's parents in which a brief developmental history is taken. Knowing about the mother's pregnancy and the circumstances of delivery may be important. Additional information may include allergies, previous illnesses, hospitalizations, and any accidents the child has experienced.

Health screening tests are used in some schools, especially those that receive government funds, such as Head Start. Children may receive hearing or vision tests in addition to medical and dental screening. Some may receive general motor coordination tests.

Observations by teachers are also useful in discovering a child's health problems. They see children for many hours during a week and can often detect problems that may not have been previously noticed. They may notice behavior that points to hyperactivity, hearing and vision disability, or poor motor coordination. Poor nutrition may be seen as a reason for the child's listlessness or withdrawal from group activities.

- Immunization of 19- to 35-month-old children was at 81 percent in 2005.
- The number of deaths due to AIDS in children under 13 has decreased from 582 in 1994 to 76 in 1999.
- Asthma is one of the most common chronic conditions among young children, affecting five million children under 18.
- The number of overweight children has more than doubled within the past 10 years and now represents almost 11 percent of all children between the ages of six and 19. Sixty-seven percent of these children have a higher-than-recommended intake of fats per day, and fewer than one out of five eat the recommended number of servings of fruits and vegetables.

SOURCE: U. S. Centers for Disease Control as reported in The State of America's Children, Children's Defense Fund, 2005.

TREATING PROGRESSIVE CONDITIONS

Certain health conditions will become progressively worse if left untreated. They may have a lasting and irreversible effect upon the child's health and ability to function in school. Examples are excessive tooth decay, strabismus (crossed eyes), and amblyopia (lazy eye). Malnutrition may permanently disturb the child's growth pattern. Behavior problems may affect learning and may become increasingly difficult to treat successfully as the child grows older. Often, though, it is hard to find the best sources of help, and they are likely to be expensive when found.

Comprehensive health care provided by some publicly funded preschool and child-care programs covers the cost of treating progressive conditions. In Head Start centers, a health coordinator works with the community-involvement worker to facilitate health referrals for medical or dental care when necessary. A Head Start Nutrition Committee, comprised of parents, plans monthly menus and assists in conducting nutrition activities for children. This committee also plans and conducts nutrition activities with the parents.

Schools that do not have the support of public funds must find other ways to work with families to treat progressive conditions. They must tap the resources of communities or seek out help from national organizations. Health departments sometimes have low-cost clinics or treatment centers. Service and research organizations such as the American Academy of Pediatrics, the American Lung Association, or the American Cancer Society have updated information for staff and parent education. They may also be able to provide information about treatment facilities.

Individuals within the school may also be helpful in providing information. Parents can often tell the director which pediatricians are best when interacting with families and children. They may know dentists who manage children sensitively as they treat their dental problems. Other directors in the community may know sources of psychological help for families.

The director of an employer-sponsored school may have another option. The business or industry that supports the center may be associated with a health-care organization that can provide health services. The role of the director is to be knowledgeable about those benefits and to suggest that parents make appointments with appropriate departments or health organizations. Hospitals that support child care obviously have their own built-in services that are probably available to families.

IDENTIFYING CONDITIONS THAT INTERFERE WITH LEARNING

Often, conditions that interfere with learning don't become identified until the child reaches elementary school. By then, significant time and chance to correct the difficulty has been lost. The preschool or child-care center can be instrumental in preventing this delay.

The most obvious vision problems usually are recognized, but only a very alert adult will recognize other conditions. Teachers should watch for the child who has difficulty with eye–hand coordination or is awkward in games. The child who avoids close work or assumes an abnormal posture when doing it may also have poor vision. Complaints about inability to see or lack of curiosity about visually interesting objects may indicate vision problems.

Children's speech is often a good indicator of hearing disabilities. The teacher may be the first person to recognize a difficulty because parents are so accustomed to understanding the child's particular speech pattern. Hearing loss in young children is fairly frequent, sometimes due to the recurring middle-ear infections suffered at this age. Some indications of hearing problems that teachers should be aware of are listed.

- Limited use of speech
- Lack of response when spoken to
- Consistent lack of attention during group activities
- Talking very loudly or very softly
- Asking for a repetition of what has been said
- Watching intently when being addressed

Speech difficulties may occur without hearing loss, and they will have an equally severe impact upon a child's learning. Language skills are intimately related to the development of cognitive skills. Problems range from delayed speech to indistinct articulation.

Delayed speech may stem from a wide range of causes. A neuromuscular disorder such as cerebral palsy, or simply shyness and lack of environmental stimulation, may lead to limited speech.

Articulation deviations are common in young children. Many children find it easier to say "b," "d," and "g" at the beginning of words and often end words with "p," "t," and "k." Double consonants such as "sp" and "tr" are difficult. If only a few words are unintelligible, the child will probably be able to say words more clearly with time. However, if all the child's words are unintelligible and the child is older than three and a half, professional help may be needed. A speech therapist should evaluate the child and possibly institute a remedial program.

Children who have delayed speech may be helped through special activities at school and at home. Both teachers and parents can encourage children to talk by listening carefully to what they say. Adults should ask questions that encourage children to respond with sentences rather than a single word. Most important, children should have interesting experiences they can talk about.

Certain behaviors may interfere with the child's ability to take advantage of the curriculum of the school. These may range from very mild patterns to severe disabilities.

Mild patterns of behavior that limit the child's learning capability sometimes go unnoticed by parents. In school, though, the behavior is usually noted. In this category are such behaviors as extreme shyness, which prevents the child from participating in group activities or making friends. This category also includes the inability to stay with an activity long enough to finish. Additionally, the category includes the child who only wants to play with one toy or one activity. Each of these behaviors interferes little with other children's rights. However, if left unchanged, these behaviors will limit the child's benefits from a preschool experience.

More severe patterns of behavior are easily identified by both parents and teachers. These are the behaviors that infringe upon others' rights. The child who hits or bites is noticed by everyone. The child who constantly moves around, creating havoc everywhere he goes, also attracts notice. Severe temper tantrums long past the time when most children have found other ways of expressing frustration can also be considered serious.

Behavior deviations can often be assessed correctly by experienced teachers. They will know that some behaviors are part of a child's normal developmental progression. Other behaviors are personality characteristics. Children with other behaviors, particularly those that persist or severely limit the child, should be referred to appropriate professionals. A detailed discussion of behaviors is not appropriate here, but suggested sources for further information appear at the end of this chapter.

Some children with special needs can benefit from participating in programs designed for children without special needs. This process is called mainstreaming. Additional

Teachers and parent can help children with delayed speech by implementing special activities at school and at home.

staff, materials, and perhaps modifications in the physical environment may be required. Although the Americans with Disabilities Act prohibits discrimination in enrollment policies, private schools can decide whether they can provide the necessary environment. Before accepting a child, both director and staff should make an honest assessment of the child's needs. The director should observe the child, discuss needs with the parents, and confer with staff members about the ways the environment and curriculum can be changed to accommodate the child. The experience for both adults and children should be a positive one, so careful consideration ahead of time is essential.

Children with special needs such as mental retardation, visual or hearing limitations, and physical difficulties can be managed fairly easily in the regular classroom. Alternatively, a child with emotional problems may be a disruptive influence in the classroom that many teachers do not have the skills to manage. One disruptive child can make it impossible for all the other children in the group to gain as much as they might from their preschool activities. The school should enroll children with special needs only if it can be a positive experience for those children, other children in the group, and the teachers.

PREVENTING FUTURE ILLNESSES

Each person involved in an early childhood program should be concerned about the problem of illnesses in children in their care. Young children are especially vulnerable to various infections and communicable diseases. This vulnerability is due to some special characteristics of this age level. Young children:

- have not developed immunity.
- have a small body structure. The distance between the nose and throat area and the middle ear is especially small. Respiratory infections are the result.
- are in close contact with other children while playing, eating, toileting, and diapering.

- use their mouths as an additional way to find out about the world around them.
- fall frequently, getting bumps and scrapes that can become infected.
- do not know how to protect themselves and have not developed routine hygiene procedures.

One way to minimize occurrences of illness in a school is to develop procedures for care of the environment. Because the requirements for infants and toddlers are somewhat more extensive than those for older children, it is helpful to look at these separately.

General precautions to prevent the spread of diseases in a child-care environment are as follows:

- Clean rooms on a regular basis, including floor scrubbing and carpet cleaning.
- Wipe tables with detergent and water after a play activity.
- Clean and disinfect toys, utensils, or any objects that children handle or put in their mouths at least once a week. Wash in a dishwasher or dip in a bleach solution (¼-cup household bleach and one gallon of water prepared fresh each day).
- Clean and sanitize bathrooms daily using a bleach solution.
- Clean and disinfect the entire play area on a daily basis.
- Clean sleeping cots or mats at least once a week. Each child should have a cot or mat with a sheet or blanket. Wash sheets or blankets each week.
- Whenever possible, clean with paper towels rather than cloth towels.
- Encourage children to wash their hands after toileting, before eating, and before participating in a cooking activity.
- Establish a policy for exclusion of children whose condition is highly contagious.
- Encourage children with runny noses to use a tissue and to wash their hands afterward.

The incidence of AIDS and other serious infectious diseases that affect children makes it necessary for staff members to take additional precautions when handling any bodily fluids (urine, feces, vomit, blood, saliva, or discharges from the nose, eyes, or draining sores). Important measures are the following:

- Staff should wear latex gloves when cleaning up any bodily fluids. Gloves should be used once, for only one incident, then discarded.
- Staff should wash their hands after handling any bodily fluids, whether they were wearing latex gloves or not.
- For spills of vomit, urine, or feces, staff should clean and disinfect the area, including floors, walls, bathrooms, and tabletops.
- Blood-contaminated material should be disposed of in a plastic bag with a secure tie and placed out of the reach of children.
- If any staff member has any known sores, or breaks in the skin, on his or her hands, particular care to wear gloves should be taken when handling blood or bodily fluids containing blood.
- Staff who may be exposed to hepatitis B or to contaminated blood should be informed about immunization.

The requirements for an infant and toddler room are more stringent because of the kinds of activities that occur there. Children crawl on the floor, are diapered, and put almost all objects in their mouths. Therefore, in addition to the general room cleaning that is done, some special procedures can increase the safety of this area of the school. They are the following:

- Cleanliness is important in this area of the school, but it should not present an obstacle to interactions with children. Cleanliness should become so automatic that children can be attended to while also having as safe and as disease-free an environment as possible.
- Vacuum carpeting daily and wet-mop vinyl floors with detergent and disinfectant. Clean all floor surfaces thoroughly on a regular schedule.
- Wipe cribs and mattresses regularly with a disinfectant. Change the sheets whenever wet or soiled. Wash sheets weekly, or as needed.
- Cover the diapering table with paper towels when being used; however, wipe it with a disinfectant after each use.
- Dispose of soiled diapers or hold for laundry in a closed container.
- Rinse the potty-chair cup after each use, and spray the seat with a disinfectant.
- Wash all toys with a disinfectant at the end of each day. Put them in a mesh bag, dip them in a disinfectant solution, and hang them to dry.
- Spray with disinfectant and wipe any large pieces of equipment that children climb.
- Disinfect food containers and utensils regularly.
- A solution of ¼ cup of chlorine bleach in one gallon of water is an adequate disinfectant for most cleaning purposes.
- All caregivers in the infant-toddler room should automatically wash their hands after diapering and before feedings or preparing food for children.

A discussion of preventing unhealthy conditions should include management of the sick child. Each school should have a child inclusion/exclusion policy statement indicating when children should be kept at home and under what conditions a child will be sent home. Such a policy might state that children will neither be denied admission nor sent home unless:

1. their illness prevents them from participating in activities
2. their illness results in need for more care than the staff can provide without jeopardizing the health or safety of other children

Children should be sent home and kept home as long as the following conditions exist, or until medical evaluation deems it safe for the child to return.

- oral temperature 101°F or greater; rectal temperature 102°F or greater; armpit temperature 100°F or greater; accompanied by changes in behavior or other signs of illness
- symptoms and signs of a severe illness: coughing, wheezing, lethargy, irritability, crying
- vomiting: two or more episodes in the previous 24 hours
- uncontrolled diarrhea
- rash, along with a fever or change in behavior
- mouth sores accompanied by drooling
- purulent conjunctivitis (pink eye)

- tuberculosis
- strep throat or other streptococcal infection
- scabies, head lice, or any other infestation
- impetigo
- chicken pox, until six days after onset of the rash or until all sores are dry and crusted
- mumps, until nine days after the onset of gland swelling
- pertussis, until five days of antibiotic treatment have been completed
- hepatitis A virus, until one week after the onset or as directed by health authorities
- rubella, until six days after onset of rash
- measles, until six days after onset of rash

The first step is to train teachers and caregivers to recognize early signs of a sick child. The most obvious symptoms are a runny nose, red throat, sneezing, and coughing. Diarrhea and vomiting also are quickly associated with a possible illness. Less-apparent signs may be "glassy" or watery eyes and a general listlessness. Irritability, fatigue, or loss of appetite might also not be recognized as portending an illness. Several staff members should know how to take children's temperatures and to interpret the reading. (An oral temperature over 99.4°F or an axillary reading over 98.0°F accompanies many childhood illnesses.)

The next step in managing a sick child is deciding what to do after the illness is first recognized. If it is at the beginning of the day during morning inspection, the child should be sent home. If the illness only becomes apparent as the day wears on, other decisions may have to be made.

Ideally, a portion of the school environment would be set aside for the care of sick children. Here children could stay and be taken care of until the end of the day when the parents can get them. Some programs do offer this kind of service. The school must have a planned environment that allows the children to be in a less-stimulating setting than their regular classroom. There also should be medical services available by telephone as needed. The Fairfax-San Anselmo Children's Center in Fairfax, California, provides this kind of service. One of the classrooms is called the "get well" room. Staffed by regular child-care workers who have had specialized training, the room can accommodate six children. Parents let the staff know about the child's evening and morning symptoms. Staff keep careful records of the child's day for parents' information at pickup time.

Some child-care centers provide care for a sick child within the regular classroom. The Frank Porter Graham Child Development Center in Chapel Hill, North Carolina, has operated such a program for more than 10 years. Children with minor illnesses are allowed to attend school and stay in their regular classrooms. Children with contagious diseases such as measles and chicken pox are excluded, but because so many children are immunized, few have been kept home. The usual caregivers take care of the children, but medical assistance is nearby when necessary. The designers of this program reason that the child is most contagious long before recognizable symptoms appear, so there is little reason to exclude children once the illness has been identified. Children in this program do not become ill more frequently than in other programs, and the diseases are no more severe.

Another kind of service for sick children is a child-care center totally devoted to their needs. These programs usually accommodate children from six months to 12 years who have colds, flu, or even chicken pox. Children are separated according to their illnesses, and nurses are available to care for them. Although this is a relatively expensive kind of child care, it is probably a bargain to the parent who might otherwise miss a full day's pay by staying home to care for the child.

Including sick or recovering children in the regular classroom may mean that staff will be responsible for dispensing medication during the day. This should be done only with signed permission from both parents and the children's physicians. Medicines must be kept in a separate place, either on a high shelf or in the refrigerator. Maintaining careful records of the time a dosage was given, the person who gave it, and the amount given is absolutely necessary. Parents and caregivers should confer daily about the continuance of the medication.

One further way to prevent future illness is immunization. This practice protects children against many of the preventable childhood diseases including rubella, mumps, measles, polio, whooping cough, diphtheria, and tetanus. Many parents have their children routinely immunized from an early age. Others are seemingly unconcerned because they do not recognize that some of these conditions are life-threatening to young children. Others think these diseases have been eliminated and, therefore, their children need not be subjected to the procedure. A few worry about the side effects of immunization.

Immunization is required before entering public school in all states and the District of Columbia. In states where the requirements for preschools and child-care entry are

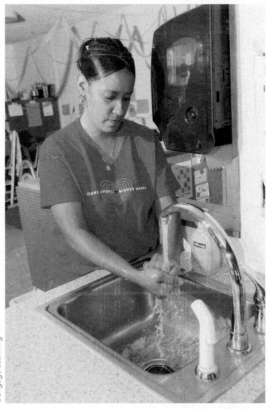

Cengage Learning

Caregivers should wash their hands after diapering and before preparing food for children.

not similar, many teachers, directors, and others responsible for policies have opted to require immunization as a condition of entrance. Visit http://www.cdc.gov/nip to view the recommended immunization schedule for children.

When, despite all preventive measures, a child in a school has contracted one of these illnesses, it is the director's responsibility to see that the parents of all children who might have been exposed are notified. A simple form can indicate that their child has been exposed to a specific illness. The form should include information about the incubation period and possible signs and symptoms.

Children should not be allowed back into the classroom until their physician certifies that they are free of contagion. This will protect staff, children, and parents in the best possible way.

INCLUDING CHILDREN WITH HIV/AIDS

Although reports from the Centers for Disease Control (CDC) indicate that the number of children with AIDS has declined since 1994, many are still infected. Despite evidence indicating that these children can attend child-care programs without harm to other children, many child-care professionals are concerned. Actually, children with HIV are at risk of contracting other childhood diseases because their immune systems do not develop antibodies to combat them. In order to relieve anxieties of staff members and parents, it is important to become educated about what the disease is, how it is transmitted, and what precautions can be taken to prevent its spread.

Children with HIV have been infected by their mothers during pregnancy or through receiving a contaminated blood transfusion. Adults acquire the disease by sexual contact involving secretions and sperm, infected blood, and contaminated needles. It is not transmitted by casual contacts such as sharing food, dishes, drinking glasses, toilets, pools, clothing, or toys. It cannot be transmitted by hugging, kissing, or touching. Children with HIV can go to school, play with friends, and participate in out-of-school recreational activities without risk to other children. The CDC and the Pediatric AIDS Foundation of Santa Monica, California, recommend that children be kept out of group activities only if they have bleeding or open sores that might expose other children to risks. When children with HIV are included in school, the precautions listed in this chapter should be strictly adhered to, especially when cleaning up any blood or blood-contaminated fluids. Schools and child-care centers should draft a policy on infectious diseases, including HIV, which is distributed to all staff members and parents. For further information about HIV, contact the Centers for Disease Control of the U.S. Department of Health and Human Services and the Pediatric AIDS Foundation.

Centers for Disease Control & Prevention (CDC)
http://www.cdc.gov
301-458-4636

Pediatric AIDS Foundation
1311 Colorado Avenue
Santa Monica, CA 90405
310-314-1459
http://www.pedaids.org

Another excellent source of information regarding health and safety of children in group care can be obtained from the National Association for the Education of Young

Children (NAEYC). It is a two-DVD set titled "Health and Safety Consultation in Child Care," Stock number 8621. The topics include how to train child-care staff and how to make health and safety improvements. There is also an interactive assessment tool and relevant forms.

> *NAEYC*
> 1313 L Street, NW
> Suite 500
> Washington, DC 20005
> 202-232-8777; 800-424-2460; fax 202-328-1846

RECORDKEEPING

Although the matter of adequate records of children's health has been touched upon, it is worth covering more extensively. Adequate records are the basis for planning for individual children, for developing policies and procedures, and for checking the attainment of health goals. Each child should have a file that contains information about health before entering school and during the time of attendance.

Each child's file should contain the following information.

Health

physician's examination prior to entrance, including general health status

any conditions that might interfere with functioning at school

immunizations

conditions the school should be aware of, such as seizures and allergies

health screening tests

continuing health care, such as illnesses, surgery, injuries, current medications

Child Development

information concerning the mother's pregnancy

developmental history from birth to school entrance

profiles done by teachers on a periodic basis

Family Information

application form including residence, workplaces of both parents, family members

emergency information including people to contact in case the child is hurt or ill

release for emergency medical treatment

people authorized to take child from school

authorization for use of child's photo or voice recording for educational purposes

permission to take child on trips away from school

financial arrangements for payment of tuition

Working parents' greatest concern is probably the health and safety of their children when someone else cares for them. A well-maintained, safe, and healthy environment is worth all the staff effort and time that it takes. The parents will be grateful and there may be a financial benefit as well. A safe, well-maintained, and attractive school will bring a more stable enrollment and a more consistent income.

CASE STUDY

Ryan Walsh is three years old and was diagnosed with hemophilia when he first began to walk. At home the family has been able to restrict his activities somewhat so that he has had few problems. However, now his mother feels he needs to be with other children and would like him to be in a good preschool. She visited several in her community and none of them had openings. She finally called a small school owned and operated by Maria Guitierrez. Maria said they did have an opening and would be willing to discuss Ryan's enrollment.

Mrs. Walsh visited the school and liked what she saw. Maria seemed willing to discuss Ryan's enrollment further and asked what special accommodations would be needed to keep Ryan safe. Outdoors at home Ryan wears a helmet, elbow pads, and knee pads, and could do so at school. Additionally, the school would need to have ice packs available at all times; these would be provided by the family. Mrs. Walsh would also see that the school had all necessary emergency telephone numbers. They agreed to pursue Ryan's enrollment further by having him come for a visit.

1. How would you feel about enrolling Ryan if you were Maria? Ryan's teacher?
2. What should Maria do to educate her staff members about managing a child with hemophilia?
3. If you were Maria, would you enroll Ryan in your program? Why or why not?

SUMMARY

The physical environment of the school should be planned carefully because it bears equal weight as educational programs.

Maintenance consists of major projects; operations are the daily tasks required to keep the school functioning hygienically and attractively.

The director should take an inventory of all buildings and equipment at least annually and should keep accurate records.

Licensing guidelines and local building and safety codes are designed to ensure the safety of children in group settings. Knowing requirements and always complying with them is important. Regular safety checks of all equipment, both indoors and outdoors, are required.

Every school should have a well-stocked first-aid kit. At least one person on staff at all times should be Red Cross certified to administer first aid.

Developing a disaster plan for meeting emergencies such as fires, floods, hurricanes, tornadoes, or earthquakes is important. An evacuation route should be posted in each classroom and in entry areas. Frequent drills will prepare staff and children for what to do in the event of a disaster.

Every early childhood center should have a set of health goals designed to promote the health and well-being of children. These goals should be the basis for health policies that guide preventive practices.

Health goals should address children's health status and include means for alleviating conditions that prevent children from learning. Health goals should also address the prevention of future illnesses.

Prevention of future illnesses is facilitated by maintaining a clean and sanitary environment.

Furthermore, staff must take additional precaution when handling bodily fluids.

Each school should have a child inclusion/exclusion policy stating when children should be kept at home and under what conditions children will be sent home.

The inclusion of children with HIV/AIDS is an issue that needs to be addressed in child care. All staff members and parents should become educated about the causes of AIDS, how it is transmitted, and what precautions can be taken to prevent its spread. Keeping accurate records of children's health is important. Records should include information regarding the child's general health status, developmental information, and family information.

STUDENT ACTIVITIES

1. Draw the floor plan of a classroom you know. How would you replan it after having read this chapter? What are your reasons for the changes?

2. Visit a school for young children. Observe the playground for an hour. What changes would you make if you were in charge? Why?

3. What methods are used to clean your school? Are they adequate? Why?

4. Visit the health department of your community. What services are available to children? Who can use them?

5. Look in the telephone book under the listing for physicians. How many pediatricians are there?

6. Where is the closest emergency hospital to your school? Is the phone number posted? Do you know the most direct route?

REVIEW

1. Why is the physical appearance of a school more than cosmetic?

2. List safety precautions that should be taken when transporting children.

3. What kinds of information are included in a disaster plan?

4. List items that should be included in a disaster kit.

5. List five general precautions to prevent the spread of diseases in a child-care environment.

6. What special precautions should be taken when handling any bodily fluids?

7. How do physical disabilities interfere with a child's ability to learn?

8. Under what conditions should children be sent home or kept home?

9. What are the current recommendations for including children with HIV/AIDS in child care?

10. What are the three categories of information that should be in a child's health file?

REFERENCE

Farish, J. M. (2006). Helping young children after a disaster. Adapted from "When disaster strikes: Helping young children cope." NAEYC Brochure #533.

SELECTED FURTHER READING

American Academy of Pediatrics. (2002). *National health and safety performance standards for out-of-school child care programs* (2nd ed.). Elk Grove Village, IL: Author.

Aronson, S. S. (2005). Maintaining a sanitary child care environment—six tips for germ control. Retrieved 2006, from https://secure.ccie.com/resources/view.

Children's Defense Fund. (2001). *The state of America's children 2001*. Washington, DC: Author.

Federal Emergency Management Agency (FEMA). (2001c). FEMA for kids. Retrieved March 30, 2006, from http://www.fema.gov/kids.

Gaines, S., & Leary, J. (2004). Public health emergency preparedness in the setting of child care. *Family and Community Health, 27*(3), 260–265.

Huettig, C. I., Sanborn, C. F., DiMarco, N., Popejoy, A., & Rich, S. (2004). The O generation, our youngest children are at risk for obesity. *Young Children, 59*(2), 50–55.

National Association for the Education of Young Children. (2004). FYI. Keeping young children safe and healthy: Child care health and safety-change and reminders for staying alert. *Young Children, 59*(2): 49.

Robertson, C. (2007). *Safety, nutrition, and health in early childhood education* (3rd ed.). Clifton Park, NY: Cengage Learning

Werner, P., Timms, S., & Almond, L. (1996). Health stops: Practical ideas for health-related exercise in preschool and primary classrooms. *Young Children, 51*(6), 48–51.

Youngquist, Joan, (2004). From medicine to microbes: A project investigation of health. *Young Children, 59*(2): 28–32.

HELPFUL WEBSITES

Disclaimer: Links to Internet sites throughout this book are provided for your convenience and do not constitute an endorsement.

American Academy of Pediatrics, sponsors the Healthy Child Care America Campaign:	**http://www. Healthychildcare.org**
Americans with Disabilities Act (ADA):	**http://www.ada.gov**
CDC National Prevention Information Network:	**http://www.cdcnpin.org**
Council for Exceptional Children:	**http://cec.sped.org**
FEMA for Kids: Click on FEMA for Kids	**http://www.fema.gov**
National Program for Playground Safety:	**http://uni.edu.playground**
National Resource Center for Health and Safety in Child Care:	**http://nrc.uchsc.edu**
National SAFEKIDS Campaign:	**http://www.safekids.org**

For additional resources related to administration including videos, links to related sites for each chapter of the text, tutorial quizzes, glossary flashcards, and more, visit the Education CourseMate website for this book at www.cengage.com/login.

CHAPTER

12

Cengage Learning

Food and Nutrition Services

Objectives

After reading this chapter, you should be able to:

- Explain why good nutrition is important in an early childhood center.
- List several principles of menu planning.
- Describe some of the mechanics of food service.

KEY TERMS

allergens

Food Guide Pyramid

A day in the life of . . .

A Family Child Care Home

Slices of watermelon were served at snack time. The caregiver saved the seeds to use for gluing to construction paper cut in the shape of a slice of watermelon. Some of the seeds were still slippery when the activity began. When one little boy tried to pick them up between his thumb and forefinger, they would shoot away from his hand. After several tries with the same result, he sighed, "These are just too quick for me."

Proper nutrition is vital to the development of young children. What children eat during the years of rapid growth between birth and five years can affect their future development. Improper nutrition may delay or permanently stunt physical growth.

A child who is ill or lethargic because of poor nutrition will have less interest in learning. An irritable child is likely to have problems in social situations. Therefore, as more children spend longer hours in group settings, the adults who care for them must assume greater responsibility for ensuring that they get an adequate diet.

Caregiver's Role

The caregivers or teachers who are with children during most of their waking hours must closely observe their eating patterns. They should be aware of children's food likes and dislikes, the amount each child consumes, and any changes in food habits. Sometimes, this information can be used to reassure parents that their child is eating well at school. Other times, parents must be alerted to changes in a child's eating patterns.

Caregivers must also know what changes to expect in children's food consumption at each stage of development. During periods of rapid growth, children eat well.

When growth slows down, they automatically consume less. Unless the adult is knowledgeable enough to realize that this as a normal change, adults may be needlessly anxious or may pressure the child to change.

Current recommendations for good nutrition should be a part of the caregiver's knowledge. As research reveals more about the body's needs, ideas about what constitutes a proper diet have also changed. For instance, previously, solid foods were introduced to infants as early as five to six weeks. In 1981, the American Academy of Pediatrics recommended that breast-fed babies do not need supplementary foods until six months of age. Formula-fed babies may need some vitamin supplements. At about six months, the ability to chew, swallow, and process solid foods is more developed. At that time, parents can gradually add cereal, fruits, vegetables, meat, and fish to the child's diet. By the end of the first year, children should be consuming a variety of foods consistent with the new **Food Guide Pyramid**.

Caregivers should know how to encourage children to make appropriate food choices while being sensitive to cultural differences. Children may eat food in child care that conflicts with parents' beliefs, causing problems for the children.

Some families eat little meat, for example, or may even be strict vegetarians. Other families avoid pork or use only foods that have a kosher mark. Caregivers need to be aware of these differences and serve food that accommodates such preferences. Another area of possible conflict with parents is self-feeding. Professionals agree that it is important to

Cengage Learning

Caregivers must closely observe children's eating habits.

encourage even babies to start feeding themselves as soon as possible, but in some cultures children are fed by an adult until age four or later. This may be true in cultures where neatness is stressed, such as Japan. The same attitude may be true in American families where food cannot be wasted. Young children who are just learning to feed themselves may also play with the food before consuming it. Many experts advise leniency in allowing children to touch their food. Some teachers even use food as a sensory experience. Parents who have experienced deprivation may be offended or angered at this kind of waste.

Menu Planning

The director's responsibility will be either to plan menus or to oversee someone else who does the planning. If a school is open all day, it may be necessary to serve breakfast, lunch, and two snacks each day. This constitutes a large portion of the child's daily intake. Therefore, it is important to plan meals that include as much of the child's daily requirements as possible.

Licensing requirements will vary from state to state but are based on the number of hours a center operates. Generally, guidelines specify the following:

- If a center is open three to four hours, it should serve a midmorning or afternoon snack no closer than two hours before the next meal.
- If a center is open five to eight hours, food service should provide one third to one half of the daily requirement.
- If a center is open nine hours or more, it should serve at least two thirds of the total daily requirement.
- If a center includes infants, they should have individualized eating plans and schedules.

Some child-care programs receive funding under the Child Care Food Program. This program provides reimbursement for meals in child-care centers and for the cost of labor and administration. The Food and Nutrition Service of the U.S. Department of Agriculture (USDA) provides the funding, which the state departments of education administer. Guidelines specify nutritional standards and serving sizes for children from birth to age 12. Head Start centers also have their own nutritional standards and serving-size regulations.

There are many ways to organize menu planning so that it is efficient. Marotz (2009) recommend the following materials to help in menu planning.

- Menu forms
- A list of available foods
- A recipe file
- Old menus with notes and suggestions
- A calendar
- Grocery advertisements for short-term planning

The main lunch dishes should include protein foods or substitutes. Vegetables and fruits should also be served. These can be as salads, with the entrée, or as dessert. Enriched or whole-grain breads or cereal products come next. The meal should include a beverage, usually milk. Snacks and breakfast can be planned to round out the daily requirements.

Many schools have cyclic menus. The first step is to make several weekly menus and test them to determine whether the children will eat the food. After making any necessary changes, the menus can be recycled every month or so. This has a decided advantage because ordering larger quantities of some foods is possible, thus saving money. It will also save the time needed to prepare new menus every week. Children like familiar foods and do not mind having the same things every few weeks or so. It is easy to make changes to some basic menus using seasonal fruits or vegetables.

Including some ethnic or regional foods will help children from different backgrounds feel more comfortable. It will also introduce all children to the concept of cultural differences or similarities.

Some schools have instituted the idea of "special day foods." These foods do not appear on the cyclic menu but are served on special occasions. The party atmosphere of a day such as this may encourage children to try foods they would ordinarily reject. Examples might be a "smorgasbord" of unusual fruits or vegetables that the children can taste-test at snack time. Another might be an "upside-down day," such as whole-wheat pancakes with fruit toppings for lunch or cheese sandwiches for breakfast. The idea is to make tasting foods an adventure.

Some schools provide snacks in the morning and afternoon, but they expect parents to supply lunches for their children. If this is the case, caregivers are still responsible for ensuring that children's lunches are as nutritious as possible. Parents can be educated about proper nutrition for their children and how to make appealing meals that will not end up in the trash can. It might be helpful to schedule a parent meeting with a nutritionist who can make suggestions for appealing brown-bag cuisine, or to include a list of suggestions in a parent newsletter.

Guidelines for Menu Planning

Some further guidelines may be helpful in developing a series of menus. The person responsible for planning meals should work within the framework of the Food Guide Pyramid developed by the United States Department of Agriculture's Human Nutrition Information Service. The newest pyramid (see Figure 12-1) shows six different colored triangles. Each color represents a different food group: orange for grains, green for vegetables, red for fruits, blue for dairy, purple for proteins, and yellow for fats and oils.

The Food Guide Pyramid is designed to be clear about which foods should be consumed in the greatest quantities. The pyramid also includes stairs along the left side and represents at least 30 minutes of exercise each day. You can view the recommendations of the USDA on the website http://www.mypyramid.gov.

GRAINS

The orange triangle is the largest and represents the grain group, including foods such as bread, cereal, pasta, and rice. At least half of the grains should be brown rice and whole grains such as oatmeal, and whole wheat. Recommended serving sizes are the following:

- 2- to 3-year-olds: 3 ounces
- 4- to 8-year-olds: 4–5 ounces
- 9- to 13-year-old girls: 5 ounces
- 9- to 13-year-old boys: 6 ounces

The following equal an ounce:

- 1 slice of bread
- ½ cup cooked rice or pasta
- ⅓ cup oatmeal

CATEGORY	GRAINS	VEGETABLES	FRUITS	MILK	MEAT & BEANS
RECOMMENDATION	Half of all grains consumed should be whole grains.	Vary the types of vegetables you eat.	Eat a variety of fruits. Go easy on juices.	Eat low-fat or fat-free dairy products.	Eat lean cuts, seafood and beans, Avoid frying.
DAILY AMOUNT	6 oz.	2.5 cups	2 cups	3 cups	5.5 oz.

OILS
- Most fat should be from fish, nuts and vegetable oils.
- Limit solid fats, such as butter, margarine or lard.
- Keep consumption of saturated fats, trans fats and sodium low.
- Choose foods low in added sugar.

Based on a 2,000 calorie diet.

FIGURE 12–1 Food Guide Pyramid.

VEGETABLES

The green triangle indicates vegetables, which can be steamed or eaten raw. Occasional stir-frying is another way of preparing vegetables. Recommended serving sizes are:

- 2- to 3-year-olds: 1 cup
- 4- to 8-year-olds: 1½ cups
- 9- to 13-year-old girls: 2 cups
- 9- to 13-year-old boys: 2½ cups

FRUIT

The red triangle includes fruits that are good sources of vitamins and minerals. In order to preserve the nutrients, eating fruits raw is best. Recommended serving sizes are:

- 2- to 3-year-olds: 8 ounces
- 4- to 8-year-olds: 12 ounces
- 9- to 13-year-old girls: 5 ounces
- 9- to 13-year-old boys: 5 ounces

MEAT, FISH, BEANS, AND NUTS

The purple triangle includes protein sources that help children build muscle and repair their body tissues. Recommended serving sizes are:

- 2- to 3-year-olds: 2 ounces
- 4- to 8-year-olds: 3–4 ounces

- 9- to 13-year-olds girls: 5 ounces
- 9- to 13-year-old boys: 5 ounces

One ounce of meat, poultry, or fish equals a one-ounce serving. Instead of meat, the following will equal one ounce of this food group.

- ¼ cup cooked dry beans
- 1 egg
- 1 tablespoon peanut butter (Do not use if there are children with allergies.)
- ½ ounce nuts or seeds

DAIRY

The blue triangle is allocated to dairy products, including milk, yogurt, and cheese. These are essential sources of vitamins A and D, calcium, and protein. Recommended serving sizes are:

- 2- to 3-year-olds: 2 ounces
- 4- to 8-year-olds: 3–4 ounces
- 9- to 13-year old girls: 12 ounces
- 9- to 13-year-old boys: 12 ounces

FATS, OILS, AND SWEETS

The yellow triangle, the slimmest, indicates that this category should be consumed in limited quantities. Fats are needed to maintain good health and to absorb vitamins A, D, E, and K, as well as beta-carotene. Fats should not be restricted for children under the age of two.

Sugars provide children with almost immediate doses of energy because they are quickly absorbed into the blood stream. However, when consumed in too great a quantity, they are stored in the body as fat that can lead to weight gain or other health problems.

Some centers may have children who are eligible for free or reduced-price meals from the USDA Child and Adult Care Food Program (CACFP). Children's eligibility is based on family income, and providers are reimbursed at specific rates that are readjusted each year. Providers in the following categories may qualify: public or private nonprofit centers, profit-making centers that receive Title XX compensation for at least 25 percent of enrollees, Head Start programs, settlement houses and recreation programs, and family child-care homes. All participating agencies must serve meals that meet the standards set by the USDA. Figures 12-2 and 12-3 show the kinds of foods to be served and the portion sizes. Further information about requirements and children's eligibility can be obtained by contacting a regional office of the USDA or by calling the National Food Service Management Institute's "Help Desk," which is funded by the USDA. The phone number is 800-321-3054.

It is important to choose foods children like. Children are sensitive to the four basic tastes: salty, sweet, sour, and bitter. Because of this enhanced taste awareness, they are more conservative in their approach to foods. Most have a very limited number of foods they like. They will often reject foods that are strong in flavor or heavily spiced. They will refuse to try new foods before they even taste them. Children do not like their foods mixed in casseroles or stew. Most want their food to be easy to manage—in bite-sized pieces or as finger foods. A list of the proven favorites can be used to plan basic menus. New foods can gradually be added to broaden the children's diet.

MEAL PATTERN	CHILDREN 1 TO 3	CHILDREN 3 TO 6	CHILDREN 6 TO 12
BREAKFAST			
Milk	1/2 cup	3/4 cup	1 cup
Juice or fruit	1/4 cup	1/2 cup	1/2 cup
Bread or substitute	1/2 slice	1/2 slice	1 slice
Cereal: cold, dry or hot, cooked	1/4 cup	1/3 cup	1/2 cup
SNACK (select 2)			
Milk, meat, or meat substitute	1/2 cup	1/2 cup	1 cup
Bread or substitute	1/2 slice	1/2 slice	1 slice
Juice, fruit, or vegetable	1/2 cup	1/2 cup	3/4 cup
Cereal: cold, dry or hot, cooked	1/4 cup	1/3 cup	1/2 cup
LUNCH OR SUPPER			
Milk	1/2 cup	3/4 cup	1 cup
Meat or alternative—One of the following combinations to give equivalent quantities.			
Meat, poultry, fish	1 ounce	1 1/2 ounces	2 ounces
Egg	1	1	1
Cheese	1 ounce	1 1/2 ounces	2 ounces
Cooked dry beans	1/4 cup	3/8 cup	1/2 cup
Peanut butter (Do not use if there are allergic children.)	2 tablespoons	3 tablespoons	4 tablespoons
Vegetables and/or fruit (2 or more to total)	1/4 cup	1/2 cup	3/4 cup
Bread or alternate	1/2 slice	1/2 slice	1 slice
Butter or margarine	1/2 teaspoon	1/2 teaspoon	1/2 teaspoon

FIGURE 12-2   Child and Adult Care Food Program, meal pattern for children.

The person who plans the menus should take into consideration the kitchen equipment that is available. When preparing food for large groups, one of the problems often incurred is that there is not enough oven space or large pans. Knowing what kitchen equipment is available is important, as is anticipating needs for preparing and serving the food. For example, a finger food can be prepared for dessert if all the small bowls are needed for the meal.

The director should consider the number of personnel available for preparing and serving food. If a school is very large, there may be both a cook and an assistant. Meals are likely to be different in this kind of school than in one where there is only a part-time cook. In a family child-care home, where the owner-operator does all the cooking, meals must be extremely simple and easily prepared.

Foods should provide appetite appeal. Remember the old saying "We eat with our eyes as well as our mouths." It helps to vary the color of foods served. A meal of mashed

Menus for Week Of _____

	MONDAY	TUESDAY	WEDNESDAY	THURSDAY	FRIDAY
BREAKFAST	1/2 orange 1/4 cup shredded wheat cereal 3/4 cup milk	1/2 cup tomato juice 2 4-inch pancakes 2 Tbsp. applesauce 1/2 tsp. margarine 1/2 cup milk	1/2 cup sliced peaches 3/4 cup milk bagel half low-fat cream cheese	1/2 banana 1/4 cup shredded wheat cereal 3/4 cup milk 1/2 slice toast 1/2 tsp. margarine	1/2 cup orange juice French toast 1/2 slice bread milk egg powdered sugar 1/2 cup milk
SNACK	1/2 cup milk 2 graham crackers melon cubes	1/2 slice cheese 4 small whole-wheat crackers apple juice	1/2 cup yogurt with fruit 2 whole-wheat crackers banana slices water	1/2 slice cheese 1/2 apple water	1/2 cup apple juice 2 graham crackers low-fat yogurt
LUNCH	1/2 cup milk 2 fish sticks 4 carrot sticks 1/2 slice bread 1/2 tsp. margarine 1/3 cup applesauce	1/2 cup milk 1 oz. meat loaf 1/4 cup peas 1/4 baked potato 1/2 tsp. margarine 2-inch square of spice cake made with whole-wheat flour	1/2 cup milk 1/2 cup spaghetti 1/4 cup meat sauce 1/4 cup green salad 2 orange wedges	1/2 cup milk 1/2 cup macaroni cheese 1/4 cup string beans 1/4 cup Apple Betty with wheat germ topping	1/2 cup milk 1/2 tuna sandwich 1/4 cup carrot & raisin salad 1/2 cup ice cream
SNACK	assorted raw vegetables sour cream dip 1/4 slice whole-wheat bread 1/2 tsp. margarine water	1/2 cup yogurt with fruit 1 graham cracker water	1/2 peanut butter sandwich (Do not use if there are allergic children.) 1/2 cup milk	whole-wheat raisin cookies 1/2 cup milk	1/2 cup milk 1/3 warm tortilla 1/2 tsp. margarine or grated cheese

F I G U R E   12 – 3   Weekly menu in a child-care center for a group of three-year-olds.

FYI

In a study on serving and food intake, Baylor College of Medicine researcher Dr. Jennifer Fisher found that preschool children ate 25 percent more when given a larger portion of food, increasing lunchtime calorie count by 15 percent.

These findings suggest that regular exposure to "supersized" portions encourages overeating among children. The study also produced a surprisingly positive result. When children were allowed to serve themselves from serving bowls, the amount they served themselves was appropriate. As Dr. Fisher reported, "We found that large portions lost the power to promote overeating when the children were allowed to serve themselves."

SOURCE: Baylor College of Medicine, 1999.

potatoes, fish, and cauliflower will hardly be appealing. The cook should occasionally change the shape of familiar foods. Sandwiches may be cut in triangles, circles, or slim rectangles. Meals should include several different textures: crunchy, soft, chewy.

A new food should be introduced along with a familiar and accepted food. For example, if the goal is to have children try a new vegetable, it could be served with their favorite chicken. An unfamiliar carrot salad could be served along with the fish sticks most children love.

Dessert should be an integral part of the meal, not a special treat when other foods are eaten. Desserts should contribute to the daily food requirement. Fruits, cakes made with whole-wheat flour, cookies with nuts or raisins, or milk puddings are all examples. Children also enjoy ice cream and fruit sherbets, which contribute to good nutrition.

Children learn when they help plan their own meals and snacks. When given limited choices, preschoolers and school-age children can plan some of their own meals and snacks. Obviously, they cannot be given total freedom because they might choose a meal of potato chips, ice cream, and chocolate cupcakes. However, if they are given information about the food groups, they should be able to plan a meal using foods from each. Children should be allowed to plan lunch once a week, once a month, or as often as possible.

Including Parents

Keeping the parents of children in the school informed about the menus is important. One of the first questions many parents ask when they arrive to pick up their child at the end of the day is "Did my child eat well today?" Parents are concerned that their children eat the right foods in adequate amounts.

Weekly menus should be posted in an easily seen place so parents know what was served that day. When they see a food they know their child likes, they can feel more confident. At home, the evening meal can then supplement whatever the child had at school and not serve the same foods.

Cengage Learning

Lunch is a time to socialize.

A parent newsletter is a great way to provide information about appropriate food choices for young children. Information can be obtained from articles in nutrition journals or from the local library. The articles can be summarized or reprinted in totality for parents. If the children bring breakfast or lunch from home, parents can be given suggestions for choosing nutritious foods and advice about how to avoid the "television advertising trap"—those appealing advertisements that make children demand the foods in their lunch boxes. Only clever substitutes will satisfy many children (see Figure 12-4). A newsletter might also give suggestions for nutritious birthday treats that parents may bring to school.

Instead of whole milk: use dry low-fat milk, cottage cheese, mild cheddar cheese, ice milk.

Instead of expensive cuts of meat: use less tender cuts, stewing chickens, fresh fish in season, home-cooked meats.

Use dried beans, peas, lentils, peanut butter (do not use if there are allergic children).

Fruits and vegetables: buy fresh fruits and vegetables in season.

Breads and cereals: use whole-grain or enriched flour, homemade cakes and rolls, whole-grain crackers.

Use brown rice and enriched spaghetti and noodles.

F I G U R E 1 2 - 4 Inexpensive substitutes with more food value.

Teachers should keep parents informed about their child's food intake. Some schools have a form that teachers complete each day indicating how much the child ate. If the school does not use a form, teachers should be alert to each child's consumption so that they can answer parents' questions.

The school should develop a partnership with parents of infants and toddlers to plan food choices. The diets of these young children need to be carefully thought-out to avoid food allergies, digestive upsets, and poor nutrition. Pediatricians have traditionally worked with parents to avoid these problems. Now the school must be included in the planning. Compounding the difficulty is the fact that babies react in different ways to new situations, including new foods. Caregivers need to be aware of those habits so that they can avoid rejection of food the child needs. Many toddlers have particular ways in which they want their food prepared or presented. No other way will suffice. Therefore, the school must have a close alliance with the parents to ensure that these youngest children are eating an adequate diet.

All parents must inform the school of their child's allergies. A large number of pre-school children have allergic reactions, although not all are to food. The common food **allergens** are chocolate, milk and milk products, wheat/gluten, peanuts, and eggs. When planning a menu item using these foods, there must be a substitute that can be served to the allergic child. Some schools ask parents to supply alternate foods on these days. Other schools keep foods on hand to use at these times.

Parents should be offered recipes of school foods that children especially like. Many children talk about a popular menu item and want Mom to prepare it at home. Quantity recipes can be translated to smaller portions so that copies are available when parents ask. Just as serving homelike foods at school brings home and school closer together, the opposite will bridge the gap as the child reenters the home routines.

Food Service for Children

The best-planned menus are useless unless children eat the food. The atmosphere in which food is presented should encourage the children to consume an adequate amount.

The classroom should be straightened before mealtime. Many teachers involve children in this task. It can also be done while the children are outdoors or having a story in another area. The teacher should put distracting toys out of sight and clear away clutter on shelves or floors.

Tables should be as attractive as possible. A centerpiece of flowers or something made by the children will add interest. Children can make their own personalized place-mats. The mat can be covered with clear contact paper for durability. The table should be set in an orderly manner with napkins, utensils, and plates carefully placed within convenient reach of the children. Special occasions such as holidays or birthdays call for special table decorations.

Mealtime furniture should be appropriate for the age level of the children. One consideration is whether to use tables or high chairs for toddlers. According to Magda Gerber (1991), Director of Resources for Infant Educarers, high chairs are confining. As soon as babies can crawl and sit up, Gerber says that they can get themselves to a table that is only a few inches off the floor. School-age children need larger chairs and higher tables than preschoolers.

Snack time.

Children should participate as much as possible in mealtime routines. They can set the table before the meal begins. Children can serve themselves from serving bowls rather than having each plate already "dished out" before it comes to the table. At the end of the meal, children can scrape leftovers from their own plates and put their utensils in a container.

Teachers and caregivers should eat with the children at mealtimes. Seeing adults enjoying food serves as a role model for the development of appropriate attitudes and behavior in the children. Mealtimes should also be a time when children and adults have a chance to talk quietly to each other. Table manners should not be stressed, nor should pressure be exerted for "clean plates."

Cooking Experiences for Children

Cooking experiences can be planned for children as part of the overall process of food service. Children are quite capable of preparing some of their own meals or snacks as part of the classroom curriculum. Directors should motivate teachers to become involved as well as provide the equipment and materials to do so. Some teachers love to cook and enjoy sharing their skills, interests, and knowledge about food with children; others see it as a chore. Those who see it as a chore may need a little extra help and encouragement.

The director should include the staff in discussions of menus and invite their suggestions for things they can prepare with the children. Starting with snacks is the easiest, because many can be done without much preparation or cooking. Even two-year-olds can spread cream cheese on a cracker with a plastic knife. Preschoolers can make a fruit shake in a blender or cut their own hard-cooked eggs with an egg slicer. School-age children can prepare a variety of nutritious snacks for themselves.

At staff meetings, discussing how teachers can set up a cooking experience to minimize the danger that children will get hurt is important. Many adults shudder at the thought of three- and four-year-olds using a knife or an electric frying pan.

Careful planning is essential. If an activity is set up properly and supervised adequately, teachers should have few problems.

NUTRITION EDUCATION IN THE CLASSROOM

The act of preparing food is fun and exciting for young children and can be an incredible source of knowledge as well. They learn many things by planning, shopping for, preparing, and serving food. They can also learn much by growing and harvesting food. Many children have no idea what corn looks like before it ends up in the supermarket or in a can. Probably few know that carrots and potatoes grow under the ground, celery grows above the ground, and peas grow on vines. In many families, there is little opportunity for children to help prepare food. In fact, many families do not frequently sit down to a meal together. They stop at the fast-food place on the way home, use prepackaged foods, or call for home delivery.

Although there is a lot of information available in magazines and newspapers about good nutrition, not everyone reads and absorbs that information. Moreover,

Learning to feed yourself can be fun.

there is a lot of misinformation and conflicting theories that can confuse even sophisticated readers. Children need to have straightforward facts that they can understand at their level. They also need knowledgeable adults who will discuss this information with them.

The child-care center, therefore, has a unique opportunity to educate children about good nutrition, their bodies' health needs, and the selection and preparation of nutritious, good-tasting food. The following are some suggestions:

- display the Food Guide Pyramid along with posters of foods included in each group
- prepare and display posters showing seeds, plants, and resulting food products
- include pictures of food preparers in the cooking area
- show different ethnic groups along with their methods of cooking and food served
- discuss concepts of good nutrition using words such as vitamins, protein, and carbohydrates
- collect and sprout seeds in the classroom
- prepare a garden plot and then grow vegetables such as carrots, lettuce, radishes, pumpkins, peas, and green beans

COOKING ACTIVITIES

The following are some simple activities that can be used with children as young as three.

Easy Pizza

Purposes: learn that familiar foods can be prepared from alternative ingredients
practice measuring
increase small-muscle coordination by spreading and sprinkling

Ingredients and Procedure

English muffins	table knives
tomato sauce	tablespoons
oregano	baking sheets
salami or other meats	oven
mozzarella cheese slices	

Spread ½ of an English muffin with 1 tablespoon of tomato sauce. Sprinkle a pinch of oregano on top. Place one slice of salami, then a slice of cheese on top of the sauce. Place on a baking sheet and bake at 425°F for 10 minutes.

Food Group Sandwiches

Purposes: reinforce knowledge of foods from the Food Guide Pyramid
expand experiences with different foods
communicate information about choices to others

Ingredients and Procedure

bread: whole-wheat, wheat pita bread, whole-wheat tortillas
fruits and vegetables: cucumbers, tomatoes, bananas, raisins, apple slices, sprouts

meat and meat substitutes: hard-cooked eggs, sliced turkey, hummus

milk: low-fat Swiss cheese, low-fat cheddar cheese, low-fat cottage cheese

fats: low-fat mayonnaise, margarine, whipped butter

Group the foods on trays labeled with their food group. Allow each child to make a sandwich using as many food groups as possible. During snack time, have each child describe the sandwich and name the groups.

Baking Powder Biscuits

Purposes: measure accurately

develop small muscles by sifting, blending, kneading, and cutting

Ingredients and Procedure

2 cups flour	measuring cups
2 teaspoons baking powder	measuring spoons
1 teaspoon salt	sifter
2 tablespoons shortening or margarine	mixing bowl
⅔ cup milk	pastry blender, fork
additional milk as needed	breadboard, rolling pin
	biscuit cutter or knife
	baking sheet
	oven

Measure and sift flour, baking powder, and salt into mixing bowl. Add shortening or margarine and cut in with pastry blender. Add milk and stir in quickly with fork. Add more milk, little by little as needed, until dough is soft and light but not sticky. Turn out on floured board and knead with floured hands until smooth. Roll lightly ¼ in to ½ in thick. Cut out with biscuit cutter or cut into squares with knife. Place on ungreased baking sheet and bake 12 to 15 minutes at 450°F. Makes 12 to 15 biscuits.

Variations: Add ½ cup grated cheese or 2 tablespoons peanut butter (do not use if there are allergic children).

Yogurt Smoothie

Purposes: measure accurately

cutting, spooning, pouring

Ingredients and Procedure

½ cup yogurt	knife
½ banana	cutting surface
¼ cup other fruit: canned pineapple,	measuring cups
fresh apricots, berries	blender
dash cinnamon	spatula, spoon
	glasses

Blend all ingredients for a few seconds. Pour into glasses. Makes one cup, but can easily be multiplied.

Mechanics of Food Service

PURCHASE

With the cost of food constantly rising, directors need to be wise shoppers when buying food. The goal is to serve high-quality meals at an affordable cost within the budget. The director should check the community for food service companies that supply restaurants and institutions. They offer large-quantity packaging, often at a lower cost than the local supermarket. If the school is a nonprofit institution, they may even give an additional discount. Some deliver, but checking the cost of that service is important. The cost may be too high or may be completely justified when weighed against the time required to shop for the food.

Newspaper advertisements are a good source for the weekly specials and for seasonal fruits and vegetables. Markets feature items that are in large supply and lower the cost to attract buyers. The school can save money by completing cyclic menus with fruits and vegetables that are on sale.

The quality of food chosen should be best suited for its purpose. Top quality, and probably a higher price, is not always necessary. Reading labels and checking grades of food before deciding is important. A can of peaches to be used in a cobbler for dessert, for instance, can be a lesser grade.

Perishable foods should be bought in a quantity that can be used quickly. Meats, fruits, vegetables, and milk products fall into this category. The quantity ordered should correspond to how much children are eating at meals.

PREPARATION

The best-planned meals will not be eaten if they are not prepared properly. Food can be overcooked or undercooked. Nutrients can also be lost in the cooking process so that the food contributes little to the children's health.

The director is responsible for ensuring that appropriate guidelines are followed by whomever prepares food at the school. This includes teachers in the preschool or after-school care rooms who help children with cooking. It also covers the person in the kitchen who puts together meals for the entire school. The following precautions should be taken.

- Prepare ahead only those foods that can safely be held under refrigeration: puddings, gelatin, and spaghetti sauce are some.

- Plan so that all foods finish cooking at about the same time so that none are held too long or are reheated.

- Use cooking methods that preserve as many nutrients as possible. Do not soak vegetables for long periods of time in water or cook them in large quantities. Do not overcook vegetables.

- Prepare foods in ways that will be appealing to children. Add a touch of color sometimes with a sprinkling of paprika or parsley. Put a dab of jelly on vanilla pudding to make it more appetizing.

- Prepare food that is easy for children to manage. Cut meat into small pieces.

Quarter sandwiches or cut them into interesting shapes. Vary the way fruits and vegetables are cut: oranges can be in slices or wedges; carrots can be sticks or "pennies." (Caution: Uncooked carrots in any shape should not be given to children under the age of two.) Figures 12-5 and 12-6 list foods that will appeal to children and are easy for them to manage.

Blender Beaters

yogurt, fruit, honey

yogurt, banana, canned crushed pineapple

milk, nonfat dry milk, berries

yogurt, frozen fruit (berries or cherries), honey

Yogurt Yummies

plain yogurt with any combinations of the following:

maple syrup, honey, brown sugar, molasses

wheat germ

applesauce, apple butter

raisins, nuts (caution: not for children under two)

peaches, pineapple, blueberries, strawberries

chocolate syrup, vanilla, cinnamon

Pancake Parade

whole-wheat pancakes with any of the following:

applesauce, apple butter, peach butter

crushed berries, sour cream

maple syrup, honey, molasses

mashed bananas with lemon juice, honey, cinnamon

mashed canned apricots combined with applesauce

berries, plums, or pears blended with pineapple juice

crumbled cooked bacon mixed into batter

Snazzy Sandwiches

grilled cheese

grilled cheese and tuna

open-faced: pizza sauce, grated cheese

refried beans, cheese in a soft tortilla

pita bread stuffed with chopped tuna

pita bread, scrambled egg, mild salsa

FIGURE 12-5   Better breakfasts.

SAFETY

The safety of food served to children in a preschool or child-care setting should be a primary concern. Food must be stored properly and prepared safely. All preparation and serving areas should be clean. Teachers, kitchen staff, and any others who handle food should observe good hygienic practices.

Food handlers must maintain the strictest standards of health practices. They should undergo periodic medical evaluations to determine their general health status and that

Apples or banana

Applesauce

Chopped celery or shredded carrots

Graham crackers

Nonfat, dry milk and honey

Cheese balls—form balls with softened cheese and roll in chopped nuts (no peanuts)

Celery stuffed with cheese spread

Pizza—use pizza dough or English muffins

Tacos or burritos—fill with cheese, leftover meat, or finely shredded carrots or zucchini

Cottage cheese with fruit

Yogurt with fruit

Ice cream in milk shakes, with fruit, or in make-your-own sundaes

Deviled eggs (avoid if there are children with allergies to eggs)

Wheat toast topped with tuna salad or cheese, broiled to melt

Tiny meatballs on toothpicks

Orange sections

Banana slices—dip in honey, roll in nuts (no peanuts)

Watermelon wedges—try seedless melons

Peaches

Apple slices, dip in orange juice to prevent browning

Granola or cereal sprinkled on yogurt

Assorted raw vegetables with seasoned cottage cheese dip

Fruit shakes—blend fruit and nonfat, dry milk in blender with a few ice cubes

Fruit kabobs—banana wheels, pineapple chunks, cherries, strawberries, orange wedges

Fresh fruit juice—gelatin cubes

FIGURE 12-6   Scrumptious snacks.

they are free of tuberculosis. Anyone suffering from an illness should stay at home until recovered.

Food handlers must maintain strict standards of personal hygiene. This includes wearing clean clothes and washing hands frequently. Hair should be tidy or contained under a net. Food preparers should refrain from smoking.

Food handling should ensure that food is clean and free of contamination or spoilage. When food is delivered, it should be inspected for spoilage. Fruits and vegetables should be washed thoroughly. Foods that need refrigeration or are frozen should be put away immediately. Bulk foods such as flour or rice should be stored in airtight containers.

Food storage should provide optimum conditions for preserving the safety and nutritive value of food. Refrigerators should maintain a temperature of 38°F to 40°F. A freezer for long-term storage should be at 0°F. Foods on the shelf should have an even, cool, dry temperature. All containers should be stored off the floor.

Leftover food that has been served but has not been eaten should not be saved. The only exception might be uncut fruits and vegetables. These can be washed and saved for serving at a later time. Food that has been left in the kitchen and held at a safe temperature can be covered and put into the freezer for later use. These foods will still be safe if hot foods have been held at 160°F; cold foods must be held at below 40°F.

Ensuring that children in a school are well-nourished, healthy, and developing positive attitudes toward eating is equally important as making certain that they acquire appropriate cognitive skills. Sadly, though, some directors see it as far less critical. Staff, parents, and children will benefit if it is a goal of the school.

CASE STUDY

Arroyo is four and enrolled full-time in a pre-K program. She has a healthy appetite, and her mother sends a large lunch plus several snacks to the center each day. Most of the food consists of starchy foods high in sugar and fat. Arroyo has gained more weight during the semester than would generally be expected, and the other children are beginning to notice. She is teased and taunted by her classmates, especially during lunch.

While visiting the classroom, the director overhears a conversation between Arroyo and several other children. One girl calls Arroyo "fatty" and another calls her "lard butt." Arroyo attempts to defend herself, but becomes upset and finally begins to cry.

1. What might the director have said to the children? What could the teacher say?
2. How could the director implement a reasonable physical education program for the pre-K group?
3. Suggest ways to educate this group of children about appropriate food choices.

SUMMARY

Caregivers or teachers must have an adequate knowledge of nutrition that enables them to be sensitive to children's dietary needs and behaviors.

Menu planning or supervision is an important part of a director's schedule. There are several principles to observe in planning menus.

- Use the six basic food groups.
- Choose foods children like.
- Plan menus within the capabilities of the kitchen.
- Fit menus to personnel available for cooking and serving.
- Include food that has appeal.
- Introduce new foods along with familiar ones.
- Consider a nutritious dessert as an important part of the meal.
- Integrate meal planning into part of the child's learning.

Ordinarily, parents are very concerned with their child's eating habits. Communicating with parents about the food served and the child's eating habits is important. The eating environment and atmosphere are important. Classrooms used as dining rooms should be neat and attractive, furniture should be comfortable, children should participate in setting and serving, and teachers should eat with their charges.

Children should be exposed to cooking experiences that are appropriate to their developmental level.

The director should give significant thought and enterprise to the mechanics of food procurement and preparation. Purchasing must be done along thrifty lines. Food poorly prepared is often wasted. Food should be easily handled by and appealing to children.

Food must be prepared and served under strict sanitary conditions. All food handlers should be free of infectious disease. Care must be taken to prevent spoilage in handling and storage.

The development of good attitudes toward food is as worthy a goal as the acquisition of any other socially desirable trait. The preschool has an important role to play here.

STUDENT ACTIVITIES

1. Prepare a poster for school-age children that shows the Food Guide Pyramid. Include suggestions for snack foods from each of the groups.

2. Plan a series of three lessons designed to teach four-year-olds about nutrition. Present the lessons to a group, then evaluate their effectiveness. Did the children understand the concepts you presented? Were there any perceptible changes in their attitudes toward any of the foods you discussed?

3. Observe two meals in a child-care center. Evaluate them using the following ratings:

	Excellent	Good	Fair	Poor
Attractiveness of setting	_____	_____	_____	_____
Cleanliness of setting	_____	_____	_____	_____
Comfort of seating	_____	_____	_____	_____
Appearance of food	_____	_____	_____	_____
Child-size portions	_____	_____	_____	_____
Teacher participation	_____	_____	_____	_____
General atmosphere	_____	_____	_____	_____

4. List the foods you liked as a young child. Why do you think these particular foods were favorites? Was it the taste, color, or ease of eating? Or were they favorites because of some association with pleasant experiences? What does this tell you about serving food to children in a child-care setting?

REVIEW

1. Why is it important to see that young children receive adequate nutrition in child care?

2. If a center is open nine hours or more, what proportion of a child's daily minimum nutritional requirement should be provided?

3. Which foods make up the largest proportion of the Food Guide Pyramid?

4. Which foods make up the smallest proportion of the Food Guide Pyramid?

5. State five suggestions for encouraging children to eat nutritious foods.

6. In what ways can a school establish and maintain a partnership with parents regarding their child's nutritional needs?

7. How can a director encourage teachers to plan cooking experiences for children?

8. Suggest some ways to decrease the cost of purchasing foods.

9. List several snacks that can easily be prepared for a group of preschool children.

10. Food storage should preserve the nutritional content of food and ensure safety. At what temperature should the refrigerator be kept? What is the optimum temperature for long-term storage in a freezer?

REFERENCES

Gerber, M. (1991). *Manual for resources for infant educarers*. Los Angeles: Resources for Infant Educarers.

Marotz, L. (2009). *Health, safety, and nutrition for the young child* (7th ed.). Clifton Park, NY: Cengage Learning.

SELECTED FURTHER READING

Books to Help Teachers Plan Cooking Activities

Cook, D. (1995). *Kids' multicultural cookbook*. Charlotte, VT: Williamson Publishing.

Jenkins, K. (1982). *Kinder krunchies*. Pleasant Hill, CA: Discovery Toys.

McClenahan, P., & Jaqua, I. (1976). *Cool cooking for kids: Recipes and nutrition for kids*. Belmont, CA: Fearon Pitman.

Nissenberg, S. (2002). *Everything kid's cookbook*. Avon, MA: Adams Media Corporation.

Nissenberg, S. (Ed.). (1994). *The healthy start kid's cookbook: Fun and healthful recipes that make themselves*. Hoboken, NJ: John Wiley & Sons.

Stori, M. (1980). *I'll eat anything if I can make it myself*. Chicago: Chicago Review.

Wanamaker, N., Hearn, K., & Richarz, S. (1979). *More than graham crackers: Nutrition education and food preparation with young children*. Washington, DC: National Association for the Education of Young Children.

Wilkes, A. (2001). *The children's step-by-step cookbook*. New York: Darling Kindersley.

Wilms, B. (1984). *Crunchy bananas*. Salt Lake City, UT: Gibbs M. Smith.

Zeller, P. K., & Jacobson, M. F. (1987). *Eat, think, and be healthy!* Washington, DC: Center for Science in the Public Interest.

Books That Help children Understand the Various types of Food.

Ahlberg, J., & Ahlberg, A. (1978). *Each peach, pear, plum*. New York: Viking.

Babcock, C. (1995). *No moon, no milk*. New York: Scholastic.

Brown, M. (1947). *Stone soup*. New York: Scribner.

De Paola, T. (1992). *Jamie O'Rourke and the big potato*. New York: Scholastic.

Degen, B. (1986). *Jamberry*. New York: Scholastic.

Fowler, A. (1995). *Thanks to cows*. Danbury, CT: Children's Press.

Fowler, A. (1995). *We love fruit!* Danbury, CT: Children's Press.

Gibbons, G. (1993). *The milk makers*. New York: Scholastic.

Julious, J. (2001). *I like berries*. Danbury, CT: Children's Press.

Kottke, J. (2001). *From seed to pumpkin* (Welcome Books). Danbury, CT: Children's Press.

Krensky, S. (1993). *The pizza book*. New York: Scholastic.

Littledale, F. (1988). *Peter and the north wind*. New York: Scholastic.

McDonald, M. (1996). *The potato man.* Danbury, CT: Children's Press.

Minuchkin, F. (1994). *Latkes and applesauce: A Hanukkah story.* New York: Scholastic.

Nelson, J. (1990). *Neighborhood soup.* New York: Modern Curriculum.

Rose, A. (1979). *Akimba and the magic cow: A folktale from Africa.* New York: Four Winds.

Scheer, J. (1964). *Rain makes applesauce.* New York: Holiday.

Smith, N. (2002). *Allie and the allergic elephant: A children's story of peanut allergies.* San Francisco: Jungle Communications, Inc.

Willems, M. (2004). *The pigeon finds a hot dog!* New York: Hyperion.

GENERAL INFORMATION

Aronson, S. S., ed. with P. M. Spahr (2002). *Healthy young children: a manual for programs.* 4th ed. Washington, DC: NAEYC.

Bernath, P., & Masi, W. (2006). Smart school snacks: A comprehensive preschool nutrition program. *Young Children, 61*(3), 20–24.

Bomba, A. K., Oakley, C. B., & Knight, K. B. (1996). Planning the menu in the child care center. *Young Children, 51*(6), 62–67.

Fuhr, J. E., & Barclay, K. H. (1998). The importance of appropriate nutrition and nutrition education. *Young Children, 53*(1), 74–80.

Goodway, J. D., & Smith, D. W. (2005). Keeping all children healthy: Challenges to leading an active lifestyle for preschool children qualifying for at-risk programs. *Family & Community Health 28*(2):142–155.

Rarback, S. (2005). Climbing the new food pyramid. *South Florida Parenting* (July): 90.

Robertson, C. (2007). *Safety, nutrition, and health in early childhood education* (3rd ed.). Clifton Park, NY: Cengage Learning.

Rogers, C., & Morris, S. (1986). Reducing sugar in children's diets. *Young Children, 41*(5), 11–16.

Sanders, S. W. (2002). *Active for life: Developmentally appropriate movement programs for young children.* Washington, DC: NAEYC.

HELPFUL WEBSITES

Disclaimer: Links to Internet sites throughout this book are provided for your convenience and do not constitute an endorsement.

Child and Adult Care Food Program (CACFP):	**http://www.fns.usda.gov/cnd/care**
Food and Nutrition Information Center:	**http://www.healthykids.com**
National Center for Health Statistics:	**http://www.cdc.gov**

For additional resources related to administration including videos, links to related sites for each chapter of the text, tutorial quizzes, glossary flashcards, and more, visit the Education CourseMate website for this book at www.cengage.com/login.

Cengage Learning

CHAPTER

13

Beginnings: A New Program/A New Year

Objectives

After reading this chapter, you should be able to:

- Discuss factors affecting the location of a school.
- Discuss costs of starting a new school.
- Identify additional requirements a school should meet before beginning operation.
- Develop procedures to facilitate routine opening-of-school tasks.
- Identify tasks that are necessary to begin a school year.

KEY TERMS

business plan

expendable supplies

family group

nonexpendable items

ongoing costs

peer group

start-up costs

A day in the life of . . .

A Director of a Church-Affiliated School

It is always fun to come back to school in September after a long summer and see the smiling, tan faces of the returning students. Last September, on the first day of school, a little girl came running toward me with arms outstretched and fell into my waiting arms. "Oh, Mrs. Channels! You missed me so much." I started to say "I missed you, too" when what she actually had said registered. I simply answered "I sure did."

Plans for opening a school must be thought out and considered as carefully as for any business. Depending upon the size of the facility, the initial investment can be large, and no one wants to lose money because of poor planning. Researching the issues that will affect the operation may take a year. Putting together a realistic **business plan** for start-up and ongoing operation, including budgets for both phases, is important. Project KickStart, a computer software program listed in Appendix A, allows the planners to lay out the necessary beginning steps and helps them organize the process.

Whether done on a computer or without one, a business plan is essential. It is a written document that describes in detail a proposed venture. Its purpose is to reflect projected needs and expected results of a new business. It helps planners to determine the project's viability, assess resources, and borrow money.

The components of a business plan are the following:

- a short description of the project, including unique characteristics and the target population
- marketing methods: how information about the venture will reach the target population
- available resources such as expertise of participants, accessible cash for initial expenses, knowledge of reasonable costs of operation
- summary of research into the need for the proposed business
- assessment of realistic risks, including potential problems and plans to resolve them
- financial forecast of income and expenses
- timeline from planning stage to financial stability

Location

COMMUNITY SURVEY

Before making the investment of time and money, the needs of the community should be assessed. This involves collecting information on the number of families with children, income level of parents, number of working parents, transportation available to families, and number of child-care facilities already in the neighborhood. Some of this information can be obtained from U.S. Census data, labor and employment statistics, school district counts, and child-care organizations. Directors of existing schools may be willing to discuss whether their schools are full or if there seems to be a need for additional places for children. The local public library is a good source to check for census and employment data.

There are various ways to survey a community with a needs assessment questionnaire. On a college campus, an article can be placed in the campus newspaper, with a request for reply by telephone or in written form. Within a business, a questionnaire can be sent to all employees. In an apartment complex or densely populated residential area, door-to-door canvassing may be an effective way to determine the need for a school.

Generally, the questionnaire should be simple, yet it should ask all the necessary questions. The sample company assessment questionnaire below may provide a beginning.

This preliminary information should indicate whether there is a need for a new school. It will probably also help when considering the kind of school to plan. If there are more school-age children than younger ones, then an after-school program with provision for summer and holiday care for children may be needed. If there are more infants, toddlers, and preschoolers, a preschool with an infant room should be successful. A large number of working parents will probably rule out the possibility of a co-op and point to the necessity for an all-day center.

COMMUNITY HOSPITAL

5329 Center Way

Emerson, PA 16112

In response to a request by employees, we are assessing the need for a child-care center on the premises of Community Hospital. It may become part of your work/family benefit package. Please complete the questionnaire and return it to your supervisor before December 15.

Name _____ Employee Number _____

Department _____ Location _____ Shift _____

Number and ages of your children _____

Do you have a child who needs special care? _____

Describe his/her special needs _____

Where are your children cared for now?

    Preschool or child-care center: cost/hr _____   per week _____

    Caregiver in your home: cost/hr _____   per week _____

    Family child-care home: cost/hr _____   per week _____

    Relative's home _____   Home alone _____

What kind of child-care service do you need?

    Part-time _____ (hrs)   Full-time _____ (hrs)

    Evening _____ (hrs)   Weekend _____ (hrs) _____

Would you enroll your child in a quality child-care center on our premises?

Please rank (1-most, 2-somewhat, 3-next, 4-least) the following benefits in importance to you and your family.

    *Prepaid medical and dental _____   *Child care _____

    *Elder care _____   *Maternity/family leave _____

Comments:

_____

_____

*These items may need to be altered to fit specific benefit packages.

LICENSING

Licensing regulations will have an impact upon many aspects of an early childhood or child-care center. Regulations provide the baseline for acceptable care of children and are meant to be minimum standards below which no program should operate. All states within the United States have licensing requirements, but they vary widely in scope. Therefore, becoming familiar with the regulations in the area is essential before proceeding further with planning. State licensing offices are listed in Appendix D.

WHY REGULATION?

Licensing requirements should achieve their primary purpose of ensuring adequate, safe care of children. Each state, though, determines what the actual acceptable level should be.

Variation among states comes from differing community needs. Some differences, however, result from disparate perceptions of what children need or from lack of official recognition of the importance of quality care. Over the years, licensing agencies have worked with professionals in early childhood education to raise the standards of acceptable care.

A good regulatory system will benefit those who provide care as well as the children they serve. A license carries with it an official recognition of the importance of the job. It can also be an advantage when recruiting children. Families will feel more secure placing their child in a licensed facility. Parents may benefit in another way because of licensing. Licensing agencies can provide parents with helpful information about standards for quality care when they choose a place for their child. Conversely, facilities can more readily justify the high cost of quality care when parents understand the standards.

WHO IS COVERED?

Not all programs are covered by licensing. Generally, programs covered by other regulations do not have to be licensed. Exempted programs might include those covered by state education codes such as the children's centers within public school systems. Laboratory schools in public colleges or universities also fall into this category. Head Start and other federally funded programs have their own standards that are usually higher than the licensing requirements.

Licensing regulations also do not apply to those who care for children of family members in their home. Even family child-care homes that care for nonfamily members may not be regulated. Some states register family child-care homes rather than include them in licensing procedures. Where this is true, inspection is not required before registration, and the programs are not monitored. Parents are informed of standards and are encouraged to inspect or monitor for themselves.

All other programs must obtain a license before they can begin operation. When operating a private for-profit school, a church-related program, an employer-sponsored–child-care center, or a cooperative, a license is required. Each school within a corporate chain must have its own license. Licenses are awarded for a specified time period and must be renewed before their expiration date.

The first step in planning a new school is to contact the state's licensing agency. They will send an application packet and a copy of licensing guidelines. The guidelines include information necessary when designing a school or choosing an appropriate building. The application packet also includes all the paperwork that must be completed.

The application process entails obtaining clearances for the building, getting staff fingerprinted, and compiling records. Completing these tasks may take three to six months. Once the application is completed and returned to the licensing agency, an appointment can be scheduled. Inspectors will determine whether all specifications have been met. If not, a period of time will be allowed to do so.

Licenses are usually awarded for a year. Another on-site visit will be made before a new license can be given. In addition to renewal, most licensing regulations include methods of enforcement. If the licensing agency makes an unannounced visit to a school and finds infractions, a notice of noncompliance will be sent. The licensee will be given a period of time to rectify the problems. If they have not been rectified when another inspection is made, a fine can be levied. Schools that do not obtain a license or operate with an expired license may be closed by legal means.

WHAT IS COVERED BY LICENSING?

Generally, licensing regulations focus on conditions that affect the health and safety of children. Statements tend to be broad and general in content to fit various situations.

Schools and child-care centers can be found in converted warehouses, storefronts, churches, or residences. Specific requirements that can apply in all these settings are unrealistic. With general statements, program monitors can interpret the regulations to fit the needs of each school.

Licensing regulations may cover some or all of the following topics:

- admission: procedures and enrollment records

- administration: general administrative procedures

- space: amount, indoors and outdoors

- equipment: usually general requirements that it be appropriate for the age and number of children and that it provide for their developmental needs

- food services and nutrition: requirements that children be served nutritious meals prepared under safe conditions

- health procedures: requirements that preadmission health reports of children be on file, that health records be maintained, that sick children be isolated, that provisions exist for emergency medical care of children

- safety procedures: requirements regarding the safe storage of cleaning supplies or any other harmful materials, regarding safe maintenance of equipment and building, regarding fire and disaster procedures

- program: requirements that the daily schedule offer opportunities for children to engage in activities that promote their growth and development, that time exists for rest and taking care of their physical needs

- staff: specifications regarding the number of children per staff member, regarding the qualifications of all staff members, regarding personnel procedures and records

- discipline: prohibitions of certain kinds of punishment; encouragements for using positive means of disciplining children

- transportation: requirements regarding safe maintenance of vehicles used to transport children, regarding methods to ensure children's safety while in transit, regarding the qualifications of drivers

- parent involvement: requirements that parents be included in planning for their children, that they serve on advisory boards, that they be given materials and information about the program's goals and policies, that they have contact with staff through conferences

Some states have now included additional guidelines for those who care for infants or elementary school children. Many of the same topics as those already listed will be covered, with specifications suitable for these age levels.

For infants, the following areas may be added:

- specifications for sleeping equipment

- provisions regarding food storage, food preparation, feeding procedures

- provisions for diapering, including equipment needed and procedures to follow

- specifications for general sanitation procedures

- procedures for meeting children's developmental needs: toilet training, introduction of solid foods

- provisions for inclusion of parents in planning

For older children, the following areas may be added:

- specifications for a play area separate from the younger children in a school
- provisions regarding special equipment or furniture appropriate for older children
- safety procedures for swimming pool activities and field trips

Licensing requirements specify the number of square feet needed both indoors and outdoors. This will limit a school to certain communities where there is enough space to accommodate the required footage. In some states, 35 square feet per child is a minimum recommendation for indoor space. To provide for maximum play space and freedom of movement, 40 to 60 square feet per child is preferable. Space used by children usually constitutes 60 percent of a school's total area, with an additional 40 percent needed for storage, a kitchen, offices, bathrooms, and so on. A fenced-in yard containing 75 to 100 square feet per child is appropriate for outdoors.

In some states, preschools cannot operate on the second floor of a building, further limiting the search for space. A ground floor school is safer because young children have difficulty managing stairs. They should have easy access to outdoor play areas. Meeting requirements for bathroom facilities also can be a challenge when looking for space for a child-care center. The bathroom should be close to the classrooms, and there should be enough toilets and basins for the number of children anticipated. Specifications for the number of windows and the kind of heating, kitchen equipment, drinking fountains, and so on, may all affect decisions.

OTHER REGULATIONS

Early childhood facilities are subject to other regulations besides licensing. Zoning ordinances in many communities specify that for-profit child-care facilities can be located

Multi-use playground equipment.

Cengage Learning

only in a commercial or business zone. Sometimes a zoning variance that allows a center in a residential area may be granted if the operation will not create undue disturbances to the neighborhood. Nonprofit programs sometimes have greater latitude in choosing a location. Zoning regulations may also require provision of off-street parking for staff and visitors, further limiting locations.

Before choosing a location, driving through the neighborhood where the school would be located is important. Is it a place where parents would want to bring their children? Does it have the right kind of environment for a school? The site should be easily visible to street traffic as the sign and school building will be the best advertising. No barriers should exist that prevent easy access to the school entrance. The ultimate consideration is whether this is a safe place for children to spend their day.

A child-care building must also meet strict codes regarding the health and safety of occupants. Before a facility can be licensed, the city will send representatives from the building, fire, and sanitation departments. Familiarity with these regulations, including any special requirements for children with disabilities, is necessary.

BUY, BUILD, REMODEL, OR RENT

Building a school on a convenient lot is a dream of many potential owners. It is probably the only way to have most of the things they want in their school. However, as costs of both land and building have increased in the last few years, this option is less feasible. One way to estimate the cost is to find a school that has been built recently, and find out what it cost to build. If that is not possible, builders or architects in the area should be able to estimate the cost of building. Realtors can estimate the cost of purchasing land.

If building a school is a hopeless dream, other options exist. Many attractive schools for young children are in renovated residences. If it is possible to find a large, older house at a reasonable price, this may be a good choice. Unfortunately, some communities prohibit schools in residential areas. Additionally, the cost of renovation is often very high. Usually, there must be additional bathrooms and bathroom fixtures. Hallways, stairs, porches, heating equipment, outdoor fences, and gates that meet safety standards also add to the cost.

Renting unused classrooms in a public school is another possibility. Dwindling populations of families with young children have left some school districts with unused space. This can be a viable solution for a child-care center, but there will likely be several problems. Bathrooms may not be adjacent to classrooms, or playgrounds may not be easily accessible from the indoor space. There may be restrictions on changing walls or adding plumbing. Furthermore, there may be no extra space for offices or other supporting uses. With careful planning, however, the space often can be adapted.

Churches often provide space for preschool programs as part of their own educational program. Sometimes they will rent space to a separate organization. Laws do not allow renting for profit-making purposes, but they may allow rental to nonprofit organizations. The main disadvantage of this kind of arrangement is sharing space with church functions. Additionally, church space designed for religious classes may not have the kind of outdoor area needed by a preschool. Often, though, there is enough space on the church grounds to install a playground.

Storefronts are usable for early childhood programs. In the author's community there are currently three child-care centers in shopping centers. Each has a large playground enclosed by a six-foot wall behind the school. In areas that cannot accommodate an attached playground, storefront schools use nearby parks where the children go for outings. An advantage of this type of site is the high visibility of the center to shoppers. This visibility may provide sufficient publicity to attract initial enrollees and to maintain enrollment. A disadvantage may be the cost of installing bathrooms, dividing indoor space, and building a playground.

Industrial sites such as a factory or warehouse are also usable as a school when a little imagination is applied. These sites may be near where parents work, allowing them to visit during the day. The rent may also be low. A factory, with its high ceilings, might be converted with a two-level design, allowing for climbing, delineation of spaces, and nooks or corners in which children can be alone. However, industrial areas are sometimes noisy and may be subject to various kinds of pollutants.

The Great Pacific Iron Works Child Development Center in Ventura, California, had to spend thousands of dollars removing soil beneath a playground when the soil was thought to be polluted by toxic wastes from a previous industrial tenant. Ensuring that the surrounding environment is safe for children is important.

If the planners already own some land, putting prefab buildings on the site may be the best solution. One California school in Santa Monica used two "temporary" bungalows unused by a school district. The buildings were attached, then divided inside to make two classrooms, offices, bathrooms, and a conference room. This choice is somewhat limiting because of the adjoining walls and the structure of the buildings, but creative use of the space is possible.

A final possibility is to buy an existing school. Each year some schools change hands for various reasons. Watching real estate advertisements is a good idea, as is checking with directors in the area and talking to realtors. A school will probably be for sale. A potential buyer should check carefully, though, as to why the school is being sold. Is it because the area already has too many schools or just that the owners no longer want to run a school? As when buying a house, investigating the building and determining necessary repairs is important. Buying a school may be a smart decision, especially for a profit-making school, because it can be a real estate investment as well as a business investment.

Before making a decision about location, listing the advantages and disadvantages of each proposed site, remembering that few schools have ideal environments, is helpful. Most school personnel learn to make creative adaptations of the space they have. Start-up costs will certainly factor into the decision. However, the least expensive choice may not always be the best choice, because minimal facilities may make a poor and unsuccessful school.

When a site for a school has been tentatively chosen, it is time to contact all the regulatory agencies that control the operation of a child-care facility. The buyer should have an inspector tour the site. Building and safety regulations specify that buildings must be free of hazards such as asbestos or lead paint, and electrical wiring must meet current standards. Adequate air circulation must exist if windows do not open. Specifications regarding the kinds of carpeting used or the number and type of exits may also be present. Exits may be required to have lighted signs and locks that can be easily opened in case of an emergency. Fire codes include requirements for the number and location of fire extinguishers, smoke and/or fire alarm systems, and the location of furnaces and water heaters.

Federal regulations that directly affect child-care centers are the 1990 Americans with Disabilities Act (ADA) and The Occupational Safety and Health Act of 1970 (OSHA). ADA requires that equal access to all facilities and services be provided to individuals with disabilities. This means that ramps must be provided where there are stairs, that doorways must be large enough to accommodate a wheelchair, and that bathrooms must be accessible. OSHA specifies that an environment should be free of any hazards that could cause death or injury to any employees. Where both local and federal guidelines overlap, the facility must be in compliance with each.

FYI

The high cost of child care makes it difficult for many families to find quality care for their children. Tuition for a four-year-old ranges from $4,000 to $6,000 a year, reaching as much as $10,000 in some centers. Low-income families are especially impacted by these costs and have few choices. Consequently, they are often forced to place their children in lower quality care.

Source: Schulman, K., & Adams, G. (1998). Cost of child care. (ERIC Document Reproduction Service No. ED426785). Retrieved from http://www.eric.ed.gov 2006.

Finances

START-UP COSTS

Before making a final decision, the start-up costs of opening a school at the chosen site must be considered. **Start-up costs** are those expenditures that must be made during the initial stage of planning before opening and before any enrollment money comes in. Renovations may need to be made; equipment must be purchased; and staff must be hired to take care of licensing, ordering materials, and interviewing parents. These costs can be considerable for a large school because the cost per child can run as high as $5,000. Figure 13-1 shows a start-up budget for a school for 70 children to be housed in a renovated school building.

Capital costs include the purchase of land and an existing school or a building. When purchasing property, the down payment is a start-up cost. Repayment of the loan is then amortized over the ensuing years and included in each subsequent year's budget. Even when renting a building, an initial outlay will include the first and last month's rent and any security deposit required (see Figure 13-1).

Everything needed to begin operation of a school must be purchased before opening day. Equipment, furniture, and learning materials all entail a significant investment. Planners can use catalogs from the various companies to estimate the cost. (Information about equipment companies is in Appendix C.) Some companies will send a sales representative to the school to assist in the task. Lakeshore Learning Materials in California offers further help by publishing a list of suggested learning materials and furniture for age levels from infants to school-age children, plus classroom layout planning grids. This information is available on the Internet at http://lakeshorelearning.com. Click on Lakeshore classroom designer. Not all schools can start out with ideal environments, but they often add to the equipment once the school gets started. Making many objects and purchasing used furniture are also options.

The director should allocate money to cover the probability that enrollment will not be filled immediately after opening the school. Full enrollment may not occur for several months or even a year. During that time, expenses will not be decreased proportionately. California licensing laws require three month's operating expenses to be set aside before a license is issued. Even if a state does not have that requirement, providing a "cushion" to fall back on during the early stages of getting a school started is a good idea.

SAMPLE START-UP COSTS

Capacity: 70 children
             Purchased school building

Start-up personnel costs	
Director—$35,000/yr. (3 months)	$ 8,750
3 Teachers—$22,000/yr. each (2 weeks)	$ 2,538
2 Asst. teachers—$19,000/yr. each (2 weeks)	$ 1,462
Secretary—$16,000/yr. (1 month)	$ 1,333
Subtotal personnel cost	$ 14,083
Employee benefits (estimated 15 percent)	$ 2,112
Total personnel cost	$ 16,195
Renovation	$ 50,000
Contract services and consultants	
Architect	$ 3,000
Lawyer (3 hours @ $250/hr.)	$ 750
Contractor (10 hours @ $35/hr.)	$ 350
Total contract/consultant cost	$ 4,100
Supplies	
Office (computer, paper, and so on)	$ 2,500
Cleaning and paper goods	$ 500
Food (breakfast, 2 snacks)	$ 900
Classroom materials and supplies	$ 2,000
Total supply cost	$ 5,900
Advertising (phone book, flyers, newspaper)	$ 1,000
Occupancy	
Down payment on building	$ 75,000
Utilities	$ 1,000
Furniture, equipment, vehicles	$ 45,000
Other	
Business license	$ 500
Insurance (quarterly payment)	$ 1,500
Miscellaneous expenses	$ 1,000
Payment into cash reserve	$ 35,000
TOTAL START-UP COSTS	$ 236,195
START-UP COST PER CHILD	$ 3,374

FIGURE 13-1   Sample start-up costs.

Personnel costs must also be factored into start-up costs. Someone must go through the lengthy process of obtaining a license; in urban areas, this can take six months. Someone must order materials and equipment and then unpack them after delivery. The building has to be readied, and any renovations must be made. Anyone who has done house remodeling knows that it can take a long time. The director should be working full-time at least two months before opening. A part-time secretary during this time can help with paperwork.

A core staff should be hired before the opening of a school and the remainder of the staff as enrollment requires it. The core staff members should start working at least two weeks before the opening day. During that time the director can have an orientation/training session. This time together helps staff to develop a good working relationship. Teachers can also set up their rooms and plan their curriculum for the initial weeks. The salaries during this time should be included in the start-up budget.

Some of these personnel expenses can be met through in-kind contributions. When directors are also owners of schools, they sometimes forgo salaries during the start-up period. In other situations, a parent who has time and energy may take on some of the start-up tasks. Teachers may also be willing to volunteer a day or so getting their rooms set up. Some equipment cost can be decreased through renovations done by a skilled volunteer or donations. However, the director should proceed with caution when expecting people to work without pay, taking care not to exploit those who are willing or who need to have a job.

Some expenses can be amortized over the first year of operation. It may be possible to delay paying some bills until tuition fees begin to arrive. Renovation costs can sometimes be handled in the same way. If the landlord in a rental property makes improvements, the director may be able to pay off the cost over the first year. Adding these costs into the operating budget is important, as is ensuring that income will be able to sustain them.

Contract services and consultants may be necessary in some settings. Legal advice is especially important when two or more people own a school. In a simple partnership either partner is liable for all partnership debts. The private assets of either one may be charged for payment of indebtedness. When the school is set up as a corporation, the corporation assumes responsibility for any debts. The individual is protected from personal liability.

Although attorneys are expensive, they are indispensable in drawing up incorporation papers or assisting in the establishment of partnerships. Having sound legal advice early is better than floundering in indecision later. Legal requirements vary between states. The owners of the school should consider the advantages of incorporation over a partnership at tax time and in relation to liability for debts.

Having an architect draw up renovation plans needed for building-safety approval or for zoning may be wise. An accountant can help to set up a bookkeeping system. A pediatrician or child development specialist can offer advice when setting up an infant room. These services are expensive, some costing hundreds of dollars per hour. Some of these services might be provided free of charge by a parent or a friend. A legal service agency can sometimes provide low-cost legal services.

Advertising and publicity are essential to a new school. Parents must know about the school in order for the school to fill enrollment as soon as possible. Some methods are relatively expensive for the start-up period, but others cost little. One form, without cost, is an article in the local newspaper. The director can contact a reporter and describe some unique feature of the program. The reporter may have enough interest to write an article, which provides free publicity.

Telephone-book advertising is excellent because parents often look there first when searching for child care. The timing may not always fit the school's need during start-up; however, because telephone books are printed only once a year. Listing is included in the cost of service installation, but a display advertisement can cost one hundred dollars per month. Next to advertising in the phone book, the radio seems to be the most effective way to publicize child care. The local radio station can run advertisements during morning commutes when parents might be listening. Cost of an advertisement will vary depending on the time when the promotion is aired.

The director may wish to purchase a mailing list of prospects for the center. Companies that supply lists can be found in the Yellow Pages under "Mailing Lists." Lists can target a geographic area, residences with children, and those in which the parents earn a certain income. For a fee of about $50, the company will provide a list that can be used on a one-time basis, and may even send the address labels. They will also rent the list for a one-year period. Comparing prices from various companies to get the best service for the least cost is a good idea. The list should be used to send an eye-catching flyer to announce the opening of the school and invite recipients to visit.

Direct mail marketing is costly and the success of the mailing depends on whether the target market has been reached. The average response from this form of advertising is one to five percent. More people will open and read the mailings if they

- are sent by first-class mail.
- are hand addressed.
- have been creatively designed.
- begin with a teaser to urge the recipient to respond.
- are consistent with recognizable color schemes and a logo.
- are sent more than once, especially at peak enrollment times of the year.

A director may include a discount offer on registration or tuition as part of the mass mailer. This may motivate prospective families to call for an appointment to tour the facility and provides an opportunity to sell the program. The director should greet parents and children warmly, explain the program, answer all questions, and offer a business card upon the close of the tour for any further questions that may arise.

An attractive brochure is an effective tool for selling a school. However, it can be expensive if the layout includes photographs or it is printed on heavy paper. It might be prudent to employ some of the less-costly methods of advertising during the start-up period but to develop a brochure that can be used for continuing recruitment once the center has opened. The contents and format of a brochure are discussed in Chapter 14.

There are several ways to publicize a new school. An open house can be held just prior to the opening. The classrooms should be attractive, with materials set out as though waiting for children to arrive. The director can conduct tours of the school, telling visitors about the program, the teachers, and the philosophy. Community groups might welcome a presentation about the school. If brochures are available, this is a good time to distribute them. Pictures, slides, or a video would be an effective addition to a talk. The director should meet with the personnel directors of large businesses in the vicinity. They may be looking for places to refer employees for child care. Local professional organizations may have newsletters to which the director can submit an article. Attending professional meetings is wise, as is talking to other directors about what has worked for them. Lastly, the director should notify a local resource and referral agency if one exists in the community. All of these can be effective ways to let a community know of the service being offered.

Another form of advertising that will help to recruit students is an attractive sign outside the school. It should be consistent with the neighborhood's style but clearly visible from the street. Once a school is in operation, the outside of the school and the playground will help sell it to prospective families. The appearance of a school is an ever-visible advertisement to any parent driving past.

Insurance costs are typically divided between start-up costs and the first-year budget. Usually, a portion of the insurance must be paid even before the school opens, and the balance is paid during the year. Insurance for schools has become problematic in recent years because the cost has increased significantly. Comparing insurers is the best way to find adequate coverage at a reasonable price. The National Association for the Education of Young Children (NAEYC) offers a good insurance package. Write to them for information. Most schools have the following kinds of insurance:

- liability and property damage: for legal protection for the owner/operator of the school
- fire damage: for buildings and contents
- fire, extended coverage: for vandalism and malicious mischief
- automobile: for any vehicles used in transporting children
- accident: for children and staff
- workers' compensation: for on-the-job injuries (required by law if 10 or more people are employed)

The following kinds of insurance should also be considered:

- burglary and robbery: for the contents of the building
- business interruption: for lost income while damaged property is being repaired
- fidelity bond: for theft by employees

ONGOING COSTS

Before going further in the decision-making process, the director should make a tentative estimate of **ongoing costs**. Chapter 10 discusses budgets in detail, but initially comparing potential income with expected costs of operating the school is most important.

Potential income is determined by the number of children enrolled in the school. That figure is found by dividing the total amount of indoor space in a building by the requirements set by the state's licensing agency. The next consideration is the amount of tuition being charged by other schools in the area. Tuition should be set near that amount. It would seem logical, then, to multiply the number of children by the amount of tuition. However, schools seldom will have 100 percent enrollment, even after the school has been established for a period of time. Most successful, established schools average 95 percent capacity. During the first year, allowing for a slow first few months, capacity may not reach more than 60 to 75 percent capacity. Estimating low income is better than having a shortfall at the end of the year. After the first year, there will be a better baseline of information with which to make the second-year budget.

Tuition income may be less than expected for another reason. During some months, children tend to become ill more frequently than others. Parents see no reason to pay for school when the child is not attending. The expenses go on, though, despite decreased attendance. A policy requiring tuitions be paid even when children are ill for short periods of time will decrease low cash flow times. Most schools excuse tuition only when a child is ill for several weeks or more.

Another factor that affects the ability to project income is that the school will always have uncollectable tuitions. For one reason or another, families fall behind in payment of fees; some even leave the school without paying. The budget should allow 10 to 15 percent of the expected income as uncollectable. Procedures for following up on late fee payments will eventually decrease that amount.

Costs should be estimated by starting with salaries, because they will take the largest proportion of total revenue. Salaries may take 50 to 75 percent of total income. The director should figure the number of staff members needed during the times when the school has the most children. In an all-day school, peak hours of enrollment may be from 8:00 in the morning until 4:00 in the afternoon. There must be enough teachers to maintain the ratio of adults to children required by licensing. The director should also estimate the number of children and teachers needed to cover the times before and after the peak times. Before

Hours		Morning						Afternoon					
	7	8	9	10	11	12	1	2	3	4	5	6
Number of Children	15	45	60								30	20
Teachers												
#1												
#2												
#3												
#4												
#5												
#6												
#7												
#8												
#9												

FIGURE 13-2 Sample teacher assignment chart.

actual enrollment of children begins, knowing how many children will be present before 8:00 A.M. and after 4:00 P.M. is impossible. After estimating the number, the director can make a chart of children and staff as shown in Figure 13-2.

The cost of the building will probably be the next largest budget expenditure. This usually takes about 15 percent of total income, but it should not exceed 25 percent. This expenditure includes the cost of repaying a loan to purchase property and renovate or of making the ongoing rental payments on the property. In 1996, a technical report, "Cost, quality, and child outcomes in child care centers " was issued by the Department of Economics, Center for Research on Economics and Social Policy, University of Colorado, which offered guidelines for determining the real costs of providing quality early childhood programs. The estimates of costs show that personnel costs are the largest portion of a budget.

All personnel	70.3 percent

The breakdown of nonpersonnel budget items in the report are as follows:

Occupancy(Rent or mortgage)	13.8 percent
Food	4.6 percent
*Educational materials/equipment and other operating costs	8.6 percent
Overhead	2.7 percent

*Other includes telephone and utilities, repair, maintenance, office supplies and equipment, insurance, health and social services, and other miscellaneous costs.

SOURCE: Helburn, S. (Ed.). Cost, quality, and child outcomes in child care centers: Technical report. Denver, CO: Department of Economics, Center for Research on Economics and Social Policy, University of Colorado, 1995

Staff Selection

Chapter 8 more fully discusses the entire process of staff selection. However, some guidelines for staffing the new school are helpful here.

Staff can be recruited through advertisements in the local newspapers or flyers sent to teacher organizations and local colleges and universities. In many programs, following affirmative action guidelines is necessary. The advertisement or flyer should state the education and experience required for the position and the method of application. If time is short, the director may request that replies be made by telephone. However, if there is time, written applications should be returned by mail or fax.

The first teachers should be chosen carefully because during the first year the reputation of a school is formed. Teachers are an important part of that process. The director should be sure that teachers know the goals of the school and that there is time to help them implement the goals.

Working Checklist

Each of the tasks necessary for opening a new school may entail many weeks of work. There may be delays when trying to meet licensing requirements. Bad weather may delay building or renovation plans. Allowing a realistic amount of time is essential, as is adding extra time for unforeseen events. A checklist of tasks with a time line will help to ensure that everything is getting done. Figure 13-3 provides an example.

Planning for Opening Day

The opening of the school should be planned for a time that will fit the needs of the community or a particular situation. In an employer-sponsored program, for instance, the time will probably not be important. When opening a private school in a community, the director needs to think about the optimum time to open the doors. Traditionally, families make plans for their children's education during the summer. Changes in child-care arrangements are often made at this time. A September opening that coincides with the school calendar often works best. Allowing at least two months before the opening date to complete all the preparations is necessary.

Existing programs, too, find that changes often take place during the summer. Families move or children graduate to elementary school. After summer vacation is the time many families decide to make a change in child-care arrangements. Thus, even in managing an existing year-round school, there will be some of the same tasks as in opening a new school.

At the beginning of a new academic year, schools receive a flurry of telephone calls from parents frantically looking for places for their children. During this time, ordering materials and preparing the classrooms are also necessary. The playground may need new sand, and equipment must be inspected for safety. If the director develops organized procedures for managing all these tasks, life will certainly be easier.

Task	Expected Completion Date	Date Completed
1. Prepare needs assessment		
2. Contact licensing and zoning agencies		
3. Seek legal advice if needed		
4. Survey available sites		
5. Figure start-up costs		
6. Choose building or decide to build		
7. Supervise building or renovations		
8. Meet with representatives from all licensing agencies		
9. Obtain building permits and clearances		
10. Start licensing process		
11. Establish a bank account		
12. Obtain insurance		
13. Prepare first-year budget		
14. Order supplies and equipment		
15. Prepare a brochure		
16. Advertise for students		
17. Write job descriptions		
18. Advertise for staff		
19. Interview and select staff		
20. Set personnel policies		
21. Prepare forms for children's files		
22. Meet with children and parents		
23. Conduct orientation for staff		
24. Conduct orientation for parents		
25. Prepare for opening day		

FIGURE 13-3   Checklist of tasks needed to open a new school.

INQUIRY REPORT

NAME _____   DATE _____

ADDRESS _____   PHONE _____

_____

Child's date of birth _____

Month–Day–Year

How did you hear about our school? _____

Brochure sent _____

Date

Application packet sent _____

Date

Additional comments: _____

_____

_____

_____

FIGURE 13-4   Sample inquiry report form.

Enrollment

During the several weeks before opening day, the most important task is to enroll children. Parents usually make their first contact by telephone. Keeping a record of each call is important, as is having a follow-up procedure. Printed cards or a report form will provide an organized method of gathering information. Figure 13-4 shows a form that can be used to record inquiries about the school. Each call should be followed with a mailed brochure or information sheet about the school. Even if the parents do not enroll their child, they may pass the information to other families. An application packet containing the application form, brochure, fee schedule, and medical forms should be sent to those parents who seem ready to enroll.

A computer will make the task considerably easier. The names and addresses of anyone inquiring about the school are entered in a database. When new programs are added or changes that would affect these inquiries are made, notifying these people is simple. A form letter can be personalized with the name of each person on the list. This list should be updated periodically.

Before finalizing any application, the director should meet with the parent and child. Some parents want to visit the school even before sending in an application. Others already know about the school and schedule a visit after they send in their application. Figure 13-5 shows a sample registration form. Whichever order is chosen for the visit, it is important that the director and the family have a chance for a leisurely visit. No child should be enrolled without it. In fact, some states require visits as a part of licensing. These visits usually take half an hour or longer; thus, they should not be scheduled too close together.

CHILDREN'S REGISTRATION FORM

General Information

Child's Name _____   Date of birth _____

Social Security # _____

Parent/guardian(1) _____   Social Security # _____

Home address _____   Home phone _____

Cell phone _____

_____

Employer _____   Work phone _____

Work address _____   Hours of employment _____

Parent/guardian(2) _____   Social Security # _____

Home address _____   Home phone _____

Cell phone _____

_____

Employer _____   Work phone _____

Work address _____   Hours of employment _____

Other people authorized to pick up child

Name _____   Phone _____

Name _____   Phone _____

Medical Information

Pediatrician's name _____   Phone _____

Address _____

Dentist's name _____   Phone _____

Address _____

My child has the following allergies and/or special needs: _____

_____

Enrollment Information

First day of enrollment _____

Arrival time _____   Departure time _____

Registration fee paid _____   Deposit paid _____

Materials fee paid _____

_____   _____
Parent/guardian(1)   Parent/guardian(2)

_____   _____
Date   Date

FIGURE 13–5   Sample application form.

The purpose of these visits is to provide information to the director and the parent. If possible, the visit should take place in the classroom where the child will be placed after enrolling, with the teacher present. The child should have some toys to play with during the visit. This is an opportunity to observe the child informally and to get an impression of the parent–child relationship. The parents will be able to ask questions about the school and express any concerns about the child's adjustment. If the parents decide to enroll the child, this is a good time to get some of the forms filled out for the child's file.

· · · · · · ENROLLMENT DECISIONS

The maximum number of children the center can accommodate will be determined by the size of the physical space and will be specified on a license. Enrolling up to the maximum allowed is possible, as is limiting the number of children accepted. The total number of children must then be divided into manageable groups. Group size will vary depending on the skill of the teacher, the age of the children, and the licensing specifications in the state.

As children are placed in groups, there is another decision to make: Should the children in each group be approximately the same age, or should the groups have a range of age levels? The first method is called a **peer group** and includes children who are near the same age, usually with about a six-month to one-year difference. The second method is called a **family group** and includes children with a wide age span. Children in this group may differ in age as much as several years. Teachers and administrators who prefer peer grouping point to the advantage when planning curriculum activities. Including materials that most of the children will be able to use successfully is easier. Those who like the family group will extol the advantage of children learning from others who are older or younger than themselves. They also feel that, especially in child-care settings, this kind of group more closely resembles the home and, therefore, is more familiar to the children. The director has to decide what suits the school, goals, and teachers.

Another important consideration is the inclusion of children with special needs. Under the ADA enacted in 1990, discrimination against people with disabilities is prohibited. This measure has an impact on early childhood education programs because it requires all public and private schools, child-care centers, and family child-care providers to make reasonable accommodations to include children with special needs. Each child's needs must be evaluated on an individual basis and then an equal, nonsegregated educational program provided. A primary legal reason for refusing admission to a child with special needs is that doing so would place an undue burden on the provider and that there is no reasonable alternative. An additional reason for denial of admission is that the child's condition would pose a direct threat to the health or safety of that child, other children, or staff members.

There are many other questions to be answered in relation to accepting children with special needs into a school. Some communities have resources such as a "Health Hotline." California has one with a toll-free number: 800-333-3212. The local resource and referral agency may provide information and materials. Every director should have a copy of Caring for Our Children, National Health and Safety Standards: Guidelines for Out-of-Home Child Care Programs, a joint project of the American Public Health Association and the American Academy of Pediatrics. The California Child Care Law Center publishes Caring for Children with Special Needs: The Americans with Disabilities Act and Child Care. The booklet covers legal concerns, insurance, and taxes. The Law Center's address is 22 Second Street, San Francisco, CA 94105.

The director should make an attendance chart showing the days and hours each child will be attending school. Most children will attend on the same days and at the same hours consistently. Some schools give parents the option of choosing to send a child two or three days a week instead of five. Attendance may vary more radically, for instance, in the case of the parent who works changing shifts. Recording this information is important so that teachers will know which children to include in their plan.

An overall schedule for the school is used to plan where each group will be during specified periods during the day. This prevents all the children from being on the playground at once and allows teachers periodic use of additional spaces in the school building. A daily schedule should allow for snack and meal times, toileting and hand washing, naps, and large blocks of time both indoors and outdoors. The day should have a leisurely pace so that children do not feel they are constantly being rushed from one activity to another. This is especially important in an all-day school because children are there for many hours.

The school should establish a file for each child enrolled. Each file should contain the following:

- registration form (see Figure 13-5)
- medical evaluation
- dietary restrictions, if any
- emergency information (see Figure 13-6)
- permission form for medical treatment (see Figure 13-6)
- permission form for field trips (see Figure 13-7)
- financial agreements (see Figure 13-8)

In addition to the foregoing information, some states currently require a form signed and dated by the parents acknowledging receipt of a child abuse prevention pamphlet. If the parents refuse to sign the form, the director must note their refusal in the child's record file.

Some directors use a running checklist that shows at a glance items what a file still needs. Another system is to put the completed files in one place, leaving the incomplete ones in another place until finished. Whatever the system, ensuring that all needed forms are in the file as soon as possible at the beginning of the school year is important.

The school must have a procedure for checking children in and out so that there is a written record of attendance plus arrival and departure times. A few teachers have had panic-stricken moments when they find a child missing and do not know if the parent has picked up the child. One school has a sign at the checkout: "Make certain you only have your own child." They had experienced children slipping out with other parents before anyone realized they were gone. A sign-in and sign-out sheet or book posted at the entrance of the school or at each classroom will serve this purpose. Computer programs can simplify this task. See Appendix A for such programs.

There should be a place for parent messages. A bulletin board in the reception area will serve for general notices. Some other method should be used to send notes to individual parents. Some schools use something like a shoe bag that hangs on the wall outside each classroom. There are pockets for each family. Others have pigeonhole slots in a cabinet at the entrance to the school. Teachers can use these to send messages to parents about the child's day or some special occurrence that might be important for the parent to know. Some schools use a form; others just use an informal note. Communicating with parents by e-mail is another possibility.

If the school has a before- and after-school program for older children, arranging for bus service may be necessary. The school can rent the buses from school bus companies or buy vehicles and employ a driver. The director should list the children who will be using the service to pick them up from home and take them to school or pick them up

IDENTIFICATION AND EMERGENCY INFORMATION

To Be Completed by Parent or Guardian

Child's Name _____ Date of Birth _____

Address _____
Street Address

Address _____
City   Zip   Home Phone/Cell Phone

Parent 1 or guardian _____

Business Telephone _____ Hours _____

Parent 2 or guardian _____

Business Telephone _____ Hours _____

Additional people who may be called in an emergency:

Name   Address   Home Phone/Cell Phone   Relationship
_____
_____
_____

Physician to be called in an emergency:

Name _____ Phone _____

Address _____

If physician cannot be reached, what action should be taken?

Call emergency hospital _____

Other _____

Names of people authorized to take child from the facility:

Name   Relationship
_____
_____

Time child will be called for _____

Signature of parent or guardian   Date
_____   _____

FIGURE 13-6 Sample identification and emergency information form.

PERMISSION

I hereby give permission for _____
                                              child's name

to participate in the following activities at _____ School.

_____   Field trip with the class. I understand that I will be notified prior to a scheduled
              trip and will be given information regarding transportation, destination, lunch
              or other food, and arrival and departure time.

_____   Pictures taken of my child to be used for educational purposes, teacher training,
              or school use. I understand my child's name will not be used at any time.

_____   Distribution of my address and/or telephone number to other parents of a
              child enrolled in this school. (Addresses will not be given out for any com-
              mercial purposes.)

                              Signature of parent _____

                                          Date _____

F I G U R E   1 3 – 7   Sample permission form.

after school; list their addresses and approximate times that fit in with parents' and the
school schedules; and use a map to chart a route for the bus driver.

    Once a route and schedule have been set, the driver should do a trial run during the
hours that would ordinarily be used. That is the only way to see whether the schedule is realistic in terms of the traffic and the distances traveled. Some adjustments may be needed.

FINANCIAL AGREEMENT

I agree to pay $ _____ per month, payable in advance for tuition for my child. I under-
stand there is no tuition allowance for absences unless my child is ill for more than two weeks.

I also agree to notify the school two weeks in advance of withdrawal, should that be necessary. I understand that without notification, I am obligated for two weeks' tuition or until the
place is filled.

I have read the Parents' Handbook and understand the school's policies regarding tuition
payment.

                          Signed _____
                                      Parent 1 or guardian

                          Signed _____
                                      Parent 2 or guardian

                          Date _____

F I G U R E   1 3 – 8   Financial agreement.

Parents

A handbook provides parents with information that will help them become oriented as quickly as possible to their new experiences in the school. It can also serve as a reference during the school year. The handbook should contain the following information:

- Philosophy: a statement of the program's ideas, beliefs, and values relating to how children can learn. "The staff members of the Child Learning Center share a common philosophy that children learn best when they can actively interact with their environment. We also share a common commitment to helping each child develop fully: physically, socially, emotionally, and cognitively. Each child is valued as a unique individual with a particular pattern of growth and manner of acquiring knowledge and skills. In your child's classroom, you will observe learning centers that contain various materials that are usable in many different ways. Children can explore the materials, solve problems, develop skills, increase knowledge, or be creative in ways that help them to solidify their abilities at one level and become ready to move on to the next level. All activities are developmentally appropriate for the age level of the children and take into account the different rates at which children mature. Staff members will allow children to engage in activities at their own level of development at a particular time. When children demonstrate readiness, teachers will encourage them to move to a higher level of functioning by gently questioning, suggesting, or providing additional materials. Staff members will also foster children's own interests by providing the kinds of materials or experiences that will increase knowledge or feelings of competence and self-esteem. In this way, every child is able to develop fully according to their own interests and capabilities."

- Arrival and departure times and procedures for signing in and out: "The Center is open from 6:30 A.M. to 5:00 P.M. Please notify staff members of the time that you will deliver and pick up your child. If you will be late for pickup, notify the school. There will be an additional charge of $3.00 for every 15 minutes past 5:00. A sign-up sheet will be posted outside each classroom. Please sign in at the time you bring your child and do not forget to sign out at pickup time."

- Health policies: guidelines for inclusion or exclusion of children who are ill. "It is our policy to maintain the health of all children and staff members by excluding anyone with a communicable illness. If your child exhibits any of the following signs, please do not bring them to the Learning Center. The signs or symptoms as well as the conditions for a return to school are described in the following table." (See Table 13-1.)

  "If children become ill while at school, you will be notified and the child will be isolated until someone is able to take them home. During the time your child is isolated, a staff member will make your child as comfortable as possible and provide whatever care is necessary.

  Some childhood diseases are undetectable during an early stage when they are highly infectious and able to expose others to the illness. If this should happen to a child at the Learning Center, you will be notified and told of the kinds of symptoms to watch for should your child become ill."

- Safety: what the school will do when a child is injured or needs medical help. "The safety of all children at our center is our primary focus and we do everything in our power to ensure that we provide a hazard-free environment. In order to do this we have established the following policies.

TABLE 13-1   ## Guidelines for Exclusion of Ill or Infected Children

ILLNESS OR INFECTION	SIGN OR SYMPTOM	DO NOT RETURN...
Temperature	Oral temperature of 101°F or more; Rectal temperature of 102°F; accompanied by behavior changes or other symptoms	Until doctor releases child to return to care
Symptoms of severe illness	Unusual lethargy; irritability; uncontrolled coughing; wheezing	Until doctor releases child to return to care
Uncontrolled diarrhea	Increase in number of stools, water, and/or decreased form that cannot be contained in a diaper or underwear	Until diarrhea stops
Vomiting illness	Two or more episodes in 24 hours	Until vomiting stops and child is not dehydrated or doctor determines illness not infectious
Mouth sores with drooling		Until condition is determined to be noninfectious
Rash	Rash accompanied by fever or behavior change	Until doctor determines it is noninfectious
Conjunctivitis	White or yellow discharge in eye(s) accompanied by eye pain and/or redness around eyes	Until 24 hours after treatment has begun
Head lice, scabies, or other infestations	Infestation present	Until 24 hours after treatment has begun; no remaining lice on hair or scalp
Tuberculosis	Cough; fever; chest pain; coughing up blood	Until doctor or health official allows child to return to care
Impetigo	Rash-blister to honey-colored crusts; lesions occur around mouth, nose, and on chin	Until 24 hours after treatment has begun
Strep throat	Fever; sore throat; throat drainage; and tender nodes in lymph	After cessation of fever or 24 hours after antibiotic treatment
Chicken pox	Sudden onset of slight fever, fatigue, and loss of appetite followed by skin eruption	Until 6 days after eruption of rash or until blister eruption has dried and crusted over
Whooping cough	Severe, persistent cough	Until 5 days after antibiotic treatment to prevent infection
Mumps	Tender/swollen glands and/or fever	Until 9 days after onset of gland swelling

(Continued)

TABLE 13-1 **Guidelines for Exclusion of Ill or Infected Children (continued)**

Illness or Infection	Sign or Symptom	Do not return...
Hepatitis A virus	Fever; fatigue; loss of appetite; abdominal pain; nausea; vomiting; and/or jaundice	Until 1 week after onset of illness or as directed by local health department; immune serum globulin should be administered to staff and children who have been exposed
Measles	Rash; high fever; runny nose; and red/watery eyes	Until 6 days from onset of rash
Rubella	Mild fever; rash; swollen lymph nodes	Until 6 days after onset of rash
Unspecified respiratory illness	Severe illness with cold, croup, bronchitis, otitis media, pneumonia	Until child feels well enough to participate
Shingles	Lesions	Until doctor allows child to return to care or if child can wear clothing that covers lesions
Herpes simplex (1)	Clear, painful blisters	Until lesions that ooze, involving face and lips, have no secretions

1. We always maintain an adequate number of adults to supervise every group of children whether in the classroom or on the playground. No child is ever left in a situation without supervision.

2. Every classroom and playground area is inspected regularly to eliminate or correct any equipment or situations that may cause injury to the children.

3. In the case of an emergency, every classroom has an intercom connection so that help can be summoned. Emergency telephone numbers are posted by every telephone in the center.

4. There is an emergency evacuation plan posted in each classroom showing the fastest route to safety.

5. When a child is involved in an accident requiring medical intervention, the parent or guardian will be notified promptly. If the parent is unable to come to the center to transport the child, a staff member will accompany them to the medical facility indicated on the child's information form. If help is needed immediately, the nearest response team will be called.

6. An incident report form will be filled out by the attending teacher and the director. One copy will be placed in the child's file and the other given to the parent. The director and staff will review the incident and determine whether some preventive measures need to be taken."

- Food: what kind of food can be brought from home; foods that will be served at school. "Your child will receive two snacks and lunch at school if they are enrolled for a full day. Our dietitian follows the Food Pyramid guidelines set by the U.S. Department of Agriculture's Human Nutrition Information Service."

  "We also make every effort to select and prepare foods that appeal to children. We often include the kinds of foods that children may be familiar with at home or are part of the family cultural traditions. Mealtimes are planned as carefully as all other experiences because they are considered part of the overall learning environment of the children. Weekly menus are posted outside the office door.

- Frequently, children are given the opportunity to prepare their own snacks. The dietitian and the teacher plan an appropriate snack, and the materials are set up as a learning center. With supervision, children can learn to cut fruit, prepare pancakes, make pizzas, and produce many other delicious edibles."

- Special occasions: how the parent can make a birthday a special occasion for the child and their class. "Children enjoy celebrating their birthdays with their class-mates, and we encourage you to bring a treat either for snack time or for lunch. Some suggestions for special desserts that are nutritious are cupcakes made with whole-wheat flour and applesauce instead of sugar and fat, frozen yogurt or low-fat ice cream, special fruits or fruit gelatin, and oatmeal cookies. Please check with your child's teacher before bringing food that contains potential allergy-causing ingredients. There may be a child in the class who will have a reaction."

- Home toys: what the child can bring to school. "We discourage children from bringing toys from home and forbid any type of weapon. It is our belief that part of the developmental process involves learning to share, and to this end we provide toys and equipment that children can share and use together. When children bring toys from home, they rightfully feel that they own the toy and should not have to share. This creates problems not only for the child, but for others in the classroom. Therefore, if your child wants to show a new toy to the class, there will be time during the first group time for them to share. The toy then must be put into the child's cubby until they go home."

- Clothing: a variety of weather-appropriate clothing for school activities. "Children at the Learning Center will be actively playing during the time that they are in school and need to have clothing that can allow them freedom to do so. They also are developing independence in caring for their own needs. Dress your child in comfortable clothing that can withstand the wear and tear of playing in the sand, climbing, digging in the garden, sliding down the slide, and all the other activities at school. Moreover, try to choose clothing that allows your child to manage his or her own toileting or putting on a jacket. Put a label in jackets or sweaters so that they are easily identifiable. Please bring an extra set of clothes to be kept in your child's cubby in case there is a need to change."

- Parent visits: how to be a good visitor. "You are welcome to visit our center at any time. In order to make your visit meaningful to you, we ask that you follow these guidelines.

  1. Stop at the office to let us know that you are visiting.

  2. After greeting your child, find a place to sit, close to your child if that is what they request.

  3. Remember that the teacher needs to focus attention on the children and cannot be available for conversations. If you have questions or comments, there is usually time at the end of a session when you can talk to your child's teacher."

Additionally, many parent handbooks contain general information to help parents understand their child's school experience better and make the adjustment easier. These kinds of information are the following:

- developmental characteristics: brief profiles of expected behavior of children at different age levels

- separation: suggestions for making separation between parent and child easier for both

- progress reports: methods staff will use to report the child's progress to parents

- information: the kinds of information parents can provide teachers

- parent involvement: ways in which parents can be involved in school activities

A parent handbook should be a useful and attractive tool to both parents and staff; therefore, significant thought should go into its writing and composition. The following suggestions may help the director who is developing a handbook:

- Think about whether some information will vary each year. Be sure that variable information is on a separate page. If changes are needed, choose a loose-leaf or stapled binding for the book so pages can be inserted as needed.

- Arrange information logically, with a table of contents. Try printing each section on a different color paper so that it is easily identifiable. You can also cut each section wider or longer than the previous one, providing a tab for ease in locating.

- Make information concise. Remember that some parents will never read the whole document. Make it possible for them to get specific kinds of information without much searching.

- Write clearly and avoid poor grammar or misspelled words. Sentences should be easy to understand; avoid professional jargon.

- Make the handbook attractive so that parents are invited to explore its contents. A computer will allow you to vary the print font, add drawings, or alter the format.

- Consider the cost, especially if you have it typeset and printed professionally. Get several estimates before deciding to use this method. If it is too expensive, consider using a copier and collating it yourself.

It is important for staff members to establish relationships with one another.

The New School Year

• • • • • STAFF

It is important that all staff members work one or two weeks before the opening of school. This is a time when each classroom environment is prepared. Teachers should have time to:

- do last-minute room cleaning
- clean and organize supply cupboards
- put away new materials
- rearrange their classroom furniture
- set up a schedule for general classroom maintenance

Staff should have time to review curriculum materials available in their classrooms and in the general storage areas. They should also have time to:

- order last-minute items as needed
- prepare lesson plans and curriculum materials for the first week of school

The time before school is an important one for the establishment of relationships among staff members. This is a time to set the tone for the working partnership between the director and staff. It is a time when the director can:

- give teachers a list of the children in their classes
- make children's files available
- share critical medical information
- prepare and distribute name tags
- discuss group schedules
- review sign-in/sign-out procedures to be used by parents
- review emergency procedures for safety of children
- encourage teachers to schedule and complete home visits
- plan procedures for the first day of school

• • • • • SUPPLIES

The beginning of a school year is a good time to do an inventory of supplies and equipment. This can be very detailed or cover only items that are most used. For instance, it may not be necessary to know how many pencils are on hand, but it is important to know if there will be enough paint.

Paint is an example of an **expendable supply**, things that get used up and have to be replaced. Also included are paper, glue, paper towels, toilet paper, and cleaning supplies. Bikes are **nonexpendable items** because they last a long time before they need to be replaced. Office equipment, outdoor equipment, and many toys are also considered nonexpendable.

Inventory should be divided into the two categories. The director should complete the inventory count and shop around for the best prices before ordering necessary supplies. Ordering in large quantities often decreases the cost. Many times it will take up to six weeks for an order to arrive, so allowing enough time for delivery is important.

Staff members are included in planning.

Setting up a petty-cash fund for each classroom is an additional way of providing supplies. A specified amount is budgeted for the year for each room, and teachers are allowed to purchase things they need. This can relieve the director of some of the responsibility and can also give teachers greater freedom to buy what they need.

FINANCES

Only a few schools can afford the luxury of a bookkeeper. Therefore, many directors have to assume that job. Before school begins each year is a good time to review whether procedures for collecting tuitions, recording income, and paying bills are efficient. Changes may be indicated. The following suggestions may be helpful for the director who is also the bookkeeper.

- Collect tuition payments promptly each month on the same date.
- Accumulate checks for a few days at a time, then alphabetize them and post them on individual ledger sheets for each child (see Figure 13-9).
- Issue a duplicate receipt when parents pay in cash—one for the parent and one for the school.
- Record all checks and cash in the cash receipts record (see Figure 13-10).
- Check individual ledgers at a specified time, usually 10 days, to see if tuitions have been paid. Notify all families who have not paid the tuition. Charging a late fee for overdue tuition is acceptable.
- Record expenditures as they are made and summarize them each month (see Figure 13-11).
- Prepare a monthly budget summary (see Figure 13-12).

Almost all of these procedures can be assisted by use of a computer and computerized methods (see Figure 13-13 for a computerized Plan Expense record).

Name _____	No. of days per week _____
Address _____	Tuition Amt. _____
Telephone _____	

Date	Item	Amt. Due	Amt. Paid	Credit	Balance

FIGURE 13–9   Sample individual ledger sheet form.

CASH RECEIPTS RECORD				
Date	Item	Cash	Check Number	Amount

FIGURE 13–10   Sample cash receipts record form.

EXPENDITURES RECORD				
Date	Item	Check Number	Amount	From Account

FIGURE 13–11   Sample expenditures record form.

MONTHLY BUDGET SUMMARY					
Date	Item	Budget Amt.	This Month (last day)	Year to Date	Balance

FIGURE 13-12 Sample monthly budget summary form.

FACILITY

The final task before the beginning of the school year is to check the overall appearance and safety of the school. It should be clean and attractive. Often parents say the first thing they look for in a school is cleanliness. Parents' first impressions will be formed by how the school looks. Is the entrance to the school appealing? Is there a bulletin board that will interest parents? Does the environment welcome parents as well as children?

KidsCare 6 Management Software - [Plan Expense]

File Edit Switch Plans Reports Help

Plan Expense 2002 Start Over

Use Budget Monthly amounts

Whole Dollar amount planned for each account

Account	Jan	Feb	Mar	Apr	May	Jun	Jul	Aug	Sep	Oct	Nov	Dec
Advertising	50	50	50	50	50	50	50	50	50	50	50	50
Auto Expense	195	195	195	195	195	2000	195	195	195	195	195	195
Checking Service Charges	10	10	10	10	10	10	10	10	10	10	10	10
Children's Enrichment	25	25	25	25	25	25	25	25	25	25	25	25
Classroom Expense	100	100	100	100	100	100	100	100	100	100	100	100
Cleaning	125	125	125	125	125	125	125	125	125	125	125	125
Consultant Health Care	25	25	25	25	25	25	25	25	25	25	25	25
Dues and Subscriptions	0	0	0	0	0	50	0	0	0	0	0	0
Equipment Rental	87	87	87	87	87	87	87	87	87	87	87	87
Food Expense	300	300	300	300	300	300	300	300	300	300	300	300
General Supplies	55	55	55	55	55	55	55	55	55	55	55	55
Insurance - Employee Grour	500	500	500	500	500	500	500	500	500	500	500	500
Insurance - Liability	300	300	300	300	300	300	300	300	300	300	300	300
Insurance - Workman's Con	130	130	130	130	130	130	130	130	130	130	130	130
Interest Expense	0	0	0	0	0	0	0	0	0	0	0	0
Landscaping	0	0	0	80	80	80	80	80	80	0	0	0
Legal and Accounting	0	0	0	0	0	0	0	0	0	0	0	0
Miscellaneous Expense	0	0	0	0	0	0	0	0	0	0	0	0
Office Expense	20	20	20	20	20	20	20	20	20	20	20	20
Payroll Services	0	0	0	0	0	0	0	0	0	0	0	0
Postal Expense	29	29	29	29	29	29	29	29	29	29	29	29
Rent Expense	1500	1500	1500	1500	1500	1500	1500	1500	1500	1500	1500	1500
Repairs and Maintenance	50	50	50	50	50	50	50	50	50	50	50	50
Taxes - Other	0	0	0	0	0	0	0	0	0	0	0	0
Totals	3776	3776	3776	3856	3856	5711	3856	3856	3856	3776	3776	3776
	Jan	Feb	Mar	Apr	May	Jun	Jul	Aug	Sep	Oct	Nov	Dec

Put cursor in any program box, then press
Control-S to spread amount for remaining months

Forecasted expenses for Nov. FLTR NUM

FIGURE 13-13 Computerized plan expense record.

The playground should also look inviting. Often this is what people see as they approach a school. It should look like a place that is safe for children and that children will enjoy. If there are any garden areas around the school, have they been cared for? Is lighting adequate for dark mornings or late afternoons? The director should try driving up to the school in the morning and look at it as a parent would. Does it have "curb appeal"? Is it a place a parent would want to stop to investigate as a place for their child? If the answer is "yes," then the school is ready for another year!

CASE STUDY

Amanda has worked for the past six months getting ready to open her own child-care center in her community. She located the site, made the required renovations, obtained a license, hired staff, and did all the many other things needed for opening day. That day is fast approaching and she still has only 43 children enrolled. She needs at least 52 full-time tuitions to break even on expenses, not to mention a salary for herself.

1.   What should Amanda do to attract additional enrollments?
2.   What else can she do to ensure that there will be enough money to pay the first month's expenses?

SUMMARY

The decision to open an early childhood center must be carefully thought out, because it entails many choices and various tasks. The first step is a needs assessment to determine whether there is a pool of prospective clients. Consulting census information about the community is one way to determine whether it will support another child-care center.

There are several options for housing a school. It is possible to build anew, remodel a residence, rent unused public school classrooms, use space in a church, renovate a storefront or industrial building, use prefab buildings, or buy an existing school.

The start-up costs of opening a center will include the cost of the land and buildings, equipment and materials, and personnel. Additional expenses will include fees for consultant or legal services, advertising, and insurance.

Before going any further in the decision-making process, it is necessary to make an estimate of ongoing costs. Potential income will be determined by the number of children the facility will support. There are some suggested ranges of fixed costs that may help. The chosen site must accommodate enough children to cover expenses.

The school should open at a time that fits the needs of the community. Often the optimum time is at the end of summer. The director should develop enrollment procedures that ensure careful attention to each inquiry. Once applications begin arriving, it is time to make enrollment decisions: the total number to accept, whether to group children in peer or family groups, and how to incorporate children with special needs into the program. There are additional tasks that must be completed such as making attendance charts, preparing an overall schedule for the school, establishing and completing files for each child, and organizing a place for parent messages. The enrollment of school-age children may require a bus schedule to take children to and from their schools.

Each new parent should be given a handbook that includes information about the philosophy of the school and specific information about rules and procedures. Having a parent orientation before school begins or within the first few weeks is helpful. Informal meetings allow time for questions and for a relationship between parents and teachers to be established. Staff members should be working at least two weeks before opening day. This is a time to prepare their room environments and to review curriculum materials.

Some additional tasks to be completed before a school is ready to open its doors include ordering supplies, setting up procedures for collecting tuitions, and giving the facility a final inspection. The appearance of the school must be clean and inviting.

STUDENT ACTIVITIES

1. Visit your local zoning agency. Ask for zoning requirements for a child-care center and a home-based center. If there are differences, ask about the reasoning behind them. Share this information with small groups assigned to the task.

2. Obtain a copy of the licensing requirements for your area. Determine the following:

   a. What is the maximum size for a group of toddlers?

   b. What is the teacher/child ratio for a group of four-year-olds?

   c. Are there any regulations pertaining to school-age children?

   d. What are the minimum qualifications for staff members?

3. Invite a director of a child-care center to visit your class. Ask them to discuss which sections of the licensing code make a director's job easier. Ask also if there are items in the regulations that should be changed.

4. Collect parent handbooks from several child-care centers. Groups can compare them and answer the following questions:

   a. Do they contain the same kinds of information?

   b. In what ways do they differ?

   c. Is the information easy to understand?

   d. Do you think essential information has been omitted?

REVIEW

1. What information should be included in a community survey to determine whether a community can support another child-care center?

2. List the possible types of housing for an early childhood center.

3. Discuss the advantages and disadvantages of using the following spaces for a child-care center: a church building, a factory, an existing school.

4. Differentiate between start-up and ongoing costs.

5. List the categories of expenses that are included in a start-up budget.

6. Which expenditure comprises the largest percentage of ongoing costs?

7. What is meant by the terms peer group and family group?

8. List the completed forms that should be included in a child's enrollment file.

9. What is the purpose of a parent handbook? What kinds of information should it contain?

10. What is meant by expendable and nonexpendable supplies?

REFERENCE

Helburn, S. (Ed.). Cost, Quality, and Child Outcomes in Child Care Centers: A Technical Report. Denver, CO: Department of Economics, Center for Research on Economics and Social Policy, University of Colorado, 1995.

SELECTED FURTHER READING

Kagan, S. L., Brandon, R. N., Ripple, C., Maher, E. J., & Joesch, J. M. (2002). Supporting quality early childhood care and education: Addressing compensation and infrastructure. *Young Children, 57*(3), 58–65.

Mitchell, A., Stoney, L., & Dichter, H. (2001). *Financing child care in the United States: An expanded catalog of current strategies.* Kansas City, MO: Ewing Marion Kaufman Foundation.

National Women's Law Center. (2000). *Be all that we can be: Lessons from the military for improving our nation's child care.* Washington, DC: Author.

Whitebook, M., & Eichberg, A. (2002). Finding a better way: Defining policies to improve child care workforce compensation. *Young Children, 57*(3), 66–72.

HELPFUL WEBSITES

Disclaimer: Links to Internet sites throughout this book are provided for your convenience and do not constitute an endorsement.

America Taking Action:	**http://www.americatakingaction.com**
Child Care Resource:	**http://childcare-resource.com**
Early Childhood Education Web Guide:	**http://www.ecewebguide.com**
ERIC:	**http://www.searchERIC.org**

For additional resources related to administration including videos, links to related sites for each chapter of the text, tutorial quizzes, glossary flashcards, and more, visit the Education CourseMate website for this book at www.cengage.com/login.

PART V
Beyond the School Itself

Including Families and the Community

Objectives

After reading this chapter, you should be able to:

- Discuss the changing roles of parents and preschools.
- List some ways that parents may participate in the school.
- State some possible goals for parent education.
- Cite several ways a school may help parents learn.
- Itemize some activities that can publicize a school.

KEY TERMS

parent conference

parent education

parent involvement

A day in the life of . . .

A Regional Director, Corporate Child Care

A few months ago, I was at one of the four centers that I supervise. The director of the center had scheduled a meeting with a group of parents who had expressed serious concerns about the program. We found that their expectations were somewhat unreasonable and their attitudes were hostile. Two parents asked for more input in the school. I suggested creating a parent association. They were enthused. We arranged another meeting for further discussion. Following the meeting, I met with the director alone and explained the role of the parent association. I told her that parents often feel a sense of ownership if they are actively involved in an organized association. She seemed comfortable with this idea.

A few days later, we met again with these parents and opened the meeting to all other parents. The meeting started out as before with a list of complaints, but the director took control. She explained her decision to establish a parent association and asked for volunteers. She got a tremendous response!

Two months later, when I again met with the director, she reported that the association changed the climate of the parent group at the center. The director's life was much more pleasant after this new group was established, and she retained enrollment.

Traditionally, parents have reared children, and schools have educated them. Recent years have brought about some changes in these two roles.

Changing Roles of Families

Changing family life has forced modification of the traditional role of parents. In the United States, more than half the mothers of children under the age of six work outside the home. Children no longer stay home until they go to elementary school at the age of five or six. Many children start in child care as babies and continue until, or even through, adolescence. Thus, parents no longer have sole responsibility for rearing their children. Teachers or caregivers share this task.

Those who are with the child while parents work are forced into new roles as well. Teachers can no longer focus only on teaching. They have to help children through each developmental stage, be concerned about their health, and provide the nurturing that once was done solely by parents.

This merging of responsibilities for rearing and educating the child has caused both parents and teachers to realize that their responsibilities overlap and that they must work closely together. This is especially true when infants are involved. Parents are understandably anxious about placing their baby in someone else's care. They want caregivers who will listen to their concerns and who will follow their suggestions about feeding, sleeping, and toileting. Correspondingly, the school needs such input to plan for the appropriate care of the baby. This need to work together changes in character but continues even when the child is older.

Parent Involvement

Even when children are in child care, research consistently shows the enormous influence parents still have on their children (Barber, 2000). They remain the primary support for the child as teachers and caregivers change. **Parent involvement** in the school becomes essential for the optimum development of the child. Follow-up studies of children who attended Head Start or those who have been in programs modeled after Head Start show lasting gains through their school years and into adulthood. One of the crucial factors in the child's development is the involvement of parents and community (Hayes, Palmer, & Zaslow, 1990; Schweinhart & Weikart, 1993).

Many parents and teachers who took part in the early cooperative schools found their involvement brought unexpected benefits. The parents learned more about their own children. They also learned some basic principles of child development. They gained comfort by finding that other parents had similar problems. In fact, they learned that some problems were merely stages in a child's growth. The school provided a support system sometimes lacking in many communities. A few parents gained enough inspiration to become teachers when their children grew older.

Beginning in the 1960s, some parents began demanding a more active role in the education of their children. It was a time of social unrest, marked by the civil rights movement. Some of the demands arose from criticism of schools in general. More specifically, the grievances were aimed at the failure of educational systems to understand minority needs. Some people felt schools were unresponsive and bureaucratic. The Head Start project was one result of this turmoil.

Early attempts to involve parents in Head Start projects were difficult for the parents and the schools. Parent participation was "built into" the legislation. However, parents sometimes felt insecure in the presence of the authority symbol of the teacher. Conversely, teachers were reluctant to include parents for fear that they might dominate the program. The partnership that Head Start guidelines mandated took time to implement.

In the successful Head Start centers, parents and professionals seem to be working together harmoniously. Parent representatives serve on advisory committees. Parents have a high degree of input into curriculum. Some serve as aides in the classroom helping the teachers directly. Parents are taught how to enhance learning through activities at home.

Nonprofit schools use parents in fund-raising, recruitment, and public relations activities. However, previously the attitude that educational aspects should be left to the school staff persisted. Now, schools are finding that parents have many skills they are willing to share for program enrichment.

Proprietary schools, too, have found that parents are willing to participate in many ways. Parents with a profession offer their skills as consultants; others use special abilities

FYI

Family-Centered Child Care: What Does It Look Like?

- Family-centered child care supports the connections between children and their families. It recognizes that children draw their identities from family. A basic belief in the value of families permeates program policies and practices. All family members are treated with respect, warmth, and courtesy.

- A family-centered program speaks the languages and respects the cultures of all families in the program. Staff members are drawn from the community the program serves.

- Family-centered programs build on family strengths. Such programs recognize stages of development in family members and work with them to meet their needs.

- Family-centered child care supports and trains caregivers. Training staff on the basic principles of family-centered child care is important. Pre-service and in-service training, peer coaching, and mentoring opportunities are provided on a regular basis.

SOURCE: Child Care Bureau, 1996.

to enrich subject matter. Satisfied parents are more willing to help the school broaden its recruitment activities.

As already noted, the steadily increasing number of child-care programs has altered the environment. When children spend many of their waking hours in school, the relationship between home and school has to be even closer. Directors must be instruments for change in this situation. Parents and teacher, guided skillfully by the director, share the responsibility for determining the best environment for the child's physical, social, and intellectual growth.

The kind and extent of parent involvement depends on the program offered by the school. As in Head Start, parent participation may be mandated with specific guidelines.

The extent of parent participation where there are no specific written agreements will depend on the philosophy and attitudes of the school. In centers where director and staff fully realize the importance of parent presence, the involvement may be broad and almost unlimited.

PARENTAL ROLES

Parents may participate in the school in several ways. They may sit on policy-making committees, play a supportive role, act as aides in the classroom, or be trained as teachers of their own children at home.

The rationale for involving parents stems from the belief that people feel a commitment to decisions in which they have participated. Research shows that parent involvement benefits both parents and children (Becher, 1986; Powell, 1989). Parents feel more a part of their children's education, and children are able to achieve more when encouraged by their parents. Additionally, in practical terms, many tax-supported programs depend on active community support for renewal of funds.

Further rationale for involving parents comes from the belief that development of decision-making and other skills will help in other aspects of their lives. Learning that their personal input can influence the school encourages self-growth and further participation outside the school.

In a policy-making role, parents may take part in planning a new program by suggesting goals. They may be asked to join in operational aspects such as hiring or helping to evaluate staff. They may also suggest topics for parent-education activities.

Some policy-making functions for parents might be:

- serving as members of an advisory committee or council
- representing parents on the board of trustees
- helping to set policies concerning finance and personnel

Some parents may fulfill supportive roles. These are tasks the parents can sometimes do at home or outside of the school. They are designed to aid or supplement educational functions. Some tasks parents may perform in a supportive role are to:

- provide parts of major maintenance projects
- act as clerical support
- plan and carry out fund-raising
- be responsible for social activities
- provide babysitting or carpool services

The real purpose of a supportive role for parents is to fulfill a mutual need; the school and parents both want the best for the children. The school may desperately need some services parents can provide.

Fathers are encouraged to participate in the school.

The supportive role may help some parents begin involvement at a comfortable level. Not everyone is ready or able to invest as much time and effort as is necessary to become competent in policy making or to serve as an aide.

When they do work as aides in the classroom, parents must learn some of the duties and skills of a teacher in order to be effective. As aides, parents may:

- perform tasks assigned by the teacher, such as helping with large-group activities or working with individual children

- prepare materials, arrange the room, and keep records of children's progress

- supervise small groups of children during specific times

In some programs, participation of parents as aides is part of the "career ladder" concept. This may be the first rung in the process toward paid employment. Head Start and many child-care centers train mothers for jobs in schools for young children.

Parents may be trained to become better teachers of their own children. In this role, parents learn:

- to recognize the child's readiness for learning

- to value various learning experiences that further the child's development

- to use common materials found around the home to enhance the child's learning

PLANNING FOR MULTICULTURAL PARENT PARTICIPATION

Head Start has met the need for parental involvement by providing home visitors who work with families in their homes. Together, the home visitor and parents plan activities for the child and determine what the child is ready to learn. Common and inexpensive household materials are used for activities. All family members are encouraged to participate. Other schools can also provide similar training in different ways. As parents become more competent, they are encouraged to become more involved in their child's school. Training parents as teachers of their own children is discussed in more detail later in this chapter.

Head Start programs, begun in 1965, required parent participation. That experience has shown that children do better when parents are involved, during later school years as well as the Head Start period. It works because parents are involved at many levels, and their diversity is honored and respected. It has a remarkable record of involvement. In 2002, over 867,000 parents volunteered in local programs, and 29 percent of the staff was parents of current or former Head Start children (U.S. Department of Health and Human Services, 2003).

Although Head Start has the advantage of funds to create a climate for multicultural involvement, all programs can adopt some of the methods that made the program successful. The following are some suggestions to help directors create a welcoming environment.

- Ask parents to assist in ways to introduce children to various cultures through books, special celebrations, art exhibits, or community events.
- Include in any discussions of cultural differences the ways in which family values such as fairness, loyalty, or honesty are shared by all cultures.
- Avoid making sweeping generalizations about children from different backgrounds. Look at the individual child, family, and neighborhood environment before labeling differences as cultural.
- Work to understand differences, but also to find common ground.

LIMITS ON INVOLVEMENT

Each community and the schools within it have their own particular characteristics. The appropriate kind of parent involvement must be tailored to fit the situation in order to be effective. Factors are: (1) number of working parents, (2) ethnic group values, (3) stability of the community, (4) size of the community, and (5) physical setting of the school.

The number of working parents, especially mothers, certainly determines the amount and time of involvement. In a child-care school where almost all the parents are working, few parents can serve as aides. Some parents may work part-time or on a flexible schedule that would allow them some limited participation. The school must realize that the working schedule of parents determines involvement.

However, some ways in which fully employed parents can be involved in the education of their children are to:

- participate in decision making at convenient times
- provide support by doing work at home or after work
- be involved in training as teachers of their own children at home

Directors must realize, and staff should be reminded, that a working parent often has little surplus energy. Reluctance to become involved in the school may be simply fatigue, not an indication the parent is not interested.

Values, attitudes, and traditions of the parents in a school may also affect the extent and manner in which parents are willing to participate. Directors and teachers must be aware of parents' beliefs when differences arise over issues involving the children. Perhaps the adults' attitudes will not change, but at least they should listen to each other and respect their differences.

There are many instances in which parents and teachers come from the same culture, but have differing values, beliefs, and practices (Gonzalez-Mena, 2001). Teachers must respect these parents even though they do not share the same views on many subjects. It is sometimes easier to understand and explain differences when a cultural label can be attached to them. It's harder to accept and respect diversity when the person looks like us. Not making assumptions about people's culture based on their appearance is also important.

Directors will be more effective if they consider the following:

- How do the parents feel about being involved in their child's school?
- Do parents and teachers have widely differing attitudes about the education of children?
- Do the families see the school and home as entirely separate entities?

The stability or mobility of the community from which the school draws children also determines the degree of parent participation.

- If the population is largely transient, involvement that takes a long time to develop will not be possible.
- If the community is relatively stable, parents can take the time to develop decision-making and teaching skills.

The size of the community in which the school is based will also determine parent involvement.

- If children are bused to school from distant areas, finding ways to involve parents may be harder.
- A school located within walking distance may naturally become a center for varied activities.

The physical limitations of the school may restrict involvement by parents.

- If the school is small and space is at a premium, many parents may feel "squeezed out."
- If certain areas can be set aside and scheduled for parents' use, they may feel more welcome and free.

INITIAL CONTACT

Parents' first visits to a school after enrolling their children are the most important for setting the tone of future contacts. As parents walk into the school, will they feel welcome? Are there ways in which the environment says "Parents are welcome, too"? Does the director or some other staff member greet parents when they enter? Does the school have an open-door policy in which parents are welcome to visit at any time?

Some schools opt for an open house to set the tone for parent relationships. Often scheduled just before the school year begins, an open house gives parents an opportunity to meet all the staff and get to know other parents.

Every contact that staff members have with parents is important. Teachers should be as responsive to the parents as to their children. Even during brief meetings when parents deliver or pick up their child, teachers should be sensitive to parents' feelings. Parents should feel that the school personnel are as interested in them as they are in their child.

A physical space reserved for parents is important. If a room can be used as a parent–teacher lounge, or a place for the parent to feel at home, big dividends will accrue. A bulletin board for parents used to announce parent meetings, community lectures, fund-raisers, books of interest, and so on is useful. The weekly food menu could also be posted. A news-letter for parents will keep them informed and emotionally involved with the school.

ENCOURAGING PARTICIPATION

Once the initial contact with parents is made, the task of encouraging continued participa-tion begins. The director has primary responsibility. The director must create the climate in which staff members work. Staff members who have high morale and who feel secure in their jobs will feel more positive toward both parents and children.

A second task as leader is to implement a program that emphasizes home–school re-lations. Teachers may need encouragement to involve parents in their classroom activities. The director can suggest ways that they can use parents as aides or in supportive roles and can let them know which parents have talents or skills they might utilize.

A third important task for the director is to act as coordinator for a program of parent involvement. Busy teachers may need help in arranging times and other specifics involved in getting parents to help with classroom activities. The coordinator can also offer positive reinforcement for parents who have participated.

The process of involving parents in the education of their children has some built-in obstacles. Parents and teachers often deal in stereotypes of each other. This makes work-ing together difficult. The parent may see the teacher as an expert and, therefore, critical of parents. This may make the parent feel uneasy and unwelcome while visiting the school. Thus, the parent may avoid contact with the school.

Teachers, conversely, may feel that the parent has unrealistic expectations for what the school should do. When these expectations are not reached, the teacher feels under attack. Again, there is avoidance, this time from the teacher.

Parents can use their special abilities to enrich the curriculum.

Parents' attitudes toward school are often based on their own experiences. If they hated school, they may need significant encouragement to participate in their child's school. Alternatively, some parents loved school and are eager to participate when asked.

Inexperienced teachers often feel they have enough to do learning to work well with children. Having to be concerned about parents is an added burden. Some may have tried to get parents involved but were unsuccessful. Justifying exclusion of parents by feeling that these parents do not care enough about their children is then easier. Negative contacts with parents may influence even experienced teachers.

Some teachers fear that parents may not regard them as knowledgeable because they do not have children of their own. A few parents do say, "You don't know what it's like being with a child 24 hours a day." Some teachers feel parents will think this even if they do not say it.

Lack of training in working with parents may also create problems. Working with adults does require special skills and adroitness. Teachers often do not understand and, therefore, are critical of the feelings parents have about their children. Teacher training programs often fail to help the beginning teacher develop greater empathy for parents.

Some teachers involve parents more easily than others. These teachers can help other teachers. The director should schedule times when beginning teachers can observe more experienced teachers working with parent volunteers. Their observations can be discussed in follow-up staff meetings.

INCENTIVES FOR SUSTAINING INVOLVEMENT

It is often as difficult to sustain parent interest and participation in a school as it was to acquire it originally. The most important incentive for parents is their children. Parents want their children to be successful in school. Feedback on children's progress in the school helps. They also want to know how to be better parents. The school can build upon these needs to foster parent involvement. If they believe they are helping their children, parents will freely help the school.

Few schools can pay parents with money. A few publicly funded programs can offer reimbursement for out-of-pocket expenses. However, mostly encouragement, knowledge, and positive reinforcement are the coin of repayment. Some employer-sponsored schools may offer limited released time away from the job to help in the school. In child-care centers, dinner meetings may be arranged just after the close of school with free child-care time.

Promoting personal growth can enhance parents' interest. In some programs, contact with the school is the first or only activity tried by parents outside home or work. If they feel successful, their feelings of worth will increase. It may be the first step to broader community activities.

Social relationships developed through parent involvement are also important in continued interest. Single parents, especially, may find friendships that become an important part of their lives. New associations with other adults offer a single parent a broader outlook than a strictly child-centered world. Family-oriented social activities will allow parents to get to know one another. Some suggestions are children's concerts, puppet shows, family spaghetti dinners, picnics, and museum trips.

Some programs should be geared solely to adult needs. Classes in nutrition or family finance might be successful rallying points. If there is room and these classes can meet at the school, parents have an additional inducement toward belonging. Even broader excursions such as trips to museums, art galleries, or theaters may broaden parents' experiences and enhance friendships.

RECORDING PARENT INVOLVEMENT

The director should keep records to show the extent of parent involvement in the school. In some publicly funded programs, this is necessary to stay within guidelines. Regardless, the records may prove valuable when attempting to evaluate the program and to determine whether changes should be made. The following records may prove useful.

- List of current committee members
- Minutes of all meetings involving parents
- Attendance records at committee and board meetings
- Copies of resolutions involving parents' work
- Correspondence relating to parents' efforts
- Evaluation of parent involvement
- Records of any citations or awards made

Thinking of the parents as part of a team consisting of the school and the home is most productive. The teacher and parents have similar aims that are sometimes frustrated by false impressions. A major aim of parent involvement is to break through these barriers in order to give the children a superior education. The teacher, director, parents, and community should be considered as a unit. Without this sense of unity, gaps in the child's education and development will occur.

Community Involvement

Community programs or organizations may ask directors of child-care facilities to provide placements for their members. Teachers of high school classes in child development often want their teens to have real experience working with and observing children. Organizations such as AARP (American Association of Retired Persons) or Grey Panthers include seniors who want to remain active in their community and love being around children.

The guidelines for including community volunteers are similar to those delineated for including parent volunteers. Some additional challenges exist when using persons outside the school. For a successful volunteer program, directors should:

1. Develop an application that includes the name, address, and phone number of the applicant, educational level, interests and hobbies, car license and insurance, work experience, health record, and a list of references.

2. Conduct screening interviews with a consistent list of questions to ask each applicant. The questions should explore specific skills and preferences for the kinds of tasks the volunteer would like to perform.

3. Establish clear job descriptions stating the time involved, and the parameters of the job.

4. Plan an orientation that includes a thorough introduction to the center and an explanation of the organizational structure of the school.

5. Provide a statement of the center's educational beliefs, program goals and objectives, and how they are being implemented.

6. Include developmental information about the children and what to expect (or what not to expect) from the children.

7. Define appropriate and inappropriate discipline techniques.

8. Clarify the steps volunteers should take when there are problems.

9. State volunteer responsibilities: general expectations, overall schedules, and written assignments.

10. Indicate to whom the volunteer will be responsible, to whom they can direct questions, who will evaluate them, and to whom they can go for help.

Prepare a short, concise handbook that is available to all volunteers. The information might include:

1. Rules and regulations of the school.

2. A sample time sheet with instructions for signing in and out.

3. A sample evaluation sheet.

4. Suggestions for dealing with children in problem situations.

5. Safety rules for staff and children.

6. Procedures for field trips and excursions.

7. Simple "dos" and "don'ts" of working with children.

Plan strategies for recognizing the volunteers for their service to the school.

1. Acknowledge all the volunteers at a party.

2. Design recognition certificates.

3. Write individual notes to each volunteer.

4. Put together a booklet with pictures of the children and describing the activities the volunteer participated in.

5. Have the children draw pictures of their favorite activities with volunteers.

Parent Education

Although the aim of parent involvement is to establish a partnership for the care of the child at school, **parent education** is designed to help parents be better informed about child rearing and family life. The director is responsible for formulating the structure of a parent education program. Teachers should be encouraged to participate as fully as possible. It might be easier for the director to do all the parent education work, but the staff will benefit from taking part.

Formulating goals is a starting point. Working on several simultaneously is a possibility, as is concentrating on one goal at a time. Goals, though, should form the base for planning parent education activities.

GOALS FOR PARENT EDUCATION

Although all the following may not be completely applicable, they may provide some ideas for developing goals. Having goals consistent with the general philosophy of the school is most important.

Establish a partnership with the family for the education and care of the child.
The director should convey the attitude of partnership to each staff member. It begins when a parent first walks into the school and talks to the secretary or director. Conveying this attitude is especially important during the time the child and parent are adjusting to school attendance.

Help parents to recognize and respect their own abilities. Most parents do a good job of rearing their children. However, they sometimes feel inadequate. An important part of parent education is to help them realize their own strengths and trust their own feelings about what is right for the child.

Provide parents with information about child development. Many parents have limited experience with young children and may feel that some of the things their children do are unusual. Knowledge of child development will help them to view behavior as developmental stages.

Explain the school curriculum and planned activities. Parents should know why the school provides certain activities and materials. They should understand why the teacher presents the materials in a specific way. They need to understand the value of free play and benefits of group participation.

Help parents understand the ways that children can learn. Some parents believe that learning takes place only when the instructor is teaching. They may not remember that children are actively learning when they are playing. Children learn in different ways. Parents can be encouraged to recognize experiences at home that may be important.

Introduce the parents to a wide variety of educational materials and experiences. The family can be helped to make use of readily available materials for the child's learning experiences. They may need guidance regarding the sources and values of toys, books, paper supplies, puzzles, and other aids such as how-to-do-it books and games. The appropriate materials for the child's age level encourage creativity and self-growth.

ACTIVITIES

An attractive parent education program will have various activities and methods from which parents may learn. Some are planned and structured; others occur spontaneously. An effective program may use some of the following formats.

One of the first opportunities for a parent to learn in the school setting is the orientation meeting. This may be held at the beginning of a school year or at various times throughout the year as new families enroll. This meeting should be an opportunity to convey general information about the school and to answer parents' questions. An evening meeting usually works best for parents who have jobs. If child care is offered during this time, more parents may be able to attend.
The director should:

- plan the meeting to last about one hour or an hour and a half
- offer simple refreshments before the meeting starts or at the conclusion. Either an "old" parent or a teacher should be asked to serve
- send written invitations to parents. If an RSVP is included, following up on any who do not respond is important
- begin the meeting on time by welcoming the parents
- introduce staff members, indicating their room assignments
- distribute a copy of the goals of the school and explain each
- explain school rules (e.g., clothing for children to wear, bringing toys or snacks from home)

- describe methods of introducing children into their classrooms and managing separation from parents

- allow time for answering parents' questions

- set a friendly tone for establishing a partnership with parents in the care and education of their children

Observation is an important avenue for learning. Parents can watch how the school operates and see the interaction between teachers and children.

Observations may be casual and unscheduled. Each time a parent is in a classroom, it is an opportunity to observe. If a school has one-way screens into the classroom, the parent may observe without intrusion. This type of observation may be especially helpful for parents who are having separation problems with their children. The parent can see that the child usually stops crying when the teacher diverts or comforts the child. This may help immensely in guilt reduction.

The one-way screen offers anonymity to the parent. Often the child acts differently when the parent is present. This is a rare chance to see the child more objectively. Within the school's child-oriented environment, the child is often different than at home.

Casual observation also has pitfalls. The parents may see something that they do not understand. Either the teacher or director should be available to explain the child's part in the total group. Many times parents have questions most easily answered by the director, as a neutral observer.

Scheduled observations of demonstration activities also help parents learn. Their attention can be directed to specific activities. They can be coached on behaviors to look for or expect. They may also be asked to note the way the teacher varies activities of the group and of each child.

If a group of parents observes, there should be time for a discussion after each session to clarify and reinforce learning. As in any endeavor, each person sees slightly different aspects of what happened. Sharing and comparing observations may be an exciting way to learn.

Group discussions are an invaluable tool for parent education, especially when led by a skilled staff member. Groups can either be structured, focusing on a particular topic, or unstructured, allowing the interests of the group to determine the topic. The structured group begins with a brief presentation of information. The topic might be stages of a child's development, aspects of the school curriculum, or how to manage situations that arise at home between the parent and child. Parents should have an opportunity to relate their own experiences with the information.

Unstructured group discussions allow parents to discuss topics that may be uppermost in their mind at a particular time. Parents have an opportunity for an informal exchange of ideas, while the leader functions as a resource for information as needed. One of the secondary results of this kind of group is that parents find they are not alone in their confusions or frustrations about the best ways to manage their children. They also learn that their child is probably not much different from other children. This is particularly important if they have never had the opportunity to watch siblings grow up or to be around young children.

When these two kinds of discussion are used at different times, along with observations in the classrooms, parents have an excellent opportunity to learn more about their own children and child rearing in general. Discussions that take place in the meetings often stimulate further conversation between parents outside of the group setting.

Lectures or panels are additional teaching methods. Experts in various fields can be asked to speak at parent meetings. The speaker should be interesting, as well as informed. A long, dull speech, especially if it is after working hours, can ruin a parent education session. It can induce sleep and seriously derail the entire effort.

Lecture topics must be chosen with care. Some topics create anxiety rather than promote knowledge. Controversial topics attract interest but must be handled skillfully. Both sides of an issue should be presented.

Films, slides, and tapes help parents learn. Many informative and interesting films are geared to parents of young children. The director should preview each film before showing it and make notes while viewing for use during the discussion period that follows.

Films made at the school should illustrate the activities and materials used in everyday teaching. Films made at intervals may show language development during the year. The same holds for other kinds of ventures. Art, music, and science all hold developmental promise. Films must be edited carefully so that nothing embarrassing to any child will appear.

Workshop participation can offer information about the curriculum. Parents may participate in the same activities as their children do. They may fingerpaint, work with wood or blocks, and sing. This gives them a firsthand feel of what the child is doing.

Another kind of workshop is one in which parents can make learning materials to use at home with their child. This can be a game, a piece of equipment, or a learning kit. This kind of workshop for parents can have a twofold benefit: they have made something for their child, and they have explored the potential of materials.

Parents can learn through participation in the classroom. Many parents have special skills or training that can be useful on a short-term basis in the classroom. It is a welcome change of pace to have a parent read a story, lead a music activity, or share a cooking experience. Some parents may be able to share stories and objects from their own ethnic backgrounds. This can be an effective way of bringing an added dimension to the classroom.

If parents show some desire to serve as aides on a long-term basis, the hurdle of training may appear. This will vary with each individual, but a brief overview followed by on-the-job instruction will probably suffice. Volunteers must understand the special goals of the school. They need to know the rudiments of interacting with young children in a group. They should begin by working under the close supervision of the regular teacher and progressing to individuals or very small groups.

Saturday or holiday sessions of a school give parents an opportunity to participate. Some schools schedule this kind of activity at least once a year. With both father and mother now working, this type of scheduling is gaining in popularity.

All communications with a parent have an educational potential. Any phone call to or from a parent is part of the parent involvement/parent education program of the school. Phone calls made when a child is home sick are especially important to remember. It tells the parent that the teacher cares. It may also give the parent a moment to talk to the teacher about the child.

Daily contacts, though routine, are important. The way the teacher answers a parent's questions about the child establishes feelings. A simple question such as "Did Johnny eat?" may be answered in detail or with a colder "Yes." Parents want reassurance that the teacher knows and cares about what the child did during the day. When that kind of feedback is given, the result can be greater trust and confidence in the school. The little efforts count.

Conferences are probably the most efficient way a school can help parents learn. They are also an effective means for solidifying parents' relationships with the school. The following are some general suggestions for the director and teacher to keep in mind for all **parent conferences**.

- Provide a comfortable setting that is free from interruptions.
- Start and end the conference on a positive note.
- Do not be afraid to tell parents that you do not have all the answers or information, but that you will try to find out.
- Assure parents that you share their interest in and concern for their child.
- Allow enough time to cover the topic adequately, but do not let the discussion become too lengthy.
- Be sensitive to each person's comfort zone regarding self-revealing dialogues. The values and beliefs learned as part of growing up in a particular culture may have a powerful influence on communication patterns and child-rearing practices.
- End the conference with a summary of the discussion and with future procedures.
- Schedule a follow-up conference if necessary.

When the conference is about a child's progress, the following recommendations may help.

- Plan conference content before the scheduled time. Be prepared to present information about the child's achievements and to describe incidents that illustrate that information.
- Be prepared to discuss suggestions for helping the child attain a higher level of functioning if there are areas in which the child needs to improve.

If the conference regards a problem, the following recommendations may help.

- Remember that parents have a strong emotional investment in their child. Empathize with parents about their concerns. "I understand how you could be really upset when that happens."
- Avoid labeling a child or making broad statements. Instead of calling a child a troublemaker, tell the parent, "At story time he will poke the child sitting next to him" or "She constantly interrupts when a teacher is reading a story to the group. She will ask a question, say she can't hear, or say that she doesn't like the book."
- Acknowledge that it is not easy to report on problems that occur at school.
- Describe the behavior or situation without being critical or making the parents feel that it is their fault.
- Allow parents to ask questions or to describe how they see their child's behavior.
- Remember that no matter how careful or gentle you might be, sometimes parents are going to be defensive or angry. They will respond with denial that the problem exists. "We never see that kind of behavior at home." They may also respond with an attitude of projection. "It's the school's problem because that teacher doesn't know how to handle my child."
- Remind parents that you have a common concern for their child.

- Avoid using educational jargon, talking down to parents, or using lengthy explanations. Use clear and concise descriptions of behavior and short explanations of developmental stages. If necessary, use a translator or speak in the parents' native language.

- Guide parents to find their own solutions to problems or be prepared to describe how you will work with the problem at school. "Do you have ideas about how you will respond to his temper tantrums now that we have talked about what precedes them?" or "Now that I understand more about why she is behaving that way, these are the things that I think will help at school."

- Do not expect a solution to every problem. Sometimes merely letting the child have time to move to another stage of development or to find their own way will change previously troubling behavior.

- Schedule a follow-up conference to discuss whether the new procedures that have taken place are working or whether another approach needs to be found. "Let's meet again in two weeks to see how our plan has been working."

- Make notes of the conference (not while the parent is present, but when the conference is finished) and place it in the child's file.

Telephone conversations with a parent sometimes become mini-conferences. These can be initiated by either the parent or by a staff member in order to report a change in the child or to better understand the child. Often parents are more comfortable talking on the phone than while sitting down with a staff member at a more formal conference. Certain topics lend themselves best to telephone conferences. For example, the parent relates what happened at home before the child came to school or a teacher describes a child's special achievement that day. The telephone is an opportunity to share information about the child.

Sometimes parents want to talk about a problem and finding time for a sit-down conference is difficult. Addressing their concerns is important, even when the telephone is the only medium for doing so. If this happens, the same guidelines should be followed as were discussed in previous paragraphs about a conference for discussing a problem.

Casual contacts between staff members and parents should also be seen as part of parent education. These usually occur when the parents leave their children at school or pick them up at the end of the day. Short, casual contacts, like telephone conversations, should be used for the purpose of exchanging information, answering questions, or discussing the program. They should not be used for discussing a problem because too much opportunity exists for a misunderstanding. In the morning both parents and staff are rushed, and at the end of the day both are tired.

The staff person who is present at the end of the day also must know any important information about the child's day at school. This means that the morning teacher needs to communicate any critical information that the parent should know. If some concern is expressed by the parent or by the teacher, a sit-down conference should be scheduled.

Home visits are another way of helping parents become more effective in the education of their own children. Head Start actually has an entire program called Home Start in which parents are taught to provide educational activities for their own children through visits from a trained professional. Most child-care centers do not have the luxury of having a staff person whose main responsibility is to work with parents in their own homes. However, home visits can be used as a way to expand and enhance the educational activities that children are exposed to in the school setting. One advantage of a home visit is that the staff member has an opportunity to learn more about the environment in which the child lives. This can be helpful in understanding both the child and the family. Another advantage is that parents can learn how to use easily available home materials to provide learning experiences for their children. The staff member might also bring materials to use at the home and demonstrate their use. Finally, both parents and children are proud when the teacher takes the time to come to their home. It helps to bridge the gap between home and school.

Information can be conveyed to parents through a parent library, a periodic newsletter, or a bulletin board. Some parents may prefer to increase their knowledge by reading. Others may resist this fiercely. However, the school should make available some books on child development—the best in the field. If the budget will not allow outright purchase, a reading list of good resources at the local library may suffice. As mentioned previously, the newsletter may keep parents informed of what is happening at the school and in the field of child development. The director and teachers can write articles aimed at parents. A centrally located bulletin board, attractively arranged, can serve as a center of interest near an exit or entrance. The board should be well maintained and up to date.

An integral part of early childhood education is the enlightenment of parents. The school has the children for only a part of each day. For each child's education to be consistent, the parents must carry the same goals into the home. To make this

Cengage Learning

Sometimes parent conferences are informal.

possible, the school must make a concerted effort to present itself to the parents. Parent education is really a cooperative enterprise on the part of the school and parents to make the child's education truly unique and whole.

The School and the Community

Schools must actively promote themselves to remain competitive. No one requires very young children to go to school. When parents choose to put their children in school, they sometimes make choices capriciously. The school is located near the home or workplace; it is convenient to transportation. It is inexpensive. The motivations are many and varied. However, the schools with full enrollment and waiting lists have made earnest efforts to promote themselves.

Probably the best form of public relations is good parent education and intense parent involvement with the school. One of the most sincere forms of advertising is word-of-mouth testimony of satisfied customers. Satisfied parents are good promoters.

A few schools have adopted easily recognized symbols to promote themselves. KinderCare uses a red tower in all its buildings and as a logo on printed material. Competing on this level, however, is not necessary. There are common, everyday ways of making the school known in the community, and even outside it.

The director usually assumes responsibility for public relations. The director should approach this self-promotion in an organized and thoughtful way. It makes sense to pursue areas over which there can be some control before launching something such as a paid campaign. Some things to think about include: (1) the exterior appearance of the school, (2) telephone-answering procedures, (3) visitor utilization, (4) brochures and pamphlets, (5) open houses, and (6) community activities.

APPEARANCE OF THE SCHOOL

Becoming habituated to the appearance of a school is easy for an employee. However, it has not happened to the casual passerby. Evaluations are frequently formed from first impressions. Sometimes it is helpful to adopt the attitude of a total stranger. What does the outside of the school look like? Are there peeling paint and fading signs or an attractive color and well-kept entrance?

Playground areas are often visible from the outside. What kind of equipment can be seen? Is it being used? Does it look sturdy and well maintained? Is the equipment designed to appeal to children or only to adults? Are there open places for children to play? When visitors enter the building, what do they see first? Is the entrance arranged so that someone will greet them? Is there a place to sit down? Is the reception area pleasant looking? Are there things that interest parents? Is the area clean and free of unpleasant odors? Sensory impressions are important in setting the tone for first-time visitors.

TELEPHONE-ANSWERING PROCEDURES

Many first contacts and first impressions are made over the telephone. The person answering the telephone becomes a front-line public relations person. Often this person is the secretary. Parents telephone for information regarding price, hours, age range, and other

A good secretary is vital to public relations.

variables. To ease the burdens on the director's time, the secretary can be trained to give this kind of routine information about the school.

The director should provide forms for recording names, addresses, and telephone numbers and should establish a procedure for following an inquiry with written information.

The secretary should be trained to know when to refer calls. Directors may want to answer questions about policy, curriculum, or goals themselves.

The secretary should be pleasant and polite when answering the telephone and should use clearly enunciated speech. An unrushed and unhurried manner may reassure a parent who already has doubts.

VISITORS

Parents of children already enrolled in the school should feel free to visit at any time. Specific times should be set aside for other visitors. For example, one or two days a week could be planned to accommodate prospective parents, community members, or others wishing to see the school. There should be a plan for what the visitors will see. Written materials are often helpful. Teachers should be informed that they will have visitors in their classrooms.

After a short orientation, the director should take the visitors to a classroom and introduce them to the teacher. They should be seated away from the center of the children's activity. Thirty minutes is about the maximum time for visitors to spend in the classroom.

Another half an hour to one hour should be set aside for a discussion after the observation. This is the time to encourage visitors to share what they have seen or to ask questions. If disparate interest groups, such as visiting teachers and prospective parents, are touring the school, meeting with them separately is best. Their questions and observations may be quite different.

Visitors should be scheduled for times when interesting activities are taking place so that they can see children working at learning centers or involved in a group activity. Discussion with visitors can focus on how the lessons further the goals of the school.

THE BROCHURE

A brochure is an effective tool for selling a school and should be a succinct portrayal of the school. It should be attractive and in good taste. Colors may be used if they are not gaudy.

The brochure may be sent out in response to a telephone call, given to parents who stop by, distributed at professional meetings, or given to the community. It is a small ambassador.

The effectiveness of the brochure depends on the carefulness of its preparation. A poor brochure is worse than none at all. A good one has few rivals for helpful publicity. Staff members or parent volunteers with special art or writing abilities may be able to help in the production.

Many people do not read brochures carefully. Therefore, the information should be condensed. The essential facts should be clear when readers skim the document.

It must contain all pertinent information. It should be a size and weight that costs minimum first-class postage to mail. The paper used should have a quality feel. Twenty-weight coated stock is often used in an 8½″ × 11″ format, folded three times. A brochure that can be mailed without an envelope is less costly.

Although total cost must be considered, counting pennies is unwise. The addition of cuts for pictures and of some color costs more. However, selective bidding by printers and a judicious selection may partially compensate. Fewer brochures for limited and controlled distribution are probably better than letting quality suffer.

A brochure should include:

- the name, address, and telephone number of the school.
- sponsorship (if any) of the school.
- hours the school is in session. Days of the week and months of the year might also be helpful.
- the procedure and cost of enrollment. If enrollments are taken only at specific times, this should be stated.
- ages of children served.
- tuition and other fees. (Using a separate sheet for tuition and fees may be wise. Reprinting will be cheaper when costs change.)
- brief statements of philosophy—in terms everyone can understand.
- a short description of the school's program(s).
- a description of unique features.
- the name of the person to contact for enrollment.
- affiliations or accreditations.

(Picture of a classroom)

ORCHARD VALLEY CHILD-CARE
CENTER
A UNIQUE LEARNING
ENVIRONMENT FOR YOUR CHILD

Orchard Valley Center
1000 Valley Drive
Orchard Valley

Place stamp
here

(Picture of a classroom)

FIGURE 14-1 Sample brochure.

PROGRAM

Orchard Valley Center is committed to providing an optimum environment for children while they are in our care. Our philosophy and goals are used to plan and implement all aspects of our program.

We believe

- each child is unique and deserves opportunities to make choices, to develop independence, and to receive reinforcement when successful.

- in providing a safe physical environment where the child can explore and can be challenged to develop optimum motor skills.

- all teaching staff should be role models for children and should plan learning activities appropriate for each age level.

- parents are the most significant adults in a child's life and should be included as partners in planning for the child's growth and development while at school.

(picture of a child)

ENROLLMENT

New enrollments are accepted at any time that openings are available. An application must be made in person. For an appointment, please call:

Mrs. Mary Anton
555-3014

A $35.00 nonrefundable registration fee is charged at the time of initial enrollment and at the beginning of each new enrollment year.

AGES

Our infant-toddler program accepts children at six weeks.

Children between ages two and five can be enrolled in our preschool program. A kindergarten classroom is available for those who are ready for a more academic program.

A before- and after-school service meets the needs of children from age six to twelve. If required, our school van will transport these children to their elementary school in the morning and pick them up again in the afternoon.

HOURS

Orchard Valley Center is open from 6 A.M. until 6 P.M. Monday through Friday.

FEES

Fees are payable at the beginning of each month and are based on the number of hours the child attends. A child may be enrolled for a half or full day, two to five days each week.

A fee schedule will be sent to you upon request.

(Picture of a child)

Orchard Valley Center is a member of the Preschool Owners Association.

In 1988, the school was accredited by the National Association of Schools for Young Children.

FIGURE 14-1 Sample brochure (*continued*).

OPEN HOUSE

An open house can publicize the best features of a school. This can be especially effective when opening a new school. There are really two parts to it: preparation of the school itself, and publicity to lure the community to attend.

As many staff members as possible should be involved in planning and preparing for the open house. The more dramatic and graphic aspects of the educational program should be highlighted. Classroom displays with children's artwork will show creativity. Block buildings, pictures, storybooks, and varied constructions all lend themselves to self-advertisement.

Room arrangements should be attractive. A story corner can be set up as though children were expected. A table set for snack time shows that proper nutrition is a vital part of the program.

After visiting the classrooms and displays, the visitors should have ample opportunity to ask questions. Staff members should be available to talk about the program or to answer questions. A guest book should be placed near the entrance for guests to write their names, addresses, telephone numbers, and comments. These names can then be added to the general mailing list.

Brochures should be displayed in a prominent place. If a brochure is not available, a simple one-page statement of philosophy and goals will suffice. Either document should include school name, address, phone number, and contact person.

The finest open houses are partially wasted efforts if attendance is minimal. Although individual notices may be sent to people on the mailing list, a more general outreach is required. Simple posters may be placed in local stores. The community newspaper may run a feature or place an advertisement. Local service clubs may make an announcement. One hint is to start early with publicity efforts—several weeks is not too long.

A school shows its best at open house.

Cengage Learning

● ● ● ● ●   COMMUNITY ACTIVITIES

Involvement in community activities is another way to make a school known. Some schools serve as part-time community centers, with adjacent meeting rooms. Others may gradually evolve into centers because of the various services offered. Either way, the school becomes known in the community for its openness and friendliness.

There are many ways to bring the community into the school. Services for parents, older people, and older children are recommended. Community members, as well as parents, will attend lectures, films, and discussions centering on child rearing if they are sufficiently publicized. Rummage sales, art sales, and used book sales attract people of all ages. Saturday art classes and general recreational activities can be offered for older children.

Fund-raisers are a good way to publicize the school as well as to collect funds. The publicity and program should include facts about the school and stimulate further interest.

Staff members should be encouraged to join one of the community organizations open to them, such as the Chamber of Commerce, community child-care task forces, women's organizations, and parent groups. Staff members should do this consciously as school representatives. In reality, the director must carry the major load of community activity.

Director and staff should also participate in professional meetings, conferences, and workshops. This leads to the exchange of ideas within the early childhood group. Another idea is writing an article for a parents' magazine or for a professional journal. Even though these methods do not reach the public directly, they can be a way of letting others know about the school. Other directors and teachers may have opportunities to refer parents to the school.

Getting free mention or presentation on radio or television may be possible if the school has innovative programs. Media people are constantly searching for human-interest stories, and few topics are as intriguing to the public as young children's activities. However, the director must go to them and sensitize them to the many possibilities open. A news release to the local media is the first step. A follow-up telephone call is often necessary.

Technology and access to the Internet has opened a new avenue for publicizing a school. Schools can now create their own home page, which is an online brochure to convey information about their program quickly and to a diverse audience. A home page may cost $100 to $200 to set up with a small monthly fee for a company to maintain and update the website.

The website should include pictures of the school. Those who access the site should be invited to send comments or questions and to sign a guest book, including their e-mail address. From this information, generating a large list of contacts is possible. They can be e-mailed newsletters, announcements of events, promotional offers, or short articles of advice for parents. If the list includes contacts such as donors, doctors, or community professionals, the website can serve to build community involvement.

CASE STUDY

Consuelo, a teacher in the infant–toddler program, decided to invite the parents to participate in a volunteer program. First she obtained the support of her director and then arranged to have several parents read stories, sing songs, and help with feeding. Kylie's mother, Marie, has spent the last two weeks participating in the program. Marie spends most of the time with her own daughter and often talks to and distracts the other staff members in the group. Consuelo overheard a conversation between Marie and one of the assistant teachers regarding another staff member. The content of the conversation was purely gossip, so Consuelo made an appointment to discuss it with the director.

1. What would you expect the director to do with this information?
2. How would you handle this situation with Marie if you were either Consuelo or the director?
3. How could Consuelo motivate Marie to continue her volunteering, and yet be sensitive to center policies?
4. If you were the director, how would you deal with the other caregiver involved?

SUMMARY

As the role of the parent has changed, the role of the school has changed to compensate.

Parent involvement in the school yields benefits to the school and to the parent.

The ways in which parents may become part of the school are many and varied.

There are also limits on what the school may expect of the parent.

Techniques for encouraging participation are limited only by the ingenuity of the school; they begin with initial contact.

Sustaining interest is as difficult as stimulating it. A major incentive and focus is the welfare of the child.

One of the major aims of parent education is better understanding of the child and of themselves.

Specific goals for parent education must be consistent with the total philosophy of the school.

Many specific activities lead directly to a greater understanding of the child: orientation meeting, child observations, lectures or panels, films and tapes, workshops, and active classroom participation.

Conferences are an effective means for educating parents as well as solidifying their relationship to the school. Sometimes conferences must be over the telephone or occur when there are casual contacts between parents and staff members.

Home visits are another way of educating parents.

One of the best forms of public relations is a group of satisfied parents. However, other methods of advertising may be used effectively.

The physical appearance of the school should be as attractive as possible.

Telephone answering, especially with regard to first contact, must be as pleasant as can be managed.

Preparation for visiting groups should expose them to the best the school has to offer. The open house as a variant on this can be used effectively.

A tasteful brochure can serve as a fact-filled ambassador.

Community groups or organizations may ask directors to provide placement for their members' children. For a successful program, directors must develop procedures and strategies that make the maximum use of volunteers without disrupting the school curriculum.

Involvement with community activities works two ways: Staff members should be involved locally and the community should feel at home in the school.

STUDENT ACTIVITIES

1. Discuss the degree of parent involvement that you think is appropriate for your school. What factors are important in determining this?

2. Talk to some parents in a Head Start program in your community. How do they feel about involvement?

3. Plan a parent education activity for your school. Use an evaluation form to check its effectiveness.

4. Interview several directors of different kinds of schools. How do their goals for parent education differ?

5. Obtain brochures from at least three different schools in your community. Compare and evaluate.

6. Write a two-paragraph news release concerning a recent event at a preschool.

REVIEW

1. Describe the changing nature of school and home since the end of World War II.

2. What are some of the benefits to the child that parent involvement entails?

3. Are there unreasonable demands that the school may make on the average parents? What are they?

4. What are some of the ways that the school can encourage parent participation?

5. What is the major goal of parent education?

6. What is one of the most tangible forms of public relations?

7. Why is the physical appearance of the school important?

8. List some of the facts to include in a brochure.

REFERENCES

Barber, N. (2000). *Why parents matter; Parental investment and child outcomes.* Westport, CT: Bergin & Garvey.

Becher, R. M. (1986). Parent involvement: A review of research and principles of successful practice. In L. G. Katz (Ed.). *Current topics in early childhood education* (Vol. 6, pp. 85–122). Norwood, NJ: Ablex Publishing Group.

Gonzalez-Mena, J. (2001). *Multi-cultural issues in child care* (3rd ed.). Mountain View, CA: Mayfield Publishing.

Hayes, C. D., Palmer, J. L., & Zaslow, M. J. (Eds.). (1990). *Child care choices.* Washington, DC: National Academy Press.

Head Start Program Fact Sheet. (2003). U.S. Department of Health and Human Services, Administration for Children and Families, Head Start Bureau. Retrieved from http://www.acf.hhs.gov/programs/research/2003.htm2006.

Powell, D. R. (1989). *Families and early childhood programs.* Washington, DC: National Association for the Education of Young Children.

Schweinhart, L. J., & Weikart, D. (Eds.). (1993). *Significant benefits: High/Scope Perry preschool study through age 27.* Ypsilanti, MI: High/Scope Press.

SELECTED FURTHER READING

Albrecht, K. (2005). Meeting the needs of today's families. *Child Care Information Exchange, 163*, 37–41.

Christian, R. A. (2006). Understanding families: Applying family system theory to early childhood practice. *Young Children, 61*(1), 12–20.

Fabre, B. (2005). Children in need of protection: Working with the foster care system. *Child Care Information Exchange, 163*, 46–51.

Gorham, P. J., & Nason, P. N. (1997). Why make teachers' work more visible to parents? *Young Children, 52*(5), 22–26.

Manning, D., & Schindler, P. J. (1997). Communicating with parents when their children have difficulties. *Young Children, 52*(5), 27–33.

Murphy, D. M. (1997). Parent and teacher plan for the child. *Young Children, 52*(4), 32–36.

Powers, J. (2006). Six fundamentals for creating relationships with families. *Young Children, 61*(1), 28.

Sturm, C. (1997). Creating parent-teacher dialogue: Intercultural communication in child care. *Young Children, 52*(5), 34–38.

Vissing, Y. (2008). Smart use of volunteers. *Exchange, 30*(6),28–31.

Wardle, F. (2001). Supporting multiracial and multiethnic children and their families. *Young Children, 56*(6), 38–39.

Wasson, J. (2000). Power pack your center brochure. *Child Care Information Exchange, 134*, 16–17.

Workman, S. H., & Gage, J. A. (1997). Family-school partnerships: A family strengths approach. *Young Children, 52*(4), 10–14.

HELPFUL WEBSITES

Disclaimer: Links to Internet sites throughout this book are provided for your convenience and do not constitute an endorsement.

Head Start Publications Management Center:	**http://www.headstartinfo.org/ publications/publicat.htm**
Interracial Voice Networking News Journal:	**http://www.Interracialvoice.com**
National Parent Information Network:	**http://www.npin.org**

For additional resources related to administration including videos, links to related sites for each chapter of the text, tutorial quizzes, glossary flashcards, and more, visit the Education CourseMate website for this book at www.cengage.com/login.

Cengage Learning

Maintaining the Quality of Child Care

Objectives

After reading this chapter, you should be able to:

- Describe the accreditation process.
- List several categories of child abuse.
- Explain how child abuse may be prevented.
- Cite a few laws pertaining to child care.

KEY TERMS

accreditation

child abuse

Child Development
   Associate (CDA)

A day in the life of . . .

A Director of a Learning Center

The culminating activity at Thanksgiving time was a "feast" with all of the pre-schoolers participating. The children ate the traditional foods of the holiday that the classes themselves had prepared (with some help, of course). This feast was held in the center courtyard of the school. It was quite a sight to behold.

I was concerned that a child who had attended our school since age three might be jaded and tired of this feasting so we planned an alternate activity for the first graders. Two first graders were watching the banquet, and one turned to the other and said wistfully, "Don't you wish you were young again?"

According to the National Association for the Education of Young Children (NAEYC), "Child care at most centers in the United States is poor to mediocre, with 40 percent of infants and toddlers in rooms having less-than-minimal quality." A Special Research Report published by NAEYC (1995) summarized the findings of a study done at the University of Colorado entitled "Cost, Quality and Child

Outcomes in Child Care Centers." That study found only 14 percent of centers offered developmentally appropriate care. As more of our nation's children spend their early years in child care, it is crucial that the quality of programs be the best they can be.

Upgrading the Quality of Programs

One way to upgrade the quality of programs is through **accreditation** offered by NAEYC. Additionally, teachers must become better trained and their salaries must be commensurate with their professional status.

ACCREDITATION OF SCHOOLS

The NAEYC accreditation service is administered by the National Academy of Early Childhood Programs. Any group program serving children from birth through age five can be accredited. Programs already accredited or in the process include half-day or full-day church-related programs, parent cooperatives, public school pre-kindergartens and kindergartens, Montessori programs, Head Start centers, laboratory schools, for-profit childcare centers, and hospital-affiliated centers.

The system is voluntary and involves a three-step process: (1) self-study by the director, teachers, and parents; (2) validation visits by trained professionals; and (3) an accreditation decision by a team of early childhood experts. Schools can pace the length of time involved in completing the process, but it usually takes from 4 to 18 months.

The self-study step is the critical element of the accreditation process. After paying a fee and receiving the accreditation manual, the director, teachers, and parents rate the quality of the program in 10 different categories. Upon the completion of the self-study, a final report is prepared and the results are reported to the academy. Academy personnel review the materials to determine whether the information is complete or whether further material is needed.

Beginning in 2006, new standards for accreditation by NAEYC are in place. The new standards are divided into four areas of focus: (1) children, (2) teaching staff, (3) family–community partnerships, and (4) leadership and administration. Included in these focus areas are 10 program standards, with a list of criteria for each. A program must show that it meets all of the standards in order to be accredited. The focus areas are summarized below, but the complete list of new guidelines can be found online at http://www.naeyc.org/accreditation. Program Standards & Criteria.

FOCUS AREA: CHILDREN

Program Standard 1—Relationships

The program promotes relationships among all children and adults to encourage each child's sense of individual worth and belonging as part of a community, and to foster each child's ability to contribute as a responsible community member.

Program Standard 2—Curriculum

The program implements a curriculum consistent with its goals for children and promotes learning and development in each of the following domains: aesthetic, cognitive, emotional, language, physical, and social.

Program Standard 3—Teaching

The program uses developmentally, culturally, and linguistically appropriate and effective teaching approaches that enhance each child's learning and development in the context of the program's curriculum goals.

Program Standard 4—Assessment of Child Progress

The program is informed by ongoing systematic, formal, and informal assessment approaches to provide information on children's learning and development. These assessments occur within the context of reciprocal communications with families and with sensitivity to the cultural contexts in which children develop. Assessment results are used to benefit children by informing sound decisions about children, teaching, and program improvement.

Program Standard 5—Health

The program promotes the nutrition and health of children and protects children and staff from illness and injury.

FOCUS AREA: TEACHING STAFF

Program Standard 6—Teachers

The program employs and supports teaching staff that has the educational qualifications, knowledge, and professional commitment necessary to promote children's learning and development and to support families' diverse needs and interest.

Program Standard 7—Families

The program establishes and maintains collaborative relationships with each child's family to foster the child's development in all settings. These relationships are sensitive to family composition, language, and culture.

Program Standard 8—Community Relationships

The program establishes relationships with, and uses the resources of, the children's communities to support the achievement of program goals.

FOCUS AREA: LEADERSHIP AND ADMINISTRATION

Program Standard 9—Physical Environment

The program has a safe and healthful environment that provides appropriate and well-maintained indoor and outdoor physical environments. The environment includes facilities, equipment, and materials to facilitate child and staff learning and development.

Program Standard 10—Leadership and Management

The program effectively implements policies, procedures, and systems in support of stable staff, and strong personnel, fiscal and program management so that all children, families, and staff have high-quality experiences.

When the director feels the center is ready, an on-site validation visit should be requested. One or more assessors appointed by the academy may visit a site. The purpose of the visit is to verify that the self-study report accurately describes the daily operations of the center. Assessors meet with the director, observe in classrooms, and interview staff. At the end of the visit, assessors and the director meet to discuss the results of the validation. At this time, the director can submit additional information concerning any nonvalidated criteria.

The final step involves an accreditation commission consisting of three to five people chosen from a diverse group of early childhood professionals. The commission reviews the information provided by assessors and can decide to grant accreditation, or to defer it until further improvements are made. If deferment is decided, reasons are given for deferment and specific recommendations are made. Deferred centers can appeal, and if there is just cause, another commission will be assigned. Accreditation is valid for five years. During this time, centers must submit annual reports. Before expiration, centers must repeat the evaluation process.

Those who have already been involved in the accreditation process report that the expense and time involved are worthwhile. Directors indicate the improvement in staff development, in morale, and in communication among staff members. Parents seem to feel a greater sense of trust in the school after having been involved in the accreditation process. Sometimes, accreditation is used as a selling point for funding requests. Even if a school already has a high-quality program, accreditation can help to achieve recognition in the community.

Information about accreditation can be obtained by writing to:

National Academy of Early Childhood Programs
1509 16th Street, NW
Washington, DC 20036–1426
800-424-2460
202-328-2601
fax 202-328-1846

e-mail NAEYC@naeyc.org
Website http://www.naeyc.org

In addition to the accreditation system developed by NAEYC, there are other rating scales that can be used to assess the environment of group programs. The Early Childhood Environment Rating Scale is a self-assessment tool for groups serving two- to five-year-olds developed by Thelma Harms and Richard M. Clifford from the Frank Porter Graham Child Development Center at the University of North Carolina at Chapel Hill. The scale assesses seven areas of a program's functioning: (1) personal care routines of children, (2) furnishings and displays for children, (3) language reasoning experiences, (4) fine and gross motor activities, (5) creative activities, (6) social development, and (7) adult needs. The result is expressed in quantitative terms that can be used to summarize the process.

Information about this tool can be obtained at the following address.

Early Childhood Environment Rating Scale by Thelma Harms and
Richard M. Clifford
Teachers College Press
1234 Amsterdam Avenue
New York, NY 10027
212-678-3929

http://www.teacherscollegepress.com

Harms and Clifford have also developed a rating scale targeted primarily for programs serving infants to three-year-olds. Information about this tool can be obtained from:

Infant/Toddler Environment Rating Scale by Thelma Harms, Debby Cryer, and Richard M. Clifford
Frank Porter Graham Child Development Center
The University of North Carolina at Chapel Hill
Campus Box 8180
105 Smith Level Road
Chapel Hill, NC 27599–8180
919-966-2622

http://www.fpg.unc.edu

ACCREDITATION OF TEACHERS AND CAREGIVERS

Upgrading the quality of programs can also occur by credentialing teachers and caregivers. The **Child Development Associate (CDA)** credential is a nationally recognized credential for early childhood personnel. It is based on the achievement of a series of competencies and is available to those who work in centers or in family day-care homes.

The model curriculum designed by the Council for Early Childhood Professional Recognition contains a set of goals and a series of graduated experiences that lead to the achievement of those goals. The goals are:

1. to establish and maintain a safe, healthy, learning environment
2. to advance physical and intellectual competence
3. to support social and emotional development and provide guidance
4. to establish positive and productive relationships with families
5. to ensure a well-run, purposeful program responsive to participant needs
6. to maintain a commitment to professionalism

The graduated experiences are achieved through three phases of work. Phase I is fieldwork in which the students participate in the daily activities of a program. They follow written materials prepared by the council that include readings and exercises to help the candidate build skills. An early childhood professional guides and advises the student through hands-on experiences with children.

During Phase II of the program, students attend courses or seminars offered through local college, university, or other postsecondary educational institutions. The instructional curriculum covers the basic components of early childhood education, but the institutions may supplement the curriculum with their own resources. Students are encouraged to relate their in-class information to their field experiences.

Phase III is directed toward integration and evaluation of the student's experiences. During this period, the student returns to working with children and simultaneously completes a series of exercises. Council-written materials contain a performance-based assessment of the student's achievement. The last step in the process is a series of interviews with a council representative in which all documents submitted by the candidate are reviewed. If the representative's assessment is favorable, the candidate receives a CDA credential, which is valid for life.

For more information about the CDA credential, contact:

Council for Professional Recognition
2460 16th Street, NW
Washington, DC 2009-3575
202-265-9090
800-424-4310
fax 202-265-9161

http://www.cdacouncil.org

INCREASED PAY FOR CHILD-CARE PROFESSIONALS

One way to increase the quality of child-care programs is to have educated teachers who understand child development and know how to work with children in groups. Unfortunately, the pay level of the average caregiver is very low. In 2006 the U.S. Bureau of Labor Statistics-Office of Occupational Statistics and Employment Projections, Washington, DC, reported that the average annual salary for preschool teachers, except special education was $22,120. The average annual salary of preschool and child care center/program administrators was $37,270. No director can run a high-quality program when there is a constant need to find and retrain staff.

SOURCE: www.bls.gov/oco/cg/cgs032.htm

The National Center for the Early Childhood Work Force launched a Worthy Wage Campaign in 1994 to improve the economic status of teachers. Their plan was to rally governmental representatives and to showcase the issue using media resources and personalities. Others have also raised public awareness of the need for improved working conditions for child-care staff. NAEYC has long been an advocate of well-trained and well-paid teachers. An editorial in *Young Children* (NAEYC, 1997) listed six things directors can do to improve staff compensation and quality.

1. "Use your annual operating budget as a working tool. Most decisions have budgetary implications." Directors should learn to read line items in the budget and track expenses for each category. There are usually alternative spending choices that could increase the amount of money available for salaries.

2. "Recognize that budget is policy: be actively involved in the development of the annual budget." The director should question items in the budget and give a rationale for any proposed changes, especially including any that would increase quality.

3. "Get support from a financial analyst or business administrator when necessary." Using a cost analysis, there may be ways to eliminate items that are not proving cost effective.

4. "Polish your leadership and negotiating skills to effectively guide the budget development process." In order to guide others into making changes, the director needs to have skills as a leader.

5. "Don't forget strong human resources skills in working with staff." Effective leaders provide support to staff, but they also support autonomy and demand a high level of professionalism.

6. "Make sure your program offers a career ladder." When staff members have equal opportunities to move up a career ladder, there will be lower turnover. Each person will know that with increased education and competency, a higher salary bracket exists.

Child Abuse

Press coverage frequently highlights sensational cases of child abuse, both in child-care centers and within families, but many more incidents go undetected or unreported. Those that occur in centers are sometimes the result of poor quality control. Prevention should be a primary concern of every director and can be achieved by choosing the very best staff members, planning training sessions, and adequately supervising all employees. The director is responsible for ensuring that everything possible is done to prevent abuse in the child-care setting and for informing staff of the laws pertaining to reporting.

All states have laws relating to **child abuse**. These are designed to protect both children and adults who care for children. The laws for each state can be found by contacting the attorney general's office.

Several categories of abuse are recognized.

- Physical abuse: a child is physically injured by other than accidental means. Severe corporal punishment may be classified as abuse.

- Physical neglect: failure to provide a child with adequate food, shelter, clothing, protection, supervision, and medical or dental care.

- Emotional abuse: excessive verbal assaults, continuous negative responses, and constant family discord may add up to emotional abuse. These cases are extremely difficult to prove and to prosecute.

- Emotional deprivation: deprivation suffered by children when their parents fail to supply normal experiences that help children to feel loved, wanted, and secure.

- Sexual abuse and exploitation: any sexual activity between an adult and child. When the activity occurs between blood-related relatives, it is called incest. Included in sexual abuse is the use of children for making pornographic photos or films.

CAUSES OF CHILD ABUSE

Although it is often believed that most child abusers are poor, uneducated, or emotionally disturbed, this is not true. Studies show that only 1 in 10 abusers can be classified as "disturbed." Most abusers are not very different from any other parents. They love their children and want what is best for them, but something happens to trigger abuse.

According to several studies, adults are more likely to abuse children when the following factors exist:

- They were abused as children themselves.
- They are young—abuse is more frequent when the parents are under age 20.
- They are isolated from others, with few friends or nearby relatives.
- They are victims or perpetrators of spousal abuse.
- They use drugs or are alcoholics.
- They have experienced stress caused by family problems, divorce, loss of a job, or unwanted pregnancy.
- They live in crowded conditions, with little privacy.

- They have low self-esteem.
- They have difficulty controlling anger.
- They have unrealistic expectations for children's behaviors.

RECOGNITION OF ABUSE

Both parents and early childhood professionals must learn to recognize the signs of abuse. Because the idea of any kind of mistreatment of children is so repugnant, there is a tendency to overlook the indications. However, children say and do things that should warn us. Often, though, it is only after abuse is finally recognized that we can look back and say, "Yes, I did see some things that made me wonder." All staff members should be familiar with signs that may indicate a child has been physically, emotionally, or sexually abused. Parent education programs should provide the same kinds of information to parents.

The state attorney general's office or licensing agency can probably supply information about what might be suspicious. If not, the following summary should be helpful.

PHYSICAL ABUSE

Physical abuse might be suspected when the following injuries are seen on a child:

- Burns: burns in places that would not be expected as the result of accident (e.g., buttocks, shoulder blades, abdomen).
- Linear marks: wraparound marks made by a strap, belt, or electrical cord.
- Bruises: multiple bruises with different colors indicating various stages of healing, bruises on many parts of the body including the genitals.
- Lacerations: multiple wounds or locations of wounds in unexpected places. Mouth lacerations, for instance, may indicate a bottle nipple has been jammed into the baby's mouth.
- Fractures: any fracture in an infant under 12 months should be suspect.

FYI

One of the most important grounds for further investigation is when a child says "My daddy hurt me" or "My mommy spanks me with a belt." The caregiver should take what the child says seriously.

Over 900,000 children were confirmed as victims of child abuse and neglect in 1998. The highest number were in African-American and Native-American families. Almost 40 percent of victims were under the age of six; infants represent the largest proportion. Domestic violence is also found in 60 percent of families where child abuse occurs.

SOURCE: Children's Defense Fund. (2000). Retrieved from the Internet, 2006 at http://www.childrensdefense.org (2002)

PHYSICAL NEGLECT

Physical neglect can be suspected when:

- there are unsanitary conditions in the home or child-care site
- there is inadequate heat or there are potentially unsafe conditions
- food is inadequate or not sufficiently nutritious
- the child lacks proper clothing for the weather, or clothing is unclean
- the child lacks proper medical or dental care
- a young child is left at home or unsupervised for any period of time

EMOTIONAL ABUSE

Although some signs of emotional abuse are the kinds of behavior occasionally seen in all children, the extent, the frequency, or the duration of the behavior should alert an observer. Abuse might be suspected if any of the following behaviors continue for a long period of time or are the only ways that a child behaves.

- The child is withdrawn, depressed, or apathetic.
- The child "acts out" or is often disruptive.
- The child is overly rigid, is afraid to misbehave, or fails to do what is expected.
- The child shows signs of emotional disturbance such as repetitive movements, or lack of verbal or physical communication with others.

Children sometimes reveal emotional abuse when they comment on their own behavior. They may say "My mommy tells me I'm bad" or "My daddy says I can't do anything right." It is important to listen and take the child seriously.

EMOTIONAL DEPRIVATION

Emotional deprivation is the most difficult to judge, but should be suspected if the following behaviors are observed.

- The child refuses to eat, or eats very little.
- The child is not able to do things that would be expected of the age level—for example, walking or talking.
- The child may have exaggerated fears.
- The child is frequently aggressive or shows other antisocial behaviors.
- The child is abnormally withdrawn or sad, or does not respond to others.
- The child constantly seeks attention from any adult, even strangers who come into the school.

SEXUAL ABUSE

Children go through periods of being curious about their own bodies and those of others. They have times when they masturbate or ask about how you get babies. Teachers and parents are often embarrassed by this behavior. They do not want to see or hear it. As a result, signs of sexual molestation sometimes go completely unrecognized. Children, too, learn to be secretive about what happens to them when they see how others react.

Additionally, abusers often frighten children by telling them that terrible things will happen to them if they tell anyone.

Sexual abuse can remain hidden for a long time. It should be suspected, though, if the following signs are evident:

- The child has bruising or inflammation of the anus or the genitals.
- There is a discharge or blood in the child's underwear.
- The child has unusual interest and awareness of sexual activities. Sometimes young children play out sexual scenes in the dramatic play area.
- The child is particularly seductive with adults, touching their breast or genitals.
- The child seems fearful of an adult or is afraid to talk about that adult.
- The child is the victim of other kinds of abuse.

Children probably least often reveal sexual abuse by talking about it. They may not even have the words to express to others what has been done to them. If they have been threatened by the abuser, they will be even more reluctant to tell their secrets. Responsive adults who are willing to let children reveal their stories in their own way can find out a great deal.

WHEN TO REPORT ABUSE

Teachers and others who have close contact with children are in a unique position to recognize signs of abuse. Therefore, they are legally mandated to report suspected incidents. They are not required to prove abuse and, if none is found, are protected from any retribution. Conversely, if mandated individuals know of abuse and fail to report it, they may be liable for fines or imprisonment.

The law is clear, but the moral dilemma facing a teacher who suspects abuse is not always clear. Suspicion of abuse can be extremely upsetting for parents or for school personnel. The normal reaction is to become angry, to feel guilt, or to want the perpetrator to be punished immediately. Everyone involved must remain calm. When adults overreact, harm to the child may be intensified. The opposite reaction may also occur. Adults can convince themselves that they must have been wrong, that nothing really happened. Nothing is done, and that may lead to continued harm to the child.

So how do teachers and caregivers know when to report? They should not report every time they see some signs of disturbance in children. Many times that is normal, transitory behavior. They should report when they have enough evidence to convince themselves that there is reasonable suspicion to warrant further investigation. If there are signs that a child's life may be in danger, it must be reported immediately.

When there are any of the signs listed in the previous section, the teacher or caregiver should make a record. They should write down what they observed, what the child said, or what the parent said. If they see bruises, burns, or lacerations on a child, they should take a picture of them. Photographs can be taken without the parents' consent as long as they are not used for any other purpose.

If there are injuries that do not quite meet the usual criteria for abuse, keeping a record is still important. Over time, it may become apparent that the same kinds of injuries keep recurring. A pattern of abuse may emerge that can be reported.

In cases of uncertainty, it helps to talk to other professionals. Teachers should talk to their director; directors can corroborate the teachers' observations. Child abuse agencies or hotlines in the area might also be helpful. They can often help to sort out impressions. The child protective agency in an area can help as well. Workers there can often clarify whether there is a reportable offense.

When ready to report, the director or teacher should telephone the local child protective services, the sheriff's department, or the police department. The following information will probably be needed:

- child's name, address, and age
- where the child is at the present time
- observations and descriptions of injuries
- information that led the director or teacher to believe abuse has occurred
- parents' names, address

If the child is in immediate danger, it is important to make that clear to the person who is taking the report. It may be necessary to follow the verbal report with a written report within a specified period. Forms for the report will be available from law enforcement or protective services agencies.

Many teachers and directors ask whether they should tell the parents about the report. Opinions vary and some states require them to do so. If someone other than the parents is the abuser, the parents may be relieved that the abuse has been discovered. They will welcome the support and concern for their child. If one of the parents is the abuser, the person reporting the abuse is likely to be the target of tremendous anger. Denial may also occur initially, and even accusations that the abuse occurred at school, not at home, may be made. The parents may immediately withdraw the child from the school. The director should be prepared for any of these reactions.

The discovery of abuse is a traumatic experience for parents, teachers, and child. The director will have to remain calm and sympathetic. It may lessen the trauma for everyone involved. The child will need to know that others understand and will be supportive. Whether the parents are the abusers, they, too, need to have support through this experience. Additionally, the director can see that the family gets support from others in the medical, legal, and child advocacy systems.

Staff members will probably need help in dealing with the abuse. They must be cautioned to respect the privacy of the child and family. Information about the abuse should never be discussed with anyone not directly involved in the incident. They should try not to be judgmental toward the parents.

Staff may also need an opportunity to talk about their own feelings of anger or guilt. If the child remains in the school, staff may react by being overprotective. They should be cautioned that the child will recover more quickly if helped to follow regular routines. Sensitive handling of an abuse situation will help everyone involved to recover.

Unfortunately, because of the upheaval discovery causes, a large number of child abuse cases never get reported. The director should encourage staff to see that it is their moral, as well as legal, obligation to protect children. When cases are not reported, there is the possibility that other children will be victimized.

ABUSE ALLEGATIONS AT SCHOOL

Some directors are faced with having one of their staff members accused of abuse. Reports may come from parents or from other staff members. If the report first goes to the licensing agency, it will be referred to the police department. If the police department receives the first complaint, they will report to the licensing agency.

The two agencies will work together to complete an investigation of the report. The staff member should receive appropriate legal representation before being interviewed by the police. Although no one is required to answer questions, cooperation is best. Thus, a quicker resolution to the problem can occur.

PREVENTION

Schools can play a vital role in the prevention of abuse.

First, directors can do much to lessen the possibility of abuse by staff members by:

- developing hiring procedures that carefully screen applicants—most states require a fingerprint check
- checking the person's references carefully
- planning and implementing in-service training for new employees, and ongoing staff development for others
- adequately supervising staff and pairing new employees with experienced ones
- holding regular staff meetings to discuss problems with children and parents, or among staff members
- developing clear personnel policies regarding methods of disciplining children
- allowing staff members the means for alleviating fatigue and burnout (e.g., adequate breaks, reasonable staff/child ratios, adequate salaries, positive reinforcement)

Second, a school and its staff can be extremely effective in helping parents manage the stresses of parenthood that might lead to abuse. Teachers and caregivers can:

- become part of an "extended family" that provides support
- educate parents about what to expect of children at different age levels
- act as models to help parents find more effective ways of interacting with their children
- provide an outlet for parents to express some of the frustrations of parenting
- share with parents the joys of watching children grow and change

Third, much can be done to lessen the chances of misunderstandings that lead to accusations of abuse at school. The director should:

- educate parents about child abuse—what causes it, signs that may indicate abuse
- establish an open-door policy and welcome parents' visits at any time, without an appointment
- share the schools' discipline policies with parents
- establish a caring relationship with parents by listening to their concerns and answering their questions

Fourth, teachers and caregivers can educate children about what is and what is not acceptable behavior between an adult and a child. From as early as 18 months, children can learn about body parts. Older children, age three to five, can learn which body parts are unacceptable for others to touch. Additionally, children should be encouraged to say "no" to an adult when they feel uncomfortable about any bodily contact. Lastly, they should be encouraged to tell an adult when they have had an encounter with someone that made them uneasy.

Prevention of child abuse is certainly a preferred tactic to reporting and punishing abuse. As more children are in group settings at earlier ages, the role of the school becomes vital to prevention. Directors, staff, and parents must be educated. Although there is no sure deterrent for child abuse, the knowledge and skills of those who care for children can help.

Laws and Issues Pertaining to Child-Care Settings

The following sections discuss some of the laws and issues important to directors of child-care programs. However, the scope of this book cannot thoroughly address every geographical area. Therefore, the reader should seek further information from the agencies or websites listed in this chapter.

REDUCING YOUR LIABILITIES AS A CHILD-CARE PROVIDER

Directors should:

- have knowledge of children's legal rights.
- develop a self-protection checklist to help reduce risks.
- comply with regulation rules.
- follow their own policies.
- screen parents before enrollment.
- communicate regularly with parents.
- screen assistant staff members.
- follow business practices: obtain medical release forms, field-trip permissions, and parent evaluations.
- report child abuse or neglect: communicate with regulators.
- get insurance to protect themselves from major risks: homeowners, business property, business liability, car, medical savings accounts and medical reimbursement plans, disability, workmen's compensation, long-term care, umbrella liability, and life.
- be aware of such legal issues as custody disputes, child abuse, and price fixing.
- understand contract issues such as late fees, termination procedures, enforcement, and the effect of the Americans with Disabilities Act.

CHILDREN'S LEGAL RIGHTS

Children have legal rights to be protected from such unlawful circumstances as:

- discrimination.
- abuse and neglect.
- personal injury.
- wrongful death.
- product liability.
- premises liability.

PERSONNEL POLICIES

Good personnel policies, as discussed in Chapter 8, are necessary to ensure the smooth operation of a school. Additionally, the following federal laws are some of those that cover certain personnel procedures.

- The Equal Pay Act of 1963 requires equal pay for men and women performing similar work.
- The Fair Labor Standards Act of 1938 (1972 Amendment) sets minimum wage, equal pay, and record keeping requirements.
- The Civil Rights Act of 1964—Title VII (amended in 1972) prohibits discrimination because of sex, race, color, religion, or national origin.
- The Rehabilitation Act of 1973 prohibits job discrimination because of a disability. It further requires affirmative action to hire and advance workers with disabilities.
- The Vietnam Era Veteran's Readjustment Assistance Act of 1974 prohibits job discrimination and requires affirmative action to hire and advance qualified Vietnam veterans.
- Executive Orders 11246 and 11375 require an affirmative action program for all federal contractors and subcontractors whose contract exceeds $10,000.
- The Age Discrimination Act of 1967 (amended in 1978) prohibits discrimination against people 40 to 70 years of age in hiring practices for any employment.
- The Family Medical Leave Act of 1993 entitles employees to 12 weeks of unpaid leave during a 12-month period. It can be used for the birth or adoption of a child, to care for a family member, or when the employee cannot work because of a medical problem. The employer must maintain existing medical coverage and reinstate the employee when ready to return to work.

SALARY PROCEDURES

Some laws require or prohibit certain procedures related to employee salaries.

- The Federal Wage Garnishment Law restricts the amount of an employee's wages that may be deducted in one week for garnishment procedures. It further restricts the amount that can be deducted when an employee is discharged because of garnishment.
- The Social Security Act of 1935 and the Federal Insurance Contributions Act provide for retirement, disability, burial, and survivor benefits to eligible employees. They require deductions from salary plus matching contribution from the employer.
- The Federal Income Tax Withholding law requires the employer to collect employees' income tax and deposit it in a federal depository. Failure to comply with this law is a criminal offense.

ON-THE-JOB SAFETY

Federal law regulates any conditions that might affect the safety and health of employees.

- The Occupational Safety and Health Act of 1970 requires employers to maintain a safe and healthful work environment, comply with all occupational safety and health standards, keep Material Safety Data Sheets in a conspicuous place, and provide employees with training in safe work practices.

For further information, visit http://www.osha.gov.

- Most states require employers to carry workmen's compensation insurance to ensure injured workers will receive necessary medical care and be compensated for loss of income.

SOURCES OF INFORMATION

More information regarding laws that may affect a school can be obtained by writing to or telephoning the following:

U.S. Equal Employment Opportunity Commission
1801 L Street, NW
Washington, DC 20507
1-800-669-4000
info@eeoc.gov

Employment Standards Administration
Office of Federal Contract Compliance Program
200 Constitution Avenue, NW
Washington, DC 20210
1-866-4-USA-DOL

United States Government—Social Security Administration
10 North Jefferson Street
Frederick, MD 21701
301-462-6765
www.ssa.gov

U.S. Department of Labor
Occupational Safety and Health Administration
Frances Perkins Building
200 Constitution Avenue, NW
Washington, DC 20210
866-4-USA-DOL

California Chamber of Commerce
1215K Street, Suite 1400
Sacramento, CA 95814
916-444-6670

POSTING EMPLOYEE INFORMATION

Certain information must be posted in conspicuous places used by employees. Both federal and state laws govern the necessary kinds of information. An attorney can provide advice for compliance within a particular state. Federal laws require the following:

- minimum wage and maximum hours: obtain from U.S. Department of Labor, Wage and Hours Division

- equal employment regulations: obtain from nearest branch of Federal Equal Employment Opportunity Commission
- age discrimination laws: obtain from nearest branch of Federal Equal Employment Opportunity Commission
- annual summary of specified injuries and illnesses: obtain from U.S. Department of Labor, Occupational Safety and Health Administration
- fire prevention and evacuation plan
- safety and health protection on the job

HOW TO CHOOSE A BUSINESS LIABILITY INSURANCE POLICY

Not all liability insurance policies are the same. To evaluate your choices among policies, use the following checklist:

- General liability coverage for accidents and lawsuits against your business. Your policy will have limits on occurrence coverage (the amount the policy will pay per accident) and aggregate coverage (the amount the policy will pay over the life of the policy—usually one year). Ideally you want a policy limit to be at least $1 million occurrence and $2 million aggregate.
- Professional liability coverage to protect yourself in case you failed to supervise the children in your care adequately.
- Legal defense in which the limits of this coverage are in excess of the general liability limits. In other words, you do not want legal fees to reduce your policy limits.
- Sexual abuse coverage with separate liability limits that cover you, your family, and your employees.
- Medical ("no fault") coverage to cover expenses when children are injured. You do not want parents to have to look for coverage from their insurance first.
- Coverage for accidents when you are away from your facility with the children.
- Renters want the ability to list their landlord as an "additional insured."
- The policy should be an "occurrence form," not a "claims-made" policy. An occurrence covers you as long as the injury occurred while you were insured, even if you are sued many years later. A claims-made policy only covers you if you are sued when you are insured.
- The policy covers you for all the hours that children are present in your facility.
- The policy should cover food illnesses and dispensing machines.
- The company should have at least an "A" rating from the Best Company.

You may not be able to get a policy that has all the features identified in this checklist. Try to choose a policy that offers the most coverage. Purchase as much insurance as you can afford. The cost of business liability insurance is 100 percent deductible.

CASE STUDY

Julia was in her first year as director of a child-care center. She was feeling overwhelmed by staffing issues, parent concerns, and curriculum implementation. Reva, a teacher in the four-year-old program, came to her to express a concern about a child. She suspected Dylan was being neglected by his parents. Dylan was rarely bathed and often came to the center in soiled clothes. Additionally, he had bruises on the inner side of his arms and on his upper thighs. Julia asked Reva to document the information and "keep an eye out" for further incidents. Reva left the director's office unsatisfied. As a mandated reporter, she thought that she should report this information to Child Protective Services (CPS). She kept notes as she was asked and continued to keep a watchful eye on Dylan.

Two weeks later, Dylan arrived at the center with a large bruise on his face. Reva asked him what had happened. His response was, "My dad got mad at me and pushed me. I fell down on the stairs, but he said sorry, then I went to bed."

Reva related this to Julia and they telephoned CPS to report the incident. The agency contacted Dylan's family. They vehemently denied any wrongdoing and were angered about the report. The family withdrew from the center immediately and did not even honor the two-week notice required in their contract.

1. How would you handle this situation if you were the director? The teacher?
2. When do you think that this family should have been reported? Could this situation have been handled differently? How?

SUMMARY

One way to upgrade the quality of programs is through accreditation, a process initiated by the National Academy of Early Childhood Programs. The voluntary process consists of self-study, a visit by a professional team, and a written evaluation.

Quality is also enhanced when teachers and caregivers have knowledge of how to further children's development. The Council for Early Childhood Professional Recognition offers a Child Development Associate credential to students who finish a three-phase program. Graduated experiences take students through fieldwork, seminars, and written materials to assess achievement. A council representative also interviews students and reviews all documents submitted by the candidate.

Increased pay for child-care professionals will also upgrade the quality of programs. When pay is low, educated teachers move on to higher-paying jobs, causing frequent turnover. The National Center for the Early Childhood Work Force and NAEYC have long been advocates for improved working conditions for child-care staff.

Prominent press coverage has highlighted child abuse. Abuse can be of several kinds: physical abuse and neglect, emotional abuse and deprivation, or sexual exploitation. There are many causes.

Certain physical or emotional results occur after abuse. Teacher and caregivers should be able to recognize each kind. Determining whether to report child abuse is often difficult. Keeping a record is always acceptable and reasonable.

Because much emotion is encountered in child abuse situations, the most consistent attitude to take is one of calm objectivity.

There are proven ways to prevent child abuse in a preschool. The director is responsible for informing the staff of these methods.

Many federal, state, and local laws pertain to child care. There are numerous sources, and most of them are listed here. It is, again, the responsibility of the director to inform the staff and parents of these laws.

It is important for child-care operators and directors to ensure that they are fully covered by insurance.

STUDENT ACTIVITIES

1. Schedule a visit to an accredited center in your community and an interview with the director. Ask the director to describe the accreditation experience and its effect on staff and parents. Was it a positive experience? What changes were undertaken as a result?

2. Write a short paper on child abuse. Focus on whether media coverage of high-visibility cases has changed attitudes of early childhood personnel. Are they more cautious about how they interact with children? Are they more aware of the signs of abuse in children in their care?

3. Visit an agency in your community that works with families where abuse has occurred. What is the agency doing to help families?

REVIEW

1. Accreditation involves a three-step process. What are the steps?

2. What is the Child Development Associate credential?

3. List the three phases of the CDA program and briefly describe each.

4. According to an editorial in *Young Children*, what are the six things directors can do to improve staff compensation and quality?

5. What are six measures a director can take to prevent child abuse by staff members?

6. What are the causes of child abuse?

7. List the five kinds of child abuse.

8. Describe the procedures for reporting child abuse.

9. Discuss the role of a school in preventing abuse.

10. Name and describe three federal laws that pertain to employees in child-care centers.

REFERENCES

National Association for the Education of Young Children. (1997). *Quality, compensation, and affordability. Six things directors can do to improve staff compensation and quality.* Washington, DC: Author.

National Association for the Education of Young Children, Special Research Report. (1995). Cost, quality, and child outcomes in child care centers: Key findings and recommendations. *Young Children, 50*(4), 41–45.

National Center for the Early Childhood Work Force. (1993). *Worthy wage campaign 1994 action packet.* Oakland, CA: Author.

Whitebook, M. C., Phillips, D., & Howes, C. (1993). *The national child care staffing study revisited.* Oakland, CA: Child Care Employee Project.

SELECTED FURTHER READING

ABT Associates Inc. (2000). The cost, quality and child outcomes study: A critique. Retrieved from Internet, April 2009 at http://www.abtassociates.com.

Morgan, G. (1983). Child day care policy in chaos. In E. Zigler, S. Kagan, & E. Klugman, (Eds.). *Children, families, and government: Perspectives on American social policy* (pp. 249–265). New York: Cambridge University Press.

National Association for the Education of Young Children. (2005). *Early childhood program standards and accreditation criteria: The mark of quality in early childhood education.* Washington, DC: Author.

Phillips, C. B. (1990). The child development associate program: Entering a new era. *Young Children, 45*(3), 24–27.

Pizzo, R. D. (1993). Parent empowerment and child care regulation. *Young Children, 48*(6), 9–12.

U.S. Bureau of Labor Statistics Office of Occupational Statistics and Employment Projections.(2006). Washington, DC. Retrieved from the Internet 2009 at www.bls.gov/oco/cg/cgs032.htm

HELPFUL WEBSITES

Disclaimer: Links to Internet sites throughout this book are provided for your convenience and do not constitute an endorsement.

U.S. Department of Labor. Various information regarding employment:	**http://www.dol.gov**
Job Accommodation Network, a service of U.S. Office of Disability Employment Policy:	**http://www.jan.wvu.edu**
National Academy of Early Childhood Programs:	**http://www.naeyc.org**
U.S. Department of Health and Human Services:	**http://www.dhhs.gov**
U.S. Equal Employment Opportunity Commission (information regarding interplay of ADA and FMLA):	**http://www.eeoc.gov**

TELEPHONE NUMBERS FOR ADDITIONAL HELP

U.S. Department of Justice operates an ADA Information Line. Specialists are available to answer general and technical questions during business hours. There is an automated 24-hour service for ordering ADA materials and an automated fax-back system that delivers technical assistance materials to fax machines or modems.

800-514-0301 (voice)
800-514-0383 (TDD)

For additional resources related to administration including videos, links to related sites for each chapter of the text, tutorial quizzes, glossary flashcards, and more, visit the Education CourseMate website for this book at www.cengage.com/login.

APPENDIX

A Computerized Data Management

In order to update this appendix, every software developer was contacted. Those who appeared in the previous edition of this text were sent a copy of the write-up and asked if they wished to revise it. Therefore, many of the descriptions are in the words of the developers. They are not meant to be an endorsement by the authors of this text. Additionally, no attempt has been made to evaluate programs because each user may have different needs, computer software, and technical expertise.

Administrative Management Computer Software

CHILDCARE MANAGER PROFESSIONAL EDITION

The Professional Edition offers a full-featured, child-care management and accounting program that gives you everything you need to run your business in one program and at one low price. With Childcare Manager Professional you get a complete contact management system to track your family, child, employee, and agency information. You also get a complete accounting package with everything you'll need to manage your center's finances.

CHILDCARE MANAGER STANDARD EDITION

The Standard Edition of Childcare Manager is designed for child-care administrators who use QuickBooks 2002 or 2003 (Pro, Premiere, or Enterprise Editions) for their general accounting needs. Childcare Manager complements QuickBooks by providing a complete system for tracking family, child, other payer (agency), and employee information. In addition, Childcare Manager provides billing and revenue management features unique to child care. These features let you link charges to children, create individual due dates, and perform weekly and monthly billings in a matter of seconds. Add Childcare Manager Standard to QuickBooks and you will have everything you need to run your center in one system (contact management, accounting, payroll) and at a price far below other systems. College and university administrators can receive a free copy of Childcare Manager to use in their classrooms by contacting:

PERSONALIZED SOFTWARE, INC.
118 S. Main Street
Phoenix, OR 97535-0359
800-553-2312
Fax 541-535-8889

http://www.childcaremanager.com
e-mail: info@childcaremanager.com

Source: Reprinted by permission of Personalized Software, Inc.

ACCUTRAK

AccuTrak is an automated claims management system for sponsors of the Child and Adult Care Food Program and has recently been rewritten as a web application at www.CACFP. Net. Family child-care providers who wish to receive reimbursements for meals served have two methods to submit their claims. Providers can go to the website and enter their current claim information, or they can complete special optical mark recognition (OMR, or "bubble" forms) for children in attendance and menu items served. These forms are then scanned into the computer using an OMR scanner.

Provider claim data is analyzed for compliance with USDA regulation, and meals are totaled by tier for various reports. The system can print reimbursement checks, create direct deposit files, or create files to interface with sponsor's accounting system.

Recent enhancements to the system analyze provider claims for possible fraud situations looking specifically for "block claiming." AccuTrak has been in production since 1998, and CACFP.Net has been in production for three years. Available from:

THE ACCUTRAK GROUP LLC
5376 Temple Court
Madison, WI 53705
608-233-7841

http://www.CACFP.Net
e-mail: Info@CACFP.Net

Source: Reprinted by permission of AccuTrak 2000 Software.

CHILDPLUS SOFTWARE

ChildPlus software is comprehensive management software for publicly funded child development programs such as Head Start, pre-kindergarten, and sponsored child-care centers. ChildPlus software provides program managers with simple day-to-day procedures, executive monitoring reports, priority enrollment lists, and special critical indicator analyses to assess how well the program is doing. The following modules are included in the software: child outcome measure, child health and disabilities, educational development, attendance, family services, parent education and training, parent involvement, parent and state billing, and administrative procedures. The software generates over 500 standard programmatic reports including application procedures, health and dental, immunization, treatment, disability, transportation, child–adult care food program, enrollment, family services, home visit, and demographic reports. ChildPlus is designed for program staff with little or no computer knowledge. Available from:

CHILDPLUS SOFTWARE
1117 Perimeter Center West, Suite W300
Atlanta, GA 30338
800-888-6674
Fax 404-252-7337

http://www.childplus.com
e-mail: support@childplus.com

Source: Reprinted by permission of ChildPlus Software.

CONTROLTEC™

Controltec is a custom systems software development and Internet business company with specific expertise in providing solutions to agencies serving children and families. Controltec's suite of products for the child-care market consists of KinderTrack™, a full subsidy management system; KinderWait™, an Internet-based waiting list for agencies servicing subsidized families; and KinderAttend™, an integrated system for paperless attendance tracking and accurate subsidy payment processing. Our newest products are SchoolAttend™, HEAPTrack, and CenterTrack. Schools and child-care agencies using SchoolAttend log in to a secured website to access their attendance data. Information tracked includes in and out times as well as meals and snacks. HEAPTrack is an Internet-based Home Energy Assistance Program that enables agencies to automatically authorize emergency energy subsidies to needy families living in cold weather areas. CenterTrack, currently being developed, is an Internet-based application that manages all facets of center-based operations. Besides offering software solutions, Controltec has extensive experience as a software systems and integration consulting firm. In this capacity, Controltec has worked with social services staff at the agency, county, and state levels. Controltec is committed to becoming the premier supplier of software solutions to the child-care subsidy market and related industries at the national level. Controltec can be contacted at:

CONTROLTEC
613 W Valley Parkway Suite 345
Escondido, CA 92025-2515
800-991-6120
760-975-9750
Fax 760-723-5255

http://www.controltec.com
e-mail: info@controltec.com

Source: Reprinted by permission of Controltec, Inc.

EZ-CARE2 CENTER MANAGEMENT SOFTWARE

Easy to learn, flexible and fast, EZ-CARE2 provides a complete center management solution. Some of EZ-CARE2's many advantages include:

- completely customizable screens for managing enrollment, staffing, and other center data
- powerful medical and immunization management
- flexible scheduling and billing options
- third-party subsidizer billing
- automatic electronic fee collection by credit card and bank draft
- easy-to-use custom reporting tools with complete control of sorting and selecting
- multisite management features
- time-clock for child and staff attendance with optional door release
- integrated accounting for QuickBooks® Interface
- Web registration system

Available from:

SofterWare, Inc.
132 Welsh Road Suite 140
Horsham, PA 19044-2217
212-628-0400

http://www.ezcare2.com/book

Source: Reprinted by permission of SofterWare, Inc.

KIDSCARE FOR WINDOWS™

KidsCare is a powerful, easy-to-use program that provides child-care professionals with all the tools necessary for successful, efficient management in one integrated system. It allows you to control the daily affairs of a center, minimizing the amount of time spent on paperwork, as well as providing you with the ability to increase the center's efficiency and profitability. KidsCare is appropriate for any size child-care operation and provides the flexibility to track all of your center's critical information. The software includes everything needed to manage enrollment, control receivables, analyze center profitability, project future enrollment, increase revenue, and minimize staffing costs. Its unique e-mail capabilities allow you to send messages and/or statements to all or selected families. And, over 100 reports give you quick, easy access to all of the information you need for yourself, your teachers, your accountant, or your board of directors. As part of our professional support program, you will receive unlimited EZ-CARE KidsCare for Windows assistance, as well as free product enhancements. New features are being added all the time, such as Staff Development, which allows you to keep track of continuing education credits, certification, and much more. Available from:

KidsCare
132 Welsh Road Suite 140
Horsham, PA 19044-2217

http://www.softerware.com/kidscare
e-mail: kidscare@softerware.com

Source: Reprinted by permission of SofterWare, Inc.

MAGGEY DELUXE FOR WINDOWS™

Maggey Deluxe for Windows contains all of the important data about your parents and children including address and telephone numbers, emergency names and numbers, immunization records, birthdays, and allergies. The menus and toolbar make data entry and retrieval fast and easy. This powerful program automatically calculates and posts tuition charges, maintains client ledgers, tracks accounts receivable, and bills subsidy/third-party sponsors. Detailed weekly financial reports quickly provide you with an analysis of the center's performance. The automatic billing will save hours each week by calculating tuition and posting it to a ledger for each client. Maggey Deluxe for Windows will enable you to closely monitor your center's revenues with accurate billing receipts, deposit summaries, and income reports that can detail billing revenue by classes. WinTime Deluxe is a unique time clock, which features a small keypad linked to your computer. Together with a monitor in the entrance to your center, WinTime Deluxe allows your parents to receive messages from the staff, see their current balance, and clock their children in and out quickly and accurately. Employees can also clock in and out, providing accurate time information for your payroll. Menus Deluxe allows you to create and maintain food menus in cycles up to six weeks long. From an inventory list, you can quickly create and change meal names and food items. Create meal calendars and USDA- compliant worksheets with ease. Paired with WinTime, Menus Deluxe can even print weekly and monthly meal attendance reports that show how many children attended the meal, how many were disallowed according to current USDA reimbursement restrictions, and how many can be claimed. Soon, Maggey Deluxe for Windows will include programs that will print paychecks, payroll detail reports, profit and loss statements, and balance sheets; allow inputting of checking and other cash expenses; and transfer all summary information to other locations or central offices via the Internet. These modules are currently available in Maggey for DOS. For more information and DEMO programs, contact:

CSMC, LTD-MAGGEY SOFTWARE

4633 N 1st Avenue Suite 1
Tucson, AZ 85718
800-462-4439
Fax 520-292-2779

http://www.maggey.com
e-mail: info@maggey.com

Source: Reprinted by permission of CMSC, Ltd., publishers of Maggey Software.

OFFICE CENTER

Windows™

Office Center is both an accounting system and information manager. The Base program is simple in design, yet powerful, and is extremely flexible. Along with a wide variety of built-in accounting and database reports, the user can design reports to accommodate individual needs. Attendance-based charges can be calculated using Office Center's time-clock accounting system. The program generates customer statements, account balance reports, year-end customer summaries, and current deposit reports. It is also possible to record, define, track, sort, and print sign-in and roll call sheets, class and bus schedules, allergy and immunization reports, date-activated future schedules, and family notes. Users may add their own data fields as well as create dozens of their own user-defined reports. The built-in word processing includes data merge, 26 letter templates, and some built-in letters. There are built-in network capabilities, designed for sharing information between computers. A program security system restricts access to information to those designated by the director. Other modules that are available are Payroll and Advances, Accounts Payable, General Ledger, Timeclock Accounting, and USDA Food Program. Available from:

EMERGING TECHNOLOGIES

P.O. Box 1539
Mt. Shasta, CA 96067
800-729-4445

http://www.etwebsite.com

Source: Reprinted by permission of Emerging Technologies.

PRE-SCHOOL PARTNER

Windows

The Pre-School Partner Combo module has been specifically designed for the daily administration of child-care and preschool centers. Its primary goal is to aid the preschool provider in the functions of family and child registration, staff management, providing billing services, collection of receivables, and the tracking of vaccinations. All this plus over 70 family-, child-, and staff-related reports. Single modules can be purchased that will address specific functions. Registration tracks family, child, and staff information and generates lists, work schedules, funding sources, and secular denomination. There are also user-defined fields available for the specific needs of each situation. This module allows the user to store frequently used letters, memos, and facsimiles. There is also a mail-merge capability. Billing permits the user to prepare and print family invoices for child-care and preschool services rendered. Quick Bill is used to print invoices for families that are on fixed recurring charges. Billable services and goods may be preset in order to speed the invoicing process, although predefined descriptions and charges can be changed at invoicing time. Accounts Receivable tracks each family's outstanding balance, and reports can be generated showing monthly activity and year-end analysis. Other modules available include Labels, Rolodex™, Envelopes; USDA Meal Program; Accounts Payable and Check Writer; Bank Reconciliation; and Report Writer. For a complete review of the software, and to download a 45-day free trial version of the program, visit the website listed below.

ON-Q SOFTWARE, INC.
13764 S.W. 11th Street
Miami, FL 33184
305-553-2400
Fax 305-220-2666

http://www.on-qsoftware.com
e-mail: webmaster@on-qsoftware.com

Source: Reprinted by permission of ON-Q Software, Inc.

● ● ● ● ● **PRIVATE ADVANTAGE**

Windows and Macintosh

Private Advantage is specifically designed to meet the demands and needs of large and small preschools, children's centers, and schools with widely varying needs. The software is available in two different versions, each having base features and add-ons. The Professional Series is the most powerful and flexible version. Private Advantage Light offers the basics but is designed for smaller facilities or for home-based programs. The Professional Series features a Client Management module that allows the user to track family and child information, scheduling, a waiting list, medical information, activity management, transportation management, and much more. The module has many reports including sign in/out sheets, birthday reports, attendance sheets, enrollment projections, weekly schedules, Full Time Equivalent (FTE) reports, emergency reports, immunization overdue reports/letters, birthday reports, some California Department of Education (CDE) reporting support, and much more. The Accounts Receivable module features family ledgers, co-family ledgers, agency ledgers, statements and receipts, reoccurring list and activity billing, pay sources tracking, tuition projections, vacation tracking, deposit tape, many useful reports, and more. The program accurately forecasts revenue that will be available for any given date in the future even if children leave the school, switch classes, or change tuitions. The Staff Management module features basic staff information, scheduling, emergency information, document tracking, staff/child ratios, vacation/sick tracking, a contact log, training tracking, and more. The Meal Management module includes monthly meal calendars, eligibility status, flexible menu setup, shopping lists, meal count sheets, production reports, meal attendance reports, meal total reports, and more. The Flexible Scheduling module allows children/staff to have a different schedule for every day of the year, hourly/daily billing, enrollment projections, staff/child ratios, integrated vacation/sick ledgers tracks up to five user-definable items, auto flex billing, and more. The Time Key module acts as a time clock for the capturing of child/staff times, allows messages to be received by the parents/staff, current child/staff ratios, many billing options, "who's here" reports, child time lists and staff time cards, and more. There is a word processing feature that includes letter templates, mail merge, and the inserting of database fields in the letters. The Custom editors allow the creation of custom reports, graphs, labels, and the exporting of information to ASCII files (text files). Available from:

DBA-PRIVATE ADVANTAGE SOFTWARE®
2777 Yulupa Avenue #302
Santa Rosa, CA 95405
800-238-7015
Fax 707-542-1521

http://www.privateadv.com

Source: Reprinted by permission of Mount Taylor Programs.

PROJECT KICKSTART

Windows

Project KickStart is a project-management program for small- to mid-size projects. It is used by child-care administrators to plan projects, create process templates, brainstorm new programs, and to communicate project details to colleagues and vendors. Project KickStart is easy to learn and easy to use. Its eight-step planning wizard provides a framework for brainstorming, planning, and scheduling projects. You'll identify goals, anticipate obstacles, allocate resources, and organize all aspects of your project. Project KickStart is incredibly flexible, accommodating hundreds of tasks and resources per project. By organizing your project step by step, you'll quickly develop a clear overview of the project and what it will take to complete it. Create a simple schedule with Project KickStart's Gantt chart. It shows the start and finish dates and the duration of each task and lets you mark tasks "Done" when completed. Print a variety of reports, to-do lists, and action plans for your staff, volunteers, and vendors. Once you've developed a project in Project KickStart, you can "hot link" to a variety of applications including Microsoft Word, Excel, PowerPoint, Outlook, Project, ACT!, and MindManager. The transfer of data lets you communicate project details in a variety of ways. For example, include your project plan in a proposal or report by linking to Microsoft Word. Create a PowerPoint presentation for parents, staff, or volunteers using Project KickStart's link to PowerPoint. Project KickStart comes with free telephone support and is the perfect combination of ease-of-use and affordability. Education and nonprofit pricing available. Download a free 20-day trial from the website.

EXPERIENCE IN SOFTWARE
2024 Durant Avenue
Berkeley, CA 94704
800-678-7008
Fax 510-644-0694

http://www.projectkickstart.com
e-mail: contact@projectkickstart.com

Source: Reprinted by permission of Experience In Software.

● ● ● ● ● SCHOOL MINDER®

Windows

School Minder is the core product in a suite of school management software products from Hunter Systems. School Minder keeps detailed student, parent, and faculty records while handling payroll, medical information, discipline, attendance, grades, and much more. Add the billing module to manage tuition. Hunter Systems is partnered with Grade Quick®, the popular gradebook from Jackson Software, to provide data integration between the classroom and front office. School Minder integrates with other Hunter products to create a completely integrated and automated administrative environment where shared school data eliminates double entry, saves time, and creates other administrative advantages. Other available software includes Master Scheduling System®, Librarian's Edge®, Lunch Minder® (cafeteria Point of Sale [POS] and management), Accountrak® (for Federal Accounting Standards Board [FASB] compliant accounting), and Giftrak® (donor development). All software products are backed by a knowledgeable training and technical support staff. Available from:

HUNTER SYSTEMS
200 Cahaba Park Circle West
Suite 260
Birmingham, AL 35242
800-326-0527
Fax 205-968-6556

http://www.huntersystems.com
e-mail: support@huntersystems.com

Source: Reprinted by permission of Hunter Systems.

Software Programs with Specialized Uses

● ● ● ● ● ELECTRONIC FEE COLLECTION

EZ-EFT™

EZ-EFT takes the hassle out of fee collection by making pre-authorized payments of tuition by bank draft or credit cards a snap. The software stores account information, creates and transmits transactions, and post-payments. All with virtually no effort.

Benefits include:

- less administrative time and cost
- minimal collection problems
- enhanced convenience for parents
- better security and control of funds
- more reliable cash flow

SOFTERWARE INC.
132 Welsh Road Suite 140
Horsham, PA 19044-2217
212-628-0400

http://www.softerware.com/ezeft

E-MAIL MARKETING WITH CONSTANT CONTACT

Build your e-mail database and conduct effective e-marketing communications with this easy, affordable service. You can create and send professional HTML e-mail newsletters, announcements, and invitations, as well as measure the success of your e-mail communications.

Features and benefits include:

- customizes signup form for your website visitors.
- over 50 professional templates available.
- hosts and manages your e-mail database (including un-subscribes and bounces).
- automatically formats for HTML and Text.
- instant reporting on opens, bounce-backs, and other critical measures.
- improves professionalism of your communications without a graphic artist.
- requires no technical expertise.
- affordable monthly rates.
- free 60-day trial.

SofterWare, Inc.
132 Welsh Road Suite 140
Horsham, PA 19044-2217
212-628-0400

http://www.ezcare2.com/cc

ONLINE REGISTRATION

Online Forms with WebLink™

WebLink is a web-based system for creating and managing virtually any type of online entry form. These forms are personalized to collect exactly the data you want. You can even offer secure credit card processing for deposits or other initial payments. All collected data can be easily reviewed through WebLink's administrative tools, and then quickly exported to a database spreadsheet.

Online forms for:

- information requests.
- registrations.
- staff applications.
- event sign-ups.
- donations.
- much, much more.

SofterWare, Inc.
132 Welsh Road Suite 140
Horsham, PA 19044-2217
212-628-0400

http://www.ezcare2.com/weblink

The following programs allow parents to view their children in their child-care setting at any time during the day.

Kinderview

8304 Clairemont Mesa Boulevard, Suite 202
San Diego, CA 92111
800-543-7075

http://www.kinderview.com

Watch Me!

4851 Keller Springs Road (#221)
Dallas, TX 75248
888-5WATCHME

http://www.watch-me.com

B Professional Organizations and Sources of Information

ADMINISTRATION FOR CHILDREN, YOUTH AND FAMILIES (ACYF)
Head Start Division
P.O. Box 1182
Washington, DC 20013

http://www.acf.hhs.gov/programs/acyf/

AMERICAN ACADEMY OF PEDIATRICS
141 Northwest Point Boulevard
P.O. Box 747
Elk Grove Village, IL 60007-1098

847-434-4000
http://www.aap.org

AMERICAN ASSOCIATION FOR GIFTED CHILDREN
At Duke University
P.O. Box 90539
Durham, NC 27708-0539

919-783-6152
http://www.aagc.org

AMERICAN ASSOCIATION OF SCHOOL ADMINISTRATORS
801 North Quincy Street, Suite 700
Arlington, VA 22203-1730

703-528-0700
Fax 703-841-1543
http://www.aasa.org

AMERICAN COUNCIL ON EDUCATION (ACE)
One Dupont Circle, NW
Washington, DC 20036-1193

202-939-9300
http://www.acenet.edu

AMERICAN EDUCATIONAL RESEARCH ASSOCIATION (AERA)
1430 K Street NW
Washington, DC 20005-2504

202-238-3200
Fax 202-238-3250
http://www.aera.net

AMERICAN FEDERATION OF TEACHERS (AFT)
555 New Jersey Avenue, NW
Washington, DC 20001

202-879-4400
Fax 202-393-7481
http://www.aft.org

AMERICAN FOUNDATION FOR THE BLIND
2 Penn Plaza, Suite 1102
New York, NY 10121

212-502-7600
800-232-5463
Fax 212-502-4777
http://www.afb.org

AMERICAN MEDICAL ASSOCIATION
515 N. State Street
Chicago, IL 60654

800-621-8335
http://www.ama-assn.org

AMERICAN MONTESSORI SOCIETY (AMS)
281 Park Avenue South, 6th Floor
New York, NY 10010-6102

212-358-1250
Fax: 212-359-1256
http://www.amshq.org

AMERICAN SPEECH-LANGUAGE-HEARING ASSOCIATION
2200 Research Boulevard
Rockville, MD 20850-3289

301-296-5700
http://www.asha.org

ASSOCIATION FOR CHILDHOOD EDUCATION INTERNATIONAL
17904 Georgia Avenue, Suite 25
Olney, MD 20832

800-423-3563
http://www.-acci.org

BANK STREET COLLEGE OF EDUCATION
610 W. 112th Street
New York, NY 10025

http://www.bankstreet.edu

CENTERS FOR DISEASE CONTROL AND PREVENTION
1600 Clifton Road, NE
Atlanta, GA 30333

404-639-3534
800-232-4636
http://www.cdc.gov

CENTER FOR PARENTING STUDIES WHEELOCK COLLEGE
200 Riverway
Boston, MA 02215-4176

617-879-2000
http://www.wheelock.edu

CHILD CARE INFORMATION EXCHANGE
P.O. Box 3249
Redmond, WA 98073-3249

http://www.ccie.com/index.cfm

CHILD WELFARE LEAGUE OF AMERICA
2345 Crystal Drive, Suite 250
Arlington, VA 22202

703-4412-2400
http://www.cwla.org

THE CHILDREN'S BOOK COUNCIL
12 W. 37th Street, 2nd Floor
New York, NY 10018-7480

212-966-1090
Fax 212-966-2073
http://www.cbcbooks.org

CHILDREN'S DEFENSE FUND
25 E Street, NW
Washington, DC 20001

202-628-8787
http://www.childrensdefense.org

COUNCIL FOR EXCEPTIONAL CHILDREN
1110 North Glebe Road, Suite 300
Arlington, VA 22201

703-620-3660
TTY 866-915-5000
Fax 703-264-9494
e-mail service@ccc.sped.org
http://www.cec.sped.org

COUNCIL FOR PROFESSIONAL RECOGNITION
2460 16th Street, NW
Washington, DC 20009-3575

800-424-4310
202-265-9090
http://www.cdacouncil.org

DIRECTOR'S NETWORK, CHILD CARE INFORMATION EXCHANGE PRESS, INC.
P.O. Box 3249
Redmond, WA 98052

800-221-2864
Fax 425-836-8865
http://www.ccie.com

ECUMENICAL CHILD CARE NETWORK
P.O. Box 803586
Chicago, IL 60680

800-694-5443
http://www.eccn.org

ERIC PROJECT
c/o Computer Science Corporation
655 15th Street NW, Suite 500
Washington, DC 2005

800-538-3742
http://www.eric.ed.gov

HIGH/SCOPE EDUCATIONAL RESEARCH FOUNDATION
600 N. River Street
Ypsilanti, MI 48198-2898

734-485-2000
Fax 734-485-0704
e-mail info@highscope.org
http://www.highscope.org

JEAN PIAGET SOCIETY
Department of Human Development
Graduate School of Education
Harvard University
Cambridge, MA 02138

http://www.piaget.org

LEARNING DISABILITIES ASSOCIATION OF AMERICA
4156 Library Road
Pittsburgh, PA 15234-1349

412-341-1515
Fax 412-344-0224
http://www.ldanatl.org

NATIONAL ACADEMY OF EARLY CHILDHOOD PROGRAMS (NAEYC)
1313 L Street NW, Suite 500
Washington, DC 20005-4101

800-424-2460
http://www.naeyc.org

NATIONAL ASSOCIATION OF CHILD CARE PROFESSIONALS
P.O. Box 90723
Austin, TX 78709-0723

800-537-1118
Fax 512-301-5080
e-mail admin@naccp.org
http://www.naccp.org

NATIONAL ASSOCIATION FOR THE EDUCATION OF YOUNG CHILDREN (NAEYC)
1313 L Street NW, Suite 500
Washington, DC 054101

800-424-2460
http://www.naeyc.org

NATIONAL ASSOCIATION FOR FAMILY CHILD CARE
1743 W Alexander Street
Salt Lake City, UT 84119

800-359-8817
e-mail nafcc@nafcc.org
http://www.nafcc.org

NATIONAL BLACK CHILD DEVELOPMENT INSTITUTE
Washington, DC 20005
1313 L Street NW, Suite 110

202-833-2220
Fax 202-833-2222
e-mail moreinfo@nbcdi.org
http://www.nbcdi.org

NATIONAL CHILD CARE ASSOCIATION
1325 G Street NW, Suite 500
Washington, DC 20005

800-543-7161
e-mail info@nccanet.org
http://www.nccanet.org

NATIONAL COALITION FOR CAMPUS CHILDREN'S CENTERS
950 Glenn Drive, Suite 150
Folsom, CA 95630

877-736-6222
e-mail ncccc@uni.edu
http://www.campuschildren.org

NATIONAL COUNCIL OF JEWISH WOMEN CENTER FOR THE CHILD
474 Riverside Drive, Suite 1901
New York, NY 11015

212-645-4048
Fax 212-645-7466
e-mail action@ncjw.org
http://www.ncjw.org

NATIONAL DOWN SYNDROME SOCIETY
666 Broadway
New York, NY 10012

800-221-4602
http://www.ndss.org

NATIONAL EDUCATION ASSOCIATION
1201 16th Street, NW
Washington, DC 20036

202-833-4000
http://www.nea.org

NATIONAL HEAD START ASSOCIATION
1651 Prince Street
Alexandria, VA 22314

703-739-0875
Fax 703-739-0878
http://www.nhsa.org

NATIONAL INSTITUTE OF CHILD HEALTH AND HUMAN DEVELOPMENT
P.O. Box 3006
Rockville, MD 20847

800-370-2946
TTY 1-888-320-6942
http://www.nichd.nih.gov

NATIONAL INSTITUTE ON OUT-OF-SCHOOL TIME
106 Central Street
Wellesley, MA 02481

781-283-2547
e-mail niost@wellesly.edu

OFFICE OF HUMAN DEVELOPMENT SERVICES
U.S. Department of Health and Human Services
309F Hubert Humphrey Building
200 Independence Avenue, SW
Washington, DC 2021

http://www.hhs.gov

PARENTS ANONYMOUS, INC,
675 W. Foothill Blvd., Suite 220
Claremont, CA 91711

909-621-6184
Fax 909-625-6304
e-mail parentsanonymous@parentsanonymous.org
http://www.parentsanonymous.org

SCHOOL-AGE NOTES
P.O. Box 476
New Albany, OH 43054

614-855-9315
Fax 614-855-9325
e-mail info@schoolagenotes.com
http://www.schoolagenotes.com

SOCIETY FOR RESEARCH IN CHILD DEVELOPMENT
University of Michigan
2950 South State Street, Suite 401
Ann Arbor, MI 48104

734-926-0614
Fax 734-926-0601
e-mail info@srcd.org
http://www.srcd.org

U.S. NATIONAL COMMITTEE OF OMEP
World Organization for Early Childhood Education
1314 G Street, NW
Washington, DC 20005-3105

800-424-4310

C Sources for Early Childhood Materials, Equipment, Supplies, and Books

ABC School Supply
P.O. Box 369
Landiisville, PA 17538

http://www.abcschoolsupply.com

Barron's Educational Series, Inc.
250 Wireless Blvd.
Hauppauge, NY 11788

800-645-3476
http://www.barronseduc.com

Caedmon Publishers
Division of Harper Collins
10 East 53rd Street
New York, NY 10022

212-207-7000

Childcraft Education Corp.
P.O. Box 3239
Lancaster, PA 17604

888-532-4453
http://www.childcraft.com

Childswork/Childsplay
P.O Box 1246
Wilkes-Barre, PA 18703-1246

800-962-1146
http://www.childswork.com

Clarion Books
Division of Houghton Mifflin Harcourt
222 Berkeley Street
Boston MA 02116

617-351-3000
www.houghtonmifflinbooks.com/clarion/

COMMUNITY PLAYTHINGS
P. O. Box 2
Ulster Park, NY 12487

800-777-4244
http://www.communityplaythings.com

CONSTRUCTIVE PLAYTHINGS
13201 Arrington Road
Grandview, MO 64030-1117

800-448-7830
http://www.cptoys.com

CORWIN PRESS INC., A SAGE PUBLICATIONS COMPANY
2455 Teller Road
Thousand Oaks, CA 91320

805-499-9734
http://www.corwinpress.com

FACTS ON FILE
132 W. 31st Street, 17th Floor
New York, NY 10001

800-322-8755
http://www.factsonfile.com

GRYPHON HOUSE, INC.
Early Childhood Books
P.O. Box 207
Beltsville, MD 20704

301-595-9500
www.gryphonhouse.com

HARPERCOLLINS PUBLISHERS
1350 Avenue of the Americas
New York, NY 10019

212-261-6500
http://www.harpercollins.com

HOLCOMB'S EDUCATION RESOURCES
3205 Harvard Avenue
P.O. Box 94636
Cleveland, OH 44101-4636

800-362-9907 ext. 2152

HOUGHTON-MIFFLIN HARCOURT PUBLISHERS
9205 South Park Center Loop
Orlando, FL 332819

800-225-3425
http://www.houghtonmifflinbooks.com

KAPLAN EARLY LEARNING COMPANY
1310 Lewisville-Clemmons Road
Lewisville, NC 27023

800-334-2014
http://www.kaplanco.com

LAKESHORE LEARNING MATERIALS
2695 E. Dominguez Street
Carson, CA 90895

800-421-5354
http://www.lakeshorelearning.com

LITTLE BROWN & CO.
1271 Avenue of the Americas
New York, NY 10020

212-522-8700
http://www.hachettebookgroup.com/publishing_publishing-groups.aspx

NASCO SCHOOL AGE
4825 Stoddard Road
Modesto, CA 95356-9318

800-558-9595
http://www.enasco.com

PLAY WITH A PURPOSE
220 24th Avenue, NW
P.O. Box 998
Owatonna, MN 55060-0998

888-330-1826
http://www.pwaponline.com

REDLEAF PRESS
10 Yorkton Court
St. Paul, MN 55117-1065

800-641-0115
http://www.redleafpress.org

SCHOLASTIC
555 Broadway
New York, NY 10012

212-343-6100
http://www.scholastic.com

SLEEPING BEAR PRESS
P.O. Box 9187
Farmington Hills, MI 48333-9187

800-877-4253
http://www.sleepingbearpress.com

WADSWORTH CENGAGE LEARNING
20 Davis Drive
Belmont, CA, 94002

800-487-8488
http://www.cengage.com/wadsworth/

State Child–Care Licensing Agencies

States

ALABAMA

DEPARTMENT OF HUMAN RESOURCES
Child Day Care Partnership
50 North Ripley Street #205
Montgomery, AL 36130

334-242-1425
Fax 334-353-1491
http://dhr.state.al.us/default.asp

ALASKA

CHILD CARE AND LICENSING OFFICE
619 E. Ship Creek Ave., Suite 230
Anchorage, AK 99501

907-269-4500
Fax 907-269-4536
http://dpaweb.hss.state.ak.us

ARIZONA

ARIZONA DEPARTMENT OF HEALTH AND HUMAN SERVICES
Division of Assurances and Licensure Services
1647 E. Morton Ave., Suite 400
Phoenix, AZ 85020-4610

602-364-2536
Fax 602-364-4768
http://www.azdhs.gov/als/childcare/index.htm

ARKANSAS

DIVISION OF CHILD CARE AND EARLY CHILDHOOD EDUCATION
P.O. Box 1437, Slot S150
Little Rock, AR 72203-1437

501-682-4871
Fax 501-682-2317
http://www.state.ar.us/childcare/provinfo.html

CALIFORNIA

DEPARTMENT OF SOCIAL SERVICES
California Community Care Licensing Division
8745 Folsom Blvd.
Sacramento, CA 95826

916-229-4500
Fax 916- 229-4508

COLORADO

COLORADO DEPARTMENT OF HUMAN SERVICES
Division of Child Care
1575 Sherman Street, 1st Floor
Denver, CO 80203-1714

303-866-5958 or 800-799-5876
Fax 303-866-4453
http://www.cdhs.state.co.us/childcare

CONNECTICUT

STATE OF CONNECTICUT
Department of Public Health
410 Capitol Ave.
Hartford, CT 06134-0308

860-509-8045
Fax 860-509-7541
http://www.ct.gov/dph/BRS/Day_Care/day_care.htm

DELAWARE

OFFICE OF CHILD CARE LICENSING
1825 Faulkland Road
Wilmington, DE 19805

302-892-5800
Fax 302-633-5112
http://kids.delaware.gov/occl/occl.shtml

DISTRICT OF
COLUMBIA

DISTRICT OF COLUMBIA CHILD CARE LICENSING OFFICE
Department of Health Regulation and Licensing Office
825 North Capitol Street, NE
Washington, DC 20002

202 442-5888
Fax 202-442-9430-9374
http://dchealth.dc.gov/services/administration_offices/
hra/crcfd/index.htm

FLORIDA

FLORIDA CHILD CARE LICENSING OFFICE
Child Care Services
1317 Winewood Blvd., Building 6, Room 381 202
Tallahassee, FL 32399-0700

850-488-4900
Fax 850-922-2993
http://www.dcf.state.fl.us/childcare/licensing.shtml

GEORGIA

OFFICE OF SCHOOL READINESS
Bright from the Start
2 Peachtree Street NW, 32nd Floor
Atlanta, GA 30303-3142

404-656-0285
Fax 404-657-8936
http://decal.state.ga.us

HAWAII

DEPARTMENT OF HUMAN SERVICES
Employment/Child Care Programs Office
820 Mililani Street, Suite 606
Honolulu, HI 96813

808-586-7050 587-5266
Fax 808-586-5229 587-5275
http//hawaii.gov/dhs/self-sufficiency/childcare/licensing

IDAHO

DEPARTMENT OF HEALTH AND WELFARE
Bureau of Family and Children Services
450 W. State Street
P.O. Box 83702
Boise, ID 83720-0036

208-334-5691
Fax 208-334-6664
http://www2.state.id.us/dhw

ILLINOIS

ILLINOIS DEPARTMENT OF CHILDREN & FAMILY SERVICES
406 East Monroe Street
Station 60
Springfield, IL 62701-1498

217-785-2688 524-1983
Fax 217-782-6446
http://www.state.il.us/agency/daycare/index/shtml

INDIANA

FAMILY & SOCIAL SERVICES ADMINISTRATION
Division of Family Resources
Bureau of Child Development—Licensing Section
402 W. Washington Street, Room W-386
Indianapolis, IN 46204-2739

317-232-1144
Fax 317-233-6093
http://www.in.gov./fssa/children/bcd/index.html

IOWA

DEPARTMENT OF HUMAN SERVICES
Hoover State Office Building
1305 East Walnut, Rm. 114
Des Moines, IA 50319

515-281-5657-6899
Fax 515-242-6036
http://www.dhs.state.ia.us

KANSAS

BUREAU OF CHILD CARE AND HEALTH FACILITIES
Department of Health and Environment
Curtis State Office Building
1000 SW Jackson, Suite 540
Topeka, KS 66612-1274

785-296-0461
Fax 785-296-0803
http://www.kdhe.state.ks.us/kidsnet

KENTUCKY

CHILD CARE LICENSING OFFICE
Office of Inspector General
Division of Regulated Child Care
275 East Main Street, 3C-F
Frankfort, KY 40621

502-564-2800-7962
Fax 502-564-9350
http://daycare.com/kentucky

LOUISIANA

CHILD CARE LICENSING OFFICE
Department of Social Services
Bureau of Licensing
1627 N. Fourth Street
Baton Rouge, LA 70821

225-922-8100
Fax 225-342 -8636
http://www.daycare.com/louisiana

MAINE

CHILD CARE LICENSING OFFICE
Office of Child & Family Services
221 State Street
Augusta, ME 04333

207-287-5060
Fax 207-287-5048
http://www.state.me.us/dhs/bcfs/index.htm

MARYLAND

OFFICE OF LICENSING
Child Care Administrations
311 W. Saratoga Street, 1st Floor
Baltimore, MD 21201

410-767-7805
Fax 410-333-8699
http://daycare.com/maryland

MASSACHUSETTS

MASSACHUSETTS OFFICE OF CHILD CARE SERVICES
600 Washington Street, Ste 6100
Boston, MA 0211108

617-988-6600
Fax 617-988-2451
http://www.qualitychildcare.org

MICHIGAN

DIVISION OF CHILD DAY CARE LICENSING
7109 W. Saginaw, 2nd Floor
P.O. Box 30650
Lansing, MI 48909-8150

517-373-8300
888-685-0006
Fax 517-335-6121
http://www.michigan.gov/dhs

MINNESOTA

DEPARTMENT OF HUMAN SERVICES
Division of Licensing
444 Lafayette Road North
St. Paul, MN 55155-3842

651-296-3971
Fax 651-297-1490
http://www.dhs.state.mn.us/Licensing

MISSISSIPPI

STATE DEPARTMENT OF HEALTH
Division of Child Care Facilities Licensure
P.O. Box 1700
Jackson, MS 39215-1700

601-576-7613
Fax 601-576-7813

MISSOURI

MISSOURI DEPARTMENT OF HEALTH AND SENIOR SERVICES
Bureau of Child Care Safety and Licensure
1715 S. Ridge
Jefferson City, MO 65102-0570

573-751-2450
Fax 573-526-5345
http://www.dhss.mo.gov

MONTANA

DEPARTMENT OF PUBLIC HEALTH AND HUMAN SERVICES
Child Care Licensing
P.O. Box 202953
Helena, MT 59620-2953

406-444-1954
Fax 406-444-1742
http://daycare.com/montana

NEBRASKA

NEBRASKA HEALTH AND HUMAN SERVICES
Regulation of and Licensure
301 Centennial Mall South, 3rd Floor
Lincoln, NE 68509-4986

402-471-1802
Fax 402-471-9455
http://www.hhs.state.ne.us/crl/crlindex.htm

NEVADA

DEPARTMENT OF HUMAN SERVICES
Division of Child and Family Services
Bureau of Services for Child Care
711 East Fifth Street
Carson City, NV 897031

775-684-4463
Fax 775-684-4464
http://dcfs.state.nv.us

NEW HAMPSHIRE	**BUREAU OF CHILD CARE LICENSING** 129 Pleasant Street Concord, NH 03302 **603-271-4624** **Fax 603-271-4782** **http://www.daycare.com/newhampshire**
NEW JERSEY	**DEPARTMENT OF HUMAN SERVICES** Office of Licensing P.O. Box 717 Trenton, NJ 08625-0707 **609-292-1018** **Fax 609-987-2086** **http://www.state.nj.us/humanservices**
NEW MEXICO	**CHILDREN AND FAMILY DIVISION** P.O. Drawer 5160 Santa Fe, NM 87502-5160 **505-827-4185 7947** **Fax 505-827-7361**
NEW YORK	**NEW YORK DEPARTMENT OF FAMILY ASSISTANCE** Office of Children and Family Services 52 Washington Street, Room 338 North Rensselaer, NY 12144 **518-474-9454 9455** **Fax 518-474-9617** **http://www.ocfs.state.ny.us**
NORTH CAROLINA	**DIVISION OF CHILD DEVELOPMENT** 2201 Mail Service Center Raleigh, NC 27699-2201 **919-662-4499** **Fax 919-661-4845** **http://www.daycare.com/northcarolina**
NORTH DAKOTA	**NORTH DAKOTA DEPARTMENT OF HUMAN SERVICES** 600 East Boulevard Ave. Bismarck, ND 58505-0250 0251 **701-328-4809** **Fax 701-328-3538** **http://lnotes.state.nd.us/dhs/dshweb.nsf**
OHIO	**CHILD CARE LICENSING SECTION** State Department of Human Services 65 East Main Street, 5th Floor Columbus, OH 43215-5222 **614-466-1043** **Fax 614-728-6803** **http://www.jfs.ohio.gov/cdc**

OKLAHOMA

DEPARTMENT OF HUMAN SERVICES
Division of Child Care
P.O. Box 25352
Oklahoma City, OK 73125

405-521-3561
Fax 405-522-2564
http://www.okdhs.org/childcare

OREGON

CHILD CARE DIVISION
875 Union Street, NE
Salem, OR 97311

503-947-1400
Fax 503-947-1428
http://www.employment.oregon.gov/EMPLOY/CCD/index.shtml

PENNSYLVANIA

BUREAU OF CHILD DAY CARE SERVICES
Office of Children, Youth and Families
P.O. Box 2675
Harrisburg, PA 17105-2675

717-787-8691
Fax 717-787-1529
http://www.dpw.state.pa.us

RHODE ISLAND

RHODE ISLAND DEPARTMENT OF CHILDREN, YOUTH, AND FAMILIES
Day Care Licensing Unit
101 Friendship Street
Providence, RI 02903

401-528-3624
Fax 401-528-3650
http://www.daycare.com/rhodeisland

SOUTH
CAROLINA

DEPARTMENT OF SOCIAL SERVICES
Division of Child Day Care Licensing and Regulatory Services
P.O. Box 1520, Room 520
Columbia, SC 29202-1520

877-886-2384
Fax 877-252-1364
http://www.state.sc.us/dss/cdclrs

SOUTH
DAKOTA

CHILD CARE SERVICES STATE OF SOUTH DAKOTA
Kneip Building
700 Governors Drive
Pierre, SD 57501-2291

605-773-4766
Fax 605-773-7294
http://www.state.sd.us/social/ccs/ccshome.htm

TENNESSEE

DEPARTMENT OF HUMAN SERVICES
Citizen Plaza—14th Floor
400 Deaderick Street
Nashville, TN 37248-9800

615-313-4778
Fax 615-313-6683
http://www.state.tn.us/humanserv

TEXAS

TEXAS DEPARTMENT OF FAMILY AND PROTECTIVE SERVICES
Mail Code E-550
P.O. Box 149030
M.C. E-550
Austin, TX 78714-9030

512-438-4800
Fax 512-339-5872
http://www.tdprs.state.tx.us

UTAH

BUREAU OF LICENSING
Child Care Unit
P.O. Box 142003
288 North 1460 West
Salt Lake City, UT 84114-2003

801-538-6152-9299
Fax 801-538-6325
http://health.utah.gov/licensing

VERMONT

CHILD CARE SERVICES DIVISION
103 S. Main Street, 2 North
Waterbury, VT 05671-2901

802-241-2158 31
Fax 802-241-1220
http://www.dcf.state.vt.us/cdd

VIRGINIA

DEPARTMENT OF SOCIAL SERVICES
Division of Licensing Programs
7 North 8th Street
Richmond, VA 23219-1849

804-726-7154 43
Fax 804-726-7132
http://www.dss.state.va.us/division/license/

WASHINGTON

DEPARTMENT OF SOCIAL AND HEALTH SERVICES
Division of Child Care and Early Learning
P.O. Box 45480
Olympia, WA 98504-5480

360-413-3284 725-4665
Fax 360-413-3482
http://www1.dshs.wa.gov/ca/index.asp

WEST VIRGINIA

WEST VIRGINIA DEPARTMENT OF HEALTH AND HUMAN RESOURCES
Office of Social Services
Division of Childcare
350 Capitol Street, Room B-18
Charleston, WV 25301-1715

304-558-1885-7980
Fax 304-558-8800
http://www.wvdhhr.org/bcf/ece

WISCONSIN

BUREAU OF REGULATION AND LICENSING
1 West Wilson Street
P.O. Box 8916
Madison, WI 53708-8916

608-266-9314
Fax 608-267-7252
http://www.dhfs.state.wi.us/rl_dcfs/index.htm

WYOMING

DEPARTMENT OF FAMILY SERVICES
Hathaway Building, Room 343
2300 Capitol Ave.
Cheyenne, WY 82002-0490

307-777-6595
Fax 307-777-3659
http://dfsweb.state.wy.us

Territories

PUERTO RICO

DEPARTMENT OF FAMILY
Licensing Office
P.O. Box 11398
Santurce, PR 00910

787-724-0772
Fax 787-724-0767

VIRGIN
ISLANDS

DEPARTMENT OF HUMAN SERVICES
Child Care Licensing
3011 Golden Rock
Christiansted, St. Croix
U.S. Virgin Islands 00820-4355

340-773-2323
Fax 340-773-6121

NAEYC's Code of Ethical Conduct: Guidelines for Responsible Behavior in Early Childhood Education

Editor's note: We need the help of all Young Children readers who are familiar with NAEYC's Code of Ethics.

Perhaps you have been involved in thinking through one or more of the ethical dilemmas that have been regularly appearing in Young Children—in staff meeting, at an Affiliate Group meeting, or with friends. Many of you have used the principles and ideals in NAEYC's Code of Ethics to help solve dilemmas you face in your work.

Because of these experiences, you have information that can be valuable to NAEYC as we review the Code for needed revisions or additions.

The Code is published on the following pages to aid your review.

- Are any of the principles or ideals phrased confusingly? How would you change the wording?

- Have you found the Code lacking in guidance for a particular ethical dilemma involving children or their families? Describe the situation for us.

Please send your suggestions regarding how we can clarify any point in the Code to:

NAEYC ETHICS PANEL
Office of the Executive Director
1509 16th Street, NW
Washington, DC 20036-1426

If you have not yet used the "case study" dilemmas we publish, we hope you soon will start discussing each one in your staff meetings.

NAEYC's Code of Ethical Conduct was prepared under the auspices of the Ethics Commission of the National Association for the Education of Young Children. The Commission members were: Stephanie Feeney (Chairperson), Bettye Caldwell, Sally Cartwright, Carrie

Cheek, Josue Cruz, Jr., Anne G. Dorsey, Dorothy M. Hill, Lilian G. Katz, Pamm Mattick, Shirley A. Norris, and Sue Spayth Riley. Financial assistance for this project was provided by NAEYC, the Wallace Alexander Gerbode Foundation, and the University of Hawaii.

NAEYC gratefully acknowledges the research and development work done for this project by Stephanie Feeney, Ph.D., Professor and Early Childhood Education Specialist at the University of Hawaii at Manoa, and Kenneth Kipnis, Ph.D., Professor of Philosophy at the University of Hawaii at Manoa.

Preamble

NAEYC recognizes that many daily decisions required of those who work with young children are of a moral and ethical nature. The NAEYC Code of Ethical Conduct offers guidelines for responsible behavior and sets forth a common basis for resolving the principal ethical dilemmas encountered in early childhood education. The primary focus is on daily practice with children and their families in programs for children from birth to 8 years of age: preschools, child care centers, family day care homes, kindergartens, and primary classrooms. Many of the provisions also apply to specialists who do not work directly with children including program administrators, parent educators, college professors, and child care licensing specialists.

Standards of ethical behavior in early childhood education are based on commitment to core values that are deeply rooted in the history of our field.

We have committed ourselves to:

- Appreciating childhood as a unique and valuable stage of the human life cycle
- Basing our work with children on knowledge of child development
- Appreciating and supporting the close ties between the child and family
- Recognizing that children are best understood in the context of family culture and society
- Respecting the dignity, worth, and uniqueness of each individual (child, family member, and colleague)
- Helping children and adults achieve their full potential in the context of relationships that are based on trust, respect, and positive regard

The Code sets forth a conception of our professional responsibilities in four sections, each addressing an arena of professional relationships: (1) children (2) families (3) colleagues, and (4) community and society. Each section includes an introduction to the primary responsibilities of the early childhood practitioner in that arena, a set of ideals pointing in the direction of exemplary professional practice, and a set of principles defining practices that are required, prohibited, and permitted.

The ideals reflect the aspirations of practitioners. The principles are intended to guide conduct and assist practitioners in resolving ethical dilemmas encountered in the field. There is not necessarily a corresponding principle for each ideal. Both ideals and principles are intended to direct practitioners to those questions which when responsibly answered, will provide the basis for conscientious decision making. While the Code provides specific direction for addressing some ethical dilemmas, many others will require the practitioner to combine the guidance of the Code with sound professional judgment.

The ideals and principles in this Code present a shared conception of professional responsibility that affirms our commitment to the core values of our field. The Code publicly acknowledges the responsibilities that we in the field have assumed and in so doing supports ethical behavior in our work. Practitioners who face ethical dilemmas are urged to seek guidance in the applicable parts of this Code and in the spirit that informs the whole.

Section I: Ethical Responsibilities to Children

Childhood is a unique and valuable stage in the life cycle. Our paramount responsibility is to provide safe, healthy, nurturing, and responsive settings for children. We are committed to supporting children's development by cherishing individual differences, by helping them learn to live and work cooperatively, and by promoting their self-esteem.

IDEALS:

I–1.1—To be familiar with the knowledge base of early childhood education and to keep current through continuing education and in-service training.

I–1.2—To base program practices upon current knowledge in the field of child development and related disciplines and upon particular knowledge of each child.

I–1.3—To recognize and respect the uniqueness and the potential of each child.

I–1.4—To appreciate the special vulnerability of children.

I–1.5—To create and maintain safe and healthy settings that foster children's social, emotional, intellectual, and physical development and that respect their dignity and their contributions.

I–1.6—To support the right of children with special needs to participate, consistent with their ability, in regular early childhood programs.

PRINCIPLES:

P–1.1—Above all we shall not harm children. We shall not participate in practices that are disrespectful, degrading, dangerous, exploitative, intimidating, psychologically damaging, or physically harmful to children. ***This principle has precedence over all others in this Code.***

P–1.2—We shall not participate in practices that discriminate against children by denying benefits, giving special advantages, or excluding them from programs or activities on the basis of their race, religion, sex, national origin, or the status, behavior, or beliefs of their parents. (This principle does not apply to programs that have a lawful mandate to provide services to a particular population of children.)

P–1.3—We shall involve all of those with relevant knowledge (including staff and parents) in decisions concerning a child.

P–1.4—When, after appropriate efforts have been made with a child and the family, the child still does not appear to be benefiting from a program, we shall communicate our concern to the family in a positive way and offer them assistance in finding a more suitable setting.

P–1.5—We shall be familiar with the symptoms of child abuse and neglect and know and follow community procedures and state laws that protect children against abuse and neglect.

P–1.6—When we have evidence of child abuse or neglect, we shall report the evidence to the appropriate community agency and follow up to ensure that appropriate action has been taken. When possible, parents will be informed that the referral has been made.

P–1.7—When another person tells us of their suspicion that a child is being abused or neglected but we lack evidence, we shall assist that person in taking appropriate action to protect the child.

P–1.8—When a child protective agency fails to provide adequate protection for abused or neglected children, we acknowledge a collective ethical responsibility to work toward improvement of these services.

P–1.9—When we become aware of a practice or situation that endangers the health or safety of children, but has not been previously known to do so, we have an ethical responsibility to inform those who can remedy the situation and who can keep other children from being similarly endangered.

Section II: Ethical Responsibilities to Families

Families are of primary importance in children's development. (The term family may include others, besides parents, who are responsibly involved with the child.) Because the family and the early childhood educator have a common interest in the child's welfare, we acknowledge a primary responsibility to bring about collaboration between the home and school in ways that enhance the child's development.

IDEALS:

I–2.1—To develop relationships of mutual trust with families we serve.

I–2.2—To acknowledge and build upon strengths and competencies as we support families in their task of nurturing children.

I–2.3—To respect the dignity of each family and its culture, customs, and beliefs.

I–2.4—To respect families' child rearing values and their right to make decisions for their children.

I–2.5—To interpret each child's progress to parents within the framework of a developmental perspective and to help families understand and appreciate the value of developmentally appropriate early childhood programs.

I–2.6—To help family members improve their understanding of their children and to enhance their skills as parents.

I–2.7—To participate in building support networks for families by providing them with opportunities to interact with program staff and families.

PRINCIPLES:

P–2.1—We shall not deny family members access to their child's classroom or program setting.

P–2.2—We shall inform families of program philosophy, policies, and personnel qualifications, and explain why we teach as we do.

P–2.3—We shall inform families of and, when appropriate, involve them in policy decisions.

P–2.4—We shall inform families of and, when appropriate, involve them in significant decisions affecting their child.

P-2.5—We shall inform the family of accidents involving their child, of risks such as exposures to contagious disease that may result in infection, and of events that might result in psychological damage.

P-2.6—We shall not permit or participate in research that could in any way hinder the education or development of the children in our programs. Families shall be fully informed of any proposed research projects involving their children and shall have the opportunity to give or withhold consent.

P-2.7—We shall not engage in or support exploitation of families. We shall not use our relationship with a family for private advantage or personal gain, or enter into relationships with family members that might impair our effectiveness in working with children.

P-2.8—We shall develop written policies for the protection of confidentiality and the disclosure of children's records. The policy documents shall be made available to all program personnel and families. Disclosure of children's records beyond family members, program personnel, and consultants having an obligation of confidentiality shall require familial consent (except in cases of abuse or neglect).

P-2.9—We shall maintain confidentiality and shall respect the family's right to privacy, refraining from disclosure of confidential information and intrusion into family life. However, when we are concerne d about a child's welfare, it is permissible to reveal confidential information to agencies and individuals who may be able to act in the child's interest.

P-2.10—In cases where family members are in conflict we shall work openly, sharing our observations of the child, to help all parties involved make informed decisions. We shall refrain from becoming an advocate for one party.

P-2.11—We shall be familiar with and appropriately use community resources and professional services that support families. After a referral has been made, we shall follow up to ensure that services have been adequately provided.

Section III: Ethical Responsibilities to Colleagues

In a caring, cooperative work place, human dignity is respected, professional satisfaction is promoted, and positive relationships are modeled. Our primary responsibility in this arena is to establish and maintain settings and relationships that support productive work and meet professional needs.

A—Responsibilities to Co-Workers

IDEALS:

I-3A.I—To establish and maintain relationships of trust and cooperation with co-workers.

I-3A.2—To share resources and information with co-workers.

I-3A.3—To support co-workers in meeting their professional needs and in their professional development.

I-3A.4—To accord co-workers due recognition of professional achievement.

PRINCIPLES:

P-3A.1—When we have concern about the professional behavior of a co-worker, we shall first let that person know of our concern and attempt t o resolve the matter collegially.

P-3A.2—We shall exercise care in expressing views regarding the personal attributes or professional conduct of co-workers. Statements should be based on firsthand knowledge and relevant to the interests of children and programs.

B—Responsibilities to Employers

IDEALS:

I-3B.I—To assist the program in providing the highest quality of service.

I-3B.2—To maintain loyalty to the program and uphold its reputation.

PRINCIPLES:

P-3B.I—When we do not agree with program policies, we shall first attempt to effect change through constructive action within the organization.

P-3B.2—We shall speak or act on behalf of an organization only when authorized. We shall take care to note when we are speaking for the organization and when we are expressing a personal Judgment.

C—Responsibilities to Employees

IDEALS:

I-3C.I—To promote policies and working conditions that foster competence, well-being, and self-esteem in staff members.

I-3C.2—To create a climate of trust and candor that will enable staff t o speak and act in the best interests of children, families, and the field of early childhood education.

I-3C.3—To strive to secure an adequate livelihood for those who work with or on behalf of young children.

PRINCIPLES:

P-3C.1—In decisions concerning children and programs, we shall appropriately utilize the training, experience, and expertise of staff members.

P-3C.2—We shall provide staff members with working conditions that permit them to carry out their responsibilities, timely and nonthreatening evaluation procedures, written grievance procedures, constructive feedback, and opportunities for continuing professional development and advancement.

P-3C.3—We shall develop and maintain comprehensive written personnel policies that define program standards and, when applicable, that specify the extent to which employees are accountable for their conduct outside the work place. These policies shall be given to new staff members and shall be available for review by all staff members.

P-3C.4—Employees who do not meet program standards shall be informed of areas of concern and, when possible, assisted in improving their performance.

P-3C.5—Employees who are dismissed shall be informed of the reasons for their termination. When a dismissal is for cause, justification must be based on evidence of inadequate or inappropriate behavior that is accurately documented, current, and available for the employee to review.

P-3C.6—In making evaluations and recommendations, judgments shall be based on fact and relevant to the interests of children and programs.

P-3C.7—Hiring and promotion shall be based solely on a person's record of accomplishment and ability to carry out the responsibilities of the position.

P-3C.8—In hiring, promotion, and provision of training, we shall not participate in any form of discrimination based on race, religion, sex, national origin, handicap, age, or sexual preference. We shall be familiar with laws and regulations that pertain to employment discrimination.

Section IV: Ethical Responsibilities to Community and Society

Early childhood programs operate within a context of an immediate community made up of families and other institutions concerned with children's welfare. Our responsibilities to the community are to provide programs that meet its needs and to cooperate with agencies and professions that share responsibility for children. Because the larger society has a measure of responsibility for the welfare and protection of children and because of our specialized expertise in child development, we acknowledge an obligation to serve as a voice for children everywhere.

IDEALS:

I-4.1—To provide the community with high-quality, culturally sensitive programs and services.

I-4.2—To promote cooperation among agencies and professions concerned with the welfare of young children, their families, and their teachers.

I-4.3—To work, through education, research, and advocacy, toward an environmentally safe world in which all children are adequately fed, sheltered, and nurtured.

I-4.4—To work, through education, research, and advocacy, toward a society in which all young children have access to quality programs.

I-4.5—To promote knowledge and understanding of young children and their needs. To work toward greater social acknowledgment of children's rights and greater social acceptance of responsibility for their well-being.

I-4.6—To support policies and laws that promote the well-being of children and families. To oppose those that impair their well-being. To cooperate with other individuals and groups in these efforts.

I-4.7—To further the professional development of the field of early childhood education and to strengthen its commitment to realizing its core values as reflected in this Code.

PRINCIPLES:

P-4.1—We shall communicate openly and truthfully about the nature and extent of services that we provide.

P-4.2—We shall not accept or continue to work in positions for which we are personally unsuited or professionally unqualified. We shall not offer services that we do not have the competence, qualifications, or resources to provide.

P-4.3—We shall be objective and accurate in reporting the knowledge upon which we base our program practices.

P-4.4—We shall cooperate with other professionals who work with children and their families.

P-4.5—We shall not hire or recommend for employment any person who is unsuited for a position with respect to competence, qualifications, or character.

P-4.6—We shall report the unethical or incompetent behavior of a colleague to a supervisor when informal resolution is not effective.

P-4.7—We shall be familiar with laws and regulations that serve to protect the children in our programs.

P-4.8—We shall not participate in practices which are in violation of laws, and regulations that protect the children in our programs.

P-4.9—When we have evidence that an early childhood program is violating laws or regulations protecting children, we shall report it to persons responsible for the program. If compliance is not accomplished within a reasonable time, we will report the violation to appropriate authorities who can be expected to remedy the situation.

P-4-10—When we have evidence that an agency or a professional charged with providing services to children, families, or teachers is failing to meet its obligations, we acknowledge a collective ethical responsibility to report the problem to appropriate authorities or to the public.

P-4.11—When a program violates or requires its employees to violate this Code, it is permissible, after fair assessment of the evidence, to disclose the identity of that program.

• • • • • ORDER THIS INFORMATIVE NAEYC BROCHURE...

Code of Ethical Conduct and Statement of Commitment

by Stephanie Feeney and Kenneth Kipnis

A code of ethics for early childhood educators which offers guidelines for responsible behavior and set forth a common basis for resolving ethical dilemmas encountered in early childhood education.

NAEYC ORDER #503

50 CENTS EACH; **100** FOR $10

Glossary

accreditation	National program for validating the quality of early childhood programs.
adventure play areas	Outdoor areas where children can use a variety of materials to build their own structures.
aesthetic appeal	Pleasant appearance derived from a well-designed environment.
AIDS	Acquired immunodeficiency syndrome.
allergens	Environmental substances that cause a reaction such as asthma, hives, or hay fever.
anti-bias curriculum	Broader approach that includes cultural aspects, as well as gender and physical ability differences.
attachment	The affectional tie that binds one person to another and that endures with time.
budget	A statement of goals for one year stated in financial terms.
budget calendar	A schedule for compiling budget data.
business plan	A written document that describes a proposed venture in detail.
caregiver	One who provides a caring, nurturing environment for children who spend long hours away from home.
child abuse	Serious harm to children in the form of physical, emotional, or sexual mistreatment.
child-care resource and referral networks	Information services for parents seeking child care.
Child Care HOME Inventory	A screening tool designed to measure the quality and quantity of stimulation and support available to a child in the home environment.
Child Development Associate (CDA)	A credential that certifies the holder has achieved a level of competency.
church-sponsored program	A child-care center or preschool organized as an extension of the educational program of the church.
clique	A group formed by school-age children as a means for strengthening bonds with peers and to be free from adult supervision.
code-switching	The use of different forms of speech in different situations.
concrete materials	Objects that children can touch, taste, smell, hear, and see.
contract	Written agreement between a child development facility and the employee that promotes job security.
cooperative school	Nonprofit enterprise, owned by all the parents who currently have children enrolled in the school.
corporate child-care centers	Business corporation operating multiple schools at different sites.
creativity	Unique ways of reacting to a situation, not just imitating what others have done.
critical job elements	Things which, if not done, would seriously impede the total teaching process.

developmentally appropriate infant-toddler program	Based on knowledge of the physical, emotional, social, and cognitive abilities of the children served.
developmentally appropriate practice	Based on a knowledge of universal sequences of growth and change and of each child's individual pattern and timing.
disaster plans	Detailed plans for evacuating children and managing a disaster.
egocentric	Children's inability to see things from more than one point of view.
employer-sponsored programs	On-site or off-site child-care facilities supported by a company or business.
ethics	The study of right and wrong, duty, and obligation.
evaluation	Process to determine whether the goals of an early childhood center are being met.
expendable supplies	Items that are used up and have to be replaced.
family child-care home	Child-care service provided in a private residence.
family group	Children whose ages vary, sometimes by several years.
Family Child Care Environmental Rating Scale, Revised Edition (FCCERS-R)	Family Child Care Environmental Rating Scale, Revised Edition.
family, friends, and neighbors (FFN) care	Child care provided by family, friends, and neighbors.
fixed expenses	Expenses that do not vary or change very little, over periods of time.
Food Guide Pyramid	Recommended daily servings of food developed by the U.S. Department of Agriculture in 2005.
for-profit proprietary school	School owned by one or more individuals, established to provide a community school service but also to make a profit for the owners.
fringe benefits	Mandated or voluntary benefits that are added to personnel expenses.
goal	Expected long-term changes in a child's behavior.
industry versus inferiority	Erikson's middle childhood stage during which children acquire skills for adulthood.
knowledge	A familiarity with a particular subject or branch of learning.
laboratory school	Early childhood center that is part of the instructional program of a college or university.
leadership	Setting a direction or vision for a group to follow.
license-exempt family child-care providers	Child-care providers who are exempt from regulation (nannies, relatives, and babysitters).
maintenance	Major expenditures on the physical plant: painting, alterations, repair.
management	Controls or directs people/resources in a group according to principles or values that have already been established.
mentor	Someone who can serve as a role model to help an inexperienced teacher gain new skills and knowledge.
morality	Our view of what is good or right, how people should behave, and the kinds of obligations we have to one another.
multiculturalism	A program that provides opportunities for children to develop a positive self-concept, including an acceptance of their own differences and differences of others.

multipurpose equipment	Equipment that can be used in more than one way.
nonexpendable items	Equipment and toys that last a long time.
nonverbal messages	Facial expression, movements, and posture.
objective	Expected short-term changes in a child's behavior.
ongoing costs	Expected costs of operating a school.
operations	Recurring, daily activities involved in the upkeep of a school.
parent conference	One-on-one meeting between teacher and parents to discuss a child's progress or resolve problems.
parent education	Activities designed to help parents become better informed about child-rearing and family life.
parent involvement	Sharing in the education of their children through participation in school activities.
peer group	Children who are close to the same age.
peers	People the same age as oneself.
philosophy	A distillation of ideas, beliefs, and values held by an individual, a group, or an organization.
preschool period	Designates the years before a child enters elementary school.
probationary period	The time before the full contract goes into effect, usually from one to three months.
provider networks	Networks provide peer support, training opportunities, and business consultation.
psychosocial area	Space that is planned to encourage interactions between adults and children, and among the children themselves.
scooter board	A 12-inch plastic or wooden square, with swivel casters (commercially produced boards are equipped with handles on the side).
self-concept	Children's understanding of their own characteristics.
sensorimotor period	Piagetian stage from birth to age two when children use all their senses to absorb the world around them.
sensory diversity	Objects and experiences that stimulate the senses.
skill	An ability that comes from knowledge, practice, or aptitude (sometimes called competency).
start-up costs	Expenses incurred before a new school can open.
statement of personnel policies	Written document covering employer–employee relations.
supervision	Overseeing staff members during the performance of their jobs.
synchrony	The back-and-forth interaction between infants and their parents or caregivers.
trust versus mistrust	Erikson's designation of the stage from birth to one year of age in which children learn to trust themselves and others.
values	The qualities that we believe are intrinsically desirable and that we strive to achieve in ourselves.
variable expenses	Expenses that vary and over which the director has some control.

Index